D1073840

THE VANGUARD OF THE ATLANTIC WORLD

JAMES E. SANDERS

The VANGUARD
of the ATLANTIC WORLD

CREATING MODERNITY, NATION, AND DEMOCRACY
IN NINETEENTH-CENTURY LATIN AMERICA

Duke University Press   Durham and London   2014

© 2014 Duke University Press
All rights reserved
Printed in the United States of America on acid-free paper ∞
Typeset in Quadraat by Graphic Composition, Inc., Bogart, GA

Library of Congress Cataloging-in-Publication Data
Sanders, James E., 1971
The vanguard of the Atlantic world : creating modernity, nation,
and democracy in nineteenth-century Latin America / James E.
Sanders.
pages cm
Includes bibliographical references and index.
ISBN 978-0-8223-5764-3 (cloth : alk. paper)
ISBN 978-0-8223-5780-3 (pbk. : alk. paper)
1. Latin America—Politics and government—19th century.
2. Latin America—History—19th century.
3. Democracy—History—19th century. I. Title.
F1413.S26 2014
980.03—dc23   2014012190

Cover Image: Watercolor by Henry Price, 1852. Courtesy of the
digital library of the Colombia National Library and the Colombia
National Library.

| For Jennifer and Chloe |

Contents

Acknowledgments

This project began in Bogotá's Biblioteca Nacional, as I read nineteenth-century newspapers for my earlier book on Colombian popular political beliefs and actions. I spent most of my time uncovering hints of how indigenous peoples, ex-slaves, and small farmers appeared in the historical record. Now and again, however, I would turn away from my intensely local pursuits and glance at the news of the world these nineteenth-century papers reported. At first, this was just a diversion, playing hooky from my real work—it was fun to see what Colombians thought about the U.S. Civil War, or Garibaldi's adventures in Italy, or Maximilian's empire in Mexico. After a while, however, I became troubled. These Colombian writers were not seeing the world in the way that I had been taught they should. They were not pining for a distant European civilization, hoping to imitate the latest fashion from Paris, and depressed about the sad state of their own barbarous republics. Instead, these writers expressed a great confidence in their own societies, the Americas as a whole, and their place in creating a new future for the world. My effort to understand this contradiction, to understand how nineteenth-century Latin Americans saw the world and their place in it, became this book.

Since this project began quite some time ago, I have accumulated more debts than seem warranted. As my partner is a librarian, I must begin by thanking all the librarians and archivists who have helped me along the way. I heartily thank the staffs of the Archivo Central del Cauca, the (old) Archivo del Congreso, the Archivo General de la Nación, the Biblioteca Nacional, the Biblioteca Luis Angel Arango, the Archivo del Instituto Colombiano de la Reforma Agraria, and the Archivo Histórico Municipal de Cali in Colombia; the Archivo General de la Nación, the Archivo Histórico del Museo Regional de Guanajuato, the Acervos Históricos of the Universidad Iberoamericana, the Archivo General del Gobierno de Estado de Guanajuato and the Archivo Histórico de Guanajuato in Mexico; the Archivo General de la Nación, the Biblioteca Nacional, and the Museo Histórico Nacional in Uruguay; and the Nettie Lee Benson Latin American Library at the University of Texas, the University of Florida Latin American Collection, the Duval County Courthouse, and the Merrill-Cazier Library at Utah State University in the United States. I would especially like to thank the Library of Congress and the wonderful staff of the Hispanic Division—Barbara Tenenbaum, Carlos Olave, and Everette Larson—and of the Newspaper Reading Room, especially Georgia Higley.

So many people have read parts of this manuscript, in various guises; spent time helping me develop my thoughts; or invited me to their institutions to present my work (but none save me are to blame for any mistakes!): Nancy Appelbaum, Alex Borucki, Andrea Cadelo Buitrago, Celso Castilho, Chris Conte, Jennifer Duncan, Frank A. Eissa-Barroso, Mike Ervin, Ann Farnsworth-Alvear, Nils Jacobsen, Brooke Larson, Marixa Lasso, Catherine LeGrand, Aims McGuinness, Erika Pani, Len Rosenband, Hilda Sabato, Clément Thibaud, Guy Thomson, Justin Wolfe, and the anonymous readers for Duke University Press. Special thanks go to George Reid Andrews for all of his support over the years. Sally Thompson of the Merrill-Cazier Library helped immensely in creating the Mexico and Uruguay maps. I first tried out some of the arguments in this book in an article that appeared in the *Latin American Research Review* 46, no. 2 (2011) and in an essay in the collection *L'Atlantique révolutionnaire: Une perspective ibéro-américaine*, edited by Clément Thibaud, Gabriel Entin, Alejandro Gómez, and Federica Morelli (Rennes: Les Perséides, 2013). Of course, this book would not have been possible without the faith of my editor at Duke, Valerie Millholland, and the support of the entire Duke editorial and production staff, especially Gisela Fosado.

A number of organizations helped fund the research and writing of this project. The John W. Kluge Center at the Library of Congress provided generous support and a wonderful physical and intellectual environment in which to work; special thanks go to Mary Lou Reker, Carolyn Brown, and JoAnne

Kitching for making my time there productive and enjoyable. I also enjoyed support from a Professional Staff Congress-City University of New York Research Foundation Grant; a Utah State University New Faculty Research Grant; a University of Florida Center for Latin American Studies Library Travel Grant; a Utah State University Seed Grant; and ongoing moral and financial support from the Utah State University's Department of History and College of Humanities and Social Sciences.

Of course, my family—beginning with my parents, James and Glenda Sanders, and especially my wife and daughter—tolerated my distraction and absences as I worked on the manuscript, yet always were there when I needed them. This book is in some sense about how we imagine the future. Therefore, I dedicate it to mine: Jennifer Duncan and Chloe Austen Sanders.

| Querétaro, Mexico, 1867 |

Prologue

Maximilian the First, archduke of the Habsburg dynasty of Europe, and supposedly the emperor of Mexico, stood on the Hill of Bells outside of Querétaro on the morning of 19 June 1867 and awaited his execution. He had arrived to rule Mexico as emperor at the behest of Mexican Conservatives disgusted with Liberal rule after their defeat in civil war and with the backing of an imperialist-minded French monarchy and its invading army. The elected republican government of Benito Juárez resisted the invasion in a long and bloody war that lasted until Maximilian's capture in 1867, after the French had withdrawn. Maximilian faced his death with the bravery, compassion, and complete political arrogance that his European aristocratic background had engendered. While in life he had often seemed to lack even basic comprehension of the Mexican political arena, perhaps facing a firing squad focused his mind on his 1864 arrival in Mexico. He had come, he claimed, to bring "the fruits of civilization and true progress." He had brought with him from Europe "the Civilizing banner of France," and his enthronement was to lead to "the rebirth of order and Peace."[1] Maximilian's understanding of his mission fits well with scholars' understanding of modernity, civilization, and progress as arising first in Europe and later being transported to an unruly and backward Latin America.

Yet, whatever thoughts were in Maximilian's head, they were soon extin-

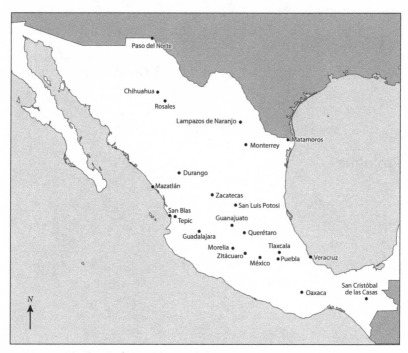

MAP P.1. Mexico after 1854. © Daniel Dalet, d-maps.com

guished by the bullets of Mexican republican soldiers. Under a blue sky, he fell in the first volley but did not die; the soldiers had to deliver the coup de grâce to his heart at point-blank range, setting his vest on fire.[2] For many Mexicans, Latin Americans, and other residents of the Americas, the bullets cut down not just a man but the very idea that civilization and modernity emanated from Europe. These bullets had killed a pirate, yes, but they also had interred forever the possibility of a return to monarchy and an abandonment of republicanism in the Americas. The Mexican Liberal colonel and writer Juan de Dios Arias argued that Maximilian's execution was a "salubrious lesson for Europe," since the triumph of "democracy" would serve as beacon of hope to "the oppressed peoples of the world."[3] Mexican patriots had not just saved their own country; they had also furthered the spread of democratic republicanism across the globe. The tree of liberty had been watered with the blood of tyrants.

Maximilian's execution was a world-historical event that ignited a firestorm of debate over the meaning and locus of modernity. The execution captured the global imagination, as politicians and essayists rushed to make sense of the news. Havana's *Diario de la Marina* devoted so much space to

FIG P.1. United States of Colombia, 1863–85. Reprinted by permission of Louisiana State University Press from *Rafael Núñez and the Politics of Colombian Regionalism, 1863–1886*. By James William Park. © 1985 by Louisiana State University Press.

covering the event that some of its readers complained; however, the paper defended its expansive investigation by arguing that the debate raised by the execution was "a universal question."[4] The news was so stunning it even inspired Edouard Manet to reconsider the then unfashionable subject of history painting, although his complex oils imagining the execution mostly seem to capture the violence of the event.[5] Beyond its spectacle, Maximilian's death raised—and, indeed, answered—questions of what modernity meant. Who was the agent of modernity? How would modernity be obtained? Where would this modernity come to fruition? In distant Buenos Aires, the exiled Chilean intellectual Francisco Bilbao had followed earlier stages of the conflict between Mexico and France. Wracked with a consumptive sickness that would kill him in 1865, he raged that the French intervention in Mexico was really part of titanic struggle of "American civilization against European civilization."[6] Republicanism defined this American civilization, providing its force and its path to the future. Although Maximilian and Mexican Conservatives saw Europe as the font of civilization, Bilbao saw only a decrepit, backward ruin: "There: monarchy, feudalism, theocracy, castes, and ruling families. Here: Democracy."[7] Much closer to events, the residents of San Felipe, a small town in central Mexico, had gathered in 1862 to decide what to do about the French invasion. They determined to fight, convinced that this battle was not just Mexico's concern, since "all nations are watching us . . . waiting anxiously the dénouement of this struggle in which humanity, civilization, and progress are so interested."[8] Perhaps more so than any other single event, Maximilian's death by firing squad seemed to confirm the triumph of a vision of modernity that celebrated republicanism, rights, and even democracy—all achieved in the Americas—as defining modern civilization. I call this countervision of civilization and progress "American republican modernity." How this American republican culture of modernity arose in Latin America after its independence from Spain, what it meant for not only that region but for the broader world, and why this republican culture collapsed late in the nineteenth century are the subjects of this book.

Maximilian, Bilbao, Arias, and the good people of San Felipe had all entered into a debate that consumed the nineteenth-century world: what did it mean to be a modern, civilized society, and what path would nations take to succeed in the race to modernity? Europe and the Mexican Conservatives' defeat (after all, Maximilian was just a proxy for them) marked the triumph and acme of the idea that the future of humanity lay in the Americas, especially those lands now called Latin America. Bilbao, Arias, and the Mexican villagers argued that democracy and republicanism defined modern civilization. And if that was so, then no part of the world was as modern as Latin America, because nowhere else had democratic republicanism been so widely adopted. Of course, the best proof of the importance of Latin American democracy was not the claims of such people but the actual, quotidian, on-the-ground practices. The vast majority of the nineteenth-century world's republics were in Latin America, but for too long historians have joined Maximilian in denigrating republicanism in nineteenth-century Latin America as a corrupt façade.[9] What if we took the assertions of Arias, Bilbao, and these Mexican villagers seriously? How would that make historians rethink the origins and meanings of republicanism, democracy, and modernity in the Atlantic world?

American Republican Modernity

When Mexican Conservatives offered Maximilian the throne, he assumed that their desire for a monarch meant that the republican experiment in Latin America had failed. Even though he fell in defeat, Latin America's importance for the development of republicanism and democracy and the shaping of the modern Atlantic world is similarly dismissed today. This refusal to grant the republican experiments in Latin America legitimacy has occluded a powerful alternative possibility for organizing society and understanding the future that emerged in nineteenth-century Latin America. As noted in the prologue, I denominate this alternative "American republican modernity." In this counter mentalité, Latin Americans did not define a modernity bound to cultured Europe and its civilization but celebrated an imagined modernity located in America, a modernity whose definition was inherently political. Latin America represented the future because it had adopted republicanism and democracy while Europe, under the boots of monarchs and aristocrats, dwelled in the past.[1] American republican modernity emphasized republican politics as a marker of modernity. This republicanism did not just involve elite gentlemen's safeguarding of abstract political and personal rights for privileged individuals; instead, popular groups (to use the nineteenth-century language for the lower class or subalterns) infused republicanism with a democratic challenge and assertions of social and economic rights. Although republicanism began in Latin America as an elite-dominated project, its legitimacy and importance grew due to the demands of popular actors to open the republican nation to people of different classes and racial backgrounds. The force of popular concerns made universalism—the idea that all people, in spite of differences of class, race, or nationality, shared a basic human fraternity and enjoyed rights and citizenship—a central tenet of American republicanism. Although universalism is now viewed with deep suspicion by the postmodern left, it was one of the most powerful tools available to challenge old hierarchies—both on the global scale, between the imperial powers of the Old World and the weak and struggling young nations of the New World, and on the local, between landlord and peasant or master and slave.

This alternative political culture can be understood only in the Atlantic context, because its Latin American practitioners understood their experiments in that framework. They saw their politics as the culmination of a tradition coming out of the Age of Revolution and spanning the Atlantic world. Although recognizing the supreme importance of the American and French Revolutions, they saw their societies as continuing and perfecting these traditions. After all, the French Revolution had failed; by the mid-nineteenth century, Latin Americans saw France as returned to monarchy, ruled by a corrupt pretender to past glories whom they referred to as Napoleon el Chico (the Little Boy Napoleon).[2] The United States, however, was almost always viewed as a great success—and, not as a nation following a distinct path, but as a sister republic traveling the same road as Spanish America. Although generally considered the model republic, the United States could disappoint Latin Americans, due to its imperial desires (which were anathema to the republican ethos) and its racial oppression.

Indeed, the center of modernity was not Europe, but the New World. By the 1860s at the latest, a broad consensus had emerged in many parts of Latin America that the future of the world lay in their societies. A similar confidence had existed at times during the wars of independence and immediately afterward, but that had soon faded as a dominant discourse, as most people in the public sphere looked to Europe as the model for civilization and progress. Yet by midcentury, although many Latin Americans still saw Europe as cultured and powerful, republican politics in the Americas had shifted the locus of civilization. In 1864 the Spanish republican Emilio Castelar termed what I am calling American republican modernity "American civilization," a civilization based not on European norms but on republicanism and democracy.[3] A Mexican provincial newspaper argued that instilling "democracy" and having "triumphed among us the latest progresses of human learning" had "made us equal to the old civilizations" of Europe. In this vision, Mexico had not only reached the same level of civilization as Europe but would "resuscitate the republican genius of France, awaking her subjects and slaves."[4] A Colombian newspaperman put it more succinctly, also in 1864: "Europe is the past. America the Future."[5] Civilization, once defined by Europe, had now passed to the Americas. Francisco Bilbao, the most important intellectual who promoted these visions of American republican modernity, proclaimed that Europe, lacking true liberty, had degenerated due to its monarchy, imperialism, and absence of justice. Europe would have to wait for America "to regenerate the spirit of old Europe." Bilbao, like a generation of largely unknown lesser politicians and provincial newspaper scribblers, asserted what for them was a simple fact about the nature of nineteenth-century societies and the future of the world: "Civilization is today America and the Republic."[6]

Certainly, nineteenth-century Latin Americans thought that their societies' experiments with republicanism and its consequences represented a key moment in world history. This alone seems reason enough for their ideas and practices to merit study. Yet I will also argue that this moment when Spanish America produced an alternative vision of what the future would be and where it would take place—a modernity in contrast to that of the North Atlantic—is both historically and politically important, not merely a quixotic challenge to the intellectual history of the Atlantic world.[7] American republican modernity challenged the dominant tenets of the nineteenth-century world: the primacy of both Europe as the imperial center and the material realities of capitalism for dictating the future. This countervision of modernity also forces a rethinking of the complexities of Latin American liberalism, because it shows that this liberalism did not simply absorb European thought and reveals possibilities and fractures in liberalism that have since been lost. Finally, although American republican modernity may be most interesting as a lost alternative or a path not taken, many of its tropes and preoccupations would reemerge in the twentieth century, in populist political and cultural movements.

In a nineteenth century that would be increasingly defined by imperialism, industrial capitalism, scientific racism, patriotic nationalism, and the growth of state power, American republican modernity presented powerful challenges. Intellectual, social, and political movements in Spanish America would appropriate and reconfigure the most powerful concepts of the nineteenth-century world: republicanism, democracy, rights, universalism, liberalism, and race. All of these potent discourses would be combined into one master narrative of the future and its meaning that would be the dominant Spanish American sense of modernity for a short but critical epoch in the history of the world. Since the fluorescence of American republican modernity was so brief, at best from the 1840s until the 1870s, it would be easy to dismiss it as a momentary and curious hiccup. However, its importance extends beyond Latin America. All of the discourses noted above—republicanism, democracy, rights, universalism, liberalism, and race—bear the stamp of the "West," and scholars and politicians both celebrate or denigrate the Western heritage and origin of such notions, seeing them as either great gifts of the European Enlightenment to mankind or products of a sinister imperial hegemony that seeks to subjugate non-Western peoples, an intention most evident in regard to race but extending to all the tropes.[8] However, if we look at Europe in the nineteenth century, although a heroic few championed the concepts of republicanism, democracy, rights, and universalism, these ideas do not seem to have been the dominant, governing ethos of most European societies. It is in the Americas, despite intense contradictions, where the ideas found fecund soil in which to grow. It is in the Americas where the ideas of the Enlightenment survived, thrived, and evolved. It is in the Americas where, as Laurent Dubois and Nick Nesbitt have shown, universalism was born.[9] And it is in the Americas where the daily practices of republicanism, democracy, and rights actually occurred in societies, where people actually experienced them on a daily basis. Unlike republicanism and democracy, liberalism and race were incredibly powerful in Europe, but it is in the Americas—especially Latin America—where both popular and elite groups succeeded in infusing individual liberalism with more powerful senses of liberty, equality, and fraternity (that is, community). It is Latin Americans who challenged the importance and meaning of race, positing universalism as a powerful opposing force. Edward Said has argued that imperialism created the habit and assumption in Europe that the gifts of history and intellect flow only one way—from metropole to periphery; yet the nineteenth-century Latin American experience does not just argue otherwise—that influence flowed from the New World to the Old—it also dismisses the claim that Europe was the metropole.[10] It is beyond the scope of this book and my own limited abilities to argue that these ideas would not have survived or obtained their eventual importance in the world without the experience of nineteenth-century Latin America. However, I will argue that it is in Latin America, and not the European West, that the progressive human potential of these discourses thrived while they withered elsewhere during the nineteenth century.

A Hidden History

Yet if this vision of American republican modernity was not unusual in nineteenth-century Latin America, why does it sound so surprising in the twenty-first century? First, as noted above, most professional scholars of modernity, beginning with Hegel, agree that Europe—and perhaps the United States—created the conditions for modernity and exported it to the rest of the world.[11] Anthony Giddens, a theorist of modernity, asserts that in the form of the nation-state and capitalism, modernity had its "roots in specific characteristics of European history" and swept out of Europe to engulf the globe—an assertion accepted even by many Latin Americanists.[12] C. A. Bayly notes how other societies tinkered with European modernity but ultimately sees modernity happening earlier and "more powerfully" in Europe and the United States.[13] For Marshall Berman, it was only in the twentieth century that modernity emerged out of Europe and the United States to transform the world.[14] If modernity touched Latin America, one scholar of world history claims, it "was corrupt and flawed."[15] For José Maurício Domingues, even Latin American intellectuals believed that their homeland had experienced only "an incomplete or a degraded form of modernity."[16] Even those postcolonial scholars harshly critical of modernity as a myth that Europe created to justify colonization and violence against "barbarous" peoples in order to civilize them, accept that modernity is European and that Latin America was "the first periphery of modern Europe."[17]

For many of these scholars, not only is modernity European, but its political elements of the nation-state and republicanism cannot really exist in Latin America (our second reason for American republican modernity's low visibility). Bernard Bailyn in his treatise on Atlantic history notes that Latin America's late joining of the Age of Revolution would end in the "collapse of Latin America's new republics into despotic fiefdoms and anarchic city-states."[18] David Landes mocks the new republics of Latin America as "a penny-dreadful of conspiracies, cabals, coups and countercoups—with all that these entailed in insecurity, bad government, corruption, and economic retardation." These societies, Landes asserts, "were not 'modern' political units."[19] Although less vitriolic, Howard Wiarda also sees democracy as essentially alien to Latin America's founding principles, which were feudal, statist, and corporatist—certainly not "modern," like the founding ethos of the United States.[20] Lawrence Harrison simply dismisses any history of democratic republicanism in the region, arguing that only in the 1990s did Latin Americans experiment with democratic institutions "for the first time."[21] Perhaps unconsciously, these scholars accept as fact, instead of opinion, the racial views of some nineteenth-century U.S. observers, who saw no connection between the revolutions in Latin America and their own republican society, since those republicans south of the Rio Bravo were a "degenerate people" with separate histories and abilities.[22] Even for Latin Americanists, it is still part of the conventional wisdom that independence in Latin America was an elite affair, and that most nineteenth-century subalterns were prepolitical simple "folk" protecting traditional lifeways from the outside world, or only conscripted into politics as cannon fodder or clients of powerful patrons.[23] The nation and republicanism meant nothing to them; in the words of Richard Morse, these were "phantom nations."[24] For many cultural theorists, since republicanism was so bound to the new entity of the nation, and the nation was an elite construct doomed to fail as a way to fully incorporate subalterns, republicanism was, a priori, a failure too.[25] For both conservative and classically liberal historians, the problem was not so much the form of the nation, but that Latin American nineteenth-century nations had failed to develop properly (presumably along European lines). Indeed, the whole period of nation and state formation from independence until capitalist takeoff (1820 to roughly 1880), far from being central to the master narrative, was nothing but a "long hiatus" in the course of Latin American history.[26] For Colombia, David Bushnell entitled his history *The Making of Modern Colombia: A Nation in Spite of Itself.* Eric Hobsbawm, hardly an ideological bedfellow with Landes, also dismisses Latin American constructions of nation and republicanism in comparison to Europe. Referring to Latin America, Hobsbawm writes: "It would be anachronistic in our period to speak of anything more than the embryo of Colombian, Venezuelan, Ecuadorian, etc. 'national consciousness.'"[27] In Hobsbawm's world map demarking republicanism in 1847, most of South America is obscured by an inset of Europe (although Switzerland was Europe's sole republic at this time), visually emphasizing Latin America's marginality.[28]

The comparison of Hobsbawm and Landes also suggests a third reason why scholars have not accorded to Latin American republicanism its due: a republican vision of modernity is not teleological in the right ways, being neither Marxist nor conservative nor classical liberal. For some Marxists, republicanism and nation are simply distractions from class-based labor organizing, which does not really begin in Latin America until the late nineteenth century (hence the unimportance of most of the nineteenth century).

For conservatives and classical liberals, the lack of order and economic development in Latin America suggest that these are not real republics, and, given the failure of capitalist development, they are certainly not successful or modern. One cannot help but also feel the deep commitment to the West—a concept used repeatedly in Bailyn's book on Atlantic history in spite of being anachronistic for the eighteenth century on which he focuses—and to protecting its role as the instigator of human freedom.[29] Latin America's history of developing both republicanism and modernity at least complicate this story by situating the development of republicanism and democracy in an Atlantic frame, centered on Latin America, instead of in a Western frame, centered on Europe and the United States.[30]

The fourth, and most important, reason this discourse has been ignored is that many nineteenth-century Latin Americans, especially the region's most eminent and influential political thinkers (letrados), would have agreed with these present-day scholars' definitions and loci of modernity.[31] Domingo Faustino Sarmiento and Juan Bautista Alberdi, so often political rivals, agreed that Europe was the "only known civilization" and that Latin America's condition in the nineteenth century was not on the cutting edge of the future, but more like "Europe in the Middle Ages."[32] For Sarmiento, arguably nineteenth-century Latin America's most famous intellectual, the choice was between European civilization or barbarism: "to be or not to be savages."[33] Many historians and literary theorists generally have accepted Sarmiento's vision as representative of Latin Americans' views of modernity (to the point of ignoring countervailing views among other intellectuals); even postmodernist-inclined cultural theorists who are highly critical of Sarmiento's essentialism assume his work defined nineteenth-century thinking in the region.[34] The great Fernand Braudel asserts: "For a long time, the only civilization that modern Latin America knew was alien to it: a faithful copy, made by a small group of highly privileged people, of the civilization of Europe, with all its refinements."[35] E. Bradford Burns argues that after independence, "civilization and the progress that led to it became identified with Europe," and as the nineteenth century progressed, elites accepted as dogma the idea that only Europe had created "a desirable civilization worthy of emulation."[36] The editors of a recent volume titled Imported Modernity in Post-Colonial State Formation claim that Latin Americans always thought that their societies were trying to "catch up" with Europe.[37] Jorge Larrain argues that Latin Americans' pining for and imitation of European modernity was a "total cultural surrender."[38] Aníbal Quijano deftly eviscerates Europe's presumption in defining itself as the center of modernity, but then he asserts that its colonial and postcolonial subjects accepted such definitions.[39] The argument that Latin Americans sought to remake themselves in the "image of Europe" is still in many ways the master narrative for understanding nineteenth-century life.[40] For most scholars of Latin American culture, it is only with the rise of a purely cultural modernism (modernismo) in the late nineteenth and early twentieth centuries that Latin America establishes its intellectual independence from Europe and begins to challenge the very concept of European, or Western, modernity.[41]

Finally, the fifth reason why Latin—or, more precisely, Spanish—America's assumption of the mantle of modernity has been subsumed in historical memory is that the period of Latin America's claim to modernity was brief. Various currents of modernity competed throughout the nineteenth century, all running parallel with one another; however, at distinct geographic and chronological moments one current might become dominant, directing the flow. In this book I trace the moments in Mexico and Colombia when American republican modernity reigned, beginning in the late 1840s. Yet since this was a transnational discourse, I also show how Colombians and Mexicans were not alone in their imaginings but shared visions with people across the Americas, such as the Chileans, Uruguayans, and Cubans who appear in this story. American republican modernity always competed with visions of modernity coming from and powerfully associated with Europe (and later the United States). After the first flush of postindependence optimism faded, visions that celebrated European high culture and wealth—what I call "Europhile cultural modernity"—predominated early in the century. As the century progressed, what we easily recognize as "Western industrial modernity" emerges, with its focus on scientific, technological, commercial, and industrial advances and, critically, an increase in state power often manifested by renewed imperial projects.[42] These competing currents dramatically shaped subalterns' abilities to make claims on state and nation in the nineteenth century. By the 1870s and 1880s, Western modernity would triumph, burying American republican modernity as a vision of the future in the nineteenth century and as a vision of the past for historians working today. The rise of Western modernity presaged by several decades the concept of the West itself, which arose only at the century's end, although the two were related. In both the West and Western modernity, Latin American societies were no longer the locus of human progress but only a distant, barely legitimate, periphery, struggling to be included in the family of nations that now represented the future.[43] Latin America could only be on the road to progress, always chasing or trying to import a distant modernity located elsewhere, at best a caboose behind Western modernity's locomotive.

However, before this collapse, a generation of Latin Americans created a vision of modernity that profoundly challenged the political, intellectual, and social history of the Atlantic world. Although most Latin Americanists tend to have leftist or at least progressive sympathies, they long have embraced the conservative vision of the nineteenth century as representing not the self-justifying views of a particular class at a particular moment in history, but as an accurate reflection of reality.[44] American republican modernity has largely disappeared from historical consciousness because a generation of letrados and politicians in the late nineteenth century chose to denigrate and dismiss it as either a utopian fancy or a corrupt farce. I will argue that they consigned American republican modernity to the dustbin of history not because it was a negligible and passing fad, but because it represented such a threat to their interests and their project of liberal capitalist development.

"All the Inhabitants of This America Are Citizens"

Given all of the reasons noted above for why scholars have largely ignored this phenomenon I call American republican modernity—the Eurocentric thesis of modernity's origins; the consignment of republicanism, democracy, and the nation's creation to the West; the teleology of some Marxist, conservative, and classical liberal thought; the vision represented by Latin America's most famous letrados; and the rewriting of history that took place in the late nineteenth century—why do I think it was so potent and even, at moments, hegemonic? Simply because if one listens to the quotidian hum and bustle of nineteenth-century political and cultural discourse, what at first seems like a low murmur at the back of the stage becomes a roar, front and center, that demands attention. If you read nineteenth-century newspapers and put yourself in the place of those who listened to nineteenth-century oratory, the discourse of American republican modernity is impossible to miss; indeed, it is omnipresent.

If we move from the letrados, the so-called great thinkers and their intellectual treatises, to the realm of everyday political thought and discourse—most accessible in newspapers and speeches (which, as Pablo Piccato argues, so expanded the public sphere)—a different vision of Latin America's place in the modern world emerges.[45] I am not arguing that there was a class difference between the producers of newspapers and those of oratory and formal literary works (indeed, most intellectuals worked in all three fields; works like Sarmiento's Facundo often first appeared serialized in newspapers), but that when writing for a newspaper or speaking to a public audience, the performer often, if not always, chose to adopt a much different discourse about modernity than he (almost always he) would have employed in more self-consciously literary or scientific texts. Letrados, often trained in Europe (the grand tour was considered essential for gaining an understanding of civilization), pitched their arguments to Europe, often published in Europe, and adopted European sensibilities.[46] The audience was also distinct. Elites and members of the nascent middle class wrote for newspapers, but they had a readership far beyond the literate. The masthead of a Mexican newspaper, La Chinaca (meaning the plebeians or a play on el chinaco—someone who fought the French), shows a gathering of men, women, and children, some with bare feet, listening as a newspaper is read aloud (see figure I.1). La Guerra—published in Morelia, Mexico—was free, and the editors urged readers "to circulate it principally among the indigenous and poor class."[47] Newspaper vendors roamed urban streets in such numbers that cities regulated their activities; for example, Guanajuato, Mexico, banned the shouting of sales pitches after 9:00 in the evening.[48] An observer in Mexico suggested that literacy there was more widespread than widely believed, with the pueblo (which in the nineteenth century could mean all people, but often implied the popular masses) absorbing a variety of printed matter.[49] As even Sarmiento recognized, poor people would gather in taverns or at cockfights for news, spreading knowledge of politics beyond what he called the civilized cities.[50] Many elites feared these taverns as places where "antisocial ideas" spread and the pueblo defined what "their democracy" meant for them.[51] Newspapers also reprinted public speeches, delivered as part of national celebrations that included dances, parades, and fireworks and that were attended by a cross section of society. Of course, the tradition of the Cuban lector, reading to his fellow cigar rollers, is famous. This is also not to say that American republican modernity did not appear in more intellectual writings (it certainly did), or that the more recognized visions of European modernity did not appear in newspapers, but the dominance of each vision varied in different media.

A brief story from Mexico in 1861 shows the power of newspapers' link to the popular classes and the public sphere of the street. As rumors spread that Conservative rebels had captured the popular Liberal hero Melchor Ocampo, crowds, made up especially of artisans, gathered in Mexico City. When further news arrived that he had been assassinated, the crowds rushed first to newspaper offices to confirm the reports, then to the Congress, where they stormed the galleries, "demanding vengeance for the illustrious victim."[52] I

FIG I.1. Masthead of *La Chinaca*. *La Chinaca* (Mexico City), 30 June 1862.

will discuss the public sphere a great deal in this work, but for now I would like to briefly propose that there were both a public sphere of the intellectuals' salons (more akin to Habermas's notion) and a broader, more chaotic public sphere of the street.[53] Historians who rely only on published texts geared to the small elite audience of the salon (and only certain canonical texts at that) miss or underestimate the importance and dominance of American republican modernity in the mid-nineteenth century.

I suppose we should pause a moment to consider, "What is modernity?" Literally thousands of pages have been devoted to this debate, with no consensus, but at least there is some sense that modernity involves industrialization and the politics of citizenship and nation-states.[54] However, debating what modernity "really" means does not concern us.[55] Marshall Berman, a central theorist of modernity, defines the rise of modernity as involving scientific advances, industrialization, global capitalism, migration, urban growth, new forms of communication, social movements, and the nation-state. Yet he also notes that the consciousness of being modern emerged in a second phase of modernity, ushered in by the French Revolution.[56] Echoing Berman, Bayly argues that modernity is something real, involving the rise of the nation-state, nationalism, capitalism's globalization, industrialization, and urbanization, but also simply a mind-set: "the idea that an essential part of being modern is thinking you are modern."[57] I will employ the second, discursive and endogenous definition: modernity does not exist as anything measurable, but is only a normative and judgmental comparison. For our purposes, only what people at a certain time thought of and categorized as "modern" is useful for understanding the power of modernity not as an analytical category, but as a potent discursive force operating in society. Following Frederick Cooper, I will study the representation of modernity, not the so-called condition of modernity.[58] I have tried to uncover what actors on the ground thought about modernity; indeed, modernity had no agency itself—if modernity had power, it was only through the actions of people who believed in it. If I have succumbed to an exogenous view (ascribing modernity to a society), it is by christening a descriptive name to a diverse, but connected and coherent, set of ideas that proliferated around the middle of the nineteenth century: American republican modernity. I hope that this approach will offer more in clarity and succinctness than it loses in analytical violence and simplification. I have also used the word "alternative" at times, but I do not mean to suggest that American republican modernity was an "alternative modernity" in the sense—used by many critics—of a reaction to the primary or authentic modernity of Europe, which Spanish Americans simply tinkered with to serve their own ends.[59] Those who embraced American republicanism saw themselves as modern and their societies as the authentic embodiment of modernity—it was Europe (and Asia and Africa) who were alternative, behind, and desperately reacting to the events and ideologies developing at the core—the Americas.[60] Mid-century Spanish America reversed the imperial gaze, classifying and judging Europe.

If modernity was only a discourse, how important was it in the nineteenth century? The invocation of modernity, civilization, and progress was the master discourse of the nineteenth-century Atlantic world.[61] Writers and speakers in the nineteenth century expressed the concept of modernity through use of the term "modern" (*moderno/a* in Spanish), but more often via the employment of the word "civilization" or its variants—although this usage was not without its own tensions—and by combining the two into "modern civilization."[62] "Civilization" did not always carry modernity's linear sense of progress; it could embrace the past as well. However, most writers assumed there were more or less civilized societies and that societies were moving toward greater civilization (modernity), or away from it and toward barbarism. Indeed, societies were on the "road to civilization" or in a "race of civilization," competing against one another to see which could move toward modernity more quickly.[63] The Cuban paper *Diario de la Marina* asserted that "civilization and barbarism are not just empty words" but encapsulated "the social state of pueblos."[64] Although social scientists still make distinctions between the economic, political, and the discursive, nineteenth-century thinkers saw such fields as tightly interconnected.[65] Indeed, as Thomas Holt has argued, to understand societies (and the operation of power) we must investigate how people understand and make sense of the world on a daily basis through newspapers, stories, song, symbols, and myths (in our study, through public speeches as well).[66] American republican modernity contained in itself an explanation of how the present operated and a plan for the future. I will argue that American republican modernity acted as a critical shaper of both politics and society in the nineteenth century and, through society and politics, significantly altered the economic sphere as well (in ways usually not pleasing to classical liberals or suitable to the needs of capital).

The discourse of modernity was so powerful due to its tight connection to defining and legitimizing the nation, especially given nineteenth-century Latin American nations' inherent novelty and hence essentially undefined character. Elites worried constantly about their new nations, and whether anyone beyond a small circle of intellectuals actually cared or even knew such nations existed. How would new nations be created and legitimized? Unlike in later postcolonial environments, elites could not rely on the state to prop up weak nations, or at least violently suppress the dissent of those unwilling to submit to the nation. The state was, in most cases, far too weak to play such a role effectively if faced with more than isolated resistance. Outside the capital city, the nation-state often consisted of little more than a handful of employees, commanding perhaps a building or two as institutional bulwarks, with little revenue to collect and spend, and almost no coercive force at its immediate disposal. By and large, the nineteenth-century Latin American state was a miserable failure, losing its territory, unable to enforce its laws and will on most of its population, collecting little income, failing to inculcate economic development, or extremely unstable and subject to coups and civil wars. However, contrary to elite fears, throughout the region many subalterns—be they Indian communalists, Afro-Latin American slaves or freedmen, mestizo campesinos, or urban artisans—often eagerly embraced the new nations and proudly, indeed vociferously, claimed citizenship when it suited their purposes to do so.[67]

Let us take the most extreme scenario—the weakest nation-state imaginable right at the moment of its creation in interaction with a social group as far removed from the supposed Creole elite nation builders imaginable.[68] Our nation-state is Mexico in 1822 immediately after independence secured the previous year, with no established institutions, still chaotic from over a decade of devastating war and with the dubious, largely self-proclaimed

Emperor Iturbide on the throne. Our social group, who should not have known or cared about a new elite, Creole nation in the slightest, is enslaved women of African descent. Yet these women wrote the emperor, eagerly demanding their freedom from enslavement as their "natural right," which they could claim as the Plan of Iguala had declared "that all the inhabitants of this America are Citizens."[69] The women did not even know exactly what the new nation would be called, but they knew they wanted to stake a claim to it as citizens. Nations could represent opportunities for those excluded from the social body and politically and economically oppressed to improve their status. Given the right circumstances, subalterns eagerly embraced nations, even if few people thought to include them as citizens, except—critically—subalterns themselves, such as the Afro-Mexican women.

Hobsbawm famously noted for Europe that "nations do not make states and nationalisms but the other way around."[70] This may have been true for Europe, but in nineteenth-century Latin America, while it is true that the state came first, it was quickly passed in power and legitimacy by the nation. Without the idea of the nation to lend the state some legitimacy, many Latin American states might well have collapsed. If the nation's currency propped up an often literally bankrupt state for elites, it also presented them with the intractable problem that they did not control the new nation. The wealthy and powerful hoped that subalterns would dutifully accept the elite version of the nation. That did not happen. Subalterns embraced the nation, but only through a process of struggling over what it would mean. Subaltern men (and, with less success, women) also assumed they would be citizens in full standing in the new nation, with rights and responsibilities they would help define. Elites could not control the new nation—they had little idea what they had wrought.[71] Either they had to accept at least a little of subalterns' assertions about what citizenship and nation would mean, or the new nation would cease to be vital and would become a sterile, imagined community. The state and elites would eventually largely succeed in taking control of the nation away from subalterns, but only beginning in the 1880s.

Discourses of modernity worked powerfully to both bolster and question the legitimacy of these new nations and their states. How societies imagine the future both legitimize their present and determine their priorities. American republican modernity, with its confident evocation of progress grounded in the Americas and based on the greatest extension possible of liberty and equality to all citizens, worked powerfully to establish these new nations as legitimate entities and their states as executors of this legitimacy, representing the people's sovereign will. Throughout this book I explore how visions of modernity molded Latin American societies—not as an intellectual history that traces how great thinkers influenced one another, but more as a history of the culture of politics (or political discourse, if you prefer) that was dominant in a society, a profound social and cultural mentalité that shaped both high and low politics.[72] I am less interested in charting how intellectuals employed certain ideas or discourses than in how and when those discourses and ideas found traction in the public sphere. Since visions of modernity deeply affected the hegemonic rules of political life in Spanish America, I also will suggest how those discourses enabled subalterns to exploit this language for their own ends. Republican modernity viewed a republican citizen body as central to the future not only of their own societies, but of the Atlantic world as a whole; therefore, subalterns' claims to citizenship and rights were a potent tool to confront the state and the powerful. Of course, elites and state makers could simply ignore the discourses. They could make beautiful speeches about citizenship, liberty, equality, the pueblo's sovereignty, and the bright American future, while brutally suppressing subaltern dissent. After all, what ruling class is not hypocritical? As E. P. Thompson noted, "only a ruling class that feels itself threatened is afraid to flaunt a double standard."[73] The problem was that Spanish American elites and the states they ruled always felt threatened in the nineteenth century. With their nations too undefined, their states too weak, their own resources too lacking, elites' position was always precarious at best. Once American republican modernity became the dominant vision in the public sphere, elites and the state could simply not afford to ignore it completely. Yet other imaginings of modernity would not be nearly so conducive to subalterns' needs. Indeed, Western industrial modernity would work directly against subalterns' abilities to claim a place in civilization, while providing states—perhaps more than nations—with a new way to legitimize themselves.

American republican modernity was truly a hemispheric discourse, and the processes outlined above operated across the Americas; therefore, we must study it on a different plane than nationalist historiography allows. The Americas were part of an imagined international community, united by steamships (and later the telegraph), and of an international print culture.[74] Therefore, I will draw on evidence from throughout Latin America, but I will focus my attention on Mexico and Colombia. So why use the term "Latin America" if the focus is primarily on those two societies? Mostly, I admit, for convenience: "Latin America" is simply more pleasing to write than "Mexico and Colombia." Yet Latin America was beginning to emerge as a self-described entity in this period.[75] Most of the time our protagonists employed a more catholic sense of being part of the Americas or the New World, but they did occasionally refer to Latin or Spanish America—sensing, correctly, that their visions of republicanism, international fraternity, and racial equality were not shared in the United States. Equally important, I am not comparing Mexico and Colombia so much as I am attempting to show the connections of a shared discourse not just between the two societies, but with ideas and events throughout the Americas.[76] Therefore, I also turn to Uruguay and Cuba to explore key moments in American republican modernity's rise and fall. In addition, moving beyond Mexico and Colombia helps mitigate the limitations of nationalist historiographies not felt by our nineteenth-century actors, such as the Chilean (but also truly world citizen) Francisco Bilbao. Yet I do emphasize Mexico and Colombia— partly because it was necessary to circumscribe the project somewhat if I ever hoped to complete it, but mostly because I found that it was in Mexico and Colombia that American republican modernity seemed to operate most strongly (especially compared to the Andean states), and there that we can see the results most sharply. Mexico and Colombia also had a very similar nineteenth-century history.[77] Both societies faced early turmoil, both had developed distinct Liberal and Conservative parties by mid-century, both suffered civil wars as these parties contested for power, both had subalterns who actively engaged in national politics, both undertook extensive projects of liberal reforms of colonial institutions, both embraced republicanism and democratic innovation around mid-century, and both started projects of regeneration to restrict this republicanism and democracy and institute capitalist export development. However, the differences—Colombia was faced with imperial intrusion in Panama, but it did not suffer foreign invasions to the same degree as Mexico in the nineteenth century; Colombia was much more stable than Mexico in regard to its governing officials and commitment to republicanism—can be as illustrative as the similarities for understanding the rise and fall of the alternative modernity I explore. I do not want to deny that American republican modernity did not flourish elsewhere, especially in the Southern Cone—in fact, it seemed to develop earliest and with the most force first in Uruguay, and its most eloquent *letrado* interlocutor was the aforementioned Francisco Bilbao.[78] Indeed, if we bother to look after mid-century, we cannot help but sense its effects in newspapers almost anywhere in the Americas. Therefore, although this work is centered in Mexico and Colombia, I hope it is suggestive of (certainly not definitive for) processes occurring across the Americas. However, American republican modernity does seem to have been somewhat less prevalent, though hardly nonexistent, in the Andean states, where the weakness of republicanism resulted from elite fears of the indigenous majority.[79] It also operated much differently in monarchical Brazil and colonial Cuba, although in Cuba American republicanism would find its last, best hope (and Cuban patriots would adopt most of its key tropes), if on a different and more compressed timeline compared to the rest of Spanish America (but ultimately suffering the same fate). Critically, it seems that the intense and sharp ideological divisions between Liberals and Conservatives in Colombia and Mexico fomented the development of competing and alternative visions of modernity by the contending factions.

A Note on the Organization of the Book

Tracing a discourse across two continents, in the wider context of the Atlantic world, throughout the nineteenth century suggested a number of narrative strategies that I hope the reader will approve. As discussed above, the book has a strong evolutionary argument, since I trace the rise, almost to the level of hegemony, of American republican modernity and then its fall as a dominant way of organizing society. However, this current of thought emerged slowly, waxing and waning in different locales and at different times, and always in competition with other currents of modernity and political thought—all of which requires an approach that is not just chronological but also thematic. Indeed, Maximilian's invitation to Mexico shows that American republican modernity always competed with other discourses of civilization for supremacy in the public sphere. These discourses would, like Maximilian, be defeated in the short term, but they would soon reemerge in triumph. After Maximilian's prologue and this introduction, the book continues in chapter 1 with the Banda Oriental (Uruguay) and the most celebrated hero of American republican modernity's pantheon of champions: the Italian Giuseppe Garibaldi. Although Garibaldi would become one of American republican modernity's most important symbols, I am more interested in his mostly local soldiers, the Garibaldinos, and for what they thought they were fighting. This chapter will introduce the first serious challenge to an older elite cultural modernity that looked to Europe, as well as suggest how Americans, in this case the Garibaldinos, thought they would export revolutionary modernity back to Europe from America. Given the scope of this project, I have chosen to delve into key moments that illuminate aspects of our story of modernity, nation, and democracy in short narrative chapters (the prologue and chapters 1, 3, 5, and 6) including those about Maximilian and the Garibaldinos, that accompany the more analytical and comparative chapters (2, 4, and 7) exploring the competing discourses of modernity more systematically. The first of these analytical chapters is chapter 2, which discusses the Europhile cultural modernity that dominated Latin American discourse from soon after independence until around mid-century (and, as noted above, that still dominates assumptions about nineteenth-century thought), and that would always weigh heavily in *letrados'* visions.

In chapter 3 we move to Mexico and the story of the San Patricio Battalion (made up of foreign volunteers and deserters to the Mexican cause) in the U.S.-Mexican War, which involves two key concepts: race and international republicanism. As in the cases of Maximilian and Garibaldi, here I am interested not so much in the foreigners themselves but in how Latin Americans made sense of them and the worlds from which they came. Mexican critiques of the war helped foment a distinct vision of international relations based on universal republican fraternity—the sister republics—as well as establish a pattern of disappointment with the failure of the United States to measure up to this ideal. Chapter 4 is the fulcrum of the book, examining in depth the discourse of American republican modernity and its effects on society. The next two chapters utilize more individual stories to explore key aspects of the evolution of modernity and republicanism in the Americas. Chapter 5 follows the life of the Chilean *letrado* Francisco Bilbao in order to excavate an Atlantic imagination of world events and nations, a roll of heroes and villains engaged in a titanic struggle between civilization and barbarism. This chapter also explores Conservative currents of modernity that always flowed alongside and challenged American republican modernity for supremacy. Chapter 6 outlines the career of the Colombian soldier and politician David Peña to trace the tight relationship between Afro-Latin Americans and American republicanism and the challenge this alliance posed to the hegemony of racial hierarchy.

Chapter 7 examines the collapse of American republican modernity and the rise of Western industrial modernity, with its celebration of capitalist industrialization, technology, science, state power, military force, and racial purity as markers of civilization. The popular classes now confronted a discourse that did not celebrate them as sovereign citizens forming part of the imagined community of the nation, but one that insisted their only place would be as pliant subjects of a disciplinary state and laborers for capitalist development. In the conclusion, I briefly turn to the Cuban War of Independence, which I interpret not only as presaging the conflicts over the color line and decolonization of the twentieth century, but also as looking backward at the nineteenth century's fraternal republican struggles to create a new type of modern society that this book has explored. I close by arguing that reinterpreting the locus and meaning of modernity forces a reconsideration of both the importance of republicanism and democracy in Latin America as well as of Latin America's role in creating republicanism, democracy, and rights in the broader Atlantic world, a creation usually credited to Europe or the United States alone.

CHAPTER 1

Garibaldi, the Garibaldinos, and the Guerra Grande

G iuseppe Garibaldi, "the Hero of Two Worlds," has become the preeminent symbol of the nineteenth-century Atlantic world's struggle for
liberty against the old regime.[1] Across the Americas, there are Garibaldi
Plazas, Garibaldi Streets, and Garibaldi statues, commemorating a man
who nineteenth-century progressives thought best represented their struggles for modernity against an ultramontane Church, kings, aristocrats, and
imperial oppression. We will return to Garibaldi the symbol later, but in
this chapter we will explore Garibaldi's adventures in the New World, especially in the Banda Oriental, where he fought in Uruguay's international
and civil war (the Guerra Grande) of 1839–51. However, of much more interest than Garibaldi himself are the local soldiers who fought under him,
the Garibaldinos (who included Italian immigrants to the Banda Oriental
and local Orientales, or Uruguayans, including many of African descent).
Recovering these soldiers' motivations and mind-sets will begin our journey to understanding the emancipatory potential that subalterns saw in
American republicanism for improving their social, political, and economic
lives. For the Garibaldinos and other popular soldiers, the war provided an
opportunity to rethink the nature of the new nation slowly forming along
the Banda Oriental, which would eventually become known as Uruguay.
The conflict would also provide an important first moment for challenging

traditional notions of the relationship among Europe, the Americas, and modernity.

Uruguay typified the unsettled nature of nation-states in postindependence Latin America. José Gervasio Artigas initiated a revolt against Spanish rule in the province in 1811, and after enjoying an initial military success, he also proposed land redistribution to his rural supporters. However, the region's independence was short-lived, as Brazil invaded in 1816. A decade-long struggle ensued between Argentina and Brazil (both of which claimed the region) and those in Uruguay who wanted independence, which was finally achieved in 1828. Almost immediately, civil war broke out. It raged intermittently throughout the 1830s and 1840s, beginning as a familiar contest for power between two political parties in Uruguay, one side called Colorados (more identified with liberalism and urban Montevideo, and at times being allied with the French and English), the other known as the Blancos (based more in the countryside, and backed by the powerful Argentine caudillo, Juan Manuel de Rosas, who ruled Buenos Aires from 1835–52).[2] The Guerra Grande of 1839–51 involved various American states and European imperial powers, due to Montevideo's geostrategic importance on the Río de la Plata—which was seen as a gateway to the commerce of the Southern Cone—as well as its role as a contested buffer zone between an emerging Argentina and the Brazilian monarchy. The involvement of Europe caused both the Colorados and Blancos to rethink the relation of Europe and the Americas not just in imperial politics, but also in determining the locus and meaning of modernity. For a time, the Colorados especially developed a discourse presaging, if hesitantly and often contradictorily, many of the tenets of American republican modernity: universalism, abolitionism, republicanism, and the meaning and locus of civilization.[3] In spite of its youth and instability, provincial Uruguay, seen as a pawn in the imperial maneuvers of the European Great Powers, would challenge the Old World's claim to monopolize modernity.

The Hero of Two Worlds

Garibaldi came to Montevideo in 1842 after being exiled from Europe and having fought for the self-proclaimed Republic of Rio Grande in its rebellion against the Brazilian monarchy. While there, he had met his future wife, the Brazilian Aninha Ribeiro da Silva.[4] Also while in Brazil, Garibaldi became acquainted with two central aspects of American republican modernity that he would also encounter in Montevideo: New World republicanism and the Afro-Americans who were often its keenest supporters.[5] During the Battle of

MAP 1.1. Uruguay (La Banda Oriental). © Daniel Dalet, d-maps.com

Rio Grande he exhorted his men: "Fire, fire! Against the barbarous tyrants, and also against the patricians who are not republicans."[6] He associated the "Brazilian empire" with "imperialists," no doubt thinking of his native land's relations with Austria. Most of the men he fought with were "men of colour," almost all "negro slaves liberated by the Republic" who were "true champions of freedom."[7] Garibaldi's political thought succeeded not in spite of, but rather because of, its relative lack of sophistication; his simple commitment to liberty against tyranny would inspire numerous followers.

Montevideo was the bastion of the Colorado Party, led by Fructuoso Rivera, which had been at war since 1839 with the Blanco Party, led by Manuel Oribe. Garibaldi's arrival coincided with a massive military defeat of the Colorados at the Battle of Arroyo Grande, and Oribe's forces soon besieged the city, expecting an easy victory. Due to his exploits in Brazil, Montevideo welcomed "José" Garibaldi (he had learned Spanish while imprisoned in Argentina) as a "warrior for the future" who fought for "the dogma of liberty."[8] He was made a colonel and achieved notoriety among his enemies and a reputation for bravery among his friends—first at sea, fighting against Rosas's blockading navy, for which the Colorados awarded him special recognition and prizes.[9] Montevideo feted Garibaldi and his soldiers (the first of several such public celebrations they would enjoy) for their bravery in the battle of el Cerro.[10] Garibaldi served Montevideo by commanding its small navy on the Rio de la Plata and its tributaries and by organizing the Italian immigrants of the city into the Italian Legion. His fame spread among the Blancos and Argentines, who cursed him as the "savage Garibaldi," a bloodthirsty pirate with no ideals (an opinion shared by many of the British diplomatic and naval officials in Montevideo).[11]

His most successful military accomplishment began with his command of a naval expedition up the Uruguay River into the country's interior in 1845 and 1846. After seizing several of the enemy's littoral fortifications, Garibaldi tried to establish a permanent presence in the country's north. Argentine forces laid siege to his base in Salto, and when Garibaldi tried to break the siege, the enemy engaged him in the hamlet of San Antonio. The Battle of San Antonio (or Salto) became legend, with stories that Garibaldi and the Italian Legion of about two hundred men, without cavalry support, defeated a force of over 1,900 (inflated from the initial reports of one thousand adversaries). The battle lasted more than seven hours, with Garibaldi losing thirty men to the enemy's reputed two hundred to three hundred.[12] Newspapers gave detailed accounts of the battle, including maps of troop positions and movements.[13] Garibaldi was immediately promoted to the rank of general, and homages to the battle quickly appeared. General Melchor Pacheco y Obes praised Garibaldi and his troops, proclaiming that the victory had taught "the slaves of the tyrant of Buenos Aires what men who fight for liberty can achieve."[14] The Colorados rewarded Garibaldi and his men with parades and honors, in addition to offering them various prizes. However, Garibaldi declared he deserved no promotion and asked that any recompense go to the wounded soldiers or the families of the fallen, who did receive a double pension (his own family lived in considerable poverty in Montevideo).[15] After the battle, Garibaldi claimed that "I would not trade my name of 'Italian Legionnaire' for all the gold in the world."[16]

For what was Garibaldi fighting? He had the opportunity for many material rewards. The Colorados offered him a seat in the Assembly of Notables.[17] In 1845 and 1847, the president gave him command of all forces defending Montevideo, although he did not serve for long either time, in part due to his inability to navigate the internecine Colorado factions.[18] At various times he could have claimed prizes for his services, yet he generally turned down all such offers. Renown was another matter, and by the end of his career on the Río de la Plata, Garibaldi was already on his way to becoming a legend, with newspapers advertising his portrait for sale.[19] Garibaldi claimed he fought for a "pueblo that fate had placed at the mercy of a tyrant."[20] Bartolomé Mitre, who would become president of Argentina, met Garibaldi while in exile in Montevideo. He remembered being inspired by Garibaldi's aura, and although he thought sentiments more than ideas motivated Garibaldi, Mitre still described him as a "passionate republican" who thought "new revolutions" would be needed across South America to solve the problems those nations confronted (revolution would become a key trope of American republican modernity).[21] Whatever the messy realities were on the ground (and for many elites the war was more about caudillos' competition for power and control of international trade than any idealistic concerns), for Garibaldi and many others in the Atlantic world, the Montevideanos' struggle became a battle between tyranny and besieged liberty and independence.[22] Yet how was the contest understood by the men and women who actually fought in the battles and suffered the siege's privations? What did liberty and independence mean for them?

Foreigners and Slaves

The army that defended Montevideo had two unusual components in a purported national struggle, foreigners and people of African descent— neither of whom most elites considered national citizens. Most of the Foreign Volunteers (as foreigners they enjoyed protection from conscription, so they were volunteers) were Italian, French, or Basque. Some toiled as small farmers, some as laborers, and many as artisans; most were not wealthy, of course.[23] Montevideo was truly an international city in 1843, with 11,431 natives outnumbered by 19,758 resident foreigners (5,324 French, 4,205 Italians, 3,406 Spanish, 2,553 Argentines, 1,344 Africans, 659 Portuguese, 606 English, with a smattering of residents from other locales around the globe).[24] Between 1843 and 1851, at least 148 members of the Italian Legion died while enlisted. This was a significant casualty rate, considering that in 1843 there were just 4,205 Italian men, women, and children in Montevideo.[25]

Why did thousands of foreigners enlist and risk their lives? Eloquent rhetoric asserted that a "spirit of liberty" inspired them.[26] Or they fought for "liberty and civilization."[27] In 1843, during a public festival, the Italian Legion marched and sang that they fought for "liberty" and against "despotic power" and "tyranny."[28] The slogans chanted during two demonstrations of the volunteer troops and local residents provide a small window into their ideology: the crowd shouted "vivas" to "the Republic," to "Liberty," to "all the friends of liberty," to "Colonel Garibaldi," and to "French volunteers," but they booed "*mueras*" to "tyranny," to "Rosas," and to "Oribe."[29] In a letter to a newspaper, "some resident foreigners" argued they would fight not out of an interest in local politics per se, but because "we are brothers in this struggle of principles and civilization . . . wherever Liberty begs for martyrs and calls for defenders." They compared their local struggles to those of the French during the Revolution and the July Days (The French Revolution of 1830), as well as to movements in Italy and Poland.[30] Much like Garibaldi, the soldiers fought for what may have been vague notions of liberty and independence, at once local (as we will see below) and connected to a sense of international movements that shared the same fraternal principles.

Did the soldiers value republicanism as one such principle? Coronel Mancini of the Italian Legion claimed that he and his comrades fought with "republican hearts," which—given that he was speaking to the French Volunteers, some of whom were monarchists—reveals the tensions carried from Europe about what liberty would really mean.[31] The commander of the French Volunteers ended his message to his troops by shouting: "Long live the King!"[32] However, many of the common French soldiers may have held more republican commitments, since during demonstrations they tended to carry symbols of "the French Republic" and sing the Marseillaise (which was banned in France at the time).[33] In 1844 these republican sentiments became more evident, and the French government ordered its subjects to cease fighting in Montevideo. The soldiers of the Legión de Voluntarios signed letters of nationalization and reformed as units of the National Guard. The Legión de Voluntarios' officers and soldiers renounced "the protection as Frenchmen the flag of France offers. Therefore, we ask to be placed under the banner of the Republic as citizens."[34] As is so often the case, it appears that the soldiers' values were much more liberal and republican than those of their officers, and the subalterns much more willing to give up the valuable protection of the French flag to commit themselves to their new nation.

Of course, the volunteers not only thought themselves part of an international movement but also paid close attention to local and personal politics. More mundane motivations for enlisting included the potential loss of their property or even their lives to Rosas's forces, a constant rumor given Rosas's xenophobic rhetoric.[35] Certainly, the chance to obtain booty from the enemy encouraged some, as did promised prizes from the Montevideano government.[36] The Colorados also proposed that foreign volunteers be given land and cattle as thanks after the war.[37] During the war, those serving the state at times did not have to pay rent on houses or farms, or the government paid their rent for them; they were exempted from certain taxes as well.[38] After the battle of San Antonio, the state promised double pensions to members of the Italian Legion.[39] Others soldiers demanded citizenship in return for their service.[40] Indeed, by the end of the war, many of the foreign legionnaires "called themselves Orientales" (as Uruguay was also known as the Banda Oriental).[41] As demands for citizenship and assertions of national identity suggest, I argue that the discursive and the materialistic are not in conflict but equated by the soldiers. "A militiaman" claimed he fought for his "political convictions" and the cause of "liberty," and against the threat of conquest by "foreign barbarity." Although he served because it was "the most sacred duty of the citizen," he also thought the troops deserved medals of honor and that they should be exempted from certain taxes and duties.[42] The volunteers did fight for liberty and republicanism, but these were not the abstract and individual rights imagined by classical liberalism; instead, they signified a broader change in society and their own conditions. This conflation of liberty, republicanism, and social change is most evident with Afro-Uruguayans.

Foreign immigrant volunteers were an important part of the Colorado coalition, but of equal importance were Afro-Uruguayans.[43] After the devastating military defeat at Arroyo Grande in 1842, the Colorado government abolished slavery in the Republic (almost), ordering all males fit to serve to take up arms, while women, children, and the aged would have to remain "at the service of their masters" as "pupils."[44] It is easy to view the decree cynically, as a last-ditch effort to survive, especially given the only tentative and circumscribed freedom of forced military service it initially granted, which even commentators at the time recognized as inadequate.[45] However, the measure succeeded in giving the Colorado government a powerful discursive weapon: Montevideo now stood for liberty and humanity, the decree proclaiming in boldface, "THERE ARE NOW NO SLAVES IN ALL OF THE TERRITORY OF THE REPUBLIC."[46] After its proclamation, the crowds in the legislative galleries erupted in "fervent applause."[47] A newspaper celebrated the decree: "Nothing is more urgent than the recognition of the rights that these individuals have from nature, the Constitution, and the enlightened opinion of our century." (Across the Americas, the opinion of the century—in other words, the force of modernity—would demand abolition, a key component of republican reforms.) The paper went on to say that now "free men" would "defend the liberties and independence of the nation."[48] An editorial urged the freedmen to fight, reminding them that it was "the Colorados who have broken your chains."[49] The hopes of the lawmakers and editorialists were not in vain. Even more important than the discursive advantage it provided, the decree succeeded in raising a large army of the previously enslaved, who did fight with great accomplishment for their own freedom.

For the Afro-Uruguayans, this crisis provided an opportunity not only for legal freedom, but also for a more complete inclusion in the new nation. Colorados did not hesitate to emphasize that the former slaves had to earn this status: "Slaves! Now you are free! Fight, you slaves, to become men!"[50] Colorado politicians did not offer freedom alone: they suggested that after the war, the former slaves would be given land and the "pupilage" of their wives and children would also be ended as a reward, so that the soldiers would be "property holders" and "padres de familia."[51] A newspaper noted that the "soldiers of color have paid in blood" for the liberty of themselves, their families, and the Republic; therefore, after the war, they would be "free men" and "citizens."[52] Colorados urged that a state official ensure that women and children be treated as "pupils" and not slaves, so that "our fellow citizens," the freedmen, would see the decree as just and not a farce.[53] The freedmen themselves acted to end pupilage by marrying pupils and then demanding that the state release their wives, due to the "incompatibility of pupilage with the status of wife."[54] Soldiers also demanded their children's release from pupilage. Since these men were vital to Montevideo's survival, the state at times acceded to their demands.[55] Freedmen now had significant bargaining power; negotiation between elites and plebeians would powerfully shape and be shaped by American republican modernity.

The Colorados' exhortations to the former slaves to earn their manhood and the freedmen's efforts to reconstruct their families emphasize the importance of gender in determining citizenship and national inclusion. Race played an equally important role. Colorados suggested that race would become less important during the war, arguing that "whites, coppered-skinned, blondes, blacks, everyone will mix together . . . in one phalanx in order to save National Independence."[56] They also promised that under the Colorados, men would not be "disparaged due to their color" and that promotion to the militia's officer corps would be decided by "merit."[57] A paper made much of the fact that in a letter the Blanco leader Oribe derided the Colorado President Rivera as a "mulato."[58] However, if Rosas and the Blancos won, the Colorados warned the freedmen would be reenslaved and shipped to Brazil, "where the poor blacks are treated worse than animals."[59] When Oribe and the Blancos created a legal defender of minors and slaves in 1845, the Colorados argued that this meant he did not recognize the emancipation they had declared and would return freedmen to slavery. The Colorados read Oribe's decree to units with former slaves, reminding them: "But now you have weapons and will die fighting before returning to live under the whip of a master. War to the death, men of color, to those who would return you to wearing the uniform of a slave!"[60] One might argue that the evidence of the Blancos' plan to return freed people to slavery was slim, but for black soldiers that would have been enough. Gambling on whether slavery would return or not under a Blanco victory was not a risk that many were willing to take. The Colorados combined legal, political, social, and gendered enticements, with a warning of what a failure to fight would mean: slaves might now be free, but they still had the status of minors; only by fighting could they improve their social standing. Soldiering would "make them heads of families and free citizens with a soul of iron and the standing of a hero."[61]

Given the limited options that the freemen enjoyed, they perhaps had little choice but to fight. However, as we saw above, they took advantage of Montevideo's perilous situation to push their own agendas. The Colorados did not take for granted that the freedmen would serve (or serve well), especially if they had no reason to do so. Since the abolition decree was so incomplete, the Colorado generals conducting the war worried that the soldiers on whom they now relied might choose not to fight if the declared emancipation appeared to be a trick or to go unenforced. When a Montevideo newspaper ran an ad offering to sell a "mulata," the minister of war rebuked the paper for running the notice, calling it a "scandal" that "one advertises the slavery of a free person."[62] Colorado newspapers also regularly reported on rumors that masters smuggled freed Montevideanos into Brazil, to turn them into slaves once again. The Banda Oriental's consul in Rio de Janeiro even succeeded in freeing three "black women Orientales" who had been sold by their former masters to a ship's captain (in two cases) or kidnapped (in the third case) from Montevideo and transported for sale in Brazil.[63] The state eagerly tried to show that it now represented the Afro-Uruguayan soldiers' interests.

Did the Colorados' efforts work? The abolition decree seemed popular: upon its announcement, crowds in the city erupted with "vivas" to the government.[64] Colorado politicians privately celebrated the act as inspiring both the pueblo and soldiers.[65] More important than the discursive advantage, hundreds, if not thousands, of freedmen joined the National Guard and certainly saved Montevideo from imminent defeat at the hands of Oribe's advancing army.[66] Within days of the decree's issuance, between eight hundred and one thousand freedmen joined the National Guard.[67] Garibaldi considered them a central component of the army.[68]

What did Afro-Uruguayans think about the decree? Those held in bondage certainly used the decree of 1842 to declare themselves free. While trying to move a number of "blacks" from one worksite to another, a master murdered one of his former slaves, who had claimed that the new decree had ended all slavery in the Republic.[69] We know the freedmen fought, and we know they used their status as defenders of the country to improve their conditions. A letter purporting to be from "Masambiques, Banguelas, Congos" would, if authentic, support the view that Afro-Uruguayans also thought that the Colorados were their allies: "Masambique, Banguela, Congos, all the blacks are going to fight for the Patria [Fatherland] and for the government that has given them freedom." The letter's authors acknowledged that "Don Fruto [Rivera] has given us liberty and removed our chains." The Blancos, who were also called the Rosistas, wanted to reenslave them, because the freedmen now shouted: "Long live Liberty! Death to the Tyrant!"[70] The letter is almost a perfect (perhaps too much so) vindication of the Colorados' strategy: freedmen would fight for Montevideo, saw the Blancos as representing the master class and tyranny, and thought Uruguay was now their homeland. Whether Afro-Uruguayans thought the Colorado politicians were cynical and desperate manipulators or true friends of liberty may never be known. However, clearer is the fact that the freedmen seized the chance the war had brought to improve their status and make a play for inclusion in the new nation as citizens. In general, war provided many opportunities for subalterns to assert their status and could act as a leveler of social distinctions, where "poor and rich" faced the same treatment and hardships.[71] In this war, blacks and whites fought together, the companies of freedmen and the Italian Legions holding the line as one.[72] In Montevideo, we see in the crucible of war the creation of a new nation out of foreigners and slaves and the melding of universal fraternity (shorn of race), abolition, republicanism, and popular citizenship that, for a time, would make American republican modernity so potentially emancipating.

Early Stirrings of American Republican Modernity

The discourse of the freedmen and foreign volunteers and the discourse that percolated throughout Montevideo's public sphere during the Guerra Grande prefigured a number of elements of American republican modernity: fraternity between people and nations, abolition as a marker of freedom and progress, and—most important—an equation of republicanism and liberty with civilization. Rosas and Oribe regularly mocked the Colorados as being the dupes and pawns of European imperialists as manifested by their reliance on the foreign legions.[73] However, Colorados did develop a counternarrative celebrating their foreign volunteers as displaying "the fraternity that exists between natives and foreigners."[74] Not just individuals but nations should embrace fraternity, and Montevideanos viewed the civil war as an international struggle for liberty, as did many across the Atlantic world who celebrated Montevideo as a "New Troy."[75] Abolition also became a powerful trope to define republicanism and civilization. A letter to the editor immediately after the 1842 abolition argued that emancipation was "a tribute to civilization" in accordance with "the principles of equality that we have proclaimed since our glorious revolution."[76] The Colorado minister of war denounced slavery as "the most barbarous of institutions."[77] The entire war could demonstrate the dichotomy not just between slavery and abolition, but also that between civilization and barbarism; in 1844 soldiers claimed they fought "to sustain civilization and liberty."[78] Civilization could mean more than simply elite culture, manners, or wealth; it could involve degrees of human freedom as well. I will discuss these tropes in depth in chapter 4, but now I will turn to the most developed aspect of American republican modernity in Uruguay: the challenge to Europe's role as master of civilization.

The Guerra Grande began with most educated Uruguayans subscribing to the dominant ideology that Europe was the font of all civilization, a more or less hegemonic intellectual position that I will explore in the next chapter. For many Uruguayan intellectuals, caudillos—such as the Argentine Rosas and Antonio López de Santa Anna, "the Mexican Rosas"—represented American barbarism that only "European civilization" could one day redress.[79] The economic success of Europe was greatly envied, and some intellectuals saw the Old World's slow progress toward constitutional and parliamentary monarchy as a great political achievement.[80]

As the war progressed, however, some Colorados began to assert that what they still called "European civilization" was part of an international struggle for "liberty, equality, [and] humanity" occurring across the globe. Europe was no longer unique or the progenitor of all progress, but part of a shared movement toward modernity, contested by the forces of reaction and barbarism. The fight on the Río de la Plata against Rosas's dominion of "assassination and barbarity" was a continuation of combat "in the streets of Paris" during the July Revolution of 1830, of Spanish and Italian struggles against "absolutists" and "tyrants, and of "humanitarian meetings" in

England.[81] Other Colorados also saw the Americas as continuing the project of the French Revolution. Melchor Pacheco y Obes, the Colorado minister of war, addressed the French Volunteers in 1843, urging them to look to their ancestors, who had destroyed the "decrepit monarchy." He argued that Americans had continued this work, taking up the banner of "free men" from "the Pampa to Chimborazo" to overthrow "the flag of the conquistador." Now European and Americans fought together: "If you fall in combat, our blood will run together fraternally with yours."[82] Although the speech generally speaks of a shared project of liberty, the implication (it was only an implication at this point) is that since a king once again ruled in France, America had surpassed Europe in moving toward greater liberty (which was beginning to be equated with modernity).

As the Guerra Grande progressed, and their European allies either abandoned them or pressured them to accept a settlement with Rosas and the Blancos, some Colorados (and their Argentine Unitario allies, who also opposed Rosas) began to use a more aggressive tone. One newspaper claimed that "civilization and humanity still do not occupy a privileged place in the councils of European Governments."[83] Another complained that Europeans looked on the war in the Rio de la Plata as evidence of American barbarism, arguing that if one looked at "the center of civilized Europe," a bloody civil war had erupted in Switzerland, whose citizens were supposedly a pacific and industrious people. Furthermore, if one turned to Ireland, one would see "repeated scenes of pillage, arson, violence and murder."[84] Instead of accepting European superiority as indisputable, some Americans began to assert that Europe suffered from many of the same abuses and trials as they did.

While much discourse stressed the similarities between the Old and New Worlds, either in their struggles for liberty or the abuses each suffered under barbarous tyrants, another discourse stressed a fundamental difference between the two sides of the Atlantic: republicanism versus monarchism. In assessing the amount of influence that European models should have on the Americas, instead of assuming that greater imitation of Europe automatically led to greater civilization, a paper noted that "the European principle of constitutional monarchy" conflicted with the "American principle of popular and elected governments." However, the author also asserted that the new American nations needed European capital and immigrants.[85] This ambivalence reflected the still dominant acceptance of Europhile modernity while also foreshadowing the tension between political modernity and economic modernity that would define the success and failure of American republican modernity. Other Colorados, in spite of their claims to support racial equality, were more explicitly racist in their conception of civilization, not easily escaping the racial and Eurocentric hegemony that had defined civilization up to that time. Even a newspaper promising a future in which race would not matter also hoped that ending slavery would encourage the immigration from Europe of "a civilized, white population," which the writer predicted would soon double the country's inhabitants.[86] Race would be the aspect of American republican modernity that often hewed most closely to the colonialist past and the racial currents of Europe and North America that celebrated whiteness; yet at times American republicanism would also present the most radical challenge to racism's hegemony in the Atlantic world by promoting universalism.

As I will discuss in the next chapter, most Latin American public intellectuals were still reluctant to assert the superiority of republicanism, given the apparent failures of many American republics in the 1840s. Surveying the Americas, *Comercio del Plata* found "hispano-americanos" in "a chaos of anarchy and disorder, drowning in a sea of blood." This sad state of affairs had caused some—especially in Mexico—to see monarchy as the answer. However, the solution was not to model states after Europe, as European papers were urging in the case of Mexico, but to adopt truly republican systems, instead of the "false republics" that currently ruled.[87] Another essay in the same paper went further, suggesting a natural progression from monarchy to republicanism, as pueblos sought "to take the reins of government in their own hands." But the opposite, moving from a republic to a monarchy, would be extremely difficult, as the pueblos would not want to give up "the idea of their own and exclusive sovereignty" and turn that sovereignty over to "only one man."[88] This type of thought implied—though not yet completely expressed—a natural progression from monarchy (the past) to republic (the modern future) in "modern history," which the writer noted that all the former American colonies, except Brazil, had achieved after independence, but that Europe had not yet mastered. The essay closed by urging Americans not to follow "European principles."[89]

A few writers went even further. They believed that the Americas formed not just one part of a shared Atlantic struggle for republican civilization, but that Americans would soon surpass their European brothers. One writer, furious that the French appeared eager to make peace with Rosas at their Montevideano allies' expense, told his compatriots to take heart in spite of French treachery: "Neither the French nor other foreigners are the ones that have given us liberty or institutions. Thanks to our own efforts, we enjoy both more and better than the French, who are more slaves of Luis Felipe [the French king]."[90] Some began to suspect that Europe was not becoming more modern but—due to its autocratic politics, which had recently crushed revolutions in Poland and Italy—was actually moving backward: "Under the rule of absolute power, who doubts that the human species regresses in Europe?"[91] After the failure of the 1848 revolutions had become evident, *Comercio del Plata* surmised that although the "people of Paris" had made great strides for "liberty, civilization and intelligent progress," they had succumbed since "the spirit of the rest of Europe is not prepared to accept republican ideas."[92] An important revelation had arrived: republicanism was as potent a definition of civilization as high culture or wealth, and this progress found a welcome in America, in contrast to its hostile reception in Europe. In the midst of a civil war and foreign invasion, Uruguayans were not as assertive of their position in the world as would be the case later in the century, but they did sense that by embracing republicanism they had accomplished something Europe had not.

Teaching Europe about Free Men and True Republicans

When a Genoese ship brought news in December 1847 of new liberal and anti-Austrian movements throughout the Italian peninsula, there was a great celebration in Montevideo. Garibaldi (now disillusioned by the Colorados' internal bickering) and some of his men prepared to leave to continue their revolution in Europe.[93] At least four native Orientales accompanied Garibaldi to Italy, including "the pardo [a free person of African or African and European descent] Aguilar."[94] On Garibaldi's departure, a newspaper saluted his "constancy and loyalty to the noble cause" that Montevideo had defended.[95] Garibaldi returned to Europe, where he already enjoyed considerable fame due to his New World campaigns; this fame pushed him to the forefront of struggles for Italian unification and independence.[96] Poems celebrating his and the Italian Legion's exploits had been published in Italy (and banned by the authorities); upon his return to the Old World, European press accounts referred to him as the "man of San Antonio," after his most famous triumph in Uruguay.[97] After news of the Battle of San Antonio had reached Italy, a Florentine broadside called for a subscription to reward the legionnaires with a "sword of honor" for Garibaldi and silver medals for his men. A Montevideano paper noted the curiosity of this call being reported "under the power of one of the instruments of Austrian oppression in Italy, to whose ears no echo of liberty sounds pleasing."[98] American newspapermen no longer waited for the ripples of the French Revolution to cross the

Atlantic but began to assume that Europe waited to hear the echoes of New World clamors for liberty. Common soldiers went even further.

Upon Garibaldi's departure, the vast majority of his soldiers stayed behind in their new home and now referred to their Italian Legion as the Italian-Oriental Legion.[99] Identities were fluid in the new nation, and many of these immigrants, like their freedmen comrades, invested powerful hopes in the new American nations, which could turn Italians into Orientales and poor men into citizens. The soldiers who remained to make their lives on the Río de la Plata requested in 1852 that the national government give them their legion's standard, citing their "service to the Republic," including at the battle of Salto. The legionnaires wanted to send their battle flag to Genoa, as an "example for the Italian democrats." Although their compatriots had been fighting despotism for over three centuries, "this banner will teach them that against the tyrant's bayonets . . . free men and true republicans can triumph."[100] We rarely have a window into subalterns' perception of world affairs, as opposed to more accessible local concerns, but these soldiers' words show that not only the wealthy and educated thought about the nature of the nineteenth-century world and its fantastic evolution. For these American soldiers—unlike the elite *letrados* I will discuss in the next chapter—America was not the student of European civilization, waiting for enlightenment and progress to wash up on the shores of Montevideo from France or England. Instead, the soldiers would instruct and inspire the Old World, showing it how to secure political progress by fomenting the type of revolution that already had succeeded in the New World—an idea that would become a consistent element of American republican modernity. After all, it was in Uruguay, not the Old World, where Garibaldi and the Garibaldinos first began to wear the famous red shirts by which they became known.[101] Like the raiment, ideas and inspiration spread east across the Atlantic.

CHAPTER 2

"A Pueblo Unfit to Live among Civilized Nations"
Conceptions of Modernity after Independence

The Garibaldinos' confidence in their own republican struggle, and their sense that Europe needed American inspiration, found little echo in most conceptions of modernity before mid-century. Elite intellectuals tended to look to Europe for civilization, and by the 1840s they despaired at the state of American progress as often as they expressed any faith in the potential of the new republican nations. It is in this period that Latin American intellectuals cemented their assessments of European culture and civilization as superior and exemplary, as well as sowing doubts about the suitability of republicanism for their own societies. These thinkers developed a vision of Europhile cultural modernity that imagined progress as best achieved by imitating European models of high culture, wealth, propriety, urbanity, discipline, and whiteness. Thus, the postindependence generation laid the foundation for the current of modernity that would continually challenge and counter American republican modernity throughout the rest of the century. Surveying the state of their new nations, adherents of Europhile modernity generally despaired at the state of American civilization (if such a thing even existed!), gloomily proclaiming that the judgment of Europe (the single truly civilized world) could only look on the new American nations as failures.

The epitome of this vision of pessimism is Simón Bolívar's famous quote: "America is ungovernable . . . those who serve revolution plough the sea."[1]

Bolívar's despair overcame the sense of potential and hope that had bloomed immediately after independence.[2] Puebla's El Farol, although still acknowledging the tutorship of "European Enlightenment," declared in 1821 that America—the former pupil—would now become the professor, as Americans "find themselves ready to give lessons to Europe, and Providence seems to destine them to be from here on the teachers and reformers of the world."[3] La Minerva Guanajuatense also reflected such provincial optimism, predicting that Mexico's industries would soon rival those of Europe and observing that they had nothing "to envy" even from England.[4] The paper somewhat bemusedly commented on a public atmosphere that dismissed "decrepit Europe" in favor of the men of "young America," who "were born to teach the world what liberty and patriotism are."[5] The Spanish invasion of Mexico in 1829 evoked paeans to American "republican virtues" as "children of liberty" in contrast to Spain's "degrading slavery," ruled over by a "barbarous King."[6] Such confidence about the Americas' role in modernity in contrast to European barbarism would soon be rare, but it would reappear as the central trope of American republican modernity after mid-century.

More common by the late 1820s were Bolívar's attitudes of looking on Spanish America with disgust and despairing over the anarchy, chaos, corruption, and general failures of the new nations and their republican systems. For Bolívar, America was not moving forward to modernity but backward, as a land dominated by "feudal lords."[7] Indeed, there was little hope: "From one end to the other, the New World is a vast abyss of abomination."[8] Republicanism was a farce and the new nations, failures.[9] In short, America was not at the vanguard of modernity, but at risk of being "the laughing-stock of the world."[10] Bolívar looked more to Europe's "wisdom and experience" and Great Britain and its constitutional monarchy as an exemplar than to any American innovations.[11] By the 1860s, the public sphere would celebrate America as the future of the world, but in 1830, instead of moving toward the future, it seemed more likely to the Liberator that America would "revert to primitive chaos."[12]

Bolívar's pessimism about republicanism and the Americas' standing in the race to civilization soon became quite generalized across Latin America, eventually becoming the master narrative (if one that was often challenged) of the letrado class. By the late 1820s, the chaotic political situation had dashed any early hopes in Mexico. Constant civil wars and coups created a revolving-door presidency, with chief executives serving on average less than a year; the caudillo and political operative Antonio López de Santa Anna alone took office on eleven different occasions between 1833 and 1855.[13] In the public sphere of daily political discourse, newspapers fretted that "the apostles of anarchy, sedition and disorder" had so corrupted the pueblo with their demagoguery that Mexico risked a "total degeneration of society."[14] Editors declared that "the Republic is visibly declining," as indicated by a collapse of "public confidence" and capital flight.[15] Due to the deterioration of the respect for property and individual liberties, they warned of the "ruin of the republic" and the "horrors of barbarous despotism."[16] Mexico was hardly alone. As the young state faced yet another armed uprising in 1832, one writer warned that if such chaos continued, "we would succumb to a military anarchy, perhaps more pernicious than that in Colombia."[17] Although they had been optimistic in 1825, by 1827 the editors of El Observador de la República Mexicana did not think the nation had moved forward toward modernity; rather, it had experienced a "fatal retrogression."[18] In the mid-1840s, many found Latin America's situation little improved. In still-colonial Cuba, El Diario de la Marina surveyed the whole of the Americas, noting the looming war between Mexico and the United States, the continued coups in Central America, the rule of caudillos in Peru, and the conflict between Buenos Aires and Montevideo. The newspaper concluded: "Such is the sad state of the American continent."[19] In Uruguay, El Constitucional agreed, sighing that nothing was more "melancholy and deplorable" than the present situation of the New World.[20] Bolívar, though often imagining himself a lone Cassandra, presaged the fears, uncertainty, and gloom that dominated the public sphere after the first blush of independence's promise had faded.

Europhile Cultural Modernity

If Bolívar epitomized the pessimism and disillusion with republicanism of the postindependence era, it was Domingo Faustino Sarmiento who, in 1845, provided the intellectual basis for analyzing the problems of the early American nations by proposing his famous dichotomy between civilization and barbarism.[21] However, while Bolívar despaired at the end of his life, Sarmiento was much more optimistic, proffering a solution to America's problems. Sarmiento would not have disagreed with much of Bolívar's assessment of America's state but thought it correctable, if Americans would follow the proper path and aspire to European civilization. Like Bolívar, Sarmiento opposed the corrupt political leadership that he saw dominating the new American states, especially his own Argentina's Juan Manuel Rosas (1835–52). Unless his regime ended, Rosas would doom Argentina to backwardness, due to his hostility to "the ideas, customs and civilization of European peoples."[22] Sarmiento famously constructed a dichotomy between cities, where "the latest progresses of the human spirit" developed, and the barbarous countryside.[23] It was in the cities where European civilization existed and from which modernity would flow: "The man of the city wears European clothes, lives a civilized life as we know it everywhere; there are laws, ideas of progress, means of instruction, some municipal organization, regular government, etc."[24] In the countryside, one found American clothes and American people but little industry, no education, no culture, and scant public life—in short, barbarism.

In Sarmiento, we see the clear linkage between what he called civilization and what academics call modernity. Sarmiento stressed that societies' civilization was not a fixed state but a continuum, changing both in time (as societies improved or vegetated) and space, since in every nation, but especially in the Americas, the modern and the backward existed side by side: "The nineteenth century and the twelfth century live together, one in the cities, the other in the countryside."[25] Barbarism ruled the countryside not just because of the ignorance of the population, but also because of its mixture of European, indigenous, and African elements, who detested labor and industry.[26] Although Sarmiento expressed some optimism that "indigenous barbarism" could be cured by education, mostly he hoped that the civilized cities would come to control the countryside, spreading European influence.[27] Sarmiento was more optimistic than Bolívar that the Americas could obtain the "genius of European civilization," but only by ensuring that the Eurocentric part of society became dominant.[28] In this manner, Sarmiento encapsulated and promoted the Europhile modernity that would define the public sphere in the 1830s and 1840s and would dominate letrado thought for much longer. Civilization was basically a cultural attribute, linked to middle- and upper-class European behavior, manners, norms of living, race, and wealth. There was some concern with economics, as Latin America must develop some industry (mostly imagined at this time as export agriculture, not industrial production) in order to create the wealth necessary to sustain civilization.[29] However, this economic concern was important mostly as a support to the critical cultural behavior that defined civilization. Similarly, unlike in American republican modernity, the type of politics (republican, democratic, constitutional, or monarchical) seemed less important than that the style was orderly and the ruling class had European sympathies. Politics were not critical in themselves, but the wrong politics (those of Rosas or the influence of the plebes, for example) could block these cultural aspirations, thus spreading barbarism.

Sarmiento's work, of course, is considered the preeminent exemplar of nineteenth-century elite political and cultural thought.[30] This is correct in many ways, but misleading in two. First, many of the views on civilization that Sarmiento expressed had filled the public sphere long before his publications appeared. Over a decade before Sarmiento's *Facundo* was published, the newspaper *Registro Oficial* noted that the fate of Mexico rested on "a war of civilization against barbarism, of property against thieves, of order against anarchy."[31] Second, Sarmiento represents the norm for the public sphere only at certain moments, not throughout the entire nineteenth century, as is often assumed. Indeed, by the time of their publication, his ideas were already being strongly challenged in the public sphere, as we saw in Montevideo. I will deal with the second concern in later chapters, but here let me examine how widespread were the views attributed to Sarmiento. Long before he made such claims dogma, a sense of civilization as defined by education, manners, order, and European norms had dominated public discourse. In 1821 *El Farol* lamented the state of Mexico's population, in particular that there was so little education among its people, a problem even in the most "civilized nations" of Europe but one that was much worse in the emerging American states.[32] Indeed, some blamed the pueblo's "ignorance" for the general weakness of the nation and national sentiments across Latin America.[33] As Sarmiento's work attests, education was perhaps the single most prominent marker of civilization under Europhile cultural modernity.

Above all, civilization was broadly defined by high cultural attributes (as opposed to political or economic measures), and its locus centered upon Europe. Mexicans desired to imitate the lifestyle of "refined Europe" even in matters as trivial as public amusements, where theaters and salons should replace back-alley gambling dens. In its pursuit of a noble "sense of pleasure," Mexico should emulate the land of the Saxons, "that great people."[34] Nothing marked elites as modern as much as having the latest dresses, pianos, pocket watches, or foodstuffs from Europe.[35] Literature, of course, formed the bedrock of any "civilized nation," and translations of the great European works should commence.[36] Sarmiento cemented these cultural traits as synonymous with cultured urban life. However, it was not just adopting Europhile elite consumption tastes that mattered, but society's broader refinement. The newspaper *Comercio del Plata* proposed that civilization was based on "sociability," which denoted the pervasiveness of such traits as industriousness, pacificity, order, lawfulness, and decorum in a population.[37] Like all nineteenth-century visions of civilization, this assumed a progression, depending on the extent to which such values had permeated society.

As the concern with sociability suggests, a society revealed its level of civilization by the educated life and manners that operated in the public sphere. Jürgen Habermas did not invent the obsession with the public sphere; it was a constant concern of nineteenth-century observers.[38] El *Observador de la República Mexicana* argued that in civilized nations there was a distinction between "popular voice" and "public opinion." Public opinion could be formed only by educated citizens: "There exists in civilized nations a body consecrated by nature . . . to teach and propose the means by which to make happy the patria."[39] "Philosophers" were those who had "civilized" the "barbarous pueblos." If societies followed the popular voice, which was formed by "violence, by terror, by factions, by ignorance," they would go down the same path that France had taken because of the Parisian masses.[40] El *Siglo Diez y Nueve* argued that republicanism, more than any other political system, relied on the good sense of "public opinion," which perhaps doomed Mexico due to the ignorance of the masses who insisted on participating in politics.[41] As the century progressed, Liberals fretted that Mexico's "ignorant and imbecilic pueblo" embraced "fanaticism" and religious superstition to such an extent that education might be impossible.[42] The proponents of Europhile cultural modernity thought that only the civilizing opinion of the public sphere of the salon mattered (following Habermas's ideal of rational bourgeois property holders); the raucous street, despite Sarmiento's love of urbanity, carried the plague of barbarism.[43] This theorization of the public sphere captured two concerns of cultural modernity. First, progress occurred due to the leadership of educated elites: it was a cultural action. Second, the uncultured and barbarous masses, whose influence must be limited, always threatened to undermine civilization.

In Mexico, many in the public sphere thought of the peripatetic Santa Anna (as Sarmiento thought of Rosas) as representing barbarism, due to his open lust for power and the support of the lower classes that he could marshal. Although Santa Anna's opponents obviously envied his political success, they often coded their criticism of him in cultural terms: Santa Anna's "sentiments little conform to the suavity of customs that inspires the lights of the century and modern civilization."[44] Of course they hated Santa Anna for his political prowess, but they expressed their displeasure in the terms of cultural modernity: Santa Anna did not act like a modern, educated, Europhile leader should. Worse, he undermined modernity with his attacks on "the aristocracy," mocking those who wore "fine clothing," "paid for seats in the theater," had a maid, or whose table settings and culinary habits seemed too luxurious.[45] Yet, for the *letrados*, going to the theater, wearing fine clothes, and having the latest china were all marks of civilization.

Although undoubtedly cultural in its emphasis, Europhile modernity did not exist in isolation. Instead, it reflected and competed with other measures of civilization developing in the North Atlantic world, especially involving the changing economic and political realities that educated elites would foment. El Farol argued that the "glory of a nation" depended on the state of its arts and sciences, its good government, and its advancements in industry, commerce, and agriculture.[46] The diplomat, politician, editor, and poet Joaquín M. de Castillo y Lanzas defined progress as involving educating the pueblo; improving the arts, agriculture, and commerce; enjoying peace; and encouraging industry.[47] Most letrados and the public sphere accepted civilization as basically a cultural phenomenon, but the promise of commercial and industrial progress provided both the most potent secondary definition and the greatest challenge to Europhile cultural modernity and American republican modernity—and it would eventually triumph over both of them.[48] In the 1820s and 1830s, however, improving the cultural life of the people, along European lines, was what allowed industry to develop. The most expeditious way to accomplish this would be to import Europeans. Large-scale immigration would provide labor and industry, ameliorate the common people's culture, and improve society's racial stock, which elites saw as dominated by "the degenerate and depraved race of the natives."[49]

While the exact measure of civilization remained open to debate, there was less uncertainty about modernity's locus and the progress of the world's nations. In the prevailing view, Latin America at best was only on the path to modernity, following Europe and the United States. Even optimists assumed that England, France, and other European states were "advanced on the road to civilization" and therefore had much to imitate.[50] Youth, which later in the century would become a great strength, appeared in the late 1820s to represent the new nation-states' fragility and insubstantiality.[51] New nations were like unruly children, lacking both a reasoning populace provided by education and the material resources offered by a history of labor, especially compared to Europe's cultural and economic maturity. Latin America was still pursuing modernity, making some advances but just as often suffering debilitating setbacks. These were due to disorder and anarchy in particular, but also to the racially problematic population, colonial past, rebellious plebeians, and lack of education.[52] Anarchy, often codified as a cultural failing as well as a political condition, appeared to be an almost insurmountable hurdle.[53] "Modern powers" had achieved their advancements thanks to avoiding internal strife.[54] The aptly titled *El Imperio de la Ley* (The rule of law) fretted that the "enemies of order" sought to "impede our progress toward civilization."[55] *Los Amigos del Pueblo* condemned Santa Anna for reducing Mexico to barbarism, since "modern civilization" had rejected such sordid Machiavellian actions as his constant plotting and coups.[56] *El Genio de la Libertad* despaired at the nation's anarchic state, claiming that "civil war has broken all the ties of society," so that only "ferocity" and "barbarism" remained.[57] In "modern times," there was no better mark of "civilization" than achieving "political order" over "turbulent anarchy."[58]

In 1839 de Castillo y Lanzas could look back to independence as bittersweet, given "our subsequent degradation." The nation had failed due to political scheming and the collapse of the social bonds that held society together, all of which had contributed to the "retardation of our progresses."[59] *El Observador de la República Mexicana* despaired over plans to expel the Spanish from Mexico, noting that this would ruin the nation's reputation in Europe and was not the action of a "halfway civilized nation."[60] As we saw in the last chapter, by the 1840s, some *letrados* had begun to challenge Europe; however, this reversal was unthinkable for many of them. Regarding the 1848 Congreso Americano in Lima, *El Siglo Diez y Nueve* mocked as "delirium" the idea that "the young, weak Spanish America would try to give laws to virile, strong Europe."[61] The public sphere constantly worried about how Europeans, as masters of civilization, would judge their new societies' missteps.[62]

A Republican Façade

If Europe were the measure of modernity, then the adoption of republicanism, hardly practiced in Europe at all, would raise grave doubts as to the best strategy for creating and governing a civilized society. Support for republicanism was constantly questioned. Of course, Mexico immediately experimented with monarchy after independence (under Agustín de Iturbide from 1822–23), which was seen as a way of limiting radical changes and controlling unruly subalterns, an overriding concern of Europhile modernity.[63] Republicanism seemed too leveling and utopian; *El Farol* argued that it could work only in a society in which everyone enjoyed an "equality" of wealth.[64] In contrast to later developments that stressed a common American republican bond, *El Sol* claimed republicanism might work in the United States but was ill-suited to Mexico, due to the country's history, religion, state of development, unruly population, and lack of education and the peonage of most of the lower class.[65] The paper argued that monarchy would best protect "liberty, property, and security."[66] At worst, republicanism could lead to a social "revolution," as had been the case in France.[67] Reflecting a little-stated but very influential theme, El Observador de la República Mexicana argued that the form of government mattered little, as long as "civil liberty" existed.[68] Although the royal sentiment was not as strong in Colombia, nevertheless constant rumors of monarchical projects regularly disrupted society there.

However, in general, ideas of republicanism as the best and most modern political system overcame monarchical sentiments. El Condor de Bolivia argued that the representative system represented the "perfection of political civilization."[69] Yet this same newspaper continually worried about republicanism's efficacy and especially about the unsuitability of the majority of Bolivia's residents for a republican system. Therefore, republicanism had to be sharply bounded to limit the pueblo's influence.[70] In 1826 the paper published an address by Bolívar in which he urged having a president for life.[71] In Colombia, however, one senator declared the Bolivian constitution an embarrassment to "this century of enlightenment and liberty," since it would make a citizen nothing but a "beast of burden."[72] Another senator, Francisco Soto, refuted those who said that without Bolívar's strong hand Colombia or Bolivia would fall apart, arguing that it mattered little to him whether a state lost any one province; instead, "as a member of the human species I wish that liberty would reign everywhere."[73] We see the germination of the idea that would come to fruition under American republicanism: that the universal struggle for liberty trumped any passing material or local concerns.

Although a few writers celebrated republicanism's liberatory potential, many more questioned its suitability for Latin America. Some began to doubt that simply borrowing republican institutions from the United States would work, due to the higher level of education there, and warned that either the institutions must change or the people must be changed.[74] El Genio de la Libertad thought that Santa Anna demonstrated the weakness of Mexico's republican institutions, as he had seized power with the support of a "mob" composed of the "most vile rabble," who should be excluded from politics.[75] Elections themselves could be a problem, if too broad a class of citizens participated. In an 1852 letter to Juan María Gutiérrez, Juan Bautista Alberdi declared that "while the law calls on the mob to vote, the mob will elect children that tell them pretty words."[76] Thus republicanism shared the same preoccupations as did Europhile cultural modernity: were the pueblo educated enough, European enough, and civilized enough for a representative system of government? As discussed earlier, Europhile modernity was not largely political, but for those who saw republicanism as representing modernity, the new republics had clearly failed. In 1832 *El Genio de la Libertad* declared that the misery of the last six years were "the fruits of the imprudent development of modern theories, the fruit of Jacobinism and the Enlightenment, of demagogic furor and party spirit."[77] A number of Guatemalans made similar claims in 1848, noting that following "the modern systems" of republicanism, liberalism, and constitutionalism and other "pretty theories" had produced only "many evils in both the Old and New Worlds." The pursuit of "lauded progress" had resulted in "uprisings, revolutions, civil and foreign wars, blood, ruination, misery, and misfortunes."[78] In 1852 the *letrado* historian and politician Lucas Alamán was also suspicious of modern politics, blaming Mexico's ills on the excessive "innovations" introduced into the nation's government, instead of maintaining tested colonial institutions.[79] Alamán and others worried that those pursuing a politically defined modernity—the American republicanism we will explore—would bring chaos to a society to which it was ill suited.

Before mid-century, a general sense of disillusionment with republicanism had solidified. A Uruguayan paper despaired at the caudillos and civil wars that dominated Spanish American politics.[80] There was a general fear that any progress that had been achieved would quickly collapse with the rise of tyrants such as Rosas.[81] Rosas and his ilk would "always invoke Republican principles" in pretty speeches but would govern as dictators; "this abuse of language" gave a republican façade to aristocratic or dictatorial policies.[82] Latin Americans had created "republics in form," but not in reality.[83] The Mexican politician and diplomat José Fernando Ramírez mocked the clubs and societies forming in Mexico in the 1840s as "no more than a farce and a parody of the meetings held by the English and the people of the United States."[84] As we shall see, opponents of American republican modernity regularly declared Latin American politics to be merely a pale reflection of true republican practices. Not everyone agreed that the failed constitutional experiments meant Latin America must imitate Europe; there was some sense that an indigenous system must develop, as proposed by the young Alberdi in 1837.[85] More common, however, were laments about failure and collapse. *Comercio del Plata* declared "anarchy" and "despotism" thrived in Latin America under the rule of "false republics," which existed only as "words" and not as a "system." The paper urged readers to reject calls for monarchy but understood why "the republican faith of almost everyone will waver."[86] In 1840 José María Gutiérrez Estrada famously proposed a European monarch as the solution to Mexico's failed experiments with every version of republicanism: "democratic, oligarchic, military, demagogic, and anarchic."[87] Conservatives found the 1848 revolutions in France particularly distressing, since they seemed to destroy the bedrock of civilization in its heartland. The *Gaceta de Guatemala* argued that it hardly mattered that France had been a monarchy, since it had an "admirable government." For progress, it mattered less how a nation-state administered power than that it fostered civilization. The newspaper cited as a cautionary tale the Caste War of the Yucatan (a rebellion of the Maya that began in 1847): "The elements of civilization are few and weak; if these make war among themselves, they will weaken and have to succumb to the weight of the forces of barbarism."[88] Republicanism could become a threat to civilization; it mattered less than the preservation of order and elite society.

In Colombia, and to a lesser extent in Mexico, few people would openly embrace monarchy, but the public sphere endlessly debated what republicanism should mean. One contest concerned centralism versus federalism, with Alamán blaming the federal system for fomenting anarchy.[89] Equally problematic was republicanism's relationship with democracy. *El Observador de la República Mexicana* argued the two had no relation, as democracy was basically mob rule, while the "representative system" should represent the "public opinion" not of the majority (democracy), but of the educated few, as in any society with "civilization."[90] The salon must dominate the street. There was a sense that too much democracy would inevitably lead to tyranny. Rosas's opponents claimed that he owed his support to the "proletariat" and the "mob."[91] Richard Warren argues that many Mexican elites thought the 1828 Parián riot represented "the inevitable culmination of the political enfranchisement of the urban poor."[92] The problem of the mass of people, and what role they would play not just in republican governance, but also in constructing the future, would be the central dilemma of cultural, republican, and Western modernity.

The Rampant Appetite of the People

In spite of being recast as a populist, Bolívar generally saw the increased participation of the poor as a threat and the pueblo's lack of discipline as leading to anarchy, due to "the rampant appetite of a people who have broken their chains and have no understanding of the notions of duty and law."[93] The people were not ready for republicanism. The "masses" themselves might be "incapable of independent action," but nefarious caudillos always rounded them up for the next revolution.[94] Race underlay Bolívar's and other elites' fear of the masses.

The supposed racial threat in the new societies terrorized the elite, who like Bolívar, saw new phantasmagorical Haitis spreading bloodshed and ruination everywhere. Bolívar decried the situation in Mexico, where "a new class of barefoot poor" had taken over power and property. These poor were, of course, racially suspect. Bolívar described Vicente Guerrero as "a barbarian from the southern coasts, the vile miscarriage of a savage Indian woman and a ferocious African" and a "new Dessalines" (Jean-Jacques Dessalines was Haiti's revolutionary ruler in 1804–6).[95] Barbarism and savagery here are encoded as Indian, black, and provincial. The poor and racially mixed were a "ferocious hydra."[96] Bolívar predicted that eventually the "unrestrained multitudes," composed of "all colors and races," would tyrannize the Americas.[97] Even later, when Liberals began to associate republicanism with modernity, many of them could not escape Sarmiento's master trope that equated civilization with white cities and barbarism with the savage, multiracial countryside, in which ruled "the men of the forests."[98] When the Caste War of the Yucatan erupted, a Montevideano paper declared it a contest of "barbarism, in its true personification, against an incomplete and weak civilization."[99] In Mexico, due to "bloody and barbarous war in the Yucatan," elites feared that "the civilized race is about to disappear from the face of the earth, overrun by the immense horde of savages."[100] After independence, the greatest challenge to the nation was no longer external—European colonial powers—but an internal enemy, its own population.

In the 1820s two great fears concerning a pueblo perhaps racially unfit for civilization crystallized for elites: that the pueblo was too interested in politics and its antithesis, that the pueblo was completely uninterested in national life. Like Bolívar, letrados feared that the pueblo would be too interested in politics and not leave governance to their betters. Even the optimists, such as Sarmiento and the newspaper El Farol, worried that unruly plebes and their "disorder and turbulence" would derail the progress planned by the letrados.[101] After all, El Farol argued, "only the wise and just man can possess true liberty," and the paper urged support for a monarchy, making only cautious reforms to the colonial system, and providing only limited freedoms and rights: "Liberty, when abused, is as disastrous for men as slavery."[102] El Sol demanded a monarchy as necessary "to impose respect on the pueblo," while republicanism would lead only to the "domination of the mob."[103] Yet letrados also fretted that the pueblo would have no interest in or knowledge of the new nation and would care only about the patria chica, the people and land in view from their village's bell tower. In this vision, due to their ignorance and passivity, the pueblo had no knowledge of, interest in, or abilities to participate in national life.[104] El Sol estimated that only half a million people in Mexico had any sort of education, while the vast majority of the other seven and a half million did not "concern themselves with the interests of the nation."[105] The idea that the pueblo cared little about the nation would become a bedrock of letrado thinking and would dominate historical understanding of the nineteenth century until the 1990s (even if events later in the century proved it a self-interested elite fantasy).

However, for most elites, the more pressing concern was not that the pueblo declined to participate in national life, but that the pueblo was not educationally or culturally (or racially) prepared to participate rationally. The problem was not that the pueblo did not follow national affairs—indeed, a newspaper claimed that reading was more widespread among the poor in Mexico than in "more civilized nations"—but that the pueblo read the wrong type of material and took the wrong lessons from it.[106] El Condor de Bolivia warned that the pueblo possessed "a poor understanding of the words Patria, sovereignty of the pueblo, liberty, equality," which had caused "convulsions to such an extreme as to dissolve the governments" of other nation-states.[107] The paper warned that the pueblo must understand that Bolivia would be a republic, not a democracy, which the paper equated with "savages in their tribes."[108] Instead, under the representative system, the pueblo's only role was to elect its ruling politicians, after which "its influence is nothing," and the pueblo must "do nothing more than obey."[109] Two decades later, Mexico's El Siglo Diez y Nueve echoed this interpretation of republicanism: the pueblo's only role was to elect representatives; after doing so, it must "blindly obey, with the most profound respect, the voice of the law."[110] This tension—between republicanism and democracy, between the elite leaders and the masses, and between the pueblo's own interpretation of its rights and the desire of the powerful to discipline those below—would be constant throughout the nineteenth century.

How would the pueblo interpret liberty, equality, and fraternity? A few writers expressed optimism as long as the letrado class was able to exercise its mastery, opining that the poor needed only "good direction so that they do not stray" in their understanding of liberty.[111] More, however, feared the people's predilections. In 1827 El Observador de la República Mexicana warned of "demagogues" who would mislead the pueblo, which "never has known liberty." Therefore, since the pueblo had broken the chains of despotic colonialism, it might as a consequence act to break "all the ties that bind it to authority, and to that necessary dependence that centuries of inequality of class has brought." These demagogues thus deluded the pueblo into thinking a "chimerical equality" was possible and desirable.[112] The terror of a social upheaval along the lines of the French Revolution—*sanculot-ismo*—loomed large.[113] Five years later, *Los Amigos del Pueblo* similarly argued that "our pueblo" possessed "a poor understanding of liberty" and that the pueblo's presumptions, coupled with nefarious leaders, would lead ultimately to bloody scenes reminiscent of the Terror in France.[114] *El Genio de la Libertad* added that the pueblo held "erroneous ideas" about the meanings of liberty, rights, and despotism. The paper attacked Santa Anna as one of the demagogues who misled the pueblo, undermining the idea that the educated classes should rule with his continual rhetorical salvos against "the aristocrats" who were the "enemies of the pueblo."[115] This would be a constant theme: the pueblo did not understand the true meaning of liberty.[116]

Even worse, a nefarious notion of equality had spread through society. Instead of signifying "legal equality" as was proper, "they [the pueblo] have wanted to pass the level" over society, replacing "equality of rights" with "that of conditions." Virtue would be the same as vice, ignorance as genius, poverty as wealth.[117] Years later, another newspaper discussed the "absurd" notions of equality that many people held, leveling "the wise man" with the "ignorant."[118] In 1832 *El Genio de la Libertad* begged for a stronger central government to control the mob, those wearing "the Jacobin cap" who preach "the insubordination of the people."[119] This was especially ironic, considering that the paper had a liberty cap on its masthead, showing the quick disillusion with popular sentiments of liberty (see figure 2.1).

The primal fear was not of an indifferent pueblo, but of an engaged pueblo. Indeed, as Marixa Lasso has argued for the independence period, politicians' declarations of subalterns' disinterest and inability to participate in national political life were not objective descriptions of reality, but biased arguments used to justify the exclusion of those below.[120] During the period of American republican modernity, the public sphere sought to elide the problem by claiming that the pueblo was truly sovereign and should and could influence the state, and that the state truly represented the pueblo. As we will see, this strategy was immensely successful in granting legitimacy to the nation-state and incorporating many subalterns into the nation. The problem was that the pueblo insisted on making its own demands and defining liberty, equality, and sovereignty on its terms. This would lead to a reaction late in the century, which once again would restrict the pueblo from participating in public life by prioritizing order and discipline over political rights.

Although the restriction of citizenship rights later in the century would signal a tectonic shift in societies' organization and political culture, the new

FIG 2.1. Masthead of *El Genio de la Libertad*. *El Genio de la Libertad* (Veracruz, Mexico), 11 September 1832.

republics' undefined nature gave elites more space to follow Europhile cultural modernity's dictates and limit the masses' citizenship. A quick survey across the Americas at this point shows that the institutional response to these fears was simple legal exclusion. Colombia's constitutions of 1821, 1830, 1832, and 1843 required property or an income for citizenship, and all but that of 1843 explicitly excluded those who were day laborers or domestic servants (the property requirement of 300 pesos would deny them citizenship anyway). Under all the constitutions most elections were indirect, with citizens simply choosing electors who then selected the officeholders, and some important officers were appointed.[121] After earlier experiments with more inclusive suffrage rights, in 1836 Mexican Centralists passed a national suffrage law that required an income of 100 pesos to vote and one of 1,500 pesos to hold office, while explicitly excluding domestic servants.[122] Local politics could be even more exclusionary. Until 1832, the outgoing *cabildo* (town council) of Cali, Colombia, simply chose the next year's officers, not even bothering with the pretense of elections.[123] Alamán thought that only the wealthiest residents should serve in local assemblies.[124] In 1830 in Ecuador, citizenship required 300 pesos of property or a profession or trade (domestic servants and laborers were excluded), and, most important, literacy.[125] In Argentina, the province of Buenos Aires enjoyed at least technical universal adult male suffrage after 1821, but most of the other provinces required a profession or literacy.[126] In Chile, renowned across Latin America at this time for its regular elections, the constitution required literacy, as well as property or income, with a moving scale that was adjusted every ten years.[127]

These limitations of citizenship were truly an Atlantic phenomenon. In Europe, qualifications for citizenship tended to be even higher. In 1848 a

Mexican newspaper applauded the lifetime appointments and restricted eligibility for voting and service to the Papal States' two councils.[128] Before 1848, French voters in national elections needed to have paid 200 francs a year in property taxes.[129] In Rouen in 1836, only 2.5 percent of the population were eligible to vote.[130] In Great Britain—even after the Reform Act of 1832, which expanded the electorate by 80 percent—only 4.1 percent of the population could vote, and these figures exclude Ireland.[131] In general, for elite Europeans, the period of the 1820s through the 1840s was one of "great social fear," to quote Foucault.[132] Attitudes were similar across the Americas as well, which is surprising given the harping on the supposed superiority of English colonial tutelage for instilling republicanism in the young United States. As in Latin America, the political class of the U.S. founding fathers assumed that gentlemen of education, civility, and talent would naturally lead, and Alexander Hamilton and others fretted over the democratic masses' violence and turbulence.[133] Before Jacksonian politics, U.S. elites still expected plebeians to display an appropriate deference.[134] By 1830, a half-century after independence, eight out of twenty-four U.S. states still maintained a property requirement for citizenship, and fifteen excluded nonwhites.[135] Echoing the debates in Latin America about who exactly would define democracy, in 1837 (after much more experience in these matters than more recently independent Latin Americans had), Noah Webster complained in a letter to William Stone: "The men who have preached these doctrines have never defined what they mean by the *people*, or what they mean by *democracy*, nor how the *people* are to govern themselves."[136] Indeed, the definition of civilization expressed by Latin American supporters of Europhile cultural modernity was little different from that expressed in the North Atlantic, where a Boston newspaper in 1818 worried that with the dispersal of the population across the frontier, and the ignorance and crudeness of life this entailed, the United States retrogressed: "The tendency is from civilization to barbarism."[137] In the period of Europhile modernity, Latin America lagged behind the United States in creating a more inclusive citizen body—but this is not the case if one compares Latin America of the 1820s and 1830s to the United States in the 1780s and 1790s, an equal number of years after it became independent. Of course, compared to Europe, Latin America was already at least an equal, if not far ahead. By the 1850s, many parts of Latin America would far surpass the United States and Europe in extending citizenship to all men, regardless of race or class. How the poor, especially those of African and indigenous descent, reacted to the possibilities and limitations created by independence is the subject of the next section, and it is critical to understanding how later, under American republican modernity, subalterns often successfully appropriated citizenship and nation for themselves.

"The Rights That God, Nature, and the Nation Have Granted Me"

Let us briefly focus on Mexico in the years after independence to trace how subalterns sought to deal with both a new nation and a public sphere dominated by the language of Europhile cultural modernity. As with the enslaved women who appealed to Emperor Iturbide, as described in the introduction, subalterns eagerly seized any new political space, investing themselves with the status of a rights-bearing citizen. Even at the moment of national creation, when the very concepts of citizen, nation, and liberty were undefined, many subalterns rushed to test the boundaries of the new political systems that were replacing colonialism's oppression. The legal dismantlement of the caste system seemed to signify immense positive changes for the vast majority of Latin America's inhabitants. As we will explore, for Indians the new nation presented complex challenges, but for those of African descent, the caste system's end was an unqualified boon. José Trinidad Martínez, a "native of Africa, born in Havana," wrote to Iturbide in 1823 to claim his freedom from a master eager to return him to a hacienda. Unlike others, Martínez did not claim that his master had promised him emancipation, just that freedom was his right, now that "the sweet echo of liberty" was heard throughout the land. He argued that slavery was nothing more than holding one man a "prisoner" in spite of his having committed no crime and that Spain made people "slaves only by the domination of their government." Now slavery would end: "With what delight, with what universal jubilee, have we celebrated the liberty that the Emperor declared in the Mexican Empire." This declared liberty must signify abolition, for how could it be "that all the inhabitants of this vast continent were free and only I a slave, without any crime other than being a descendent of Africans"? Martínez asked that Iturbide order his master to free him, "restoring to me the rights that God, nature, and the nation have granted me."[138] Martínez assumed, logically, that the caste system's end and the declarations of liberty from Spain would apply universally and thus necessitate a general emancipation. Afro–Latin Americans often embraced the new nations with fervor and joy, and as we will see, they were the strongest proponents of popular liberalism throughout the nineteenth century. Yet Martínez's question—could he be left out of this liberty?—nagged and worried him as much as Indians would fret over their place in the new republics.

The petition above was not Martínez's first letter; he had drafted another a few months earlier. Martínez was illiterate and could not sign his name, and the two documents were clearly written by different scribes. The earlier letter was in a large, blurry script, while the later was written in a small, neat hand (so delightful to historians). Yet each petition makes the same arguments. In the earlier petition, Martínez asserted that the mere existence of slavery "is opposed to and attacks the individual liberty of every citizen." Furthermore, he declared that he had been enslaved "without having committed any crime other than to be black." He assumed that Iturbide meant for slavery to be abolished, and that the only reason it had not been was that "in your vast dominion the vestiges of Spanish rule are maintained." Finally, he claimed freedom as part of the "rights of man" that had been granted by "nature."[139] It is always easy to dismiss any document produced by a subaltern as inauthentic, reflecting the intent of the scribe or country lawyer who wrote it. Yet as these two letters show, the common denominator was not the scribes, but the slave Martínez. The content and discourse of petitions varied greatly, depending on the social situation of the supplicants. One might ask why Indians did not use the same soaring rhetoric of liberty that slaves employed, if lawyers had determined the content? The contrasts among petitions show that scribes alone cannot account for the strategies employed in subalterns' demands. The vast body of evidence reveals that—contrary to the claims of past generations of historians and of some self-interested contemporaries—subalterns knew of, were interested in, and sought to take part in the life of the new nation-states. Martínez's claims also reveal how quickly the rhetoric of the Atlantic Age of Revolution penetrated into the lower classes.

Yet few subalterns had Martínez's confidence, even if they were equally eager to test the new regime's intentions. Desiderio Antonio de Meza, "born a slave," wrote to "Your Majesty Iturbide" in 1822 for help in obtaining the freedom that had been promised by his master. De Meza did not go so far as his female compatriots and claim citizenship, but he did ask for Iturbide's "protection" as "father of all the unhappy." The slave asked that Iturbide "allow him to enjoy his liberty, a good that the supreme Author of nature gave to every creature and only inhumanity and tyranny have tried to usurp."[140] Also in 1822, "Indians and others" from Tlaltenango, Zacatecas, complained of the local authorities, who "were resisters to the new system" and "enemies of order and liberty."[141] Indians from Maravatío, Michoacán, complained because local authorities were not allowing them to vote, keeping the "system of the old government" intact and ignoring the new constitutional system and their "right of citizenship."[142] However, in 1822 it was still very unclear who would be a citizen, whether all citizens would be equal, and what citizenship would mean. As the brief discussion of legal requirements above indicates, elites and the state would move to exclude most Indians and Afro–Latin Americans from citizenship due to their poverty or illiteracy. Eventually, many subalterns would have great success in claiming citizenship that was not legally theirs, forcing elites to redefine the institution. However, claiming rights and citizenship not legally recognized leads to recognition only under certain conditions. First, you can force the issue due to your own accumulation of power (either through armed insurgency or providing indispensable military support to elite leaders). This was the case only rarely in the early years of Mexico and Colombia. Second, your calls for citizenship and rights can resonate with the dominant, legitimating discourse of society. If a society declares that it is at the vanguard of human freedom, in which the pueblo is sovereign, it is hard to ignore that pueblo's demands without creating a serious dissonance that weakens the legitimacy of the state, nation, and ruling class. However, if as in early Latin America, the dominant discourse of Europhile modernity declared the pueblo to be an ignorant, uncivilized mass that hindered progress and did not understand liberty, it is much easier to ignore the pueblo's demands because doing so dovetails with the dominant discourse in the public sphere.

Certainly, subalterns tried to find a voice to which the new governing system would respond. In a petition about a land dispute with a nearby hacienda, the village of Santa Marta Chichihualtepec, Oaxaca, first celebrated the new political situation after independence: "We enjoy our complete liberty, shed of the yoke that had so much oppressed us everywhere." The campesinos (country people, roughly) did not hesitate to flatter "Your Majesty Iturbide," who had achieved independence for "all the inhabitants of America" and who only wanted the "complete happiness of his children." They had traveled to Mexico City to celebrate Iturbide's coronation and to seek justice against the "great tyranny" of the *hacendado* who had taken their land, stolen their livestock, and had them thrown in jail; in short, this local lord had abused "our rights." They begged Iturbide to relieve them of the "miseries and indignities" they had suffered, and to act quickly because they were "dying of hunger at this court due to the lack of resources we have, as we only are eating some hard tortillas that we have brought."[143] The petitioners used a variety of strategies, old and new. They united traditional and colonial appeals for protection, citing their humble and lowly station and intense poverty.[144] Yet they combined this with a new language of constitutionalism, independence, and rights, which they cleverly associated with Iturbide, while linking a picture of colonial oppression and tyranny with the *hacendado*. These villagers were testing whether the new language of sovereignty, constitutionalism, and rights would mean anything for them. Subalterns would soon learn that it would not. Increasingly, as the power of Europhile modernity overwhelmed the initial optimism of independence, the new public discourse of republicanism and rights explicitly excluded subalterns.

Indigenous peoples were caught in a particularly vexing dilemma. Many, such as the villagers of San Miguel el Grande, Oaxaca, eagerly desired "to escape the oppression" they had suffered under "Spanish residents" who had usurped their land. However, to do this they needed to act in concert, using their Indian communities' tested political and economic resources. We already saw how Afro-Mexicans were eager to exploit the possibilities engendered by the destruction of the colonial caste system. Indians had a more complicated and contradictory relationship to that system. The Indians of San Miguel were not even sure how to identify themselves in 1823, given the dismantling of the system, and they settled on "those who the Spanish government denominated indios." However, they were sure that they wanted to continue to protect their communities, sending representatives (who were so poor they could only remain for a brief period) to Mexico City. When the community tried to raise more funds to pursue their case, the local mayor jailed the indigenous leader Juan Marcos Patlán for illegally collecting taxes from the indigenous community. Unsure of the legality of their traditional community governance, the Indians claimed the contributions were not taxes, but strictly voluntary. This stance typified their predicament. Did the new government consider them Indians or citizens, equals or subjects? As we will see in chapter 4, indigenous communities would seek to combine the categories of Indian and citizen in ways that subverted the assumptions of elites' liberalism. Now, however, they struggled to find purchase for their claims—using complaints about their miserable condition, appeals to custom, and bargaining with the powerful—promising: "We are ready to sacrifice our lives in service . . . to the patria and to Your Majesty Iturbide."[145] These indigenous villagers held an intense interest in the new state and nation, but they proceeded cautiously, hoping to discover exactly how the state and nation felt about them.

Subalterns generally do not ignore the state and nation, as elites sometimes complained and as historians often assume, but try to influence it as best they can. Obviously, they prefer, as did Martínez and the enslaved women who wrote to Iturbide, to do so from a position of dignity, strength, and inclusion as citizens. However, if this is impossible, they will use a rhetoric that fits the situation. In the 1820s in Mexico, we see that subalterns continued to use a colonial strategy of deference and submission, begging for protection from patriarchal authorities. They generally did not mention rights and citizenship, nor did they make outright demands as their due.[146] Instead of demanding rights as citizens, many petitioners, describing themselves as "humble servants," just begged the state or local authority to fulfill its "obligations."[147] In response to the petition and visit of the illiterate village officers from Tlanelhuayocan, Veracruz, national authorities reported that the visitors had begged for help and the return of stolen lands by emphasizing not their rights but their "great misery."[148] The indigenous village of San Damián, Tlaxcala, also petitioned for lands in a dispute with a hacienda, similarly citing "our poverty" and "our pressing misery."[149] The residents of another village wrote to Iturbide, placing themselves "under his protection" and pleading for access to water that a nearby hacienda had appropriated, leaving them "naked," in a state of "misery and lack of food." The villagers based their argument not on rights but on "customs."[150] The residents of an indigenous village in Oaxaca wrote to Iturbide, appealing to "his mercy and pity" for the "indigent class." They were engaged in a land dispute with the Miraflores hacienda and admitted they could not prove that the land in question belonged to them, instead appealing to the long tradition of support they had under Spanish law and their "ancient privileges." The Indians lamented how the hacendado had burned their houses and thrown their poor families into the forests. Finally, they tested the new monarch's mettle, not by making any personal demands on him, but by subtly questioning his power: "Sir, will such criminal conduct remain unpunished?"[151] Instead of demanding rights, they probed to see if older colonial norms still applied, to see if the new rulers would fulfill the same bargains that underlay the Spanish empire. In contrast, petitions from wealthier residents more often employed a language of citizenship.[152]

These petitioners chose to deemphasize or omit calls for rights and expressions of political change, returning instead to tried-and-true strategies of pleading for protection with justifications based on customs or extreme suffering. They had to beg for a favor, not demand a right. Of course, many other subalterns would persist in using a language of national inclusion, rights, and citizenship.[153] However, the power that language commanded in the public sphere was much reduced, as it did not call on the same themes as the dominant, legitimating discourse of Europhile modernity. The poor could claim to be citizens and decry violations of their rights all they wanted, but the powerful could easily dismiss such claims as nonsense, without contradicting their own ruling ideology or exposing it as hypocrisy.

As long as Europhile cultural modernity saw the masses as generally unfit for civilization, and thus for citizenship, a discourse of rights found little purchase. However, Europhile modernity's visions of degraded plebeians did create space for the miserable to entreat their civilized betters for aid. Of course, our knowledge of what subalterns really thought is limited, but we do know how they interpreted the public sphere's limitations. The poor would always push to improve their political and social condition, but the public sphere, to which they played close attention, told them what strategies would be most successful. At times open revolt, so often doomed to failure, was the only option, especially for people totally excluded by society—be it the Maya of the Yucatan or the indigenous peoples of the northern deserts and plains. More often, popular groups listened and tried to figure out what strategies they could employ to fulfill their own agendas.[154] Europhile modernity gave them very little space for maneuvering. Many subalterns simply retreated and guarded their *patria chica* as best they could (which is very different from not understanding or caring about the world beyond the view of the campanario). Others tried as best they could to position their demands in the spaces provided by Europhile modernity, which often meant appealing to the powerful's elitist and racist visions. In a public sphere that regarded them as barbarians, there were few other options. As the public sphere's vision of the world changed, slaves, Indians, artisans, and campesinos would be ready to claim the nation as their own.

The Failure of the Nation

While subalterns struggled to claim a place in the new nations, by the 1840s elites and *letrados* seemed ready to abandon the national project altogether, the public sphere ringing with declarations that Mexico had failed to become a civilized nation. The president of the Chamber of Deputies, Luis Gonzaga Solana, declared in 1845: "One doubted if we belonged to this century's civilization and if we were deserving of liberty, observing that for so long a time, like the degraded and vile pueblos of Asia, we were governed without any laws, without any rules nor principles, than that of the sultanic will and blind caprice of an unchecked ambition."[155] Conditions had deteriorated so far in Mexico that a politician could openly question whether Mexico even belonged in the family of civilized nations. As war with the United States loomed, Conservatives began to push openly for reestablishing a throne, declaring monarchy a rational system adopted by Europe's "most civilized countries."[156] Newspapers published in Mexico by the Spanish expatriate community encouraged equating civilization and monarchy, claiming that in "modern Europe" the people loved their princes for the well-being they provided.[157] Articles began to appear that stressed how a monarchy would extend many of the same rights, while providing a bulwark against disorder.[158] The 1846 U.S. invasion of Mexico would bring the most vociferous denunciations of the Mexican national project's stagnation in the race to civilization.

Most Mexicans understood the U.S. success in the war as a result of their own failed political institutions, due in part to an ungovernable pueblo. Therefore, monarchy might well be the answer (as proposed by El Universal in particular).[159] Others expressed shock at the lack of national identity that allowed the pueblo to stand idly by while the gringos invaded. Ramírez argued that although generally in world history foreign invasions strengthened feelings of nationality, in Mexico "quite the contrary has happened."[160] Yet Ramírez contradicted himself, for he also feared that the pueblo might use the destruction caused by the war to erect on the country's ruins an "empire of Liberty: in other words, that of outright democracy."[161] He thought the pueblo envisioned this democracy as "abolishing all the landed proprietors and other privileged classes."[162] It is easy to dismiss words like "liberty" and "democracy" as empty concepts debated in salons, with no importance in the fields and workshops of Latin America, but Ramírez and his ilk knew this was not the case. He knew the power of this discourse and feared the pueblo's appropriation of it. Thus, Europhile modernity had to limit the pueblo's role in creating civilization, by looking to Europe and the high culture represented by the letrado class. Elites reserved the right to invest liberty with a meaning to their liking. In spite of complaining about the pueblo's lack of interest in and unwillingness to sacrifice for the survival of an elite-controlled nation-state, what Ramírez and many others truly feared was that the lower and middle classes would claim liberty and democracy, and even Mexico itself, as their own.

The U.S. invasion only increased elites' desperation over the problem of the pueblo. After the war, El Siglo Diez y Nueve warned that if Mexico did not embrace "order and civilization," then "before long our very nationality will disappear." The paper looked to Europe for civilization, in the form of immigrants.[163] When it gained its independence, Mexico had seemed called to a great destiny; now other nations looked on Mexico with disdain.[164] The war, above all else, marked the "failure of the nation."[165] Alamán similarly lamented the "complete extinction of public spirit that has caused any idea of national character to disappear."[166] Instead of accompanying the rest of the world in making "giant strides on the path of progress," Mexico did not just remain in place, stagnant and abject, but "even moves backwards."[167] The question was not if Mexico was modern—according to these thinkers, it clearly was not—but if Mexico had even the hope of one day pursuing modernity. Perhaps Mexican society was simply doomed to backwardness and barbarism.

El Siglo Diez y Nueve concluded that "all the misfortunes that our patria has suffered" were due to the pueblo and its lack of education. The nation would never be able to progress with a republican and democratic system unless it could teach the pueblo its rights and duties and instill in them a love of order. Now, however, due to democracy, the pueblo followed only bad men, a course that led to revolution and anarchy.[168] Since the "mass of more than half of our population" had no investment in the nation and no understanding of "liberty," the paper argued that it was "a pueblo unfit to live among civilized nations."[169] Mexico had fallen to the wayside in its race to modernity—largely, many in the letrado class claimed, due to the failure of its non-European, ignorant, and backward people.

The problem of the pueblo had culminated with the failure of the nation, the vehicle for modernity in the nineteenth-century world. A letter written by "various Mexicans" in early 1848 encapsulates our themes thus far. Surveying the wreckage of the war, the writers declared: "In Mexico there has not been and there is not now that which one calls national spirit, because the nation does not exist." They lamented that in spite of Mexico's abundant natural wealth, society was very weak due to the masses' lack of education and the resulting poor government. They argued that "a nation is nothing but a great family . . . united by links of interests and by heartfelt affections" (an imagined community, if you will). However, the writers declared it impossible that Mexico could become such a nation, due to the "diverse classes that make up our degraded society." Factional politics and civil wars had destroyed the order of the colonial era. The best solution would be to improve the pueblo, but even though Mexico counted three million people of at least some European ancestry, the majority of these were illiterate. Far worse, four million Indians—who "in their semi-savage state hardly can be considered part of society"—made up the majority of the population. The writers were not Conservatives, since they held the clergy and Spanish colonialism for this ignorance. The only way to improve the pueblo would be to encourage foreign immigration. Then society could slowly reclaim the state from the agents of anarchy. Of course, the writers looked to Europe and the United States for other answers, warning that if worst came to worst, they might have to succumb to one of the "European monarchs." Republicanism, the nation, the people, and even modernity had all failed: "This country and its population does not belong in any manner to the civilized world."[170] Bolívar's predictions seem to have come true.[171]

However, the vision of modernity dominant in the public sphere would evolve both dramatically and quickly. As we saw in Uruguay, by the 1840s, many in the public sphere had begun to challenge the tenets of Europhile cultural modernity—especially the ideas that Europe was the font of modernity and must be imitated, that civilization was best measured by the adoption of European high culture, and that, therefore, the masses were barbarians unfit for political life. As we will explore in the subsequent chapters, by the 1850s Europhile modernity rapidly waned in its influence in the public sphere, jostling for position, mostly unsuccessfully, with American republican modernity. Yet even at those times and places when we might call American republican modernity hegemonic, such as Mexico after Maximilian's defeat or Colombia during Liberal rule after 1860, many of Europhile modernity's basic tenets that we explored in this chapter remained powerful among the members of one exclusive club: the letrados. Even if not heard in political debates, campaign speeches, public festivals celebrating independence, or newspaper columns, Europhile modernity never disappeared in the private libraries and salons of the most wealthy and educated, and in many ways it remained the letrados' dominant ideology, misleading historians and cultural theorists to this day.[172] However, while this gloomy picture dominated the letrado class and most of the public sphere through the 1840s, even in the darkest days there was a countercurrent that imagined American republics as creating progress. Furthermore, in only a few years this radically different vision of republicanism, nation, and modernity would emerge from being a dismissed alternative to rule the public sphere. The vision of the pueblo as unfit for civilized life would radically change under American republican modernity, which would see in the pueblo—in particular, a racially mixed pueblo—the bedrock of a New World civilization of sister republics that would challenge Europe and redefine the future of the world.

CHAPTER 3

The San Patricio Battalion

For Mexican state builders, the U.S.-Mexican War (1846–48) marked the low point of their project, since after the war Mexico would lose over half of its territory to the United States. The pretext for the war was a boundary dispute between the newly admitted U.S. state of Texas (formerly a Mexican province) and Mexico, but the cause lay in U.S. westward expansion and ideas of Manifest Destiny. With its overtones of racism, nationalism, greed, and imperialism, the war might seem a strange place to look for examples of the universal fraternity that would emerge as a key component of American republican modernity. Yet a small band of mostly Irish soldiers, known as the San Patricios, who deserted from the U.S. Army to join the Mexican Army, belied typical U.S. attitudes toward Latin America. These men challenged the reigning discourse in the United States by casting their lot with people of another race, another nation, and a supposedly inferior civilization. The war itself helped lead to a reconception of civilization and international affairs, leading many Mexicans and Colombians to embrace a vision based on fraternity instead of one based on state power. Finally, the war also allows us to examine how Spanish Americans thought of the United States, the New World as a whole, and their shared but troubled destiny as citizens of sister republics.

The San Patricio Battalion

As the United States maneuvered for war with its southern neighbor in 1846, General (later President) Zachary Taylor marched his army through Texas toward the border. Although the war would stoke U.S. nationalism, almost half of Taylor's soldiers were foreign born. Irish, many fleeing their homeland's great famine, made up the largest foreign component. Even before the war officially began, some of these disgruntled enlisted men stole across the border into Mexico to join the enemy's forces. One of these deserters was John Riley, born in County Galway, Ireland. He would become the leader of the San Patricio Battalion, eventually commanding over two hundred men—both fellow deserters and foreigners who were already living in Mexico when war broke out.[1] The San Patricios would participate in the most important engagements of the war. The battalion saw action in the north, before leaving Monterrey, and fought in the bloody battle of Buenavista. When the U.S. forces shifted their focus from an attempt to drive overland and instead followed Hernán Cortés's path to Mexico City from Veracruz, the San Patricios also marched south. They would meet their former compatriots at the ferocious battle of Churubusco, on the outskirts of Mexico City. Observers agreed that the battalion "fought heroically" in its various engagements, especially in the U.S. campaign against Mexico City.[2] During the battle of Churubusco, the San Patricios manned cannons, refusing to yield since they knew that doing so would mean their deaths; three times they pulled down white flags hoisted by other soldiers who wished to surrender.[3] In 1849 N. C. Brooks, a U.S. historian, declared that Riley had shown "undaunted courage" in the battle, and that he and his men had succumbed only after exhausting their ammunition.[4] The battalion suffered devastating casualties defending the approach to the capital, losing 60 percent of its men to death or capture.[5] U.S. soldiers immediately massacred a number of San Patricios who had surrendered, but most were bound for later execution.[6]

Why did these men choose desertion to a largely unknown enemy and finally sacrifice their lives in service to Mexico? The historian Robert Miller, focusing on testimony of the men during their trials, concludes that there were a combination of causes: the desire to flee brutal military life and discrimination against foreign-born soldiers or Catholics; the lure of women and enticements of cash, promotions, or land; and even drunkenness.[7] Certainly, these factors played some role. A U.S. newspaper reported that after the battle of Buena Vista, Riley visited some captured American soldiers, promising them land and money if they would switch sides.[8] Potential monetary rewards played a part as well, and the Mexican government made many claims about the ampleness of future compensation: officials and the Congress proposed land, cash, and freedom for runaway slaves, for example.[9] No doubt some San Patricios hoped to obtain land by deserting; some had enlisted in the U.S. Army believing they would receive property for their service.[10] The brutal discipline meted out in the U.S. Army pushed others to desert. William (Guillermo) McLaughlin and John (Juan) Davis had deserted the U.S. forces outside of Veracruz and enlisted with the Mexicans. They claimed that all the Irish soldiers "are very discontented and desire the opportunity to desert, due to their officials who mistreat them." The two San Patricios claimed most of the Irish were recent emigrants, who had arrived in the United States to find themselves with "the alternative to die of hunger or take up arms." Many men had initially signed up with the U.S. Army after recruiters had gotten them drunk.[11]

Did the soldiers have any ideological motivation, however? Certainly Mexicans believed the converts fought for the reasons above, but also because the U.S. invasion was one of the "most unjust of causes."[12] Mexicans thought the men fought for their republic. The battalion's flag bore the legend "Long Live the Mexican Republic."[13] Riley himself emphasized that he fought due to "the advice of my conscience for the liberty of a people which had had war brought on them by the most unjust aggression."[14] A broadside written (perhaps in part by Riley) to entice other Irish deserters argued that Irishmen should join the Mexicans "for that love of liberty for which our common country is so long contending, for the sake of that holy religion which we have for ages professed. I conjure you to abandon a slavish hireling's life with a nation who in even the moment of victory treats you with contumely & disgrace."[15] In this vision, Mexico did not just represent Catholicism, but it was also the true land of liberty and opportunity, where the Irish would not face the discrimination and humiliations they had endured in the United States. As we will see below, race played a critical role in the war for Irish, Mexicans, and Anglos. The San Patricios also spoke through their actions. Americans would claim that the "dastardly deserters" fought desperately at Churubusco, taking "deliberate aim at their former officers."[16] If true, the attacks on officers suggest the San Patricios' bitterness at the harsh discipline they had escaped and their hostility toward the officers (who were of a different social class than the deserters). We should also not casually dismiss motivations for land or property as strictly mercenary. As for other subalterns, for these soldiers the political and the economic were not independent fields; both were tied to notions of personal liberty and equality. It is difficult to know what the San Patricios were thinking, but it should not surprise us that their decision to fight for Mexico involved multi-faceted and complex motivations. We should also be careful not to dismiss political concerns simply because the San Patricios (reasonably) chose not to emphasize these while being court-martialed. Although we have a small window into the San Patricios' mind-set—especially their ideological motivations—much clearer are the critical debates that their desertion and ultimate fate opened in the public sphere over questions of race, nationalism, and civilization.

After the battle of Churubusco, General Winfield Scott would show the captured men no mercy. As U.S. forces assembled for the final assault on Mexico City and the Castle Chapultepec guarding its approach, Colonel William Harney, a sadist and butcher from the Florida Seminole Wars, took responsibility for hanging thirty of the San Patricios. The prisoners included a wounded man who was already dying; Harney insisted on hanging him anyway. Harney constructed the gallows with a view of Chapultepec. He forced the condemned to stand on wagons, nooses already around their necks, and watch as the battle commenced; hours later, only after the U.S. flag over the castle signaled victory, did he order the wagons moved, leaving the men to hang.[17]

Mexico City observed in horror both the execution of some San Patricios and the branding and scourging of others. A group of priests, including the archbishop, joined by a number of society ladies from San Angel and Tacubaya, tried unsuccessfully to intercede on the doomed men's behalf.[18] Later, other Mexicans would plead for and eventually secure the release of the San Patricio prisoners of war who had been spared execution; subscriptions would be taken up to aid the foreign veterans.[19] The historian and poet José María Roa Bárcena remembered the hangings' effect on the besieged Mexico City: "The execution of the enemy's deserters who formed our San Patricio Company, who fought like lions, increased the sadness and horror of those unforgettable hours."[20]

"Improper in a Civilized Age"

The executions opened a debate between the invaders and the invaded over the nature and locus of civilization. Ramón Alcaraz, a Mexican officer and a chronicler of the war, condemned the executions, noting that although many of the San Patricios had fallen in battle, "those who survived, more unfortunate than their companions, suffered soon after a cruel death or horrible torments, improper in a civilized age, and from a people who aspire to the title of illustrious and humane."[21] Alcaraz's translator, Albert Ramsey, stung by implications that the United States was not nearly as civilized as it claimed, tried to defend General Scott in 1850 by asserting that the Mexican army also punished deserters harshly.[22] Scott attempted to place the blame on the Mexicans for enticing the deserters, and thus necessitating such severe chastisement.[23] Other U.S. historians, beginning with Brooks, have followed suit, blaming the Mexicans or asserting that although harsh, such punishments were the norm.[24] Their arguments, quite unconvincing given the strangeness and brutality of the executions, reveal the power of discourses of civilization. According to one definition, the United States was more civilized than Mexico, as it had won the war—proving its potency as a society. According to another, however, by behaving in a manner appropriate to a republican and rights-bearing people, the Mexicans had greater claims to civilization.

Even years later, questions concerning the civilized behavior or lack thereof appears still to smart some U.S. historians, but for men like Ramsey it was a critical affair, this question of who was civilized and who barbarous.[25] In 1849 Brooks claimed the war would benefit Mexico by bringing it into closer contact with the United States, so that Mexico might learn from her conqueror and thus "diffuse knowledge and virtue among her ignorant and half-civilized multitudes."[26] Sergeant Thomas Barclay thought Mexico had to fail in its contest with the "Anglo Saxons," who formed the "civilized countries" that "strive to keep up with the spirit of the age." Mexico, in contrast, showed no signs of progress: "Everything betokens ruin and decay."[27] The war correspondent George Kendall bragged in 1847 that the U.S. conquest of Mexico ranked as one of the greatest of "modern achievements."[28] In the United States, power (be it state, military, or industrial) was emerging. as the benchmark of modernity.

The Mexican public sphere contested the assumption that power proved civilization. Remembering the executions and tortures of the San Patricio prisoners of war, El Monitor Republicano asked how such brutality was possible, casting doubt on U.S. claims to be the standard-bearers of civilization: "These are the citizens of a republic that calls itself free, and that pretends to be the most enlightened in the New World?"[29] In general, the Mexican public sphere questioned how a people who boasted of being "the apostles of civilization" could justify attacking another country, raping women, desecrating churches, and generally spreading destruction.[30] After the war, Mexicans and Spanish Americans in general would craft a new definition of civilization in international affairs that would contest the dominant vision coming from Europe: power proved civilization. Incipient now, Spanish Americans' rejection of power as civilizing would flower during the next foreign invasion that Mexico would endure.

In the contest to define civilization, Mexicans—perhaps surprisingly, given elites' own racism—turned to race and racial equality.[31] In the previous chapter, we saw that many Spanish American letrados fretted about their society's racial composition, assuming that the European civilization they desired required European races. However, the harsh reality of U.S. racism forced a sea change in racial thought in Spanish America, especially the relationship between equality and modernity. The experience of the San Patricios is illustrative. A New York newspaper described the scene after the 1847 surrender of Monterrey, in which Mexican forces were allowed to withdraw. As the American soldiers watched their enemies march out of the city, a group noticed the "renegade Riley" seated on a gun carriage: " 'Riley, ye desartin' thafe, ain't ye ashamed of yerself?' said one of his former messmates, an Irishman and one of the best soldiers in the company. The color entirely forsook the face of the runaway. 'Whin ye desarted why didn't ye go among dacent white people, and not be helpin' these bloody nagers pack off their vermin?' continued the speaker, his comrades keeping up a running accompaniment of groans and hisses." The paper went on to note that among the ranks were other deserters as well, including "runaway negroes."[32]

Even if apocryphal, the story reveals the intense efforts to racialize republicanism in the United States while simultaneously justifying the war. In this case, Mexicans are cast with blacks as the racially suspect, while the Irish who fought in the war could become white (but only if they differentiated and separated themselves from a Mexican and black racial other).[33] The soldiers' racism, or the U.S. newspaper's presentation of such racism, played three important roles. The first was to police the lines of republicanism in the United States. The demands for equality promoted by popular republicanism, drawing on the Declaration of Independence, were incompatible with both the slaveholding South and the Manifest Destiny West. Race excluded Indians and African Americans, thus making republicanism much more suitable to the U.S. economic system and continued expansion.[34] Second, race divided subalterns (separating the Irish from "nagers") and helped define a slippery nationality for both sides. We have already explored Mexicans' uncertainty regarding their nation, but the United States, with an army of immigrants, faced similar issues. Third, as we will explore below, race justified a war that to many citizens of the United States seemed patently unjust. How could one invade a sister republic? Casting Mexicans as a race of "nagers" and "vermin" made such a question irrelevant. No ties of kinship, no sister republics, could exist in such a racial typography.

The need to racially "other" Mexicans pervaded U.S. interpretations of the war and its relation to civilization. Many in the United States thought their civilization was due to the purity of the Anglo-Saxon race, while Mexico's mixed-race population doomed it to degradation.[35] For Private Samuel Chamberlain, Mexicans were simply "greasers."[36] Columbus Delano, a U.S. congressman from Ohio, opposed the war because he worried that the annexation of Mexico would lead to racial mixing with a mongrel people that "embrace all shades of color," resulting in a "slothful, ignorant race of beings."[37] The journalist Thomas Thorpe declared the Mexican soldier to be a "degraded being" who had inherited the worst attributes of the various races. The miscegenation evident in the Mexican wounded whom he encountered shocked and dismayed him; such diversity should not exist "in one people."[38] Thus, the San Patricios were doubly threatening: first as Irish to the Anglo-Saxon purity of America, then as traitors who joined an even more questionable and multiracial people, breaking down carefully monitored racial borders.

After Mexico City's capitulation, the treatment of the remaining San Patricio prisoners of war raised such questions anew. A debate broke out between El Monitor Republicano and the occupiers' English-language newspaper, the American Star, over the fate of the remaining San Patricios who had not been executed at the Battle of Chapultepec (including John Riley, who was sentenced to lashing and branding instead, since he had deserted before the declaration of war, and thus was technically just a deserter, not a traitor).[39] On 2 October 1847 El Monitor Republicano published a very mild request for leniency for the remaining San Patricios, some of whom still faced a death sentence. This request provoked a furious reaction from the American Star, which accused the Mexican paper of meddling in U.S. affairs and for encouraging an attack against a U.S. wagon train.[40] The American Star further demanded why Mexican women were so concerned with bringing food to the San Patricios, while ignoring their own beggars who filled the streets.[41] El Monitor Republicano refused to cede ground, castigating the United States for behaving barbarously. The paper described the prisoners as being chained and forced to wear iron collars studded with barbs and hooks that prevented the men from moving their heads. The men bore the marks of whippings and beatings and had been branded on the face with the letter D for deserter.[42] As it had after the executions at Chapultepec, the paper accused the United States of barbarity, and it claimed that the "civilized world" had rejected such tortures, "the most inhuman example of cruelty and barbarism."[43]

Of course, terror and horror were not unfortunate side effects of the punishments, but their goal. The San Patricios' actions risked breaking down both racial and national barriers between the United States and Mexico. The state employed such horrific violence to restore and cement a certain racial and national order that drew sharp divisions between whites and "nagers" and between North Americans and Mexicans.[44] As Peter Linebaugh and Marcus Rediker noted for the seventeenth and eighteenth centuries, power's great fear was the union of the lower classes against its designs: race and nationality worked to undermine any such union.[45] By the nineteenth century, such divisions seemed deeply ingrained in American life, but the San Patricios showed that these divisions were not natural or eternal but could be overcome. Although the scattering of foreign men who joined the Mexican army posed little military threat to the United States, despite their bravery, their symbolic meaning was much more dangerous. The U.S. press eagerly categorized the San Patricios as un-American. The Brooklyn Daily Eagle derided the deserters: "These men are not of American birth, we believe almost to a man they are not."[46] Discourse, brandings, whippings, iron collars, and executions all served as bulwarks for a racial and national order.

While U.S. power brokers erected increasingly rigid racial divides, the war encouraged some Mexicans to enunciate the differences between the two warring societies' visions of equality and race. Politicians regularly warned that Mexicans in general, but especially Afro-Mexicans, faced enslavement if the United States triumphed—which, given the establishment of slavery in Texas, would not have seemed unreasonable.[47] The state of México's Legislature warned that one would soon hear in "our fields the snap of the whip and the brutal yelling of the slave overseer."[48] Due to the U.S. horror of racial mixing, castas (those of mixed racial ancestry) risked the worst treatment, and even "the extermination of the men of color" was a possibility.[49] Given the racism of the United States, Mexicans wondered how U.S. society could be truly republican; instead, it was a "hybrid republic, with popular institutions and a refined aristocracy of blood" that constantly abused and degraded its "people of color."[50]

These encounters accelerated the long process by which many in Spanish America began to define racial equality as key to both republicanism and civilization, a foundation of American republican modernity. El Monitor Republicano argued that Mexico enjoyed the "sympathies of the civilized nations" due to U.S. aggression and its modernity based only on "fire and blood." Mexico stood for the "cause of human liberty," in contrast to a nation that profited from slavery and "exploits a man and marks him with a brand of servitude as if he were a beast." Mexico supported "equality," while the United States was "a nation in which only one race dominates, humiliates and degrades all the others." The paper warned that if the U.S. conquest succeeded, anyone not of "European origin" would lose their "political rights" and be subjected to a situation little different from slavery. Therefore, Mexico's cause was the "cause of civilization."[51] Now, shockingly, it was not European life or military power that defined civilization, but equality. And this equality was not simply a legal equality; it extended at least into the social realm of race. Mexicans also tried to gain the moral upper hand during peace negotiations: Alcaraz stated that the Mexican negotiators attempted to ensure that slavery would not be allowed in any ceded territory. Although U.S. power was undeniable, its place in civilization remained doubtful, as its embrace of slavery violated the "principles of equality and manumission," earning it the "censure of humanity."[52] U.S. journalists and politicians bragged that they were bringing civilization to an inferior and racially suspect people, but Mexicans reacted by questioning the invader's claims to modernity. As universalism and equality cemented their prestige in American republican modernity in the coming years, the Spanish American public would increasingly employ U.S. racism as a mark of Latin America's superior progress. However, the contest within republicanism between racial nationalism and universalism would endure throughout the nineteenth century. For a moment universalism triumphed. However, by the 1880s racism, in both the North and South Atlantics, would renew its hold over visions of modernity.

The New Russians of the Americas

The transformation of Mexicans' thinking about civilization to include a republicanism marked by universalism and equality initiated American republican modernity's ascension in the public sphere. The position of the United States in such a schema was intensely problematic, since most Latin Americans recognized the aggressive northern giant as the most successful republican nation. For those letrados beholden to Europe, this mattered little, but if civilization was redefined by republicanism, where did that leave the United States and Latin American relations with it? In spite of Mexicans' suffering under U.S. invasion, surprisingly quickly that action came to be seen as exceptional in most of Latin America: it marked a divergence from the proper behavior of the United States as a New World sister republic. Most of the discourse of American republican modernity presented Latin America and the United States as kindred spirits, opposed to European monarchy, aristocracy, and colonialism. Instead of a competitor, the United States was seen as a fellow traveler, with many Latin Americans acknowledging U.S. political and economic success.[53] Yet time and again, the United States would betray Latin Americans' expectations—never more so than during the U.S.-Mexican war, at least until the Spanish-American War destroyed the sister republic ideal. The terms best suited to describe Latin Americans' contradictory views on the United States are "expectation" and "disappointment."

Disappointment with the United States over the invasion of Mexico was so bitter precisely because expectations were so high. Under Europhile modernity, letrados might admire the United States for its incipient economic growth and relative stability, but they still tended to think that only Europe could provide the "elements of culture and civilization" necessary for modernity.[54] However, around midcentury, as American republican modernity began to challenge Europhile modernity for dominance in the public sphere, the importance placed on the United States as a republican model increased. In fact, newspapers were much more likely to see the United States as a positive "model" than Europe, especially since the former had both political success in republicanism and economic success in its commercial, agricultural, and increasingly industrial growth.[55] Politically, a Uruguayan paper applauded the "unlimited democracy" in the United States that ensured "rights" and "social privileges" to all and "to each citizen consciousness that no one is superior to himself."[56] Although eventually it would be U.S. economic power that fascinated the Latin American public sphere, before the U.S.-Mexican War if the public sphere discussed the United States it was mostly as a political model.[57] Around midcentury, politicians such as the Colombian Tomás Mosquera, urged Latin Americans to look to the United States, instead of Europe, as a political or legal guide.[58] He declared: "The republican principles of North America are, for me, social perfection and the most sound."[59] Of course, even Domingo Faustino Sarmiento had urged his countrymen to imitate U.S. education policies.[60] As politics became the definition of civilization, the importance of the United States increased and that of Europe decreased. In the 1870s, Colombian politicians crafting a new state constitution would note that they looked to the United States—which, since the independence of Spain's colonies, "has served as a guide along the path of the Republic and liberty."[61]

The U.S. invasion thus shocked and deeply disappointed those who viewed the New World, save Brazil, as a joint project of "sister republics."[62] As the war loomed, El Republicano warned that dissension among American republics was the secret plan of European thrones, who would use the instability both to discredit the republican system and to reestablish monarchies in the New World. Instead of waging a fratricidal war, the United States should join Mexico in "common cause" against Europe. Feeling bewildered and betrayed by the U.S. violation of the republican spirit, the paper pleaded with its neighbor to follow the better angels of her nature and once again act as a sister republic.[63] A Uruguayan paper lamented that "the model for democratic governments" had now adopted "the principle of military conquest."[64]

Although American republican modernity was still only developing as a strand of thought in the public sphere, already a sense that republics should behave differently from monarchies as a sign of their progress and modernity had emerged. As the war began, the Boletín de la División del Norte referred to the bombardment of Matamoros, noting this was not how "civilized peoples" behaved; indeed, the war as whole was not the work of a modern republic, but an act from the "time of feudalism."[65] Similarly, after Veracruz endured artillery barrages, a letter from "Los Nuevo-Leoneses" lamented that the United States had "forgotten the republican principles that it had feigned to profess."[66] The United States risked abandoning its claims to civilization in its pursuit of conquest; perhaps it was not at republicanism's vanguard after all? A writer from Morelia argued that the United States had too many "contradictions" to be a republic—slavery, its severe penal code, racism, and the pervasiveness of "monetary interest"; republicanism could not accept such "contradictions," and even "one could cause the entire system to die."[67]

While a few writers questioned U.S. republican credentials, more bitterly predicted that the war would destroy the proud North American political system. In a speech in Mexico City, the entrepreneur José María Godoy lamented the passing of a United States that once had "demonstrated to the world that it is practical to govern great human associations by means of those principles of Democracy" that Europeans had mocked as utopian. Now the United States had started down "the baneful road of Conquest driven by a mad greed that some day it will lament with tears of blood."[68] El Corresponsal del Ejército warned that the war would cause the U.S. economy and institutions to collapse, as its people's "industrious hands will not want to put down the rifle, once habituated to a life of adventure."[69] El Monitor Republicano predicted that, "drunk on a bloody and diabolical glory," the militarization of U.S. society would lead to a "Republic corrupted by conquest and gold."[70] If the United States persisted in its belligerence, its army would overwhelm its political insitutions and "bury the liberties of the American republic," as had happened in Mexico (thus underlining the essential similarity of the two sister republics).[71]

Of course, across Latin America people followed news of the war, most sympathizing with the Mexican defense; even the San Patricios' fate attracted attention.[72] In Uruguay, El Nacional predicted that the war would ruin the "present greatness" of the United States, as it would be tempted to invade other nations and would descend into sectional division over the gains of the conquest and the question of slavery.[73] Mexicans struggled to interpret their neighbor's behavior, turning to the Atlantic to reframe the United States: no longer the model republic, it now resembled the stereotypical barbarous power in the Atlantic world, Russia. Enrique Stolz, a Pole, expressed his solidarity with Mexicans given his nation's oppression by Russia, exhorting the Mexicans to fight against "the new Russians of the American Continent."[74] Stolz's speech echoed existing Mexicans' fears that their country would be the Poland of the New World.[75] The sister republic ideal seemed to be yet another casualty of the U.S. invasion.

The open wound of the war would endure for the rest of the century in U.S.–Latin American relations, continually aggravated by filibusters (unauthorized invasions of Latin America by U.S. citizens) or gunboat diplomacy, and encouraging a defensive nationalism and racism to fester that would dominate the public sphere by century's end. Indeed, the war and subsequent U.S. interventions may have created the idea of a "Latin America," confronting a rapacious Yankee or Anglo-Saxon North America.[76] Yet, in spite of the war's long reach and even before the U.S. withdrawal, both North and South Americans worked to resuscitate the sister republic ideal. They would succeed, in the short term creating a sense of a collective destiny for the New World, but a future imperial adventure, the Spanish-American war, would finally sunder that ideal.

Even as the war raged, Mexicans hoped the vision of "two sister republics" would encourage the United States to demand only Texas and not additional territory; weakening Mexico too much would only encourage European aggression and monarchical projects, which would be in neither country's interest.[77] During the fighting's height, some Mexicans seized on rumors that England, Spain, and France planned to use the war as an excuse to interevene in Mexico. La Opinión Nacional hoped that such an invasion would cause the United States to end the war and unite with "all the continent" against an attempt to impose a New World monarchy.[78] As the United

States pursued its vision of Manifest Destiny and Anglo-Saxon exceptionalism, Spanish Americans desperately tried to revive a sense of American fraternity against European imperialism.

Spanish Americans were heartened by the opposition in the United States for its failure to follow republican principles. The public sphere in Latin America seized on U.S. opposition to the war as a way to revive the sister republic ideal.[79] News of dissent within the United States was eagerly reported, from the Southern Cone to Mexico.[80] As we have seen, many North Americans assumed that their race and superior civilization allowed them to conquer a barbaric, inferior foe. Others struggled to justify a war that so obviously clashed with a public discourse based on republicanism, liberty, and fraternity. Some claimed that the war was not an invasion of one republic by another, but a republican crusade against incipient monarchism, inspired by a rumor a European prince would take the Mexican throne.[81] Subsequent events would show that this was not a complete fantasy, but more importantly it allowed republicanism, and republican fraternity, to remain central to U.S. visions of civilization. Of course, many U.S. politicians realized how atrociously their country had behaved and that the war had thoroughly transgressed the country's founding ethos. In his memoirs, Ulysses S. Grant—who, like so many Civil War veterans, had first tasted battle in Mexico—condemned the war as unfitting to a republic: "To this day [I] regard the war which resulted as one of the most unjust ever waged by a stronger against a weaker nation. It was an instance of a republic following the bad example of European monarchies, in not considering justice in their desire to acquire additional territory."[82] Grant echoed the Spanish Americans who had predicted the war would weaken if not destroy U.S. institutions: "The Southern rebellion was largely the outgrowth of the Mexican war. Nations, like individuals, are punished for their transgressions. We got our punishment in the most sanguinary and expensive war of modern times."[83] Not just Spanish Americans, but North Americans as well, expressed intense disappointment in the model republic's failure. The U.S.-Mexican war reveals that nation-states can violate and ignore their own discourses of civilization, yet such disruptions are not easy or free, and, as is the case of the U.S. Civil War, may carry unbearable costs.

While the United States struggled to justify its behavior, another strategy that Spanish Americans employed to overcome the war's taint was to emphasize the basic commonalities between American societies, which would become another trope of American republican modernity. Europhile modernity often stressed the differences between the United States and the new nations to its south; letrados, such as Juan Bautista Alberdi, would maintain this bias, focusing on religion, different colonial histories, and the distinct natures of their populations (especially the working classes).[84] He argued that, unlike the United States, Argentina was not ready for unrestricted liberty and equality, because most of the population was not prepared for citizenship.[85] However, by midcentury under republican modernity, more and more thinkers stressed that American societies seemed fundamentally the same. Thus, if Latin America lagged behind the United States, that was due to the region's later entrance into the race to civilization or to the backwardness of Spanish colonialism.[86] In 1848 El Monitor Republicano again emphasized how unjust and unnecessary the war was, since Mexico and the United States should enjoy a neighborly fraternity, as both had identical systems of government, similar interests in preventing the reestablishment of European monarchies in the New World, and similar histories of struggles for independence.[87]

After the war, Mexicans hoped a renewed sense of the sister republic ideal would transform the way civilized nations interacted, thus preventing future disasters. "Modern civilization" had rejected the right of force, championed by kings. Instead, republics should respect and treat each other as "sisters." El Monitor Republicano hoped that the 1848 Pan-American Congress would provide a forum for republican nations to peacefully resolve their disputes.[88] Yet this dream quickly died, as the United States moved into Panama to construct the transisthmus railroad. Commenting on this latest intervention in 1856, Francisco Bilbao celebrated the U.S. political system while lamenting the U.S. desire for domination and lack of New World fraternity: "The Yankee replaces the American." The United States had elevated patriotism, industry, and riches over morality, charity, and justice. Bilbao lambasted the United States for still allowing slavery and for its treatment of Indians. North Americans had abandoned "the universal cause" to pursue "individualism." The threat of U.S. imperialism and filibusters was particularly disappointing because it originated from "that nation that should have been our star, our model, our force."[89] Once again, the United States betrayed the sister republic ideal. Expectation and disappointment orbited one another as the twin poles of Latin American relations with the United States.

The contradictory roles played by the United States—sister republic, model, and imperial aggressor—raised the issues of the Monroe Doctrine, foreign interventions, and the relationship between American societies. Although filibusters and U.S. interventions threatened the American community of sister republics, the specter of European intervention revived it.[90]

Indeed, the 1862 French invasion of Mexico (called the French Intervention; see chapter 4) caused some to imagine the Monroe Doctrine not as a U.S. policy of imperial expansion, but the shared responsibility of the New World sister republics. Some Mexicans urged "Tio Samuel" (Uncle Sam) to intervene directly, citing the long-standing U.S. pledge to resist European "monarchical" intrusions into the New World.[91] Other Mexicans claimed a hemisphere-wide sentiment to repel European imperial advances, transforming the Monroe Doctrine from a nationalist, singular tool of expansion to a fraternal, multifocal element of New World solidarity.[92] Indeed, after the French Intervention, the famed Mexican writer, teacher, and politician Ignacio Altamirano asked why the United States had not done more to enforce the "celebrated Monroe Doctrine" that "your wise President proclaimed."[93] U.S. politicians credited Mexico for defending the doctrine as they had not, praising the "action of President Juárez to vindicate the honor of the Republic and the Monroe Doctrine on this continent."[94]

Some Spanish Americans even proposed a much more aggressive version of the Monroe Doctrine. In 1862 a writer in Morelia proposed that the Americas unite in "a general alliance, offensive and defensive, established in a treaty, committing the united American continent to take the initiative against the Old World."[95] La Bandera Nacional pushed the doctrine much further in 1864, claiming North Americans had a duty to intervene in Mexico as Mexico's allies against the French. The paper interpreted the doctrine as "the establishment of an alliance among the American Republics under the banner of liberty and justice in opposition to the tyranny of kings and emperors."[96] The fate of the hemisphere, if not the entire Atlantic world, hung in the balance: "The question of the establishment of a throne and crown for Maximilian will be decided by the French and Austrian armies on the side of monarchy, and those of Mexico and the United States on the side of democracy and republicanism."[97] Under American republican modernity, the Monroe Doctrine was not necessarily seen as promoting nefarious U.S. ambition. Indeed, the provincial paper in Matamoros quoted above could celebrate it as part of a panhemispheric commitment of sister republics to protect democracy against European imperialism, involving but not dominated by the United States. In Peru, a letter from the townspeople of Pisco celebrated the arrival of U.S. warships as marking the "American Union" of "the young Republics of Columbus's World" who stood together as "sisters" against "European despots."[98] Many Latin Americans did not reject the Monroe Doctrine out of hand, instead hoping they could reconceptualize it as a truly American union.[99] Of course, that would not happen. U.S. imperial adventures regularly tested this New World fraternity, eventually giving rise to a patriotic nationalism that replaced republican universalism.

Thus, one reaction to U.S. aggression was the attempt in both the United States and Latin America to revive the sister republic ideal of pan-American unity and common purpose.[100] However, countering this thrust was the desire to differentiate Latin America from an aggressive United States, using the schema of race.[101] Mexican President José Mariano Salas, alarmed by U.S. imperialism, asserted that the "Hispanic-American race" would be supplanted by "the Anglo-Saxons."[102] The state of México's legislature went so far as to call it a "race war" between people whose ancestors came from the northern part of Europe and those whose ancestors were from the southern part.[103] The focus on Europe is revealing, as it excluded all the other peoples who inhabited both the United States and Mexico. As we have seen, others did try to widen the threat that the "Anglo-Saxon race" posed not just to the "Spanish," but also to Indians and Afro-Mexicans.[104] Mostly, however, letrados focused on the Spanish race. In 1847 President Pedro María Anaya urged Mexicans to fight the invaders, claiming that if they met with a stout defense, "never again will they say that the Spanish race, heroic in the Old World, has degenerated in Columbus's Continent."[105] By employing the concept of the Spanish, Anaya excluded the vast majority of his countrymen.

While this discourse's anti-imperialist nature arouses sympathy, this should not disguise the language's deeply conservative nature.[106] Lucas Alamán approvingly cited President Salas's rhetoric on the threat of Anglo-Saxons to Hispanic Americans in his 1852 *Historia de Méjico*.[107] Again, Alamán focused on European peoples, their origins, and their descendants in the New World. Tellingly, he generally thought of both Indians and castas as marked by their total ignorance and debasement, with a propensity to thieving and drunkenness—especially those castas of African descent.[108] As Aims McGuinness has shown, even Liberals who championed the unity of "the Latin race"—in the words of Justo Arosemena—against Yankee imperialism could not include "upstart blacks" in their essentially European "Latin" vision.[109] This was an elite discourse—Hispanic-Americans were just that, wealthy Americans of Spanish descent. Such Hispanophilia and Anglophobia cast the wealthiest and most powerful Latin Americans as subaltern, thus occluding the violence and exclusions the dominant class practiced against the poor, mestizo, black, or Indian, focusing instead on the relative humiliations suffered by elites at U.S. hands.[110] The celebration of such discourse is not just anti-imperialistic, it is also a celebration of patriotic nationalism, racism, and elite privilege that would eventually triumph over universalism by century's end. The conservative nature of the discourse of division is even clearer when we consider the United States, where by the 1820s Jacksonians had already promoted a racial difference between North and South America as a way of protecting slavery from republican critique and uniting regional divisions of the United States under a shared whiteness.[111]

Generally, the Hispanophilia inspired by U.S. racism and the U.S.-Mexican War was not particularly strong around midcentury, except in moments of direct imperial intervention. However, over time it would grow more and more powerful. Yes, it served as a response to U.S. imperialism and racism, but it also converted a feeling of universal nationhood into a patriotic nationalism that would eventually lead Latin Americans to look to Europe; abandon the idea of a New World community; openly embrace racism; and exclude the vast, subaltern majority from national belonging because they were not of the Spanish race. History would show that universalism, inclusive nationhood, and republican fraternity were always fragile, easily overcome by calls for patriotic nationalism and racial exceptionalism in both the United States and Latin America. Indeed, the argument I would like to make here and in chapter 7 is that U.S. imperialism undermined universalism and fostered racial thinking in Latin America by reinforcing an elite, racist patriotic nationalism.

Patriotic nationalism and racism would be countered by incipient ideas of universalism, however. The inclusionary nationhood and international solidarity of American republican modernity, reflected in the relations between Mexicans and the San Patricios, would dominate the public sphere after 1850. The U.S. invasion of Mexico did establish a pattern of disappointment with the United States that would play out time and again in the nineteenth century, culminating with the U.S. seizure of Cuba and Puerto Rico. However, before 1898, as we will explore in the next chapter, the public sphere viewed the United States not as a distant and distinct society to be imitated (as was the case with Europe under cultural modernity), but as an essentially similar sister republic. Certainly the United States enjoyed certain advantages and successes, but a fundamentally American republican modernity saw the whole New World as sharing a destiny and a project of civilization. The New World would create a new civilization—a new path to modernity—based not on imperialism, racism, and aristocratic privilege, but on liberty, equality, and fraternity as the bedrock of society, accomplishing what Europe had failed to do. The Americas, North and South, would remake and redeem the world.

CHAPTER 4

Eagles of American Democracy
The Flowering of American Republican Modernity

I n 1860 El *Ferrocarril* of Chile complained of Europeans' continued assertions of dominance and superior civilization (and many elite Americans'
acceptance of those views), demanding: "Where is our inferiority?" The paper argued that Europe was built both on an "ancient lie—the divine right
of kings—and now on a brand new sophism—constitutional monarchy."
Therefore, because of republicanism, the Americas enjoyed a "decisive superiority" over Europe. The New World had already progressed further down
the road of modernity and civilization than had Europe: "America, throwing
off the iron collar of colonialism, already has completed the great revolution, the great transformation, the grand execution of the past," while
Europe still suffered monarchs and caudillos. Finally, the essayist asserted
that the influence of America would spread to Europe, as "democracy will
destroy current European society."[1] This article encapsulated the two central
tropes of a new vision of modernity that came to dominate the Spanish
American public sphere after mid-century. First, the Americas, not Europe,
formed the vanguard of the future, "the vanguard of civilization."[2] Second,
the primary definition of civilization was now political: democracy and republicanism represented the future, while monarchy signified the past. The
New World no longer needed to pine after the high culture of the Old. Indeed, Europe must now look to America, because the continuing American

revolutions would soon overwhelm Old World hierarchies and traditions. Modernity would emanate from the Americas to transform the world as a whole.

What I call American republican modernity was a fluid, though coherent, way of envisioning the race to civilization that so obsessed nineteenth-century societies. I will begin by examining the two key tropes mentioned above: the locus of modernity—now imagined in the New rather than the Old World—and its essential nature, now seen as political rather than cultural. I will then uncover some of the finer points of this vision regarding universalism, imperialism, colonialism, nation, and race. I will next explore how this discourse conceived of subalterns, and—more important—how it nourished quotidian practices of democratic republicanism in Mexican and Colombian societies. Then I will suggest how subalterns used aspects of American republican modernity and this new political space to further their own agendas. Finally, I will conclude by uncovering some of the tensions and contradictions within American republican modernity—especially the problem of economic development—that foreshadowed the collapse of that discourse's near hegemony by the last quarter of the century.

We have seen that many of the key aspects of American republican modernity had already appeared in Uruguay in the 1840s, challenging the dominance of Europhile cultural modernity. In this chapter, we will focus mostly on Colombia and Mexico; American republican modernity commanded the public sphere by the 1850s in the former and the 1860s in the latter. Why at these times? Although the discourse was not limited to Liberals, they were its greatest proponents; therefore, the rise of American republican modernity is tightly linked to Liberals' ascension in both countries. In Mexico, Liberals came to power in 1855 after the Revolution of Ayutla (1854–55) deposed the caudillo Antonio López de Santa Anna. They instituted a sustained program to remake Mexico society called La Reforma (The Reform), which sought a radical break with the colonial past—represented by the Church, a corporate and caste ordering of society (including indigenous villages), and monarchy. Liberals instead embraced a future based on liberal republicanism, imagining a nation of rights-bearings citizens and individual, rational economic actors. However, Conservatives rabidly opposed such changes, rebelling in the War of the Reform (1857–61). After suffering defeat, Conservatives turned to Europe, allying themselves with an invading French army and inviting Maximilian to assume the throne of Mexico. This alliance instigated a long, bloody international and civil war (the French Intervention) from 1862 to 1867, which ended with the Liberals triumphant under President Benito Juárez and Maximilian dead. In Colombia, Liberal rule began earlier, when José Hilario López won the presidency in 1849, and lasted longer, but it was equally contested by Conservatives, who failed to take power in an 1851 rebellion but succeeded in 1854 due to divisions among Liberals. In turn, Liberals launched their own successful rebellion from 1859 to 1862. They ruled until the 1880s, withstanding a major conservative rebellion in 1876–77. In both Mexico and Colombia, Liberals enacted numerous reforms that ended special legal privileges for the Church and armies, restricted corporate ownership of property (aimed at the Church's economic power and indigenous villages' assumed economic isolation), enacted federalism, reduced monopolies, abolished slavery (this had already been accomplished in Mexico), extended citizenship to all adult males, and passed constitutions guaranteeing a wide array of rights (freedoms of speech, press, association, to bear arms, and to petition).[3] In a speech remembering the heady days of 1848, the Colombian Senator (and former president) Tomás Mosquera recalled how he had been asked to join the newly minted Conservative Party. He had demurred, noting how Conservatives in Europe maintained "the monarchal tradition," whereas he, though sympathetic to many Conservative ends, believed in "progress."[4] In both Colombia and Mexico, Liberals would imagine Conservatives as tied to Europe, while they, along with their brothers across the Americas, would reform the world, forging a new modernity.

The Land of Democracy Versus the Land of Tyranny and Human Degradation

In the dusty provincial town of Chihuahua in 1868, a crowd that had gathered to celebrate Mexico's independence listened as an unremarkable orator made a very remarkable assertion about the origin and spread of modernity in the nineteenth-century world: "The Eagles of American democracy, crossing the Atlantic, will import into the Old World the modern doctrines of political association, thereby emancipating those peoples."[5] The speech, made in the context of Mexico's victory over Maximilian and his French army, celebrated the restoration of a republic in Mexico. The speaker, Manuel Merino, equated this transformation with modernity, while assuming this modern system's influence would eventually spread across the Atlantic to a Europe still ruled by monarchies, equated with the past. Merino, addressing the residents of an isolated and remote province of Mexico, asserted a key component of American republican modernity that had become commonplace by the late 1860s: modernity—which he defined as "American democracy"—would emanate from the New World to transform the civilization of the Old.

The inexorable current of modernity that defined the nineteenth century had shifted across the Atlantic. Since modernity had emerged as a concept in the late eighteenth century, it had always been seen as occurring right now or in the near future (at least somewhere). However, Europhile cultural modernity had looked to Europe's high culture—in a sense, to past achievements. For American republican modernity, the nineteenth century was the moment of progress. There was little doubt that the nineteenth century, "this luminous century," was a unique period that would usher in the modern age.[6] In Cañete, Peru, Federico Flores declared that "the nineteenth century, the century of enlightenment, the century of progress and civilization, belongs to America; retrograde Europe must give way, as in the past Asia gave way."[7] Europe could not join this movement because monarchy belonged to the past, the Middle Ages. A provincial Colombian politician, condemning a rumored attempt to establish a monarchy in Ecuador, noted that monarchy was a form of government that "the century has rejected."[8] The nineteenth century—in the words of Juárez, "the first century of the pueblos"—belonged to the Americas.[9]

While youth and the spirit of the age found a home in America, Europe seemed old and the cradle of the dark past. The professor, essayist, and dramatist Gabino Ortiz, speaking to the Morelia National Guard in 1862, mocked: "The decrepit nations of Europe, the rotten thrones of their sickly dynasties, the rancid and strange institutions that rule them, all feel the convulsions of their final agony. In order to distract themselves from the frightening spectacle of a past from which they flee, from a present that escapes them, and from an inevitable future, they turn their sights on young America, object of their envy, hatred and insatiable greed."[10] Addressing perhaps four thousand men, Ortiz assumed this modernity would happen in "young America," a discourse powerfully resonant in the public sphere.[11] Youth, a weakness under Europhile cultural modernity, became the American republics' great strength, ready to foment and inculcate modernity, while Old Europe clung to the past and its worm-eaten traditions.

Indeed, European influence no longer carried civilization, as cultural modernity had assumed, but rather transmitted the fatal malaria of past decay. Instead of bringing civilization, Juan Cervin de la Mora claimed in a speech to artisans, the European invasion of Mexico would only "regress us to the times of horror and barbarism."[12] American republicanism associated feudalism and the Inquisition with Europe, the origin of the "fanaticism" that

New World societies struggled to destroy.[13] When Spain invaded Mexico in 1862 (a prelude to the French Intervention), *La Guerra* mocked the Spanish pretension to bring "the inquisition, the cowl, and stocks" back to Mexico; such Old World "fanaticism" was inappropriate in the century of enlightenment.[14] *La Bandera Nacional* staunchly rejected Europhilia, smugly deriding those Conservatives who "endlessly repeat, with a childish mien, that all of Europe is superior to America, above all, the educated and the soldiers."[15] *La Opinión Nacional* argued that "European enlightenment is more words than deeds." The paper recognized that Mexico still did not enjoy some European material successes, but instead it had "our triumphant democracy," which had far surpassed Old World accomplishments.[16] The contrast with the origin of progress under Europhile cultural modernity could not be starker.

As we will explore in the next section of this chapter, the reason the Americas advanced while Europe stagnated was political, specifically the adoption of republicanism and democracy in the New World. When the French invaded Mexico, a Guadalajarense paper argued that Mexico "represents the interests of the New World, land of democracy, combating the interests of the Old World, land of tyranny and human degradation."[17] *La Chinaca* declared that democracy's future lay in the Americas: "Today we defend the banner of the democratic idea" against European tyrants; thankfully, "God has placed the Atlantic between the two continents as the distance between Heaven and Hell."[18] *El Monitor Republicano* declared: "The democratic republic is the natural government of America, just as monarchy is natural to Europe and the most stupid tyranny has extended its roots throughout Asia and Africa."[19] America was the future: it enjoyed a democratic, republican system of government, while the rest of the world dwelled, to a greater or lesser degree, under despotism.

Returning to Peru, we find that Federico Flores described the race to civilization, and the divide between Europe and America, in historical terms. America began to gain in the race with the independence of the United States, followed by that of the South American nations: "Democracy triumphed." Since then, America had taken the lead: "The Old World has sunk and will sink further into decadence; it continues converting its proverbial culture and progress into nothing but ruins; this has come to pass because those states do not have republican governments." Meanwhile, American republics, following the law and "the will of the people," were "every day moving closer to the apex of civilization." Perhaps Europe once held a claim on modernity, but no longer. And, unlike Europe, America would not retrogress as France had after its revolution, degenerating from republic to monarchy.[20]

Europe had tried to achieve modernity—with the French Revolution—but the forces of retrogression had triumphed. The rioplatense-born Héctor Varela had a similar, if chronologically deeper, historical understanding; writing from Paris, he had founded El Americano to introduce Europe to the true progress of "Latin America." He argued that the rise of New World societies marked the end of the "Middle Ages" in which Europe and Christianity were champions of civilization. Now, however, the Americas had progressed beyond Europe in their adoption of "the democratic doctrine," liberty, rights, and state institutions, but most especially "the Republic," which was "the definitive form of our spirit." Varela asserted: "Taking this point of view, one can say that the New World is the most potent incarnation of the modern spirit." The New World was modern, and if Europe would listen, it could learn valuable lessons to help bring about "universal democracy."[21]

The modern world's genesis was in Latin America. "Decrepit Europe retrogresses in all parts," the professor and diplomat Jesús Escobar y Armendáriz argued, adding that "we are heading toward a universal Republic" that had already been achieved in Mexico and much of Latin America, even if Hungary, Poland, and Italy were still struggling against despotism in Europe.[22] The New World was now civilization's best hope. Dipesh Chakrabarty argues that outside of Europe, modernity is always imagined as something that happens elsewhere, an argument echoed by some Latin Americanists—one of whom declares that nineteenth-century Spanish Americans always felt modernity flowered "somewhere else."[23] Such a sentiment would have seemed to belong to only the most conservative or Europhilic letrado in 1860s Mexico or Colombia. On the contrary, the Chilean Francisco Bilbao understood that civilization was not a fixed concept; he proposed that there was a vast struggle between "American civilization against European civilization."[24] Bilbao proclaimed that Europe had now declined due to its monarchies, imperialism, and its lack of true liberty and justice; it would have to wait for American influence to incite republican revolutions if it hoped to progress once again.[25]

Americans did not just assume that their societies no longer blindly received civilization from Europe, but they also declared that American modernity would transform Europe.[26] Indeed, this idea that the new Latin American republics might be a threat to Europe had appeared occasionally by the 1840s (as in Uruguay), but it would became a powerful trope throughout the subsequent decades. In Mexico, El Republicano criticized the editors of El Tiempo, who had promoted monarchism by arguing that it was the government of "the most civilized and liberal countries of Europe." El Republicano countered that the New World had its own destiny and that its republics were the future: "The American continent is called, by its nature, to be the complete antithesis of the Old World." Those who discredited the republican system hoped to reintroduce monarchy, which would serve European interests since "the thrones that exist there do not want to see even one flourishing republic in the world," because that might incite their own people to rebel and establish republics.[27] Spanish America's revolutions and wars were not negative in this reading (as they were under Europhile modernity) because they had engendered republican modernity; instead, the lack of revolution marked Europe as backward.

By the 1850s no hesitancy remained for many in Colombia concerning the Americas' future. In 1852 President José Hilario López warned of a monarchical project in Ecuador, Colombia, and Peru. This plot was an attempt to destroy the "democratic Republics" that had vanquished the colonial, monarchical system and had launched Nueva Granada (Colombia) down the "path of progress." For López, Nueva Granada was a shining light in the Atlantic world, proving that "liberal institutions are not the privilege of one race." He was confident that the "strength of public opinion" supported republicanism, but he warned of the nefarious dealings of those proposing "ultramontanism" and "Europe's cause of retrocession."[28] López's speech to Congress, subsequently distributed throughout Bogotá as a broadside, encapsulates our themes thus far. The public understood Republicanism was the path to progress. However, dangerous opponents—American Conservatives and European dynasties—wanted to destroy Spanish American republics' powerful examples, lest their influence triumph universally.

The challenge to Europe found its most forceful enunciation in Mexican society during and after the French Intervention (1862–67). In this era, Mexican Liberals not only asserted that the Americas were more modern than, and would influence, Europe; they also claimed that American republicanism was a direct threat to the backward European status quo. When the French invaded in 1862, El Voto del Pueblo claimed: "Luis Napoleon has made war on us because he fears America, because he hates republics, and because he sees in Mexico democracy and La Reforma made real." If Mexico "had stayed in a state of barbarism and fanaticism" and had not "transformed itself through La Reforma and launched itself toward a future of progress and liberty; if [Mexico] had not adopted as dogma the sovereignty of the pueblo and exposed as a lie and sarcasm the divine right of kings," then Napoleon III would not have needed to invade.[29] Here barbarism is explicitly linked with colonialism and monarchy. Mexico was not blindly receiving modernity from Europe and imitating it, or even developing its own modernity apart from Europe; with victory, Mexico would bring modernity to Europe, which would imitate the Americas.[30] In 1871 El Aguijón mocked France for still being ruled by a monarch as laughable as Napoleon III, calling him "the Jester of the Tuileries."[31] Mexican papers predicted the French pueblo would soon awaken from its slumber and inspired by "our 57"—La Reforma, in other words—would execute another monarch to initiate a modern future.[32] Critics of modernity have applauded twenty-first-century historiography for dismantling the totalizing claims of European modernity (which some assume non-Europeans accepted in the past), but I contend that nineteenth-century Latin Americans had already dismantled Europe's claims to modernity and its power to define barbarism.[33] Nineteenth-century historical actors were provincializing Europe long before postcolonial scholars' theoretical contortions.[34]

Although most of this discourse assumed republicanism in general threatened the ancien régime, Juan González Urueña, writing from Morelia, explicitly focused on equality. He argued that European monarchs feared "the spread of, as much in the Old World as the New, the ideas of republican equality and political and religious liberty, all of which are undermining slowly but surely their thrones' support."[35] If allowed to spread, such ideas would eventually destroy Old World monarchies. As we will explore in the next chapter, the French Intervention in Mexico was seen as only part of a larger project to eradicate the contagion of New World republics, including the United States, for which Mexico would be a base from which to support the aristocratic Confederacy in the U.S. Civil War. Therefore, "the cause of Mexico is the cause of the American continent; what's more, it is the cause of humanity."[36] The Atlantic world was a vast arena in which the forces of equality, enlightenment, and republicanism confronted those of aristocracy, superstition, and monarchy. Yet by staking the justification for American defense on equality, Mexican elite republicans established in the public sphere a notion that subalterns could easily seize and exploit. Equality was a threat to both European thrones and members of the Latin American ruling class and the incipient capitalist development that they hoped to foment.

Equality, liberty, fraternity, and universal democracy had become particularly American values. As the French Intervention loomed, La Guerra had stressed fraternity among the peoples of the earth as monarchs' greatest fear. The paper argued the French had invaded so "that in the New World, liberty's endeavors to conquer the sacred rights of humanity will be sterile in their results, because thrones tremble when democracy moves to realize the pueblos' destiny, universal fraternity."[37] Once the American republican system had toppled these European thrones, "in their place will arrive the rule of Enlightenment and liberty, the happy reign of universal democracy. This is humanity's destiny."[38] Although Europe had previously influenced America, Chile's El Independiente argued, "the current is entirely changed. American civilization works visibly and powerfully on Europe's pueblos."[39] The flow of modernity had reversed, now following the Gulf Stream from the New World to the Old.

I suspect many readers from the North Atlantic will quickly dismiss this rhetoric as empty boasting. For our purposes, I am most interested in this discourse's importance within Spanish American societies. However, it bears noting that Spanish Americans' claim to influence the Old World does not lack logic. It is easy to mock the conspiratorial paranoia of Francisco Bilbao, who in 1864 claimed that European monarchs plotted against American republics: "We now know the ancient and secret pacts of their diabolical alliances to do away with all the Republics in the world."[40] Yet it is also true that almost all the world's republics were in the Americas, and if republicanism was a threat to monarchies, as the monarchs certainly believed it was, then the Americas were the last, best hope of republican values. The Americas kept republicanism alive and meaningful at a time when it had all but disappeared in the Old World. It is beyond this study's scope to prove American influence on Europe. However, such an effort, requiring serious studies of republicanism's diffusion, will be undertaken only once Spanish America's importance in democratic and republican innovation is not summarily dismissed.

Political Modernity: The Inextinguishable Volcano of Democratic Ideas

As the fusillades against Europe attest, Mexicans and Colombians were redefining not just the locus of modernity but also its meaning, privileging a political definition of civilization. By the 1850s, American republican modernity had flowered in full in Colombia. The Liberal Party had come to power in 1849 and adopted numerous political reforms, including universal male suffrage and a long list of rights for citizens, regardless of class or color.[41] Colombian elites did not just imagine themselves as mere followers of Atlantic political currents; rather, they saw themselves as in "the vanguard in America"—along with other New World republics, including the United States—in creating modern political systems.[42] Bogotá's El Neogranadino declared that "we are not behind, but rather in front of the movement of universal civilization."[43] Popayán's La Union thought Colombia was in the vanguard, as it had established "the will of the pueblo" superior to all other powers and eliminated every "hierarchy" (including that of race) and "element of repression" from society.[44] The New World represented progress and the future in the Atlantic world; the Old World, even including prosperous England, was aged, tired, decadent, monarchical, beset by violence, and weighed down by the feudal past.[45]

American republican modernity regularly assumed that a retrograde feudalism had reigned in colonial and early postindependence Spanish America, until the adoption of effective republicanism. Before the arrival of the midcentury liberal reforms, Belisario Zamorano described the nineteenth-century Cauca region as stuck in "the tyranny of the Middle Ages."[46] Indeed, monarchy was regularly equated with a barbaric past. Juan de Dios Restrepo, writing from Buga, evoked the clash of civilizations—European monarchy versus American republics: "The situation of America is dire; the fight is between the colonial system and the modern liberal spirit, between the paganism of the Roman priests and the evangelical Christian idea, between those who dream of reestablishing slavery, privilege, monarchy, theocracy and those who believe that all of those abominations should remain in Europe."[47] Republican modernity in the Americas was thus contrasted with European backwardness, characterized by slavery, aristocracy, and monarchy. American modernity centered on republican politics and its associated political ideas—liberty, equality, fraternity, rights, and democracy. Republicanism had replaced wealth, urbanity, and European high culture as the accepted definitions of modernity in the Colombian (and in much of the wider Spanish American) public sphere.

Francisco Bilbao summed up this vision of "civilization" that I call American republican modernity as one that respected the "integrity of human rights, in politics, religion and society." He directly rejected definitions of civilization that privileged concepts of "utility, of wealth, of beauty." Speaking for all Americans, he declared: "We reject such civilization—that is, the civilization that old Europe represents."[48] Thus Bilbao denied the central construction of civilization under Europhile cultural modernity, mocking those who "confuse civilization with fashion." However, he also refused to accept new material definitions of modernity coming from the North Atlantic, arguing that science, industry, and commerce did not represent civilization and warning that it was "despots and tyrants" who now bragged about their steamships, railroads, telegraphs, machinery, and fancy palaces as signs of modernity.[49] He declared that railroads built to carry slaves, telegraphs used to organize repression, and palaces built by the poor to honor kings were not marks of modernity, but rather of backwardness.[50] Europe had tried to seduce America with "the tripartite prestige of its science, its power and its wealth," but America had stuck fast to the "idea of the Republic," representing "the victory of the modern idea."[51]

Thus, American republican modernity was in a long-running contest both with older visions of Europhile cultural modernity and newer visions of Western modernity emerging from the North Atlantic. Bilbao, like others, directly rejected both. We have already seen how in Uruguay there was a sense that while "European civilization" involved palaces, fashion, opera, and wealth, civilization was also defined by a society's success in establishing an order based on "free men" who supported "liberty, equality, [and] humanity."[52] In a speech in 1864 in Chihuahua, Mexico, Carlos Pacheco dismissed Europhile modernity's longings. Such things as "ridiculous courtiers and their ceremonies" and "their pompous titles of nobility," which had once defined civilization in the Atlantic world, now only marked Europeans as backward.[53] Under cultural modernity, wealth and European luxury were the marks of civilization. In contrast, under American republicanism tales of European opulent hotels, splendid carriages, grand balls, and "Oriental luxury" were marked as wasteful, backward, and corrupting, more akin to an imagined stagnant Asian despotism than to American republican progress.[54] With France's invasion of Mexico, the distinction between wealth and politics as modernity's markers was clear. Referring to the invasion, Colombian President Mosquera declared that his country was prepared "to defend the republican system at all costs, preferring the liberty of the savage in our forests to slavery in gilded palaces."[55]

Ultimately, much more challenging to American republicanism than the older cultural ideas were the new visions of Western modernity coming from the North Atlantic that privileged state power, military force, technology, science (and scientific racism), commerce, and industrialization. Eventually, as we will explore in chapter 7, this vision would triumph in Latin America. However, immediately after midcentury, the Mexican and Colombian public spheres' conception of modernity still downplayed economic, technological, and cultural accomplishments in favor of moral and political benchmarks. Facing a Europe intent on imposing its civilization on Mexico, the physician Carlos Santa María directly rejected "European progress"— defined for him by steamship, canals, railroads, industry, arts, and sciences— arguing instead that "the true happiness of social life consists in enjoying liberty and independence." "The comforts of material life," order, and "respect for property" that Europe offered carried too high a price: "degrading slavery."[56] Similarly, Severo Cosío, formerly governor of Zacatecas, thought that the French could not offer modern liberty or rights, but only "progress of a dazzling and corrupt materialism."[57] France "wants a monopoly of commerce, [and] the superiority of races to change the destiny of the New World, which is the home and haven of the human species and of democracy."[58] This vision recognizes Europe as having achieved economic development and increased state and technological power, but at the cost of monopolies, racism, and the repression of democracy.

Europe's imperial aggressions especially forced Spanish Americans to consider the relation between power and modernity; as state and military power emerged as a key trope of modernity in the North Atlantic, Spanish Americans directly rejected it. El Constitucional argued that when Europe would come with its cannons and warships to bombard Mexico's ports, "we will answer them via the transatlantic cable with one word: 'Democracy.'"[59] Another writer argued: "It is not with cannons that you introduce or foment civilization. . . . Civilization relies on another class of moral force, which illuminates and carries human fraternity to the ends of the earth."[60] Mexico City's El Globo encapsulated these themes: Europe (and even the U.S. North) thought their warships and newly engineered rifles "the best expression of human progress," while Mexico, suffering "the lances of empire" of an invading France, insisted that its "republican virtue" and democratic constitution best defined nineteenth-century civilization.[61]

Furthermore, Europe's political backwardness would eventually undermine its material successes, since its oppressed masses would one day rise up and destroy the palaces, factories, and railroads that European elites erroneously believed made them modern. Although Europe might have "material progress and artificial wealth," these were only the "tinsel of civilization" that states used to distract from "the masses' misery." European monarchs' rejection of "popular sovereignty" since 1789, and the continued immiserization of the masses this entailed, meant that "the inextinguishable volcano of democratic ideas" would continually erupt in Europe. As long as the war raged between the "old regime and the pueblo's aspirations," Europe would continually endure bloodshed and the majority of its inhabitants would be condemned to poverty.[62] As La Unión noted, by incorporating the masses into politics, Colombia would prevent the kinds of internecine class struggle seen in Europe, where "the rights of man are not recognized."[63] This judgment of Europe makes clear that wealth was only a false measure of civilization; democratic politics was the only true yardstick.

I am not arguing that American republican modernity did not value locomotives, telegraphs, and steam-powered factories, but that it saw them more as the eventual product of a republican modernity than as part of its essential character.[64] Political liberty was American republican modernity's key aspect; once this was obtained, other aspects of civilization—economic and cultural—would follow. In a speech celebrating independence, Máximo Castañeda declared that as a consequence of Mexico having established liberal republicanism, and "the sacred principles of equality and universal reform," peace and material progress would follow.[65] Similarly, a Uruguayan paper argued that the U.S. political system "is the true font of the prosperity that country has obtained."[66] Political modernity would engender economic progress; economic progress without political modernity was unstable, ultimately hollow, and doomed to fail. After 1870 many Liberals would abandon this calculus, deciding that political modernity did not engender economic development but, rather, actively hindered it.

In Colombia in the 1850s, however, politics still led to the future. When the radical Liberal Ramón Mercado described the liberal reforms that would lead to "civilization" and progress, his lengthy list consisted almost entirely of political accomplishments concerning extending rights and liberties: the abolition of slavery, granting freedom of expression, ending monopolies, creating a government that followed "public opinion," and allowing citizens greater participation in the judiciary. In general, these reforms undid the work of previous governments that had represented the "aristocracy," whose constitution was the largest obstacle to "ideas of progress." In sum, Mercado's vision of democratic republicanism had triumphed over "barbarism."[67] Luis Bossero, in the first issue of El Estandarte Nacional in 1856, tied "the march of civilization, the progress of noble ideas, and the emancipation of the human species" together. Here civilization is clearly political, advancing with the triumph of "liberty against despotism."[68] One speaker at a celebration of Mexican independence declared simply that "liberty is that light" that brings "civilization [and] progress."[69] Now civilization was no longer wealth (indeed, the aristocracy was its antithesis) or the city or European culture; instead, it was democracy, republicanism, and liberty.

Liberty's centrality to political modernity made constitutions supremely important as engines of and testaments to civilization. Colombian President José María Obando celebrated the 1853 constitution as "the most democratic code that has governed any pueblo."[70] Although he later condemned Obando's treason, Francisco Bilbao agreed that the 1853 constitution "has consecrated all the great conquests of the modern spirit."[71] When the nation, again under Conservative rule after 1854, debated whether to replace the 1853 Liberal constitution, which had implemented universal adult male citizenship and suffrage, Barbacoas's Municipal Council wrote to support the current constitution, "the great thesis of democracy." The council members argued: "There is not one disposition in our constitution that is not the genuine expression of the philosophy and the civilization of the century." They warned against any changes, since they were opposed to "all that is not government of the pueblo for the pueblo."[72] Here we have a provincial legislature—in European eyes, a backwater in the jungles of the Pacific Coast—arguing that a democratic constitution, of the pueblo, was the best expression of the nineteenth century's civilization. This was not a discourse of lettered elites in the salons of Bogota or Mexico City, but a quotidian language with profound depth and reach, both spatially and socially.

In Mexico the 1857 constitution held a similarly vaunted position, seen as the culmination of La Reforma.[73] In the 1857 Constitutional Congress's justification of the new charter to the nation, the members stressed how everything in the constitution emanated from "the dogma of the pueblo's sovereignty," noting that all "modern societies" used the representative system.[74] This constitution, "the most democratic the Republic has had," would propel the nation "along the path of progress and reform, civilization and liberty."[75] The Congress also stressed how quickly modernity moved in the nineteenth century: "Humanity advances day by day, necessitating incessant innovation in its political and social mode of being."[76] Only through "political and social revolution" could Mexico maintain its position in a nineteenth century whose "spirit's movement does not rest."[77] Liberals saw La Reforma as having made Mexico modern, finally fulfilling the promise of independence.

If constitutions represented a hoped-for (if rarely achieved) republican stability, revolution figured as a necessary step on the path to modernity. While disorder, anarchy, and civil wars had so distressed the public sphere under Europhile modernity, now some people celebrated civil wars as a necessary step to secure progress. Flores argued that such wars were the response of people trying to secure a liberal government and "democratic principles." Worse than having a civil war was to be like Europe, stuck in the past with monarchs blocking the road to modernity.[78] Much more radically, Mercado celebrated Liberals' taking power (electorally) in 1849 as a "social revolution."[79] In 1850 and 1851, while Mercado served as Cali's governor, a popular uprising against Conservative landowners and slaveholders erupted in the Cauca Valley. Poor men and women attacked prominent Conservatives, destroyed fences enclosing commons, and invaded and torched some haciendas. Although all Conservatives and many Liberals condemned the attacks, Mercado sought to explain them as resulting from the continuation of slavery and the domination of landholding by a small group of "oligarchs" and "pseudo nobles" who exploited the poor.[80] The poor simply could not endure the situation any longer, now that "the star of equality shone in their eyes."[81] The disorder was regrettable, but it was an understandable part of the "democratic revolution."[82]

Indeed, civil wars were an unfortunate necessity to establish the republican future and overcome the Old World inheritance of colonialism and religious fanaticism.[83] Montevideo's *La Nación* argued that Latin America's numerous revolutions had engendered "an accretion of liberties."[84] In a speech to celebrate independence on 16 September 1861 in Chihuahua, Manuel Ojinaga (a Liberal who would die fighting the French) stressed the chaos and even violence of the independence era, but he noted the struggle was necessary to obtain "liberty" and, thus, "civilization."[85] Postindependence civil wars were due to those who had not given up on the past, those who "have conspired by every excessive means to implant in our young nation the anguished and invalid institutions of Old Europe."[86] That same year, President Juárez remarked that although the War of the Reform had caused much destruction, it was a "progressive revolution" that had inspired the pueblo to demand "democratic institutions" and to institute "radical reforms."[87] Unlike under North Atlantic or Western visions of modernity, order was desirable, of course, but not fetishized. When European powers invaded Mexico, Ortiz declared, "I prefer the dangerous storms of liberty to the ignominious peace of slavery."[88] In an 1862 speech in El Paso del Norte, the doctor Mariano Samaniego surveyed the world and saw an immense international conflict (in Italy, the United States, and Mexico), a series of revolutions that pitted the forces of "progress" and "civilization" against those of "retrogression." He noted that people feared the word "revolution," but he argued that the recently ended civil war had been an "indispensable revolution" since it had resulted in "the triumph of liberty and of civilization."[89] Escobar y Armendáriz compared revolutions to the great volcanoes of Vesuvius, Etna, Popocatepetl, and Chimborazo, explosive forces that would not stop erupting until the world was transformed.[90] El *Estandarte Nacional* imagined revolution as an omnipotent force that swept across societies, the "work of modern times."[91] In 1868 *La Opinión Nacional* certainly recognized the value of peace after the defeat of Maximilian and years of devastating war, but it also emphasized that more important were successful resolutions of political questions in favor of a democratic republicanism, encapsulated in "modern constitutions" based on popular sovereignty.[92] Progress could be made during times of disorder, and order alone did not signify modernity or civilization.

The embrace of revolution at the expense of order resonated powerfully with the trope of American republicanism's threat to Europe described above. As France's invasion loomed, *La Chinaca* defended the Americas and democracy against European accusations of anarchy. The paper began by noting how "calls for liberty" and "democracy" had been crushed so thoroughly in Europe by monarchs that many European peoples "almost do not feel their chains." Thus, the "banner of liberty" had passed to America, whose revolutions had indeed created disorder but also happiness for the vast majority, who were now freed from their former masters. The paper warned: "This example was dangerous." Europe needed to employ its "iron rod" to crush "American anarchy" or risk having the people of the Old World be inspired by the example of the New: "It was necessary that there be order and that the citizens become slaves."[93] Under Europhile modernity, anarchy had been proof of America's barbarism, and order had been necessary to imitate Europe. Under Western modernity, order would be the prime precondition of civilization, without which societies were doomed to poverty and barbarism (and thus order would become the justification for persecuting and excluding subalterns). Yet under American republicanism, order—though fervently desired—was secondary to democratic liberty, which would provide subalterns with valuable discursive space to engage the nation.

Although Mexican writers looked forward to a new dawn of peace and prosperity after the War of the Reform (1857–61), they did not regret the violence and saw the war as necessary to impel modernity forward. In 1861, in a speech in Hidalgo de Parral celebrating the Liberals' triumph, José María Camarena declared that the past revolution had been a "step on the road to civilization"; while destructive, it had also paved "the way of human progress." Revolution was the path to "the future" as long as it advanced societies toward republicanism and "liberty, equality [and] fraternity." He claimed that "in order to establish ourselves we have needed a true renewal, and renewal is almost always destruction." Indeed, since revolution was necessary to achieve modernity, that excused the inevitable disorder and devastation that had ensued. Camarena's vision was not only abstract, but it directly spoke to subalterns as well. Camarena saw revolution as a contest between those promoting human liberation and equality and those defending the ancien régime of aristocrats and the idle rich, a discourse that subalterns could turn to their own ends. He mixed his very nineteenth-century celebration of progress and civilization with a much older justification that would also have resonated with many of the lower class. Almost as if a forerunner of liberation theology, Camarena declared Jesus Christ an "artisan" who was the "father of democracy" and who had "proclaimed equality of men and had to fight against the power of kings." Meanwhile, he referred to Conservatives as "vampires" who wanted to repeat the atrocities of the conquistador Cortés.[94] Camarena was just one politician speaking in one small town in northern Mexico, but the tropes of his discourse on revolution and modernity—the necessity of revolution to secure progress, the valuation of republicanism and democracy over order as markers of modernity, and the rhetorical celebration of the popular over the wealthy—resonated across the Americas around midcentury. We will now explore some of the nuances of this vision.

The Rights of Man in Society: Universalism and American Republican Modernity

The vision of modernity held by Camarena and his contemporaries assumed a universalism of humanity. We have already seen how Mexicans and Colombians embraced a teleology of history leading to "universal fraternity," "universal reform," a "universal republic" and "universal democracy."[95] As we saw above, this universalism assumed the diffusion of republicanism, liberty, and rights throughout society. Universalism also affected the proper relations between peoples—the fraternity of nations—to which we will turn next. Most important, universalism conditioned relations within society. In this section, we will examine how American republican modernity imagined the impediments to and buttresses for universalism. Imperialism was the greatest obstacle to universalism between societies. Within societies, American republican modernity decried colonialism's legacies that hobbled modernity, celebrated new nations' exertions to overcome these obstacles, and promoted universalism's triumph over race.

Universalism and Imperialism

After the French invaded, Mexicans' ideas of how civilized societies should comport themselves in international relations crystallized. *La Chinaca* envisioned two competing forces in international relations: on one side, "the barbarous principle of conquest and force," and on the other, "the rights of peoples."[96] The French had claimed they were invading Mexico in order to civilize the locals, a justification Mexicans particularly resented.[97] Instead,

Mexicans claimed the French had only brought "murder and arson, executed as instruments of civilization."[98] Mexicans accused the French of having invaded a sovereign nation for no reason and, by murdering and pillaging, having behaved in a barbaric manner: "Which of the two nations is civilized, Mexico or France? Which of the two will have to cover its face in shame when confronted by humanity, justice and true civilization?"[99] The Municipal Council of Paso del Norte (now called Ciudad Juárez) condemned the French for not respecting the "principles of modern civilization" and instead following the rules of conquest of the "Middle Ages."[100] A broadside that circulated in Mexico City after the French defeat argued that Europeans, and especially the French, had abandoned "modern diplomacy" in their wars of conquest around the globe. The broadside criticized not only the invasion of Mexico but also Europeans' "war in China." It denounced French atrocities in Mexico: "They marched into Puebla and acted as if they were dealing with a horde of savages, as if they were in Algiers, killing in the name of civilization."[101]

While Europe was embarking on its second great wave of imperial conquest, creating a wave of colonialism that would define modernity until this day, Mexicans proposed a countermodernity that rejected the equation of civilization with power and violence. Escobar y Armendáriz blamed the current state of Asia and Africa on ancient European colonial excursions—"the barbarians of the North," from Alexander the Great to the Crusaders—and lamented that when Napoleon III invaded Mexico, "he tried to civilize [it] with 50,000 bayonets."[102] Europe was not only lacking civilization in this view, but actually responsible for exporting barbarism by trying to impose monarchy, increase European states' power, and recapture their former colonial tributes.[103] Europhile modernity had been turned on its head. This critique of modernity prefigured that made by postcolonial scholars, who point out that European modernity's costs and violence were borne by colonial peoples. As Stuart Hall and Aníbal Quijano argue, modernity is a product of colonialism.[104] Long before twentieth-century decolonization or postcolonial studies, however, Mexico had not accepted this modernity; instead, it had rejected the neocolonial French project and mocked European pretensions to civilization.[105] Francisco Bilbao also denounced the French (and, indirectly, Hegel) for claiming that civilization was a "Spirit" that created the "modern world," a force that triumphs—thus justifying the imperialist adventures of the French in Algeria, China, and Mexico.[106] For Bilbao and other followers of American republican modernity, Hegel's "Spirit" was not a brutal, overreaching power that forcibly subdued other peoples, but the transformative force of liberty and republicanism that would create a universal fraternity of man.

Colonialism

If imperialism threatened this fraternity in the present, colonialism—and its lingering effects from the past—still exerted enough force to prevent modernity's reign. According to this view, modernity began with independence, when the Americas broke free from a barbarous Spain and "exchanged liberty for slavery, justice for arbitrary despotism, enlightenment for ignorance and fanaticism, civilization for heinous customs of barbarism, and finally, our new institutions for those stale ones of subjecthood."[107] The colonial era represented backwardness: domination by an ultramontane clergy, indigenous communal landholding, the caste system, and economic stagnation.[108] Spain had enriched itself but left nothing of value behind in the New World; instead, it had only brutalized its colonies' inhabitants both physically and intellectually.[109] The broader public sphere's vision of Spain under American republicanism contrasts sharply with elite *letrados'* growing embrace of the Iberian heritage as defining their societies (as discussed by Rebecca Earle), an understanding that would dominate later in the century.[110]

Independence, however, was only the first step. The new nations' problems could be blamed squarely on Spanish colonialism and lingering European influence. A Montevideano newspaper complained that after independence the colonial inheritance remained, and only revolutionary reform could truly defeat colonialism, "casting off of us the habits that 300 years of servitude have instilled."[111] Mercado argued that independence had not really changed the colonial system, since "the war against Spain was not a revolution"; it had not ended slavery or the power of the Roman Catholic Church or the aristocracy, and most people were still excluded from a role in governance.[112] It would take the "social revolution" of liberal reforms to truly remake society, a revolution carried out by the poor and dispossessed who "contributed to the triumph of Democracy."[113] In 1852 Colombian President López declared in a speech that "a social revolution" had occurred since "the reign of democracy and liberty had arrived" to destroy the "feudalism of the Middle Ages," which still oppressed society—specifically referring to slavery.[114] In Mexico the failures of the era before La Reforma were presented in simplified form as the aristocracy's success in maintaining its colonial prerogatives in spite of reformers' efforts. Santa Anna's complex political career—during which he won support from and supported federalists, centralists, proto-Liberals, and proto-Conservatives—could now be summed up as his attempt to organize an "aristocratic government."[115] Opposing reform, of course, were Conservatives, who Liberals believed wanted to return Mexico to the "colonial regime."[116] Only after the consolidation of La Reforma did Mexicans express equal confidence, but by the 1860s, they were echoing López's optimism. This confidence belies Walter Mignolo's assertions that Latin America was trapped by colonialism's remnants and an unsuitable Atlantic republican tradition and that "decolonization" was not an option in the nineteenth century.[117] Yet Colombians and Mexicans did not think themselves doomed by European colonialism. Instead, they saw their societies leading the way to the creation of a new American democratic republicanism that had destroyed colonialism. The old metropole—not the young New World—was trapped by the past.

Nation

The division between the broader public sphere of the street (as seen in newspapers and oratory) and the more intellectual public sphere of the salon, discussed in the introduction, is most evident in attitudes toward Europe, but it is perhaps just as important for evaluating Latin American nations. For American republicans in the public sphere, as opposed to letrados, the nation did not seem to be a problem; indeed, the vibrancy of new American nations in contrast to decadent European states seemed obvious.[118] Independent nations were a mark of modernity in the nineteenth century, while older pan-national empires and monarchies seemed retrograde and doomed to disappear as peoples liberated themselves.[119] Since this had already happened in America (except for poor Cuba and other Caribbean islands), while peoples such as the Irish, Poles, Greeks, and Italians still struggled to secure their national rights, America had already surpassed Europe in creating modern nations.[120] Indeed, although American republicanism stressed universal fraternity between republican nations, the nation still became the vessel of modernity.

While under Europhile modernity the nation was weak and membership circumscribed to the few letrados, adherents to American republicanism generally expressed great confidence in the nation and the pueblo's knowledge of and interest in this new identity. In provincial Chihuahua, the captain of a local volunteer militia in 1861 thought that "the nation," when threatened by reactionaries, "has in itself an irresistible force."[121] The editor and pharmacist José María Jaurrieta boasted that "the entire nation" would rise up against the French.[122] Ortiz assured national guard soldiers of victory over the Europeans, since the Mexicans were "great and powerful with our love of country."[123] The nationalism of American republican modernity was not an aggressive one; rather, it was defined around a community of shared rights and responsibility, resembling the "revolutionary-democratic" nation described by Eric Hobsbawm and William Sewell.[124] Even during the midst of European invasion, Manuel Muñoz, speaking in Villa de Allende, Mexico, argued that Mexicans did not hate the French people, since hatred between pueblos was a tool used by despotic governments to serve their designs.[125] The classic European view of nationhood focused on cultural differences, but nationhood functioned very differently in mid-nineteenth-century Latin America. A universal fraternity should unite separate nations, just as a universal citizenship should unite people within the nation.

Nineteenth-century Latin Americans realized the nation was a political construct, whereas many Europeans saw it as organic or spiritual. Indeed, Mariano Murillo, a Chihuahuense soldier and politician speaking to rouse his listeners to oppose the French, defined the nation as "ourselves collectively considered," an imagined community. Instead of seeing this as a weakness, he saw it as a strength, since the nation was united voluntarily, instead of being the construct of parties or rulers.[126] Another orator rallying the pueblo against the French declared that while citizenship in the past might have held little value, "today all Mexicans know that the title of Citizen is not a word with no meaning" but guarantees "the rights of man in society." The speaker expressed confidence that the pueblo would fight the French to defend the rights they had newly won in La Reforma, as they understandably had not done against the U.S. invaders, since at that time their citizenship was meaningless.[127] In this conception, the nation had power due to the effectiveness, validity, and legitimacy of the pueblo's citizenship. Faith in American republican modernity and faith in the nation went hand in hand. After the war, the Liberal lawyer and politician Higinio Muñoz argued that the crucible of combat had helped ignite the "fire of love for the country," uniting such diverse groups as artisans, laborers, the young, and the lettered. Meanwhile, "the old nations of the opposite hemisphere" had no community, only subjects bowing to princes.[128] While in the eighteenth century and twentieth century, both Creole patriots and nativists hoped to construct a postcolonial nation based on deep indigenous pasts, in the mid-nineteenth century the nation emerged out of a faith in the future.[129]

Universalism and Race

However, American republican modernity had to confront the problem of race, which would seem to defy universalism. Those who embraced this vision of modernity generally were reluctant to recognize racial distinctions, at least rhetorically (although cultural distinctions were another matter). Long before the much-celebrated racial democracy of the Cuban War for Independence, the discourse of American republican modernity also stressed the fraternity of man, if in equally incomplete fashion. José Manuel Estrada, an Argentine defender of Catholicism, stressed the unity of the mixed "American race," calling it "a new race in history."[130] Murillo welcomed "everyone, everyone universally, without notice of sex, nor differences of color, nor unjust preferences of fortune," to an 1862 Mexican independence celebration, thus emphasizing the universal fraternity that was part of American republicanism.[131] A Colombian writer embraced universalism even more fervently, declaring that race did not exist but was based on "ridiculous accidents" and that societies should extinguish racial distinctions.[132] Former President López remarked that "there is not a more savage banner that that of skin color." He argued that those predicting a race war were usually just trying to justify slavery. However, he had great faith that "a good political system" would sooner or later lead to racial mixing to such an extent that racial division would be impossible.[133] Presumably, López saw this as a process of whitening, but his views also revealed a sense of universalism, in which the old hierarchies of race would disappear. Latin Americans' pride in their societies having advanced, at least institutionally, beyond racism was a key element of their modernity, and this rhetoric reflected republican law, which did not recognize racial distinctions.

Of course, central to this idea of universalism was slavery's abolition. In Colombia and Uruguay, abolition became one of American republican modernity's central tropes. As we saw in chapter 1, after Uruguay's circumscribed abolition of 1842, a newspaper declared that President Fructuoso Rivera "had washed away the black mark that had tarnished the luster of the Republic."[134] Emancipation and the abolition of racial limits to citizenship, while a military necessity, were also related to the American republican vision of modernity. Uruguayans thought that true republicanism did not tolerate slavery or racial discrimination, but that "monarchy requires class distinctions and social hierarchies."[135] In Colombia, Conservatives moaned that "the red democracy" that had taken hold in the country by 1850 had incited slaves to misbehave.[136] In a speech to celebrate the abolition of slavery on 1 January 1852, Governor Vicente Fontal spoke directly to the newly emancipated, reminding them that their "democratic government," in the hands of the Liberal Party, had freed them and made them "citizens." There could not be a "true Republic, where the enslavement of a great number of our brothers endures."[137] Slavery had become anathema to American republican modernity.

Beyond emancipation, Liberals regularly accused Conservatives of racism. A speaker at a meeting of Cali's Democratic Society blasted Conservatives for denying racial equality.[138] La Chinaca rejected the racism of Conservatives who claimed European superiority, crowing that after the battle of Puebla, the French knew the prowess of "Indian and Mestizo Mexicans" in combat.[139] Mexico's victory had proved wrong those "wise ambassadors who had assured [the French and Maximilian] that our brutish Indians would humbly and reverentially inquire of the health of the Spanish sovereign." La Chinaca explicitly blamed the letrado class for spreading false notions of Mexican barbarism in Europe. The French had expected to find "a mob of mulattoes . . . a tribe of savages, a horde of mestizos and brutish lepers," but had instead encountered a force of "modest but intrepid citizens."[140] Here two views of Mexico emerge. For the letrado and scientific elite (científicos-positivist technocrats), Mexico was barbarous and racially suspect, according to the European standards of modernity they accepted as valid.[141] For the public sphere, however, Mexico was not made up of uncultured Indians, mestizos, and mulattoes, but simply of citizens. One vision is geographic, cultural, racial, and "scientific"; the other is political.

With abolition, the question of citizenship rights and racial equality came to the fore, and Spanish Americans took great pride in noting the absence of legal segregation and caste laws. When La Unión declared Colombia "the vanguard in America," it explicitly justified this boast by noting: "Men of color are as esteemed as whites, each enjoying the same rights and guarantees."[142] Colombians knew this was not the case in much of the Atlantic world and rightly trumpeted their achievement (we can note, of course, that racism existed in Colombia, but nonetheless such a statement would have been inconceivable in the United States). In Mexico, El Globo asserted: "Our Republic is the model for democracies . . . giving a lesson of progress to her powerful neighbor to the North, since she does not organize her social rankings according to tints of color nor racial distinctions."[143] Although the United States was usually recognized as a model republic, due to its political stability and economic progress, Mexicans felt that North American racism was a fatal flaw in U.S. claims to modernity. Modernizing visions' power is clear here, both as a cause and effect, because considering antiracism as a central element of modernity was impossible for most in the United States. La Voz Nacional celebrated Union victories in the Civil War and the apparent desire to end slavery, which the paper claimed had always been a stain on

U.S. institutions; the United States was not in the lead, but just now catching up to the modernity already conquered by its American neighbors.[144]

It is of course both easy and necessary to point out the contradictions and limits to republican universalism. Universal male citizenship automatically excluded women from the citizen body. There were other limits to universalism beyond gender: Indians who would not abandon their identity as Indians were often excluded from citizenship and brutally persecuted. Citizenship could be a double-edged sword, a powerful tool used by subalterns to demand their rights, but also a requirement that previous identities, such as Indianness, be abandoned. I do not mean to suggest that these exclusions are not critical, and I will close this chapter by showing how these contradictions would fatally undermine American republican modernity. However, the trend in historiography has been to dismiss republicanism, democracy, universalism, and equality as meaningless for the vast majority. Therefore, we will first examine American republican modernity's conception of the pueblo and then investigate whether the pueblo appropriated elements of American republican modernity for its own ends.

Conceptualizing the Pueblo

American republican modernity's flowery and romantic rhetoric, with its embrace of liberty, equality, and fraternity, represented a sharp break with past conceptions of the pueblo. First, we will examine what this discourse meant by the "pueblo." Then we will turn to the images of class, wealth, and power that American republican modernity manipulated. Next, we will consider notions of sovereignty, especially popular sovereignty.[145] I will argue that the conceptualization of the pueblo under American republican modernity would provide subalterns with much more room to maneuver and many more discursive tools to appropriate than its conception under Europhile modernity (or, later, Western modernity).

Many writers used the word "pueblo" with a double meaning, to embrace all the people in society but also to refer to only those citizens suited to play a role in public life. However, by using "pueblo" without stating such conditions (as they had been openly stated earlier), the lower classes could claim that they were indeed the pueblo, whatever the writers' intentions. By choosing not to explicitly limit the pueblo (for whatever reasons), politicians and intellectuals gave the lower classes an opening.

Under American republican modernity, however, a new vision of the pueblo emerged that explicitly included the poor at the expense of the indolent, corrupt elite, imagined as retrograde Conservatives.[146] In Cali in 1849, El

Sentimiento Democrático defended the pueblo against those of the "first circle" who had declared that "the pueblo is insolent, is barbarous, is immoral." On the contrary, the paper argued, this self-proclaimed elite should bear these epithets. The paper noted that all men were flawed, but that the remedy lay not in the pueblo's exclusion, but only in "fraternity and democracy with all their consequences."[147] El Pensamiento Popular declared: "The time of the pueblo's blind obedience to certain families and persons, due to imaginary titles, is over."[148] Here the pueblo clearly is the masses as opposed to powerful elite families, echoing Hobsbawm's revolutionary, democratic conception of the nation as one that emphasized "common good against privilege."[149]

In Mexico, El Monitor Republicano remembered Mexican independence as "the triumph of the pueblo over the privileged classes, the victory, bloody but inevitable, of democracy over aristocracy."[150] La Libertad made a clear distinction between "those that pretend to be masters and lords, in order to suck the pueblo's blood, and that same pueblo that dies from hunger, sunk in misery and forgotten."[151] La Chinaca claimed that true Mexicans were not men such as Juan Almonte, who—traveling in great luxury—had visited the courts of Europe seeking a monarch for Mexico, but "the poorest artisan, the lowest shoemaker."[152] Under Europhile modernity, only those who had the means to travel to Europe and absorb its civilization mattered. In contrast, under American republican modernity, those same letrados now seemed traitorous at worst and superfluous at best. The pueblo—here marked as poor, but including the middle class and elite Liberals—now had more standing.

This shifting definition of the pueblo also marked a change in the meaning of public opinion and in whose opinion mattered, evolving from only an emphasis on educated property holders or letrados (the salon) to become more inclusive (the street).[153] Previously, public opinion belonged to the educated elite; now, President López directly cited "the movement of opinion" in western Colombia concerning slavery's abolition, driven by the desires of "the poor classes and slaves" who "perceived that a new era of liberty is coming."[154] Another politician wrote to López in 1852, urging him to end the apprenticeship system and arguing that such policy would "strengthen public opinion."[155] As the French invaded Mexico, El Siglo Diez y Nueve was sure that "public opinion" would fortify Mexico's soldiers and make them "invincible."[156] The public sphere suddenly was much enlarged, now including slaves, the poor, and soldiers, heralding changes to notions of sovereignty as well.[157]

The public sphere no longer just included the lower class in the pueblo, but it also often condemned the upper class as barbarous. While questioning North Atlantic modernity's racism was quite common, most elite and middle-class proponents of republican modernity did not question the class divisions that underlay much thinking about modernity. However, many of them did. Public speakers often attacked their Conservative or monarchical foes as being representatives of the upper class. During Uruguay's civil war, El Nacional urged the French expatriates to enlist: "If you and your fathers had listened to the prudent courtesans, to the rich, to the nobles," you would not have toppled "the sanctum sanctorum of despotism."[158] In Colombia, Roldanillo's Democratic Society directly associated powerful Conservative families with aristocracy and backwardness by envisioning Colombian politics as a contest between "the feudal class" and "the disinherited."[159] Liberals in Popayán distributed a broadside proclaiming they believed "that only the pueblo is sovereign," while their Conservative enemies "disrespected the popular masses," holding that only the educated elites from the best families could rule.[160] In Cali, Liberals mocked Conservatives' pretentions that a small, educated class should rule over the debased, racially heterogeneous mass of society. El Caucano tittered at the Conservative Arcesio Escovar's fear that the "monster of the democratic republic" had allowed the "predominance of the barbarous element."[161] Once dogma, the idea that the pueblo was too barbarous to participate in politics had become an object of ridicule.

In Mexico as well, the public sphere resounded with denunciations of the wealthy and powerful as traitors, and with celebrations of the honorable poor's steadfastness. The Municipal Council of Bravos District in Villa del Paso promised to fight the French to protect their "popular institutions" against the "ominous yoke of the privileged classes' tyranny."[162] A manifesto signed by various soldiers blasted the rich and those "who wanted to be aristocrats" for supporting the French.[163] Guanajuato's El Calavera mocked its opponents as supporting an "aristocratic and monkish republic."[164] For Liberals, the enemy was the clergy and "the Mexican rich, who want to be nobles."[165] Liberals certainly only meant the nefarious elements in the upper class—Conservatives and monarchists—but the pueblo would have heard something else. From being civilization's outcasts, the internal barbarians threatening to destroy their own societies, the poor and middling classes suddenly were the nation, and the rich were now the barbarous vampires, threatening modernity with their sloth, privileges, and freeloading. La Bandera Nacional declared: "Our backward aristocracy is not progressing down the path to civilization and does not understand the demands of the century."[166]

Under Europhile modernity, the pueblo were ignorant barbarians, threatening to overturn the fragile civilization that educated letrados had constructed by securing ties to Europe; under Western modernity, the pueblo, due to its demands and political participation, would become a threat to the economic modernity that capitalists and state builders hoped to create. Under American republican modernity, however, the pueblo was the nation, and its members deserved their place as citizens. In 1861 a Mexican Liberal speaker appealed to his "cocitizens" to resist Conservatives, who were the army, the clergy, and "wealthy landholders" enjoying "ill-gotten riches"; all of these groups were "cannibals who fed themselves on human blood."[167] Similarly, orators such as those rallying resistance to the French Intervention regularly peppered their discourse with allusions to slavery and enslavement.[168] Although slavery was a fairly standard political metaphor for any kind of oppression, for many subalterns it was not an abstract concept or a stand-in for loss of rights but a real condition, remembered and experienced by many. Subalterns regularly heard discourse condemning Conservatives or foreign invaders as those who pretended to be "masters," before whom the pueblo would not even be allowed "to lift our humble faces." However, the pueblo would reject such domination, instead insisting on the title of "citizens worthy of belonging to a free people."[169] This elite speaker, Chihuahua's governor, referred to the looming European invasion, but—as we will see below—subalterns seized this exact language to confront the economic oppression of enslavement or wealthy landholders who monopolized land. Whatever elite Liberals' intent, it is a short move from elite orators' celebrating the pueblo's defense of its rights to real subalterns acting to demand and protect those rights.

Conservatives warned of the immense dangers that Liberals created by "fomenting hatred of the poor against the rich."[170] Many Liberals had similar fears, worrying that their more radical fellows would foment "a class war" with such provocative language.[171] Conservatives certainly realized the power of language; El Imperio (with its title helpfully clarifying its views) complained that the rebels resisting Maximilian kept using potent words such as "colony," "Duke," "subject," and "slave."[172] Living under American republican modernity, Conservatives were not nearly as sanguine as contemporary historians that this discourse was just for show.

More than just vilifying the Conservative rich, American republican modernity celebrated an equality much more potent than classical liberalism's legalistic conception. *La Chinaca* noted that in Europe the poor had to "humbly remove their hats before their master," but that in Mexico "all men are equal."[173] Interactions with the pueblo, both efforts to recruit subalterns and subalterns' own projects, demanded equality's redefinition from simply a legal matter to encompass social and economic terrain. As with slaves and former slaves in Montevideo, subalterns themselves had long imbued equality with more expansive visions of social and economic rights. When the need arose for Liberals to bargain with subalterns for support, the public sphere began to embrace similar notions. *La Guerra* denounced those who supported the European invasion, claiming such Conservatives saw the intervention as "killing [the] equality of classes, that foolish equality that causes the pueblo to swell with pride." Instead, Conservatives planned to restrict equality and, if they took power, "would elevate themselves above the *lower class*."[174] Here equality has an explicitly class dimension. A broadside printed in Bogota made clear that the attacks on Conservatives in the Cauca region were the result of past Conservative domination, especially the institution of slavery, "the division of property," and an "oppression so long, opprobrious, and brutalizing." The broadside argued that "the theory of equality has changed the thinking of those populations, the memory of so many humiliations and injustices has upended everything."[175] For subalterns, equality was perhaps the most important idea they could appropriate to improve their lives.

Although equality was critical rhetorically, even more important institutionally for subalterns were the new conceptions of sovereignty gaining dominance in the public sphere. Liberals liked to refer to their mission as "the popular cause."[176] It may seem commonplace that politicians would refer to their ideas as popular, but for the nineteenth century it was still a revelation that enjoying popular support validated a government or a political movement. This was a startling change in notions of sovereignty. *La Opinión Nacional* argued that "modern principles" demanded that "the popular will, legitimately represented, is the supreme law."[177] Liberals regularly asserted that it was the pueblo that now held "sovereignty."[178] *El Monitor Republicano* posited that "public power" came from the "true, spontaneous, general and simultaneous emission of the pueblo's suffrage." Power should not be in the hands of one man (a monarch) or "a reduced circle, under the pompous title of notables."[179] As American republican modernity matured, a reconfiguration of sovereignty and the theory of republican government occurred.

Certainly historians are correct to note Liberals' contradictions and elitist employment of *soberanía popular* (popular sovereignty) that worked as much to exclude the pueblo (on the grounds of race, gender, education, or rationality) as to promote inclusion.[180] However, contemporary Conservatives, such as Lucas Alamán and the editors of El Universal in Mexico, had no doubts about the potential (and, for them, dangerous) power that notions of popular sovereignty gave to the lower classes.[181] Conservatives condemned Liberals for claiming to act in the name of the pueblo, as this only fostered the "antipathy of classes." If Liberals insisted on using such language, the pueblo would eventually act on its own, ending with the destruction of "all virtue, property and knowledge" and with "the revolutionary knife" against the throats of all the wealthy.[182] Colombian Conservatives rejected as "pure democracy" the Democratic Societies' assertions that elected officials must follow the pueblo's will. Following the will of the uneducated masses would only lead to the rule of "the most poor, ignorant, miserable and abject class of society."[183] A Guanajuatense paper with the evocative title El Obrero del Porvenir condemned efforts in the 1870s to reform the state constitution, claiming it would allow an oligarchy to form and the governor to serve perpetually, replacing what the paper praised as a "democracy" with the "abortion of a parliamentary government."[184] Whatever elite Liberals' intent in the 1850s and 1860s, by constantly declaring the pueblo sovereign, they gave subalterns a potent tool to wield in their interactions with the state and nation. However, this discourse of popular sovereignty would have meant little without the daily enactment of democratic and republican political practices.

The Quotidian Practice of Democracy and Republicanism

Did all of this talk matter? In Colombia and Mexico, a discourse of political modernity and the practice of politics tightly intertwined. The reason writers in these Latin American societies embraced a modernity that focused on democratic republican politics and rights is that—on paper and in reality—they had achieved much by the 1860s. The "popular sovereignty" that politicians rhetorically celebrated found lived expression in a rich repertoire of politics practiced by elites, the middle class, and subalterns (which a new generation of scholars have uncovered, even if they are not yet fully recognized by Latin American history's master narratives).[185] Mexicans and Colombians voted in elections, vigorously campaigned for favored candidates, pressured representatives from legislatures' galleries, marched in demonstrations, joined political clubs, sent petitions, served as citizen soldiers in national guards, organized boycotts, attended political ceremonies and speeches, and interpreted abstract political theories to make them meaningful for their daily lives. The practices of democracy and republicanism were not only the concern of a few letrados in capital cities; they formed part of citizens' quotidian lived experience.

I certainly would not claim that voting is the most important element of democratic republicanism, but the right to vote is at least symbolically important and easily measured. In 1853 Roldanillo's Democratic Society celebrated "direct and secret suffrage, this holy conquest of enlightened reason."[186] El Pensamiento Popular exulted that the pueblo marched to the polls in the hundreds as Colombia wrestled with abolition, voting to ensure "the liberty of the slaves and the march of Democracy."[187] Institutionally, Colombia (and Argentina) enacted unrestricted adult male suffrage in 1853, eliminating all property and literacy requirements.[188] Mexico came close to doing so in 1857, only demanding that the prospective voter have "an honest way of making a living."[189] The Mexican constitution of 1857 and the Colombian constitutions of 1853 and 1863 also made liberal promises of a broad range of civil rights to be enjoyed by citizens: association, press, speech, religion (less so in Mexico than Colombia), due process, bearing of arms, and to petition. Both countries would try to abolish the death penalty. Mexicans and Colombians could claim they had overtaken Europe on the path to modernity because they had created political institutions that were much more republican and democratic than those in the Old World. In comparison, while in 1855 only three out of thirty-one U.S. states still maintained property restrictions for citizenship, twenty-five had enacted racial restrictions.[190] In 1810, 47 percent of U.S. states had racial restrictions, but in 1855 the number excluding non-whites had increased to 81 percent. While Latin America was making great strides in expanding the citizen class, the United States retrogressed. So did France, where the 1850 suffrage law reduced the number of eligible voters in some municipalities by over 75 percent.[191] In Europe, universal male suffrage would not generally be achieved until well into the twentieth century.[192]

Conservatives' horror of universal adult male suffrage reveals the importance of these developments. An 1859 letter to Colombian President Mariano Ospina noted that after the voting in Palmira, "an Indian, a black and a half white were elected."[193] Pedro José Piedrahíta, writing from Cali, claimed that since "universal, direct and secret suffrage was established," the result had favored candidates who preached to the "democratic masses," while the support for "property holders and intelligent citizens" had diminished. He complained that in the most recent elections the electoral tables were surrounded by "blacks," many of whom voted twice because, to Piedrahíta and his fellows, all blacks looked the same and could thus vote again and again. He disgustedly asked: "How does this Democratic Republic seem to you?"[194]

Conservatives' fears reveal two other ways the pueblo practiced politics: campaigning for candidates and even serving in offices. Concerns about fraud did not prevent candidates from campaigning vigorously or necessarily diminish the enthusiasm for elections of many in the pueblo. In Colombia candidates proffered food and drink to entice citizens to attend campaign events, entered taverns to press the flesh, and even dressed in peasant garb to appeal to rural voters, sitting down and "drinking *aguardiente* [cane liquor] with the Indians."[195] These politicians actively courted voters with ubiquitous promises to lower taxes and pledges of support for a variety of local concerns.[196] Although the middle class and elites dominated most regional and national offices, politicians with close ties to the pueblo could and did win important elections, as did the Afro-Colombian scholar and soldier David Peña, the subject of chapter 6. Indigenous men regularly held local village offices in Mexico and Colombia.[197] These candidates and their campaigns often found vocal support in the numerous political clubs that sprang up in cities and towns across Latin America.

Perhaps the most important evidence of Latin America's vibrant democratic culture is the rich associational culture that created a public sphere to debate the meanings of republicanism and liberty and then act to put those meanings into practice. Carlos Forment has emphasized how critical associational culture was in fostering a democratic tradition. Clubs and associations sprang up all across Latin America in astounding numbers; Forment discovered 7,056 voluntary associations in nineteenth-century Argentina, Cuba, Mexico, and Peru alone.[198] In Buenos Aires, after the fall of Juan Manuel de Rosas in 1852, numerous electoral clubs appeared in the city, boasting hundreds of members each and seeking to influence public opinion and bring out the vote on election day.[199] In an effort to revitalize republicanism and citizenship in Peru, 114 men formed the Independent Electoral Society in Lima in 1872. The society was intentionally multiclass, including intellectuals, artisans, bankers, merchants, farmers, and soldiers.[200] Colombia's Democratic Societies, which in the southwest counted many Afro-Colombians as members, had a similar multiclass and multiracial membership. The clubs acted as mutual aid societies; offered literacy classes; hosted speeches and debates; organized National Guard units; and, most important, served as an amplifier for their members' concerns, sending petitions demanding redress for issues of citizenship, land, slavery, and education.[201] The clubs created a public sphere open to democracy and republicanism.

Political clubs, and the readings of newspapers aloud and the political oratory heard there, allowed subalterns to engage with American republicanism's discourse; numerous civic festivals and country lawyers helped as well. On the anniversary of Liberals' retaking of Chihuahua from Conservatives during the War of the Reform, elite organizers planned a private celebration, but others in the community claimed an "equal right" to the anniversary, and the party was made public.[202] The pueblo attended these civic festivals "without class distinctions"; even women came, wearing ribbons with political inscriptions braided in their hair. In Paso del Norte, the organizers noted with approval the attendance of Indians, who—presided over by their governor—contributed their songs and music.[203] Towns, cities, and villages hosted festivals to swear allegiance to new constitutions or celebrate independence days, creating a public sphere that imagined nation and democracy as intertwined. Speeches were ubiquitous, spreading the discourse of American republican modernity, but "patriotic juntas" made sure to organize parades, music, fireworks, dances, and sporting events; they also distributed charitable donations to widows and orphans.[204] These celebrations united rich and poor, men and women, and constituted an important alternative to religious celebrations, especially masses and saints' days, that tended to have a conservative cast. Through drinking, dancing, and debating, the nation came into being. Also spreading such discourse were local scribes or country lawyers (often despised by elites) called tinterillos, who helped individuals and villages draw up petitions and legal documents.[205] Newspapers, oratory, public petitions, denunciations (such as pledges to resist the French), and festivals all reached deep into the provincial countryside, opening up the world of the patria chica.[206] Subalterns would absorb American republican modernity's discourse, reframe it to reflect their needs and values, and turn it to their own ends, all of which, along with the bargaining we will explore below, were critical to making the practice of republicanism meaningful.

Elections, campaigns, festivals, and clubs were all venues of politics that were recognized, at least usually, by the state and elites as central to democratic republicanism. However, Mexicans and Colombians engaged in numerous other political practices to influence their representatives and make their citizenship effective. They marched in demonstrations to protest foreign deals, support a political party, fete their heroes, or contest constitutional changes.[207] They packed legislatures' galleries, applauding their favorites and booing their opponents (much to the chagrin of those suspicious of democracy, as opposed to just republicanism).[208] They organized boycotts of liquor if they disapproved of the monopolies they saw as a continuation of colonial rule.[209] They sent thousands of petitions—about land, slavery, taxes, pensions, suffrage rights, and local officials—demanding the state accede to their demands as citizens.[210] And they served as "armed citizens" in national guards, both gaining the standing of the citizen soldier vis-à-vis the state, but also appropriating the power that the threat of armed force contains, as we will explore below.[211]

Yet this active and expansive repertoire of politics would have meant little if Liberals and subalterns also had not engaged in a wide-ranging bargaining over the meanings and outcomes of republicanism, creating the popular liberalism whose study (pioneered by Guy Thomson and Florencia Mallon) has transformed our understanding of the nineteenth century.[212] Popular interpretations of liberalism (and republicanism) varied widely among distinct subaltern groups, but they often focused on obtaining social and political equality regardless of social status (a point that we will explore further in chapter 6) and greater economic equality.[213] Issues of land, so dear to rural subalterns, provide a window into seeing how interactions between elites and popular classes, facilitated by democratic republicanism, transformed classical liberalism. Sometimes this challenge was indirect, as when Mercado declared that "equality" reigned, ending "odious privileges" and "dividing among all men with more equity the common inheritance."[214] A similar debate erupted between newspapers in Cali. El Hombre called the editors of El Pensamiento Popular "barbarians" for promoting an equality of property and the equal sharing of all of God's bounty.[215] El Pensamiento Popular primarily referred to rights and political equality in its discourse, rather than directly to landed property, but it is hard to imagine what else the pueblo would have thought of when they heard about an equality of God's "natural gifts."[216] This language resonated with a long popular tradition of speaking about land and water as the common inheritance from God. El Pensamiento Popular encouraged this reasoning, asking why some had "thousands of acres" of land while others had none, and asserting that the masses' poverty was the result of "tyranny and the usurpation and cruelty exercised by their oppressors."[217] Concerning land more concretely, Francisco Bilbao argued in 1844 that Latin America's revolutions were incomplete because only political change had occurred; true liberty could be achieved only by breaking up old feudal property holdings and raising salaries to a level that supported "human dignity."[218]

This debate did not just flow through newspapers and oratory; it also entered the halls of government. Discussions in provincial legislatures, which the public attended in the galleries, allowed Liberals and subalterns to share a similar discourse. A manager of a Conservative family's massive hacienda in the Cauca reported one such meeting in 1864, in which Liberals argued that "already the aristocracy of pride had fallen, and now it is necessary that the aristocracy of wealth falls too; to possess more land than one is able to cultivate immediately is a crime, which holds the pueblo in poverty." The unnamed speaker continued that this inequality was the result of the "conquistadors," who took all the good land for themselves while leaving only the most sterile and barren for the "Indians."[219] In Mexico, *La Bandera Nacional* pushed the state to act, hoping that after victory over the French, the nation would reward soldiers and punish the "aristocracy." The paper proposed continuing the work of Sebastián Lerdo—the author of the Liberals' 1856 law that sought to eliminate corporate and communal property holding—but instead of just appropriating ecclesiastical property, it suggested confiscating the lands of those supporting the foreign invaders. This "agrarian law" would then distribute the land to the soldiers who had sacrificed so much for the national cause.[220] Property is sacred to classical liberalism, but popular liberals forced at least a consideration of equality and justice when considering land distribution.

Land certainly obsessed subalterns most, as we will see below, but Liberals and popular groups negotiated about a range of issues, reflecting values and discourses emerging out of American republican modernity. During Uruguay's Guerra Grande, the state set prices for subsistence foods, so that the populace "would not be the victim of an insane greed."[221] Colorado papers often urged the state to reward or protect the government's popular followers, be it supporting subaltern land claims, suspending rents, denouncing unjust prices at the butcher, or exempting the poor from some taxes.[222] In southwestern Colombia, Governor Miguel Burbano objected to a proposed law allowing corporal punishment of vagrants as neither in the spirit of the nineteenth century nor of a "Republican Government."[223] In Mexico, *Diario de Gobierno* declared in 1863 that the French Intervention was a great battle between "our revolution" and a rebellious clergy. The paper warned that if the clergy won, Mexico would endure forced taxation on behalf of the Church, "monopolies in favor of the rich," conscription, more taxes in general, no personal freedoms, the Inquisition, and foreign monarchy, among other travesties. However, if the "liberal revolution" triumphed, the pueblo would enjoy a full panoply of personal rights (speech, press, religion) and the "liberty to eat," "liberty to move," the end of sales and religions taxes, the end of the death penalty (except for traitors), and the end of corporal punishment. The list, clearly designed to appeal to the poor, reveals that the "liberal revolution" went much beyond the tenets of classical liberalism. However, in its radically antireligious stance—"the end of miracles and appearances of saints"—it shows the disconnect between a popular religiosity and elite intellectual thought, even if both might share an anticlericism at times.[224] Certainly much of the list, such as municipal liberty or freedom of commerce, might mean one thing to elite Liberals but have radically different meanings of personal and local freedoms for subalterns. In general, subalterns used the practices of democratic republicanism to promote their own visions of social and economic justice.

Scholars might respond that the democratic and republican practices of Latin America were replete with fraud and corruption. However, what matters most is that, first, Latin Americans thought these political practices, however imperfect, were working and a path to modernity; and that, second, a comparison with Europe and the United States reveals considerable corruption and fraud, yet few claim such malfeasance totally invalidates their political histories.[225] Yes, fraud existed. Yes, elites often trampled on democratic republicanism when they could. Yes, many subalterns—especially women, but also those trapped by brutal bosses and patrons—found little space in which they could participate in political life. Yet if we survey the world in the 1850s and 1860s, we can easily argue that Latin America (and the United States) enjoyed a level of quotidian republican and democratic practice far exceeding that of most of the world. Moreover, although we might point to the greater regularity of U.S. elections and respect for the results, we might just as importantly note Latin America's greater progress in including Afro-Spanish Americans and many indigenous peoples. Mexicans and Colombians did not just assert their superior claim to modernity due to their republicanism, they practiced it daily. Their voting, campaigning, marching, petitioning, orating, and associating all attest to a rich democratic republican culture that flourished in the mid-nineteenth century; and bargaining, which we will now explore further, suggests that these practices had meaning for people's everyday lives.

A Sovereign Pueblo: Subaltern Appropriation of American Republican Modernity

How did American republican modernity's discourse filter down below the level of newspapers and politicians' oratory? Did subalterns use this discourse, and did it matter to them?[226] In attempting to answer these questions, I use the term "subaltern" in its most wide-ranging, catholic sense—not, in this case, as a substitute for "lower class." Subalternity may be any level of subordination in regard to national elites; thus, subalterns might be the lower class, but they might also be provincial power brokers or middle classes in contrast to the national state. This follows both of Ranajit Guha's definitions for subaltern: the one denoting a "general attribute of subordination," and the other employed as shorthand for nonelites, the "people."[227] My book *Contentious Republicans* examined the local social and economic conditions that shaped different lower-class groups' particular understanding of republican politics.[228] Here I am more interested in investigating American republican modernity's reach into and across society, both geographically and socioeconomically. I argue that American republican modernity's political emphasis provided subalterns with a much more efficacious and emancipatory vision of progress that they could exploit, compared to other conceptions of modernity that ruled the public sphere earlier and later.

Subalterns encountered American republicanism's discourse at festivals and in speeches, political clubs, and the public readings of newspapers. They also participated directly, at least as signatories, in petitions and protests (assuming that they only signed, instead of participating more broadly, presupposes a level of elite power for which there is little evidence) that both crafted and applied this discourse to their own lives. In 1862 Manuel Muñiz, the local authorities, the National Guard, and 198 residents of the small town of San Felipe, near Guanajuato, gathered at a public meeting to decide the town's response to the French invasion. Their protest reveals the extent to which American republicanism's tropes had permeated provincial life and this language's power to bridge class divides, while still serving as a tool for popular groups to claim a place at the table of the nation. Although *letrados* often fretted about the limited penetration of national life into the countryside, these provincials had no doubt that the "nation" would triumph over a "foreign power" and the "ridiculous idea of establishing a monarchy in Mexico."[229] As we explored in the prologue, even the people of this small town thought that the world was watching Mexico's struggle and that civilization's fate rested with them: they imagined a modernity based on independent national life, popular sovereignty, republicanism, and liberty in contrast to a retrograde aristocracy, monarchy, and colonialism.

The broadside created in the meeting also recasts Mexican history to reflect this worldview, depicting Mexicans as heirs to the pre-conquest Indians who had been conquered and exploited by Spanish colonialism, "the most oppressive slavery." However, the independence period allowed the "enslaved race" to overthrow their tormenters, as part of "the progressive emancipation of humanity." Since that time, the "retrograde men" had been struggling to roll back the changes engendered by independence. Of course, this fight now continued with the French—joined by traitorous Mexicans—replacing the Spanish. The protest was almost surely written by a local intellectual of the middle or even provincial upper class, but it has a surprisingly popular cast. While the town represented the "sovereignty of the pueblo," its enemies were the "privileged classes" who invoked the monarchy of the "Old World." The pueblo here is cast as humble natives, struggling against slavery and the abuses of the foreign invaders and Mexico's own "degraded and vile" wealthy, who plotted to retain their colonial prerogatives.[230] This discourse made clear to which imagined community Mexico truly belonged. Indeed, belying the idea the nation was seen as alien, Latin American subalterns' appropriation of the nation seems much stronger than that of their European counterparts at this time.[231] This petition presents a number of themes that were present in the discourse of many Mexican and Colombian subalterns during American republican modernity's ascendance: first, for subalterns, the nation was real, and they claimed citizenship in order to be a part of it; second, subalterns sensed a powerful connection between American republicanism's condemnation of the traitorous rich and their own struggles with *hacendados*, local officials, and bosses; and third, subalterns embraced popular sovereignty as a meaningful relationship between citizens and the state.

American republican modernity provided rich veins of material that subalterns could mine. Most potently, subalterns eagerly appropriated the identity of the rights-bearing citizen (often in contrast to the aristocracy and the idle rich).[232] A protest from a small northern Mexico mining town signed by fifty-four "citizens," many illiterate, promised that the signatories would fight against the French. The undersigned, most probably miners, claimed that they were "true republicans" who hated monarchy, since it was fit only for "vile slaves": "We do not want to be the lackeys or lapdogs of any monarch." They attacked their enemies as the "notables" and moneylenders who were in league with the French.[233] These miners thus demonstrated that an identity of true republicans served as an antidote against the deference expected by both foreign monarchs and the local gentry. Subalterns easily related American republicanism's condemnation of the traitorous rich to their own experience with bosses, landlords, and local potentates. Slavery, merely a metaphor for elites, was a meaningful lived experience for subalterns.

As noted above, political clubs played a key role in subalterns' investment in American republicanism. In a speech to an artisans' society in Mexico City in 1848, a Mr. Portugal contrasted the hard work of artisans, who were the best "citizens" and who "gave value to nations," with that of those who protected their colonial privileges to ensure "the despotism of the privileged classes."[234] In 1877, the members of Cali's Democratic Society, having just defeated Conservatives in the 1876–77 civil war, demanded their back pay, pensions, and, most important, the distribution of land as a reward for their service. The veterans claimed they had fought for "liberty" against the Conservatives, who saw them as the "slaves of these so-called feudal lords." This war had pitted those who enjoyed "great wealth and immense landholdings" against "the poor masses." Now the soldiers demanded payment from a Liberal state that claimed to rule in the name of liberty and republican democracy. They demanded land so that they could fully be "citizens of a free people."[235] The Democratic Society's claims sum up the power that republicanism, citizenship, and military service offered subalterns: it gave them an opportunity to be indispensable to the state (Liberals would have lost the war without the Democratic Society's support) and a discourse of republican and democratic rights with which to make their demands resonate with the state's and nation's dominant ethos.

A common argument is that such language is just flowery boilerplate, inserted by tinterillos to impress the powerful. Certainly, subalterns often sought to shape their language to please the state. However, not all did so. There were plenty of standard, colonial-style petitions that just stressed the supplicants' misery, begging for mercy and protection.[236] Subalterns did make a choice to use this language and, as I have explored elsewhere, tailored their usage to their specific needs and political beliefs and practices.[237] For our purposes, what is more interesting is how reigning visions of modernity allowed, encouraged, and made more efficacious certain types of subaltern discourse. Of even more interest, if not completely resolvable, is the question of how the interaction of subalterns and elites pushed the public sphere to embrace a much more radical and emancipatory discourse than elites alone might have developed. Indeed, republican discourse was perhaps more crucial to subalterns, who had little access to the legal maneuvering, than to elites, who often simply used the law, instead of moral or political arguments, to justify their claims.[238]

Of course, subalterns did not abandon older justifications and identities when assuming citizenship (as many Liberals had hoped they would) but combined them with American republican modernity's discourse. Indians from San Andrés, Guanajuato, petitioned to secure their lands and to have recognized their rights to gather wood and other forest products from the nearby mountains. They cited their ancient, colonial titles to the land, mixing this with their claims to have rights in "our Republic." They closed by noting that their treatment was a "fate of miserable slavery, unworthy of any country truly Catholic and civilized."[239] This indigenous village thus combined in one petition the tenets of Catholicism, ancient inheritances, modern rights to petition and justice, and appeals to a civilization that did not allow citizens to be treated as slaves. Although subalterns had no trouble appropriating the discourse of republican modernity, they did not abandon corporate identities, tradition, or the values of an older moral order.

In addition to citizenship, Colombian and Mexican subalterns embraced popular sovereignty.[240] In 1866 a petition from over six hundred Caleños, most of whom could not sign their names and many of whom were Afro-Colombians, demanded the state president immediately suspend a law that imposed a tax on the production and sale of *aguardiente*. Afro-Colombians, especially many Afro-Colombian women, owed their livelihoods to the small-scale distillation and sale of *aguardiente*; the tax crippled their ability to survive. The local Democratic Society, led by Peña, took up their cause, urging the state president to act, even though they acknowledged that he had no legal authority to suspend the law. More important than legal niceties, however, was the "popular will" that demanded the law's abrogation. The Democratic Society argued that in "republican countries" the executive must respond when the pueblo demanded succor, and the state president needed to prove he was a "magistrate fit to lead a free people." If the legislature expressed outrage at his bypassing its authority, the state president could comfort himself by knowing he enjoyed "an approbation that is more valuable, that of the sovereign pueblo."[241] Here, the pueblo asserted that ultimately direct democratic action—in this case, a petition—mattered more than the legislative process of republicanism. As we have seen, politicians and writers regularly referred to the pueblo as sovereign; these Colombians now insisted that the political class abide by its rhetoric.

Notions of popular sovereignty and popular citizenship even allowed Indians to confront Mexican and Colombian Liberals' hostility to communal landholding. Trinidad García and others from Huimilpan, Querétaro, wrote to state officials in 1856 to reclaim some land unjustly taken from them. They acknowledged that the new government frowned on "pueblos possessing goods in community" but claimed there should be "exceptions." Their strongest argument was that the governor or president was beholden to them as the nation's servant: a "republican magistrate" should dedicate himself "to serve the pueblo that elevated him."[242] Indians did not hesitate to use Liberals' discourse against them, even in direct contradiction to Liberals' economic program. In Colombia in 1871, Indians from the Aldea of Cajamarca similarly wrote to the Cauca state president to insist that their *resguardos* (communal landholdings) not be divided. They noted that, under colonialism, they had been "beaten down by Spanish greed into the most degrading state of slavery and misery." But now an "enlightened republican government" ruled, one that "proclaims equality."²⁴³ Of course, for elite Liberals, equality meant ending *resguardos*. Yet for Indians, the rule of equality and a republican government signified their new status as citizens who had the power to protect their rights and be heard by the state. Indians from Mocondino, also in the Cauca, expressed confidence that an "essentially democratic government," in defense of which "we have shed so much blood," would accede to their wishes not to have their communal lands divided.²⁴⁴ Of course, dividing *resguardos* into individual and marketable landholdings was a central component of Liberal ideology, but the contradictions of the democratic system prevented Liberals in the Cauca from ever making much progress in this regard. The pueblo, using rhetoric and force, simply pushed back too hard. Although many historians tend not to take seriously Liberals' exclamations of popular sovereignty, subalterns certainly did.

Behind these calls of popular sovereignty was the still radical notion that the state had a responsibility to serve the majority instead of the privileged few. A group of "carpenters" petitioned the Banda Oriental government to raise import duties, arguing that "the most civilized governments of the world do not disdain to follow their people's advice."²⁴⁵ In Cali in 1853, poor residents petitioning to claim commons land that haciendas had usurped expressed confidence that since now the Town Council's members were "directly designated by the pueblo," the poor could expect justice.²⁴⁶ Migrants who were settling the frontier between Cauca and Antioquia wrote to the National Congress to ask for help in a land dispute. After the migrants had settled on and cleared lands known as Aldea de María, which they claimed were public, a group of "monopolistas" asserted title to the lands. The migrant petitioners were sure the state would act, "rejecting, as it should reject, the influence of the few" in favor of the needs of thousands of settler families. The settlers noted that they had seen some "aberrations" in the state's past behavior, but they now were confident that the government would not abandon "two thousand five hundred unfortunate souls to the yoke of their oppressors."²⁴⁷ In a democratic republican system, subalterns insisted that the rights of the many outweighed the investments of the few.

Indeed, local elites used similar language themselves and feared openly contradicting it. In Veracruz in 1848, popular sentiment mobilized against the tobacco monopoly. Over five hundred people "of all classes" turned out at a meeting of the Town Council to present a petition demanding the monopoly's abolition. The council approved the petition, to the "Vivas!" of the crowd. The assembled citizens then demanded that the council suspend enforcement of the monopoly immediately, while the central state acted on the petition. The council did not want to do this because the monopoly was national law, "but considering the dangerous consequences to public tranquility" if they did not act, they assured the crowd they would immediately request the tax administrator to stop enforcing the monopoly. The pueblo celebrated with an impromptu demonstration, roaming the city with music and fireworks and climbing church towers to ring the bells in celebration.[248] The governor wrote to Mexico City warning that it would be very difficult to keep the peace if the monopoly were not overturned. He claimed that he wanted to obey the national government but was caught between the law and "the opinion and desires of so many in the state."[249] Notions of popular sovereignty, backed up with popular action, mattered.

As in Veracruz, the pueblo did not just suggest officials accept popular sovereignty but actively demanded that the state fulfill republicanism's promises. After the Revolution of Ayutla, Mexican villages eagerly adopted that movement's discourse. A number of villages in Chiapas, partnering with sympathetic Liberal politicians, petitioned the new national government to remove various officials who had served Santa Anna's regime. The villagers declared that these officials had served "the dictator," had created "misery for a multitude of citizens," and were therefore unfit to serve a government with "revolutionary legitimacy."[250] Another hamlet's letter complained that Santa Anna's officials had represented only greedy "aristocrats." The village had signed on to the Plan de Ayutla in the hope that it would "save the Nation from the dangers that threatened it" and that with the revolution's victory, "misery would turn into abundance, oppression into liberty." The letter closed by demanding that the state fulfill "the promises made to the Nation."[251] The villagers contrasted politicians' greed with their desire for progress through good government. Another petition from residents of the town of Comitán, described how—after adopting the Plan de Ayutla—the people took it upon themselves to remove Santa Anna's officials, who had made "slaves" out of many of the region's residents. They asked how could it be fair that a "hard dictatorship reigns in Chiapas while the rest of the Republic enjoys Liberty."[252] This village employed Liberals' enshrinement of liberty and the association of reaction with slavery. These letters echoed that of Angel Corzo, a powerful local Liberal politician, who claimed that the officials in question represented an elite clan that "has become tyrants over the pueblos of Indians of this state." The pueblo had adopted the Plan de Ayutla and, thus, now had a right to demand satisfaction, as guaranteed in the plan. Corzo's letter went further than the others, threatening a new uprising if the state were to ignore the "promises of the revolution."[253] Provincial elites were in an especially close dialogue with their popular neighbors: neither could easily ignore the other, and both groups confronted the national state. If the national state justified itself via a republicanism based on legitimate revolution, popular sovereignty, liberty, and rights, villagers assumed that they had the right to call on the state to fulfill its promises (and if the state did not comply, that they too could rebel). If the state claimed legitimacy through American republicanism, it remained legitimate in subalterns' eyes only as long as it kept its revolutionary promises.

Subalterns did not hesitate to hold officials' feet to the fire, demanding the change Liberals had promised in the Revolution of Ayutla. In 1856 villagers from Huimanguillo, Tabasco, claiming status as "citizens," compared the Liberals' new government, "so good and just," with the previous administration, implicitly asking the state to prove this change; they assumed that the new state "is interested in the general welfare of all the inhabitants."[254] The pueblo of Chico, Veracruz, represented by the renowned orator José María Mata, wrote to the president to complain about Santa Anna directly, who had stolen an image of the Virgin Mary from their church and taken it to his hacienda. They hoped for better treatment from the new government, since "the fall of the dictator has caused Mexicans to enter into the enjoyment of their legitimate rights."[255] Rafael Cataño, a former guerrilla who had fought in Oaxaca "against the reaction" and was now accused of deserting the army, protested that his rights must be respected or the constitution would be nothing but "weak leaves of paper."[256] This was exactly Liberals' conundrum: would blatant dismissal of subaltern demands reveal their projects of nation and state building as nothing but insubstantial words?

Since Liberal elites defined their societies and justified their rule using American republican modernity's discourse—the sovereignty of the people, republicanism, democracy, and rights—it became much harder to simply ignore subalterns, who did not hesitate to question the nation's viability.[257] The Colombian and Mexican states were simply too weak to attempt to rule without some political legitimacy. A petition from over forty residents of Paso del Bobo, Veracruz, most of whom could not sign their names, demanded the Liberal state allow them to keep renting from the state—at the same rate—land that had been seized from Santa Anna, from which two other renters had evicted them. The petitioners claimed the intended *hacendados* wanted "to live by the sweat of the pueblo," but hoped the new government would look after the rights of "citizens." The citizens continued: "We expect that neither your Excellency nor the law will permit that the pueblo lives under oppression, as it would be, for us, as if the fight in which our poor Patria is now engaged in order to enjoy Liberty had been lost."[258] These illiterate citizens thus made a direct connection between revolutions for liberty and their need for land. If their concerns were not heard, then the revolution and the nation-state's legitimacy, regardless of the outcome of any battle, were already lost.

Subalterns especially expected to be heard if they felt that the nation and state owed them due to their past sacrifices as soldiers. In Uruguay the question of land rents in and around Montevideo became a flash point during the Guerra Grande. Rents incited such passion because the vast majority of Montevideanos did not own property; an 1843 census counted 849 property owners and 4,020 renters.[259] A letter from some Montevideanos demanded that rents be suspended for the war's duration, especially those owed to the city's enemies. They warned that while they fought in the civil war, there was also a "war between landlords and renters." The writers asked how it could be just for those who had sacrificed so much to suffer at the hands of landlords fighting for the enemy.[260] Another letter asked how those "citizens" who had sacrificed for the republic in the war could be subject to "the tyranny of the landlords"? Although the landlords "will invoke the right to property," the writers argued that if rent payments were suspended for soldiers, they would not be stealing the landlords' property but only putting limits on "greed and tyranny." Furthermore, they asserted that the rights to property "are not of the same sacred nature as those of personal labor."[261] A similar letter from "ten employees of the Republic" also demanded a suspension of rents, asking why landlords' rights to property should be "inviolable and sacred" while "the labor, personal service and blood" of the renters were not considered so.[262] For popular republicans, the right to one's labor power mattered more than the more abstract right to property cherished by elite Liberals. This tension between the demands of republicanism for equality (of types of rights) and for fraternity (in time of war) conflicted with liberalism's concerns for liberty (of property), reflecting the uneasy coexistence of popular republicanism with elite liberalism. In this case, during war, republicanism partly superseded classical liberalism, and the state temporarily suspended rents (or offered to pay them) for those serving the government.[263]

During war, Liberal elites celebrated citizen soldiers and their role in the body politic, calling the National Guard "soldiers of democracy" and "armed citizens."[264] This rhetoric strengthened the citizen-soldier persona, an identity subalterns expropriated in both Colombia and Mexico.[265] Indians from the village of Teremendo, Michoacán, petitioned President Juárez to return land to them that a neighboring hacienda had usurped. They claimed that the *hacendado* had been allied with the "French forces" that had persecuted the Indians, many of whom had died in the war, due to "our firm adhesion to the national cause." The *hacendado* was also Spanish: "We poor Indians still suffer thousands of cruelties from the Spanish, who have remained on our soil, owners of uncounted riches acquired through usury, usurpation and more iniquitous means." If no action were taken, the Indians threatened to act on their own, intimating a "pernicious disturbance."[266] This petition echoes the themes of subalterns' appropriation of American republican modernity: the evil, traitorous rich; the loyal poor who serve the nation; and the right to rebel to ensure justice. National Guard soldiers from the village of Tetela de Ocampo refused to surrender their weapons after a rebellion in 1868, reminding the state that they still enjoyed "rights as free men" whose fellows "were sacrificed while defending republican institutions."[267] In Colombia the residents of the village of Quilcacé, many of whom were former slaves or descendants of slaves, demanded help from the Liberal state in a land dispute. The petitioners justified their request by reminding Liberal officials of "the services the village made to the cause of the federation [the Liberals in the 1859–62 war] and due to the bloody sufferings that it endured because of its adhesion to that cause."[268] Soldiering gave even those with little traditional status in the eyes of elite Liberals—in this case, poor and largely illiterate Afro-Colombians—a powerful identity as citizen soldiers from which to make their demands. Similarly, the Palmira Democratic Society petitioned for access to commons and public lands that haciendas had enclosed. The Society reminded the Colombian president that "the poor class" has made "the very valuable contribution of their blood in order to defend our institutions. . . . These individuals have, at the very least, an unquestionable right to be protected by a liberal government."[269] States ignore their subaltern subjects all the time, but it is harder to do if those states have legitimized themselves via republican revolutions, subalterns have fought in those revolutions, and they still have their rifles and machetes from the revolutions.

Although subalterns eagerly embraced many of the key concepts used to define republicanism, they did not as often engage the concepts of modernity or civilization and progress directly, although some certainly did. In Uruguay soldiers in the Guerra Grande claimed they fought "to sustain civilization and liberty," implying that civilization was not only elite culture and wealth but had a political component as well.[270] Gatherers of forest products near Tumaco wrote to the Colombian president to protest that investors now claimed the forest as private property, complaining that these capitalists wanted to impose the "tyranny of feudalism," the Middle Ages being a well-known shorthand for backwardness.[271] Indians and whites from a couple of villages near Amoles, Querétaro, protesting a confrontation over land that had left three people dead, exclaimed that such violence deserved the "reprobation of the civilized world."[272] Sebastiana Silva petitioned Popayán's local government for help in the return of her son, who was forced to work as a domestic servant (a not uncommon arrangement for poor children). She demanded her son's return, but the family where he was in service refused, "as if we still were in the barbarous times in which the government allowed the slavery of men. Today, thankfully, we have a republican and democratic government that will not allow such monstrosities."[273] Silva was poor, illiterate, and a woman, but she still expected a republican and democratic government owed her a response. She cleverly manipulated American republican modernity, equating slavery with barbarism and calling on the state to justify its own claims to democratic, republican legitimacy.

Subalterns were more likely to directly employ the trope of modernity when elites represented them. Juan José Baz, writing for a client in jail because of a debt he owed to a hacienda near Puebla, declared such treatment unsuited to a modern Mexico. He argued that Mexico still suffered from "legacies of feudalism, truly painful for the poorest class of society." *Hacendados* loaned money to workers to ensure that they were in debt; if the workers tried to leave, they were hunted down and beaten, as if "a slave." Baz argued to President Ignacio Comonfort that such cases should be civil matters, not criminal, and suggested that ending such treatment would earn him the thanks of millions, as well as creating "a considerable number of citizens." Baz closed by arguing that the state must act "in order to end suffering unworthy of civilized man."[274] Baz was a powerful politician in his own right, yet we see how he could bend American republican modernity's discourse to argue in favor of the poorest class in society—debt peons.

Certainly in the close quarters of small towns, the lower class, middling actors, and provincial elites came together, each influencing the notions of civilization dominant in the public sphere. The Democratic Society of San Pedro, a parish of Buga, requested that their town remain the provincial capital, justifying their petition by reminding the state of both their service in the past civil war and their "right of sovereignty." They claimed Buga, unlike its rival, Cartago, had fought for the "emancipation of the masses" and now hoped to enjoy the "fruits of republicanism." Cartago, meanwhile, was a Conservative town of "barbarians," nothing but a "den of oligarchs" who had opposed "democratic opinion."[275] Barbarism had previously been used to describe the poor and uneducated. Now, the Democratic Society recast the antidemocratic oligarchs and wealthy as barbarians. This petition, whose signatories included not only the local priest and officials but also over 160 men (most of whom only made their mark), had turned the world of civilization and barbarism upside down.

Much more directly appealing than notions of modernity were the tropes defining civilization and modernity under American republicanism—republicanism; democracy; popular sovereignty; and the universal extension of citizenship, rights, liberty, equality, and fraternity. Many of the poor and the working class were able to take advantage of this discourse, asserting their citizenship and claiming rights to promote their own agendas, be it to protest unfair monopolies, protect landholdings, demand pensions, or simply participate as equals in the political system. Their claims are now well documented in the state and nation formation literature.[276] How the public sphere envisioned modernity played a key role in determining the effectiveness of subalterns' claims to citizenship and nation. Subalterns sensed the congruence of their understandings of liberty, equality, and fraternity (which varied across different subaltern groups) with those of American republican modernity. Subalterns could not pretend to be educated in the ways and manners of Europe, and thus they had little to appropriate from Europhile cultural modernity. Western modernity's focus on order and labor would provide little space for most subalterns, relegating them to being means of production. However, American republican modernity, with its political path to the future, gave them a powerful discourse to make their own. This language of citizenship and rights would not have resonated with discourses of modernity based on technology, high culture, or economic development. Yet for a modernity based on republican freedom, subalterns' appeals and language carried great weight. In an era when the state was weak to nonexistent and nations were still undefined, elites did not have the power to simply ignore discourses of nation, modernity, and republicanism that were critical to creating a new political system. Thus, they could not simply dismiss subaltern claims to citizenship, since the political systems they sat atop rested on American republican modernity's discourse. If citizenship, rights, and popular sovereignty had no meaning, then the new nations and their elite leaders had no meaning or legitimacy either.

Limits and Contradictions

Once unleashed, popular republicanism would be very hard to rein in again. By the 1870s and 1880s, elites would eventually realize the dangerous threat that American republicanism's language posed and how little they controlled it. In the projects of the Porfiriato (1876–1910) and the Regeneration (formally dated 1885, but actually beginning earlier), both Mexican and Colombian elites would redefine civilization and modernity to largely exclude subalterns (and a discourse of citizenship and rights) from the political sphere. They would be aided in this endeavor by contradictions within liberalism that opposed American republican modernity's emancipatory potential.[277] Liberals were American republican modernity's greatest proponents, but elite liberalism was a distinct philosophy. Liberalism contained conceptions of the pueblo, Indians, women, order, and economic development that conflicted with much of American republican modernity's discourse.

While discursively inclusive of the poor and often excluding the venal wealthy from the national family, Liberals' discourse nevertheless maintained a strong sense that the true citizens who must lead the nation belonged to "the middle class of society, where one finds morality and enlightenment."[278] Although Liberals often celebrated the pueblo, they did not hesitate to condemn the lower class for its "religious fanaticism," ignorance, and other bad habits that the poor had inherited from colonialism.[279] Liberals eventually embraced (or nearly did) male universal citizenship, but they had a long history of excluding subalterns; even during the Guerra Grande in Uruguay, when subalterns had immense leverage as soldiers, the still reigning constitution of 1829 did not grant citizenship to servants, day laborers, or enlisted soldiers, and after 1840 it also required literacy.[280] And when citizenship was awarded (as opposed to subalterns' conception of citizenship as a right), subalterns were expected to know their duties and limits. In spite of its name, El Amigo del Pueblo declared that its program was to inform the pueblo of its rights but also of its "duties," and that the pueblo must educate itself out of its colonial ignorance in order to obtain the "reason" necessary for civilization.[281] Of course, whenever groups of the lower class opposed Liberals—due to local history, for religious reasons, or in opposition to a particular Liberal policy (which was especially the case with Indians)—Liberals denounced the poor for their abasement and fanaticism.

Reinforcing Liberals' suspicion of the poor was the long history of racism, especially that of letrados, emerging from the colonial epoch and Europhile modernity. Many Liberals could never escape the racism that always considered civilization the provenance of white Europeans, while "blacks" and Indians would remain "barbarous" until educated and disciplined.[282] Liberals usually publicly promoted racial universalism in speeches and newspapers, but in their letrado texts—meant for a more refined local or foreign European audience—they pursued a different tact. Miguel Lerdo de Tejada, brother of the future president, published a geographic survey of Mexico in 1856, notably dedicated to Alexander von Humboldt. He deduced that Mexico's population was one-sixth "pure European," three-sixths "pure Indian," and two-sixths "mixed European, Indian and African." He argued: "This diversity of races that composes the Mexican Republic's population has been and will be the major obstacle to its prosperity and growth."[283] In an essay written in Europe that was not published in his lifetime, Juan Bautista Alberdi recanted his faith in the Americas and republicanism, urging the adoption of monarchy, in imitation of Europe. He believed that American republican experiments were doomed due to the lack of European population: Indians could only create a "savage reaction . . . far from being a civilizing movement."[284] In order to civilize the Americas, one needed European immigration.[285] Another Liberal intellectual, José María Samper—who in his youth, although not his middle age, was a great proponent of American republicanism—did not hesitate in his survey of Colombia to ascribe characteristics to races, especially "mulatos," many of them virulently negative.[286] He particularly denigrated "zambos," whose degradation resulted from the "evident inferiority of the mother races": Indians and Africans.[287] Despite the depth of his racist thought, Samper still had great faith that American civilization and its "democratic society" could benefit from racial mixture, creating a new "race of republicans."[288] Yet it was clear he imagined Europeans providing spiritual and intellectual qualities, while more physical qualities might come from other races.[289] Publishing in Europe, like so many letrados, Samper embraced geographic and "scientific" thinking on race.[290] In terms of race, the divide between the public sphere of the salon (where a science-inspired racism reigned) and that of the street (where universalism dominated) appears especially sharp.

However, many Liberals believed all the problems of the pueblo—their ignorance, fanaticism, culture, laziness, and even race—could be solved by the implementation of a disciplinary program. Although earnestly orating about the triumph of popular sovereignty and democratic republicanism, Liberals often thought only a disciplined, rational pueblo could exercise these rights.[291] An undisciplined pueblo whose members did not follow their elite leaders would undermine the "principle of authority" and lead to "social dissolution."[292] The great disciplinary tool was education; Liberals often looked to the United States, "our great model," as an example.[293] Liberals believed that education would make the pueblo rational and restrained citizens, aware of both their rights and duties.[294] A Colombian Liberal official urged action to improve education: "When the democratic form has been established successfully in a pueblo, it is necessary to shape, educate and give to the pueblo, via instruction, the baptism of civilization."[295] Democracy still intensely frightened the Liberal elite; only education could make the pueblo safe for democracy.

As worrisome as the pueblo was in general, one group posed even more problems for Liberals' sense of universalism and a unified citizen body. Indigenous people living in semi-autonomous villages, with their own local governments and communal property holdings justified by a colonial legal identity of "indígenas," threatened liberalism's economic (private property) and political (individual rational actors as citizens instead of corporate bodies) underpinnings. Certainly, many whites believed that if Indians wanted to be "citizens of a free and independent Republic instead of the vile and abject slaves of a despotic and tyrannical foreign monarch," they had to renounce their communal landholdings and local self-government.[296] Of course, those hacendados who coveted indigenous communal landholdings exploited a discourse of modernity that equated Indians' attachment to their traditions with "barbarism." Nonindigenous residents of Silvia, Colombia—then known as Nueva Granada—petitioned to have the local resguardo divided, arguing that the new republican system guaranteed "equality of rights to all New Granadans"; therefore, Indians should lose their special communal rights to property and government. In this interpretation of universalism, Indians' identity must be eliminated completely: "To the embarrassment of N.G. [Nueva Granada] within its own territory there today exist, forty-two years after Independence, groups of men with the name 'communities of Indians.'"[297] Of course, if a pueblo rejected Liberals' universalism, this marked them as barbarians. Liberals in the Cauca denounced the Pasto region, marked as Indian and religiously benighted, as an area with "little civilization."[298] In general, as Fernando López-Alves argues, state makers imagined a homogeneous nation as ideal, thus casting indigenous peoples especially as a problem.[299]

Even when Liberal officials hoped to forge some sort of relationship with Indians, their prejudices interfered. The governor of Jalisco, Mexico, wanted to establish a special court to help with land disputes involving those "who are called Indians." The governor thought that a more accessible judicial system would prevent rebellions and seemed to also hope that such a court would improve indigenous villagers' conditions, but he could not bring himself to even recognize them as Indians.[300] In Colombia, Liberal *letrado* politicians such as the novelist Jorge Isaacs, even when promising to protect Indians from predatory *hacendados*, did so as lordly benefactors, bragging that they would come to indigenous villages "diffusing civilization and well-being to their populations."[301] Instead of universal republicanism's egalitarian promise, elites clung both to the exclusionary rationalizations of a colonial, *letrado* Europhile modernity that saw Indians only as barbarous impediments and to classical liberalism's requirement of elite rationality to merit inclusion in the public sphere. Liberals simply could not see Indians as true citizens.[302]

Even more brutally persecuted, of course, were indigenous peoples, usually on the frontiers, who had not submitted to the national state. When *La Alianza de la Frontera* celebrated President Juárez's homage to La Reforma and liberty, it also announced attacks by the Apaches, calling them "barbarous Indians."[303] Indians such as the Yaqui or Maya were condemned as barbarians who wanted to destroy civilization in bloody caste wars.[304] From the pampas to the rainforests of Colombia to the North American deserts, these indigenous people faced genocidal violence and total exclusion. Even the most progressive visions of modernity in the nineteenth century could classify them only as the barbarous other.

Although non-Indian women did not face these levels of state violence, they suffered a political exclusion even more complete than that of Indian men. Women's classification as irrational and fundamentally alien to citizenship was not incidental to liberalism and republicanism, but central. Indeed, as scholars of European and Latin American republicanism stress, liberalism's reliance on rationality and the establishment of a private, domestic sphere (of women) separate from the political public sphere (of men) actually isolated women politically more thoroughly than they had been under colonial or monarchial rule.[305] A Caleño paper noted that elections' turbulences and disputes were not suited for women, who must therefore be excluded from such scenes. Anyway, the paper cavalierly asserted, if given the suffrage a woman would vote only according to her husband's or lover's desires; lacking a man, "she would give her vote to the most handsome, even if he were dumb as a mule."[306] Women had no place in the "public plaza" but should attend to their duties of education and motherhood: if women engaged in politics, this would corrupt both politics (introducing irrational actors) and women (turning them away from their domestic responsibilities).[307]

Notions of rationality, masculinity, and honor underlay the identity of citizen at the heart of American republican modernity. Radical republicans mocked Spanish kings as fratricidal (Enrique de Trastámara), foolish (Juan II), tyrannical (Felipe II), idiotic (Carlos II), or female (Isabel II).[308] Liberals thus classified the rule of a woman as little different than that of a despot or moron. For radical republicans, the fact that Europeans tolerated rule by tyrants, the mentally disabled, and women only showed Old World backwardness; given "rational" choices, disciplined male citizens would elect educated, responsible men to representative rule. Nineteenth-century republicanism was gendered as male, with other forms of government coded as female—all the more obvious when female monarchs ruled in England and Spain. American republicanism did not just cast Europeans as feminine but also questioned American Conservatives' commitment to a male public sphere. Liberals blasted Conservatives for "exploiting the fanaticism of the fairer sex and making them take an active part in politics."[309] Liberals also assumed that "women's inclination for monarchy" would lead them to support Conservatives.[310] Women found very little play in masculinized republicanism.

This new republican exclusion combined with the continued importance in the republican era of colonial notions of honor. Sarah Chambers argues that honor became democratized after independence, as poor men could claim to be honorable, but their claims relied on masculine behaviors and controlling wives and daughters.[311] Petra Hinojosa de Gutiérrez and three other women wrote to the commanding officer of Morelia to pledge their "patriotism" and aid to the soldiers who fought against the European invasion. Yet they had to claim that "awakening and enlivening the natural sentiment of liberty and independence" was the work of men; women's role was to nurture love of the "patria" and to support the soldiers by collecting resources.[312] This is a subtle but fascinating division: men practiced republican politics, while women fostered the more primordial sentiments of national feeling. Of course, universalism has a logic of its own that is hard to deny. Therefore, when discussing women, Liberal men elided universalism's internal logic by tending to revert to older definitions of modernity, focusing on issues of "culture" and "morality" as central to women's role in marking "the thermometer of civilization."[313] In general, gender exclusion made republicanism, which was intimidating due to its challenge of so many traditional hierarchies, seem much less threatening by embracing patriarchal rule. A fairly common formulation was that the family underlay society, which in turn underlay republicanism.[314]

Crucially related to these limitations of class, race, and gender was the central contradiction between American republican modernity and liberalism: the need for capital to create economic development along the lines of the North Atlantic versus republicanism's political utopia of equality. Countering American republican modernity's progressive potential throughout the 1850s and 1860s were the competing currents of both a lingering Europhile and an emerging Western modernity, as well as the ideology of elite liberalism to which republicanism was linked, if often uncomfortably. Although American republicanism did not measure modernity in economic terms, it did assume that political modernity would bring economic growth, as defined by elite (but not popular) liberalism. Ideally, the social peace between elites and popular groups that democracy and republicanism should engender would create a more stable economic base than that currently sustaining a feudal Europe riven by class conflict.[315] While Juárez in Mexico and his counterparts in Colombia imagined a modernity that subalterns could seize to promote their claims in the public arena, these Liberal rulers planned an economic future that would doom many subalterns to entrenched poverty, especially Indians losing their collective lands and artisans losing their workshops due to industrial imports.

Whenever Liberals' discourse moved away from politics to state power or trade, Latin America became removed from the civilized world, once more looking in from the outside. The Colombian Tomás Cuenca, in promoting a controversial canal treaty for Panama, argued that if Colombians refused to make a deal, the English would build the canal elsewhere: "Civilization and the world's commerce are knocking at our door, and we should hasten to allow them in, before they go elsewhere and leave us without anything but the pain of our indolence."[316] Even at the height of Colombia's confidence in its political future, doubts nagged elite Liberals about their true position in the world. Politically, Colombia had created the most modern nation on the face of the earth, but Cuenca, by equating civilization with commerce, returned Colombia to a passive state, waiting for North Americans and Europeans to bring modernity to them. Some fretted that Colombia would cede too many rights to the English, but Cuenca brushed aside such concerns, saying that only England—"the center of universal commerce"—had the immense credit, wealth, "colonial possessions," and fleet necessary to complete the project.[317] Despite the intense hostility to colonialism in the public sphere, Cuenca could now present England's colonies and its imperial impulses to control the proposed canal as positives, as harbingers of progress.

These tensions had existed since American republican modernity's emergence. In Uruguay, during the Guerra Grande, the Colorado government had to reassure landowners that it would limit the amount of land it intended to expropriate and give to the landless who had served it.[318] Elites worried that the subalterns they needed as allies during the war, such as the former slaves, might not be so eager to accept their previous lot once hostilities ended, urging the freedmen to "change your military uniform for the simple clothing of the laborer."[319] As we have seen, during moments of crises subalterns used their indispensability to bend liberalism's tenets, such as suspending rents on property or even seizing property from traitors for redistribution.[320] Elite Liberals fretted over when and how the state would restore the status quo of property rights once the war ended.[321]

In Colombia, moderate Liberals, such as those represented by El Hombre, often looked back to Europhile modernity, stressing property as a marker of civilization: "Property is that which has civilized the world and that which has created sciences, arts, industry and all the physical and moral improvements."[322] El Hombre accused the more radical El Pensamiento Popular of inculcating "the poison pill of socialism and communism, gilded with the pretty words of the masses' emancipation, unlimited liberty, absolute equality."[323] If democracy and equality were the measure of modernity, what would that mean if the pueblo decided equality meant property's equitable distribution? In the case of the villagers of Paso del Bobo mentioned above, who demanded the right to keep renting land at the past rate, the hacendados confronting them responded by calling the petitioners "criminals" who had "perverse habits" and preached "the most detestable doctrines against work and property."[324] The Juárez regime was caught between the contradictions of its emancipatory discourse and its desires for capitalist economic development.

Questions of order were equally troubling. Certainly, the destruction of the War of the Reform caused many to doubt Mexico's future, at least for the moment.[325] Although revolution trumped order in much public debate, especially during the French Intervention, as Florencia Mallon has noted concerning plebeian soldiers and national life, a reaction quickly occurred.

In early 1868 the politician and writer Francisco Zarco urged Mexico to show the world that the nation could now follow "the path of order and progress."[326] The diplomat Manuel María de Zamacona was more direct, insisting that force be employed immediately to punish bandits and deter crime, as part of a more general disciplinary project.[327] In only a few years, Zamacona's and Zarco's words would seem less like an anomaly and more like part of the dominant discourse of modernity—not just in Mexico, but eventually throughout most of Latin America.

However, we should not assume that this economic liberalism made American modernity meaningless.[328] While La Reforma's economic program was a precursor to Porfirio Díaz's regime, simply ignoring the importance of the political and the discourse of modernity obscures both why Juárez's economic program failed and why political life and visions of the future had to change so significantly under the Porfiriato. Of course, the Spanish American public sphere could not help but marvel at the technological achievements of the age: "the century of steam power, of electricity, of enlightenment."[329] Elites fretted about disorder, socialism, popular demands, and unruly plebeians' influence in a democratic system. Yet for all these concerns, political considerations still dominated modernity's definitions in the public sphere. After midcentury, American republicanism was more powerful than economic liberalism in both Colombia and Mexico. Even as some Liberals worried about the lack of economic development, there was a confidence in the public sphere that such material concerns were not true measures of civilization and that eventually American republican modernity would produce the long-awaited economic prosperity (if not imagined by many subalterns as necessarily individual, as opposed to more fraternal, prosperity). In spite of classical liberalism's doctrines that citizenship could only emerge from the rational, male property holder produced by capitalist economies,[330] the radical republican and subaltern adherents to American republican modernity insisted that citizenship came first; it was a right of primordial importance. For republicans, politics created the citizen; for Liberals, economics did. Yet during this era, it was the political that triumphed, and the political that defined modernity and the future.

Of course, middle-class and elite republicans yearned for affluence and capitalist development. However, they could not escape the contradiction between the necessities of capitalist development and the political space opened up by American republican modernity. Ultimately, the contradiction could not be resolved; for the economic program to achieve some success, American republicanism's political and social project would have to be subsumed. The Colombian Regeneration's and the Mexican Porfiriato's political projects sought to control popular political demands precisely in order to satisfy capital's needs. Concomitantly, their cultural and intellectual projects sought to replace American republican modernity with Western modernity as the prime orientation of the public sphere. By the 1880s both the Porfiriato and, to a lesser extent, the Regeneration would succeed in doing so.

In the 1860s and even 1870s this future was not yet clear, as American republican modernity still held sway in the public sphere. Returning to Chile's El Ferrocarril that opened this chapter, the paper argued that Europe was really not that wealthy anyway, especially if one traveled beyond its great cities, and that it was doomed to be poor due to its political system: "Therefore, one can say with certainty that in Europe while there is poverty there will be despots, that both evils coexist, and that the latter will only disappear if the former does as well."[331] While elite writers aligned with "Western modernity" tended to equate modernity and civilization with economic wealth and high culture, American republican modernity's quotidian language focused on the achievement of the most modern political systems—meaning those republics that guaranteed the most rights to the greatest number of people. As President Manuel Mallarino of Colombia (then New Granada) asserted, "The Granadan people, if not as prosperous and powerful as others whose existence measures centuries, is without a doubt as free as any in the New or Old Worlds."[332] This discourse of American republican modernity profoundly and powerfully shaped both elites' efforts at nation and state making and subalterns' struggles to make these new nations and states their own.

CHAPTER 5

Francisco Bilbao and the Atlantic Imagination

M ore than any other single writer, thinker, revolutionary, or politician, Francisco Bilbao embodied the spirit of American republican modernity. His writings and thought depicted an Atlantic world consumed by a titanic struggle between modernity and retrogression, republicanism and monarchy, universalism and aristocracy, independence and imperialism, rationalism and ultramontanism, liberty and slavery, civilization and barbarism. How Spanish Americans like Bilbao created a shared imagination of the republican Atlantic world and that world's heroes and villains is this chapter's main subject. Although not unknown today, Bilbao has not received the same scholarly attention as other nineteenth-century letrados.[1] Yet Bilbao is a much more interesting figure and, I would argue, a more original thinker than Sarmiento, Alberdi, Alamán, Samper, or Sierra. His radical republicanism and universalism prefigures almost all of the key contributions of the considerably more celebrated José Martí. Bilbao challenged Europe's claims to modernity much more thoroughly than did Rubén Darío's cultured modernism.[2] With his radical reconfiguration of modernity, Bilbao was one of the most important and innovative thinkers not only of Latin America, but also of the nineteenth-century world.

Francisco Bilbao was born on 9 January 1823 in Santiago to a father from Chile and a mother from Buenos Aires. Bilbao's education began at home;

FIG 5.1. Portrait of Francisco Bilbao. *Las obras completas de Francisco Bilbao*, edited by Manuel Bilbao, 1:iii.

his father, Rafael Bilbao, had trained as a lawyer but worked as merchant and a government official. Rafael had long ago sided with the opposition against the dominant conservative politics in Chile, standing with those in favor of reform, the "democratic system," and a break from imitating the metropole.[3] Indeed, Francisco's peripatetic Atlantic life began as a result of Rafael's radical views: as an eleven-year-old boy, Francisco would accompany his father into exile in Lima in 1834, not returning to Chile until 1839.[4] Within a few years after Francisco's return he would be infamous.

Bilbao entered the Instituto Nacional after his return and studied to become a lawyer. At school and in the local literary society, he found teachers such as the Venezuelan Andrés Bello, the Chilean José Victorino Lastarria, and the Argentinean Vicente López. Bilbao also absorbed European works of history and philosophy by Gibbon, Voltaire, Rousseau, Volney, Dupin, Herder, Vico, Coussin, Quinet, Michelet, and especially the liberal defrocked priest Lamennais (whose work Bilbao translated into Spanish).[5] Bilbao first gained public notice by speaking at the funeral of the anticlerical politician José Miguel Infante in 1844; his oration provoked an outcry from the capital's Roman Catholic hierarchy. During the resulting confrontation between the clergy and Bilbao's fellow young rationalists, Bilbao wrote "Sociabilidad Chilena," in which he attacked the Church, the Chilean oligarchy, and the hacienda system. He was only twenty-one. The clergy reacted with fury.[6] Santiago's *fiscal* (prosecutor) filed charges against Bilbao of blasphemy, immorality, and sedition. Many of his friends abandoned him as priests denounced him from the pulpit, but his own family stood by him, his father praising him for "favoring oppressed humanity."[7] On the day of Bilbao's trial, spectators filled the tribunal and plaza central, and when Bilbao appeared shouts of "Viva el Defensor del Pueblo!" rang out.[8] As revolutionaries have throughout history, Bilbao used the trial to further promulgate his ideas, defending himself by arguing that his suggested radical reforms of still extant colonial institutions were the only path to progress.[9] The court acquitted Bilbao of sedition but convicted him of blasphemy and immorality, punishing the young author with a fine of 1,200 pesos or—failing payment—six months in prison. Bilbao did not have the money and turned himself over for incarceration, but his friends quickly raised the necessary funds from the assembled crowd. His supporters then carried Bilbao through the streets of Santiago, shouting and clamoring riotously along.[10]

Bilbao was now famous, confronting a clergy and an entrenched conservative political elite that would be his lifelong sworn enemies. Although he seemed to enjoy the support of the young intelligentsia, the state and Church struck back, expelling Bilbao from the Instituto Nacional, punishing his supporters among the student body and faculty, and confiscating and destroying copies of his essay. Bilbao left Santiago, first for Valparaiso and soon afterward for Europe, to continue his education.

Like most intellectuals of his generation reared under Europhile modernity, Bilbao looked to France for guidance. He arrived in Paris in 1845 eager to study with the historians Edgar Quinet and Jules Michelet, and to meet Hugues-Félicité de Lamennais in person. While infatuated with Paris, Bilbao quickly realized that he had not left behind in Chile the struggles between the forces of progress and retrogression; the same battle raged in France. Quinet's class at the Sorbonne was soon closed by Louis Philippe's government, the French professor observing that Bilbao had fled Chile under persecution of the "Jesuit spirit" only to find that same spirit dominant in France.[11] The events of this time molded Bilbao's imagination. News of Poland's rebellion against Prussia reached Paris in March of 1846, inflaming passions throughout the city. Of course, the events of 1848 would stun the Atlantic world as a whole. That year is regularly cited as massively influential in Latin America, but Bilbao was significantly disillusioned by it. He saw the year's events in France as a failure of republicanism, especially the French refusal to aid Hungary or Poland.[12] Although most Latin American intellectuals who took the grand tour of the Old World returned with an intense Europhilia, Bilbao journeyed back to America filled with doubts about Europe's place in the modern world, doubts that blossomed into his embrace of America as the future of humanity.

Bilbao returned to Chile in 1850, taking a post in the office of Statistics while considering his options. He had become increasingly disenchanted with traditional politics, as neither faction in Chile seemed to represent republicanism and democracy.[13] Chilean politics instead appeared to be just a contest among caudillos, hungry for power. Bilbao had become convinced that only a complete change in the pueblo's manner of thinking would make progress possible. Critically, the Catholic Church's stranglehold over education must be broken. Bilbao's anticlericalism and rationalism would be hallmarks of his thought. The Church represented only barbarism and the colonial past to him, and he believed it was embraced by postindependence leaders as a way to control the masses. In April 1850 Bilbao helped found Santiago's Sociedad de la Igualdad (Society of Equality) in order to make connections with the capital's artisans and put into practice his ideas about education. Only an alliance with the people could create true republicanism and break apart the old oligarchic politics. The society promoted universal suffrage and universal fraternity, reason over the Church's teachings, and the pueblo's sovereignty. Bilbao's continuing attacks on Catholicism led the Church to excommunicate him, causing many of his Liberal allies to abandon him. Some sought to expel him from the Society of Equality, but the society's members decided to allow him to remain. Nevertheless, the society faced growing hostility from Chile's conservative government, including armed attacks on its meetings by presumed state agents and sympathizers. By November 1850, only a few months after its founding, the Chilean state disbanded the society for subversion.[14]

Many members of the Society of Equality, including Bilbao, concluded that open revolt remained their last option. Bilbao actively participated in the planned coup of Pedro Alcántara Urriola against President Manuel Bulnes in April 1851, but betrayal and poor organization doomed the rebellion. Bilbao fled the country, settling in Peru.[15] He had to promise Peruvian President José Rufino Echenique that he would not involve himself in local politics, but Bilbao could not resist. Soon he was agitating for slavery's abolition and fulminating against the Jesuits. He was forced into exile again in Guayaquil, Ecuador, but he returned to Peru because his father was imprisoned in Lima. He then joined the successful revolt against Echenique led by Ramón Castilla, but his anticlericalism made him an unpopular and dangerous figure. He went again into exile in 1855, returning once more to Europe.[16]

Bilbao had left Europe already disillusioned with the Old World's self-proclaimed civilization, and his return to France in 1855 strongly confirmed his doubts about the long-trumpeted European superiority. France under Napoleon III seemed but a pale shadow of its former glory, now ruled by a petty, laughable tyrant; it had become a society suspicious of foreigners, having abandoned universal fraternity in favor of a paranoid police state. According to his brother, Manuel, instead of the modern, all Francisco found was "silence about the blood" of Napoleon's rule and the "terrible future" that awaited France.[17] Europe was no longer the future or the guide to civilization, but simply a corrupt collection of aristocrats, monarchs, and empires, all wallowing in a medieval feudalism. Bilbao now fully embraced his vision of America as the future of humanity that would spread liberty and equality across the globe to regenerate a decadent Europe.

Bilbao sailed again for America, arriving in 1857 in Buenos Aires, where he would live until his death. He quickly became embroiled in local politics, to his eventual disquiet. He lent his skills to the Federalists, whom he saw as looking to the United States and American unity, instead of the Unitarians, whom he claimed imitated Europe. He saw Juan Manuel de Rosas as a nothing but a dictator who had falsely exploited federalist sentiment, but he thought the new federalists represented American republicanism. Bilbao would eventually break with Justo José de Urquiza and other federalists over their caudillismo, but he would continue to agitate for slavery's abolition in Brazil, for support of Mexico against the French (the subject of some of his finest and most powerful writings), and for reason and individual sovereignty in relation to God (which would lead the bishop of Buenos Aires to attack Bilbao in a pastoral).[18] Thousands of miles to the north, Chihuahua's *La Alianza de la Frontera* would celebrate his book condemning European aggression and backwardness, *La América en peligro*.[19] After years of wandering, Bilbao would finally find some domestic happiness, marrying Pilar Guido y Spano in 1863. However, their only son would die in infancy, and Bilbao's lifelong battle with illness would intensify. Suffering from pneumonia and perhaps also tuberculosis, and coughing up terrifying volumes of blood, Bilbao would succumb on 19 February 1865, dying with his brother and wife by his side. Manuel gave perhaps the most fitting eulogy, declaring his beloved brother had worked his whole life to inaugurate the "paradise of humanity: the Republic."[20]

The Struggle for the Soul of the Atlantic World

One of Bilbao's earliest biographers lamented that Bilbao never achieved independence from the thinking of his mentors, such as Lamennais, Quinet, and Michelet, a view also held by a number of subsequent scholars.[21] However, I argue that Bilbao was a critically original thinker in terms of the importance of American republicanism and modernity. His writing helped inspire and in general best exemplified the discourse I have called American republican modernity. Bilbao and his legion of comrades, writing in capitals and provinces from Argentina and Chile to the United States, imagined an Atlantic world involved in a vast and titanic struggle of civilizations, pitting America, modernity, liberty, and equality against Europe, retrogression, despotism, slavery, and aristocracy. The quotidian discourse of mid-century Spanish America reveals a clearly defined Atlantic imagination of heroes and villains contending for the future of humanity.

Bilbao imagined this epic contest taking place in the hearts of men (thus his visceral hostility to ultramontane Catholicism) but also within and between peoples and nations. He saw the French invasion of Mexico as part of a plan to destroy the independence of nations, with the ultimate goal "the extermination of the Republic in the world." Although Bilbao's rhetoric was overheated, he foresaw the coming wave of European imperialism more clearly than most.[22] Of course, on the side of the angels were many European peoples and nations, and on the side of the devils many Americans; allying with the French were those conservative Americans who pined for monarchy, for dictatorship, for a return to the colonial order, and, crucially, to "dominate and civilize the masses."[23] Geography was ultimately less important than visions of modernity: in Bilbao's words, "American civilization versus European civilization."[24] Bilbao was specific about the sides and terms of this conflict that spanned oceans and continents, fought "from Mexico to Chile": "Political faith against religious faith, reason against religion, hope against tradition, union against isolation, federalism against centralism, labor against land, the logic of sovereignty against oligarchic constitutions."[25]

For American republican modernity's supporters, their most tenacious and powerful enemies were the conservative clergy and their "retrograde and fanatical" followers.[26] Bilbao was rabidly anti-Catholic, seeing the Church as the largest obstacle to progress. For Bilbao, Catholicism was compatible only with monarchies and theocracies since it insisted on blind obedience to authorities and denied reason and the pueblo's sovereignty, both of which were central to republicanism. Thus Latin America's Catholicism helped explain any problems and setbacks that republicanism faced in the Americas.[27] Bilbao blamed Paul and the subsequent Catholic hierarchy for distorting Jesus's true message. Instead of the Nazarene's "social revolution," the Church promoted the "enslavement of women" and an authoritarian despotism.[28]

Liberals across Spanish America shared Bilbao's preoccupations, often engaging in ferocious attacks on the Church and especially the Vatican. A Bogota newspaper declared that of 262 legitimate popes, 153 were incompetent, corrupt, or unfaithful. The paper asked what other institution in world history had such a poor record.[29] Mexico City's La Opinión Nacional equated the clergy and militarism with a feudal past and celebrated Liberal martyrs, such as Melchor Ocampo, who had died so that "man should be the priest of his own conscience."[30] Liberals saw conservative religiosity as a means of enslaving the masses, and they classified zealots as "enemies of democratic institutions" and "executioners of humanity and civilization."[31] However, some Liberals had faith that the pueblo, or at least groups such as artisans, had escaped the clerics' sway by distinguishing "between religion and fanaticism."[32]

Within the discourses of both liberalism and American republican modernity, a wide variety of approaches to religion and the Catholic Church coexisted. Most Liberals claimed they were not anti-Christian, instead embracing a religion that promoted charity, the Golden Rule, fraternity, science, public health, and enlightenment while rejecting fanaticism and intolerance.[33] In both Mexico and Colombia, Liberals viewed the Church hierarchy as the staunchest opponent of all progress, motivated by both retrograde views and a desire to protect its own power and wealth and that of the Conservative "aristocracy" with which the Church was allied.[34] Some made a clear distinction between religion and "the Church," the latter equated with the Inquisition, indulgences, and taxes.[35] Others embraced Catholicism; for example, José Manuel Estrada espoused many ideas of American republicanism but combined them with Catholicism, which tempered liberty with morality.[36] In general, however, many saw the Church as impeding modernity. Those who planned to reestablish the Jesuits in the Americas, for example, were assumed to "want to detain the course of the century."[37]

While the nuances of rationalism, religion, and the Church's temporal power engendered endless debate, at moments of crisis the lines between progressives and retrogrades became clear. During the 1876–77 Colombian civil war, sparked by debates over secular education, priests openly revolted with Conservatives. The Liberal president of Cauca State, César Conto, wondered: "Is there anything more absurd than the attempt to start a religious war in America in the last third of the nineteenth century?"[38] Cali's Democratic Society celebrated the Liberals' victory over "the ultramontanists and theocrats" who were the "eternal enemies" of both democracy and "all progress."[39] During Mexico's War of the Reform, Liberals described Conservatives as barbaric religious fanatics who "only are happy under the whip of their master, passively eating the bitter bread of the slave."[40] Maximilian's invasion similarly crystallized anticlerical feelings. Morelia's La Guerra accused Conservatives of treason for inviting the French to invade, claiming that Conservatives had plotted "to saturate our atmosphere with the black smoke of the inquisitorial bonfires."[41]

As debates about the Church suggest, seeing Latin America's civil wars and electoral and ideological contests as central to an Atlantic-wide campaign between the past and the present was not just a trope of Bilbao, but widespread. As early as the 1840s, when Europhile modernity was still dominant, some began to imagine an international republican struggle that engulfed the Old and New Worlds, as we saw in Montevideo. By the 1860s such conceptions were widespread, and Latin America was no longer just part of this struggle but the key to its success. Mexico's La Chinaca understood the wars of the 1860s to be tightly interconnected: on one side stood Mexico, Cuban patriots, and the U.S. North in the Civil War; on the other side stood the Confederacy, England, France, and Spain (desperate to keep Cuba). This vast international struggle pitted aristocrats, monarchs, and imperialists against "the fraternity of everything intelligent, progressive and democratic in the world."[42] For the Liberal politician Eduardo Urueta, celebrating President Benito Juárez's triumphant entrance into Mexico City after Maximilian's defeat, on the enemy side stood the clergy, military despots, "the rich," European powers, and even the United States, if it returned to expansionism.[43]

This international struggle was reflected internally in the numerous civil wars between Liberals and Conservatives, not just in Colombia and Mexico but across the New World.[44] Instead of cataloging New World states' ills and failures, as under Europhile modernity, newspapers now eagerly tracked new liberal revolutions that would add more Spanish American nations to the American republican fraternity.[45] For La República of Zacatecas, 1866 marked a decisive turning point in this struggle, with "Europe in particular" learning many lessons. Slavery had been abolished in the United States, Mexico was victorious, and in Europe "the pueblos . . . told their sovereigns: enough oppression, enough of armies. When will you allow us to enjoy our liberties and rights?"[46] In this vision, the struggle between civilization and barbarism in the Atlantic world was not between cultured urban *letrados* and barbaric backland plebeians, but an international contest between republicanism and monarchy, between citizens and aristocrats, between freedom and slavery, and between sister republics and European empires.[47] Although some scholars see the Age of Revolution as marking the last moment when Spanish America and North America shared a common experience, midcentury writers still saw a common project and destiny for the Americas.[48]

Rhetoric contrasting America and Europe was so ubiquitous that it could be appropriated for commercial exploitation, with advertisements exploiting this struggle for material gain. A North American photographer working in Lima stated in an advertisement: "It is undeniable that there exists a vast European conspiracy against the liberties of America and it is also undeniable that the best way to defeat it is Union and mutual protection." Therefore, reaching not a little, he suggested that Limeños have their photographs taken at his shop as a way of expressing American solidarity.[49] More important, this discourse regularly appeared in speeches meant for general consumption. The Atlantic imaginary was not only shared by the *letrados* but was also a common referent throughout the public sphere.

France's invasion of Mexico confirmed the "European conspiracy" to destroy American republicanism. Mexicans warned that Maximilian's invasion was an attack on "all the interests of the Republics of the immense American continent."[50] Many Mexicans actively hoped (and even assumed) that the United States would directly intervene in the war as their ally; after all, the Old World threatened them all, and mutual protection was the duty of sister republics and in the spirit of the Monroe Doctrine (as interpreted by Spanish Americans).[51] It was, of course, Mexican monarchists who opposed any U.S. involvement during the French Intervention, claiming the Monroe Doctrine and protestations against monarchy were only a cover for U.S. ambition.[52]

The U.S. Civil War's bloody spectacle acted both to atone for past U.S. aggression (as Ulysses S. Grant noted, the United States seemed to paying a dreadful price for its sins) and to reanimate the idea of the sister republics. Spanish American papers eagerly followed the course of the war, celebrating Union victories.[53] Spanish Americans understood the war as no different than their own struggles between Liberals and Conservatives, between those pushing for expanded citizenship and rights and those seeking to restrict human freedom.[54] Moreover, the Confederacy was linked not just with Conservatives but also with U.S. filibustering and European imperialism. Latin Americans assumed that England and France under Napoleon favored an independent Confederacy.[55] As Spain, England, and France invaded Veracruz in 1861 to recoup Mexico's defaulted loans, *La Guerra* speculated that England had really joined the invasion to position its navy to break the Union blockades of Confederate ports. The paper predicted that if this were true, "a continental war will erupt."[56] Mexican papers reported rumors that the Confederacy's long-range goals included invasions of Mexico and Cuba.[57] Many Mexicans (and North Americans) thought the Confederacy would ally itself with Maximilian's French invaders.[58] *La Bandera Nacional* reported that the French had sided with the Confederacy and clamored for the Union to join Mexico in common cause to rid the New World of European monarchical imperialism, even claiming that a friendly North American army would be welcome on Mexican soil.[59] Some North Americans agreed; the Union's military governor of Texas urged U.S. support for Mexico and linked the Confederacy with Maximilian's monarchy and French imperialism.[60] Bilbao clearly saw the U.S. Civil War as a struggle to end slavery, closely linked internationally with Mexico's resistance against French imperialism.[61] In Mexico, such an understanding was common. For example, in the celebratory speech cited above, Urueta applauded the U.S. "great war of abolition."[62] Bilbao, often suspicious of U.S. imperial intentions, in 1863 celebrated a now possible "alliance with the United States, purified of slavery," that would make American civilization invincible against its European and domestic enemies.[63] A competing identity of pan-American republicanism challenged racial nationalists' promotion of divisions between Latin America and North America.

The Americas' triumph in this struggle seemed secured by the dual victories of the Union over the Confederacy and Mexico over France. In the banner year of 1866, the tide seemed to have turned inexorably in favor of liberty: "Any attempt to compromise the development of the free peoples of the Americas will now be useless and sterile."[64] In a speech, the professor and diplomat Jesús Escobar y Armendáriz celebrated Mexican and and U.S. triumphs over European reaction: "Its [Europe's] efforts to sustain the rebellion in the United States and perpetuate slavery are in vain. Grant has made Richmond [the Confederacy's capital] surrender and the world has celebrated."[65] The Mexican Congress asserted that Mexico's victorious resistance to French colonialism had helped secure the future of all the Americas and shown Europe the vitality of American "progress." Now, the American republics would unite in an alliance "for the good of civilization and humanity."[66] Meeting in Baltimore to celebrate Mexico's triumph, soldiers from the U.S. Grand Army of the Republic extolled Maximilian's execution as having "erased with one blow monarchy's prestige in our continent."[67] Matías Romero, the Mexican ambassador to the United States, replied that the French invasion had been not just an attack on Mexico but "an attempt to overthrow popular government and the free institutions of this continent."[68] Americans, North and South, imagined the New World as at the vanguard of civilization, facing Europe's retrograde institutions with a moral and physical force that could not be denied.

Visions Competing with American Republican Modernity after Midcentury

Those Conservatives and letrados opposed to American republican modernity also imagined an Atlantic world in a grand contest between civilization and barbarism. However, for Conservatives, on the side of the angels were those defending a Christian civilization that protected an orderly, hierarchical society against barbarous subalterns and their revolutionary Liberal leaders, whose plans would lead only to anarchy and dissolution. Most letrados, be they self-declared Conservatives such as Lucas Alamán or writers more associated with Liberalism such as Sarmiento or Juan Bautista Alberdi, tended to look to Europe for validation and were suspicious of popular sovereignty; in this regard, Bilbao was more the exception than the norm for the lettered elite.[69] However, in this section I mostly will concentrate not on letrados but on the counternarratives to American republican modernity in the public sphere of the street and in the political arena during the moment of American republican modernity's ascension (1850s–1870s). These conservative visions drew on Europhile modernity, with its focus on European high culture, education, and manners, but they also prefigured many aspects of an emerging Western modernity, which emphasized economic progress, technological evolution, state power, and racial hierarchy. Even during its heyday, American republican modernity always competed with other discourses of civilization for supremacy in the public sphere.

While American republican modernity celebrated the Americas, Conservatives were much more likely to still look to Europe for a path to the future, as epitomized by Maximilian's invitation—"true civilization" could come only from Europe.[70] Juan Almonte and José Mariano de Salas thanked Napoleon III and Maximilian for bringing order to Mexico and for sacrificing "their blood and treasure, without any other ambition than to elevate us to the level of the most civilized pueblos."[71] Mexico's *La Sociedad* declared it was in "cultured Europe" that the "lights of the century" shown most brightly, and Europe's "civilizing influence" was still needed to reform Asia, Africa, and the Americas.[72] Upon hearing news of Maximilian's execution, colonial Cuba's *Diario de la Marina* worked itself into hysteria, demanding "a crusade of European civilization against Mexican barbarism." If that was not possible, then Mexico must be completely isolated from "civilized peoples" so it could not spread its infection of barbarism and anarchy.[73]

For many Mexican, Cuban, and Brazilian Conservatives, if not for Colombians or most Spanish Americans, monarchy defined European civilization. As Erika Pani has discussed, Maximilian's monarchy was not an aberration or only a foreign imposition, but represented long-standing political currents.[74] *Diario de la Marina* declared that civilization was based on two great principles, "law and authority," and supported by two great institutions, the Church and monarchy. The paper smugly noted how orderly Cuba was becoming "more wealthy, more civilized" every day because the "principle of authority" reigned," while the rest of the Americas regressed into fratricidal bloodshed.[75] Mexico's Assembly of Notables, who gathered in 1863 to formally establish a monarchy, argued that Mexico should imitate the most powerful nations in "Western Europe."[76] The assembly did not reject the idea of modernity, claiming to support "modern monarchies"; the "magic word" of monarchy was the only sure path to "civilization."[77] Brazilians argued that Mexican Conservatives had looked to their country's orderly monarchy for a political model to escape republican anarchy.[78] Many Spanish America *letrados*—even those such as Alberdi who were not publicly associated with conservatism—were also suspicious of republicanism, fretting that Europeans would learn about the extent of "our backwardness and our misery."[79] Sarmiento dismissed claims of American centrality in 1865: "South America is too low down in the human current" for European governments to pay any attention to it.[80] The Colombian *letrado* José María Vergara y Vergara mocked those Americans who thought the "universe" looked to them, derisively snorting: "The universe is watching the new opera premiering in Paris."[81] In an unpublished essay written in the 1860s, Alberdi went even further, arguing that Americans must embrace Europe in every way possible, including monarchism, "not because monarchy is better than a republic in itself, but because it is the government that prevails in civilized Europe, with which we must live united in order to have civilization."[82] In short, America was "backward" while Europe was "the only known civilization."[83]

Around midcentury, American republican modernity's opponents shared that discourse's insistence that the question of modernity was essentially a political one; they just differed on the types of politics, the definition of liberty, and the role of popular groups. If monarchy was unacceptable, then republicanism should at least be orderly and led by educated elites. The Church should play a central role in limiting democratic excesses. Alamán declared that only the Church stood as a bulwark against these nefarious modern ideologies of irreligiosity and open class warfare.[84] *La Sociedad* declared that the Church was the "cornerstone of society" and "the dike against the torrent of immorality." Furthermore, "the Pope, as temporal sovereign, represents property and public power: on these two bases society rests."[85] Without religion, society would descend into depravity and socialism: "A civilized barbarism will triumph in the world," just as barbarians overran Rome.[86] Hundreds of residents of Ipiales, Colombia, petitioned against a plan for secular public education; the petitioners declared that if society abandoned its religious principles, "we will regress to being barbarians, yes barbarians."[87]

If religion provided one of the key cultural touchstones for Conservatives, opposition to American republican modernity's universalism was another. Conservatives and *letrados* talked more openly about race—in this period, before scientific racism became dominant, still largely understood as an amalgam of cultural, legal, and biological traits—and its importance in defining civilization. Under Maximilian's rule, Durango's *El Telégrafo* declared that Mexico's problems were due to the "absolute lack of homogeneity" of race: "Our society is formed of three races that are entirely unfriendly and separate from one another, due to their education, customs, language and even memories." The difference among these races was the difference between "civilization and barbarism." Nonwhites were unfit for citizenship, generally drunken, and ignorant of political life.[88] Colombian Conservatives regularly cast doubt on Afro-Colombians' fitness for citizenship, claiming that the latter were "ignorant men" who "do not deserve the title of true Granadans."[89] Race also provided Conservatives with a way to deal with the horrifying doctrine of equality. Cali's *Ariete* argued that God had created inequality among men and "never will the color black be equal to the color white."[90] The powerful Conservative politician Sergio Arboleda, who openly spoke of "inferior races," even condemned legal equality: "I see another obstacle to industrial progress in the titular absolute equality with which the three races that form our pueblo should obey the same legislation." He urged a return to Spanish legislation that recognized "the fact of inequality in our races."[91] Some Conservatives still felt restrained, at least in the midcentury public sphere of the street, from openly embracing a codified racism, given the preeminence of the idea of racial equality in the wars of independence. Soon, however, Western modernity's scientific racism would encourage public discussion of race and modernity.

Conservatives blamed the fetishization of equality, the presence of barbaric races, and the decline in religious sentiment for fomenting chaos and anarchy. Disorder was the most important rebuttal to American republican modernity's claims to the future. Although most Conservatives did not support monarchy, they certainly sympathized with many monarchists' critiques of republican-induced anarchy. Mexico's Assembly of Notables argued that republicanism's chief failures in Mexico included the decline of authority and the concomitant disorder that had sunk Mexico into "unspeakable barbarism."[92] The assembly mocked the "delights of liberty" that republicanism had bought to Mexico: extortion, violence, injustice, robbery, arson, and death.[93] In a public address in 1868, Ignacio Gutiérrez Vergara— the Conservative governor of Cundinamarca, Colombia—argued that security and protection of property was "the primary goal of the government in every civilized society." He declared that "peace and order are the fathers of prosperity" and that their attainment marks all "civilized nations."[94] He planned to achieve this order by encouraging public opinion to limit those involved in politics, which should be only the elect few, a guiding principle of Conservatives' views of subalterns' role. Employing one of the most potent metaphors of midcentury, Gutiérrez compared progress to a locomotive, with peace and order acting as the rails that guided it. Without this guidance, progress could lead to catastrophe.[95]

Order was an end in itself, of course, but it was also crucial to instigating the economic development that was becoming modernity's hallmark in the North Atlantic. In an 1861 speech, Ignacio del Campo—later an official under Porfirio Díaz—argued that Mexico must prepare to be "linked to the civilized world by the telegraph and railroads," which would bring "marvelous machines" and commerce from afar by establishing peace, order, and guarantees of favorable treatment for foreigners.[96] Campo thought that Mexico had to look elsewhere for a technological and commercial modernity. This was a discordant note in 1861, representing an important elite, but minority, view; however, two decades later, it would become hegemonic in the Mexican public sphere. Liberals' own concerns about order after the French Intervention would soon drive many to radically rethink their commitment to republican modernity.[97] It would still be some time before economic development became the hegemonic definition of modernity;

however, such an idea was germinating even while American republican modernity reigned supreme.

In the 1860s and 1870s, the solutions to the problem of anarchy were still inchoate—including religion, discipline, and monarchy—yet they were beginning to coalesce around ideas that would become central to Western modernity's political project in the last quarter of the century: a massive augmentation in the state's power and a reduction in popular participation. Conservatives (and many Liberals) had long decried the state's weakness.[98] The Conservative paper *La Cruz* argued that the form of government—be it democracy, aristocracy, or monarchy—did not matter; the only important point was that it effectively exercised authority. While Liberals celebrated popular sovereignty, Conservatives dismissed it: "The crowd, with a leader to direct it, is not government."[99] Conservatives equated overparticipation in politics with barbarism. For example, one Caleño wrote to Colombian President Mariano Ospina in 1859 to warn him of the coming "democratic explosion" planned by Liberals meeting in their Democratic Societies. However, he assured the president that the "property-owning and civilized people" supported him and his calls for order, while only "men without morality or fortune" composed the opposition.[100] Conservatives were often horrified by the poor—especially blacks or Indians—voting. After denigrating blacks who had come into Cali to vote as drunken, sinister creatures of the forest, "as in Africa," Pedro José Piedrahíta lamented that the Liberals "want to sink us in the stinking mud while the civilized world looks on."[101] In general, although many Conservatives supported republicanism, democracy enjoyed little support. *El Clamor Nacional* claimed that Liberal politicians spoke of the progress of "true democracy," which Conservatives thought meant undisciplined plebeians participating as equals in the public sphere, the collapse of social hierarchy (including slavery), and the destruction of landed property.[102] In 1861 *El Porvenir* wailed that if the Liberal "hordes" won the civil war, property would disappear: "Everyone will be poor, everyone will be equal." The paper mocked "these fathers of democracy" for whom "property is theft" and "authority is tyranny," "the family is a farce," and "religion a lie."[103] Although the technology, strategy, resources, and even ideology required for a more powerful state were still largely lacking around midcentury, there was a growing sense that the masses' influence on the nation and state must be sharply curtailed. Pasto's Conservative Governor Antonio José Chaves emphasized the need to strengthen the police and the law's authority, which while perhaps "repressive," would work to establish the "morality" that was the essential base of progress. He warned that "without morality there is neither civilization nor industry."[104] Chaves was more than willing to trade some repression for order, and he saw civilization as resting not on rights but on the morality of the population, a morality that force and authority could instill.

Liberals in the public sphere tended to express confidence in the nation, but Conservatives had their doubts. The Colombian *letrado* Arcesio Escobar argued that a true Colombian nation did not exist: "Why? Because the barbarism of the pueblo impedes it." Under democracy, Colombia risked becoming an *oclocracia*—the rule of the mob—resulting in "the tyranny of the ignorant and depraved masses."[105] Escobar adopted Europhile modernity's intense fear of democracy and of a racially and culturally suspect lower class, which made a true nation—a white and European nation—impossible. Pasto's *El Espectador* would have concurred with Escobar's views of the apocalyptic dangers of a demagogic democracy. During the 1859–62 civil war, the paper saw the rebellion against Conservative rule as upending "the constraints of morality, respect for the law, inviolability of marriage, the sanctity of the family and the security of property, all these bases upon which society rests." In short, Conservatives fought for "the cause of civilization over barbarism."[106] El *Espectador* presented the main alternative to American republican modernity as, under Europhile modernity, mostly concerned with morality, religion, and culture but also worrying about order and state power, prefiguring the rise of Western modernity late in the century. These Conservatives' visions would burgeon in the 1870s, especially as many Liberals became disenchanted with their republican experiments and increasingly eyed the North Atlantic when searching for a path to the future; yet in the 1850s and 1860s, the radical republican imagination of American progress still reigned in the public sphere. While Conservatives looked to figures such as Maximilian, Napoleon III, and Pope Pius IX to save their vision of civilization, American republicans celebrated a pantheon of heroes fighting for liberty and equality.

The Legion of Honor and Bestiary of the Atlantic Imagination

While the midcentury public sphere envisioned a general contest between Europe and America, the discourse of American republican modernity contained a complex imaginary of both American and European heroes, villains, and victims. Listeners to speeches and readers of newspapers easily identified common references to both individuals and countries as allies on the side of good or opponents aligned with tyranny.[107] This roll call mostly focused on actors and states in the Americas and Europe, but it occasionally touched on Africa and Asia. Of course, at any one moment individuals and nation-states might figure more or less prominently, but at midcentury certain peoples and places shone brightly in Spanish Americans' understanding of the world.

In some ways, given the broad strokes with which most writers and orators painted, nations—along with symbols such as the liberty tree, liberty cap, and the Marseillaise—were more powerful referents than individuals.[108] As long as American states were governed by generally republican institutions, they were all sister republics, even if some were behind others on the road to modernity.[109] For example, by 1856 Bilbao saw Colombia as best representing "all the great conquests of the modern spirit."[110] Cuba and Brazil stood as anomalies, although American republicans hoped that each would soon join the sister republics' ranks. During the French Intervention, some Mexicans argued that after defeating their invaders, they should extend the fight against imperialism and Europe by removing the Spanish from Cuba and Puerto Rico.[111] Colombian politicians actively debated direct involvement in support of Cuban patriot rebels, and in 1871 the government of Cauca State reported that some citizens had departed for Cuba to join the rebellion.[112] Under the headline "Progress," one Mexican paper welcomed rumors of republican revolts in Brazil, "wishing the insurgents the best of luck."[113] Haiti now also tended to stand apart, signifying now mostly a race war instead of a republic.[114] At times some would remember Haiti's brave struggle against France, but the country was mostly forgotten and effaced from the fraternity of republics.[115] Of course, the United States remained a problem. We have already discussed the country's wavering commitment to the ideal of sister republics. Bilbao and others feared the unbridled individualism in the United States (decades before José Enrique Rodó published *Ariel*), its filibustering imperialism, its retention of slavery, and its racism against blacks and Indians.[116] However, in general, American republicans still looked on the United States as "the first Republic."[117] Yet essentially the United States was no different than other republics: a universal fraternity of man should unite all Americans. After the French invasion, El *Independiente* of Chile (in an article circulated in Mexico), argued against the European-imposed idea that the "Latin race" should be opposed to "the Anglo-Saxon race," which had only been developed to justify the French invasion. Instead of embracing "latinism," the New World should adopt "the American sentiment" and "the fraternity of all peoples."[118] As we will explore later, the championing of *hispanismo* and a Latin identity was not only a project of emancipation from gringo imperialism, but also a Conservative effort tied to European imperialism and the promotion of whiteness and a Europeanized cultural vision of civilization.

In Europe it was the new nations, yearning for statehood, that garnered the most sympathies. Latin Americans celebrated certain nations—Italy, Poland, Ireland, Greece, and Hungary—as representing transnational republican fraternity in contrast to the older empires that oppressed them.[119] Poland was an eternal victim of retrograde, monarchical repression and thus worthy of republican sympathy.[120] In the face of the French invasion, a Mexican paper declared that "our cause is that of unhappy Poland," which, like Mexico, faced attack from "barbarous enemies."[121] Italy was the great hope, a seed of American liberty that would sprout in European monarchies' decrepit pleasure garden. Popayán's *La Unión* declared that Italy would become the "sentinel of American rights, stationed at the gates of European monarchies."[122] Cali's *El Caucano*, which regularly fulminated against European cupidity and barbarism, declared: "When we speak of the Old World, we do not speak of you, young Italy! You are the America of Europe."[123]

Countering Italy, Ireland, Poland, Greece, and Hungary were the despotic trio of Russia, the Habsburg Empire ("the prison keeper of nations"), and the formerly tyrannical but now largely impotent Spain.[124] For Bilbao, the oppressor states included Russia, Austria, Prussia, and—after the invasion of Mexico—France.[125] Russia occupied the zenith of despotism in the American imagination. Even more conservative and Eurocentric papers such as Cuba's *Diario de la Marina* could employ czarist Russia as a metaphor for the most barbaric oppression and Poland as its most suffering victim, if at other times the czar was celebrated as the most enlightened of rulers.[126] The Atlantic world was widely enough imagined to be employed in speeches to soldiers. In an oration to celebrate the entry of Republican troops in Querétaro in 1867, for example, Juan de Dios Burgos compared the victory to an imagined Poland, rising from its oppression to confront the despotic czar.[127]

England and France (at least until its Mexican adventure) held more contradictory places, neither unqualified heroes nor villains. Bilbao saw England as deserving praise for its liberty at home but condemnation for its tyrannical foreign policy.[128] England was clearly prosperous and had a long tradition of rights; wealthier Liberals also found appealing its strong property laws and limited democracy—which, although perhaps unacceptable by American standards, surpassed that of most of Europe.[129] Celebrated for its enterprise and tradition of rights, England was still a monarchy and colonial power.[130] A paper from Durango warned that Ireland and India would "imitate one day Mexican heroism" and revolt against England.[131]

France was even more problematic than England. France was seen as having a glorious republican history, and though it was now obscured by fools and pretenders such as Napoleon III, there was always the hope that the French people would awaken from their slumber and throw off the monarchical yoke.[132] American republicans fondly recalled the glories of French revolutionary triumph, appropriating French symbols for their own ends.[133] In 1850 the Democratic Society marched through the streets of Cali, "singing their Marseillaise."[134] The French fascinated Americans for having decapitated their monarch, but many realized that this republicanism had not endured and that France had returned again and again to despotic rule.[135] Although modern historians often categorize caudillos as a particularly Latin American problem, nineteenth-century Spanish Americans thought of it as a more universal contagion, one that plagued Europe equally—for example, in the case of Napoleon and his pretenders.[136] However, while the French had killed one king, América had ensured the death of kingship: "If America has not decapitated kings, it has decapitated monarchies."[137]

Early in his career, Bilbao had thought the French the origin and epitome of modernity, but his time in Europe and the rise of Napoleon III, along with the maturation of his own thought, soured Bilbao on Paris.[138] Bilbao claimed that although France was the "initiating nation" on the path of liberty, it had soon stumbled; except for a few months, the French "have never practiced liberty."[139] After the French Intervention, such condemnations became the norm. Mexicans celebrated the French revolutionary past but lamented that the country of the Marseillaise, Victor Hugo, and regicide was now the land of despotism, the clergy, imperialism, and rule by a petty despot. Although once France had led the way on the path to modernity, its people now could do nothing more but "cry for their lost liberty."[140] While many Spanish Americans acknowledged Europe's, and especially France's, past achievements in republicanism and rights, they noted that such movements had long since failed on the far side of the Atlantic.

Spain, due to its weakness, was not generally seen as a villain because of its current actions, but it was blamed by Americans for the colonial past. Bilbao castigated Spain for the legion of difficulties the Americas faced: "With Spain came Catholicism, monarchy, feudalism, the Inquisition, isolation, silence, depravity, the genius of exterminating intolerance and the culture of blind obedience."[141] In short, "Spain is the Middle Ages. We are the future."[142] Escobar y Armendáriz declared in a speech that with the coming of Cortés "the slavery of our fathers began."[143] In general, Spain's significance lay in its past actions, not in its rather sad present state. Although Bilbao harshly condemned Spanish colonialism, he simply mocked contemporary Spain for its despotism and backwardness.[144]

American republicanism had less interest in Asia and Africa. If considered at all, such peoples were seen either as victims of European oppression, deserving sympathy, or—following a long-standing European tradition— as the subjects of despotic states, outside the flow of history.[145] The great struggle centered around the Atlantic basin, pitting America against Europe; but a large part of the eastern Atlantic, Africa, seemed forgotten. However, as we saw in the last chapter, many Spanish Americans did condemn European imperialism in Africa and Asia. Bilbao argued that European despots engaged in imperialism to distract their populaces from oppression at home.[146] Although mainly concerned with the Americas, he also condemned European imperialism in Rome, India, China, and Algeria.[147] In speeches, other orators also excoriated European aggression in Asia and Africa, especially in China and Algeria.[148] However, American republicanism embraced its own version of Orientalism, casting China and especially the Ottoman Empire as autocratic and backward regimes, doomed to fade as history progressed.[149] Curiously, the Orient also figured as simply part and parcel of the Old World. Thus, in contrast to Said's study, Europe and the East merged as retrograde.[150] After Maximilian's execution, when Mexicans mocked the intense mourning in Europe's courts, they took delight in noting how "the sultan of Constantinople is heartbroken over Maximilian's sad end."[151] In general, the globe's nations were arrayed in a vast struggle of liberty, republicanism, and modernity against despotism, monarchy, and retrogression. European powers were oppressors: of their own people, of those subject nations yearning for independence, of their remaining and new colonies.

Of course, famous and infamous individuals strode the historical stage, as themselves but also as symbols and proxies in the Atlantic arena. After the assassination of the Mexican Liberal Melchor Ocampo by Leonardo Márquez, Ocampo's comrades quickly presented his murder not only as an event in Mexican history, but as part of the centuries-long struggle between the partisans of progressive republicanism and their Conservative enemies. This "Conservative Party" had murdered Ocampo just as it had Socrates, Jesus of Nazareth, and Savonarola and, more locally, Hidalgo, Guerrero, and Morelos. Thus the classical world, the biblical world, and the modern world formed a singular chain of meaning, sites of a long struggle that had found a new theater in Mexico. The list of villains included many religious figures and institutions, led by the Inquisition and many popes and stretching from Herod to Ignacio de Loyola. Joining them were such Europeans as Philip II of Spain, Charles IX of France, and various Austrian potentates. The list also included figures from New World history, such as Cortés (the vilification of Cortés began long before twentieth-century *indigenismo*) and the general and viceroy of New Spain, Félix María Calleja del Rey. Finally, such nefarious men were joined by the contemporary Mexicans who continued the struggle against liberty and equality, such as Alamán and the assassin Márquez.[152] At such moments as Ocampo's martyrdom, these names of heroes and villains would be drawn up in great lists, in which the living and dead, the classical philosopher and contemporary politician, the European and American were placed side by side as part of a millennium-long battle spanning the Atlantic world that was culminating in the nineteenth century.

Certain villains constantly reappeared in this discourse, luminaries whom American republicans loved to hate. Spanish American scoundrels included Argentina's false federalist and demagogue Rosas, Paraguay's López, Venezuela's Monagas family, Ecuador's Flores, Chile's O'Higgins and Bulnes, and Mexico's Iturbide and Santa Anna.[153] Some, including Bilbao, even saw Bolívar as having betrayed the masses in his quest for political order and condemned him for his autocratic, Napoleonic tendencies (although, of course, he remained the Liberator for others).[154] Brazil and its emperors were the Latin American exception, condemned for both their continued embrace of slavery and of monarchy.[155] Concerning North America, filibusters, especially the notorious William Walker, were decidedly villains, promoting a European-style imperialism and racism while violating American republican fraternity.[156] Although most European kings and emperors, from Nero to Louis XIV, and many popes, especially Pius IX, earned condemnation, a few figures enjoyed special prominence.[157] Of course, after the French Intervention, partisans of American republicanism across the New World universally scorned Maximilian.[158] His patron, Napoleon III, became a figure not just of hatred, but also of mockery—"the pygmy."[159]

American republicanism celebrated a pantheon of heroes as well, drawing connections across time and space. Bilbao could celebrate two seemingly distant figures in a single phrase: "Túpac Amaru and Washington initiated the torrent" of rebellion that engendered independence.[160] The association of an Andean leader of indigenous revolt and a U.S. Founding Father might seem strange to present-day readers, but for Bilbao they were allies in the struggle for American liberty. In general, Jefferson and Washington represented the best of the North American republican experiment.[161] Ranking with these North Americans were Spanish American heroes of independence, especially Miguel Hidalgo y Costilla in Mexico.[162] After the defeat of the French, Juárez emerged as a major emblem of American republicanism: as one Mexican noted, "Juárez, independence, liberty and democracy are, for us, the same thing."[163] From Spanish Democrats in Europe to Unionists in the United States and Liberals in Bogotá, Atlantic republicans celebrated Juárez as having joined with "the immortals, Washington and Lincoln," as champions of liberty.[164]

Yet American republicanism's most powerful symbol was not American by birth, but nonetheless tightly linked to the American continents: Giuseppe Garibaldi. While other Europeans, such as Kossuth, Mazzini, and Castelar, were also viewed as fraternal democrats, none sparked the fires of the mind as did Garibaldi.[165] Bilbao called Garibaldi "the embodiment of the spirit of universal democracy."[166] In 1859 R. M. Arana, a Liberal partisan, wrote to the president of Cauca State, Tomás Mosquera, promising local support for Mosquera's planned rebellion against the Conservative government. Arana claimed that his followers "possess an Italian soul" and that Mosquera would be "our Garibaldi," leading them from triumph to triumph, "carrying liberty to the oppressed pueblos."[167] In 1863, as Mexico prepared to battle the French, the Junta Patriótica of Mexico City named "José Garibaldi" as its honorary president.[168] During the French Intervention, *La Chinaca* equated the Mexican struggle against foreign domination and a retrograde clergy with that of Garibaldi.[169] Indeed, Garibaldi's anticlericalism, if not as central to his appeal as his republicanism, had a wide approval.[170] He was frequently written about in American newspapers—at least one of which bore his name—that eagerly followed his campaigns for liberty against papal and imperial power until his death in 1882.[171] Garibaldi stood as a hero for struggling against "the Austrian yoke" that condemned his brothers to "slavery," in the context of an Atlantic world in which his former American compatriots had already succeeded in this fight against aristocracy and imperial power.[172]

While Garibaldi's legend loomed over the Americas, it was of particular import in Uruguay. Montevideanos remembered him as "the great democrat of the century" whose loss was felt by the entire world—he was a "universal" hero.[173] After his death in 1882, there were four days of mourning in Montevideo, with funeral services, parades, the closure of public offices, cannonades, and numerous other tributes to the man "who in both worlds had fought for the cause of liberty."[174] An orator at his funeral service asserted: "Garibaldi was in modern times the most austere and tireless apostle of the Universal Republic." He was a saint in "the cult of democracy."[175] Angel Floro Costa denounced those who claimed Garibaldi as mainly Ital-

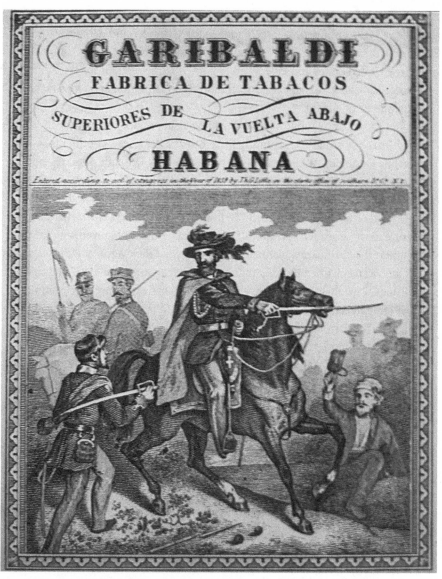

FIG 5.2. Tobacco label featuring Giuseppe Garibaldi on horseback, 1859. Library of Congress, Print and Photograph Division, Tobacco Label Collection, LOT 10618–15.

ian: "Garibaldi is a Oriental citizen" (Uruguay is also known as la República Oriental). Moreover, just as Uruguay owed much to Garibaldi, Garibaldi owed much to New World, "where his spirit received the poetic education of liberty." Garibaldi had first heard in Montevideo the "magic eloquence" that he used to inspire Italians.[176] However, for Conservatives, Garibaldi was a

SMOKING TOBACCO

MANUFACTURED BY

C. ELIAS, Agent,

No. 58 JOHN STREET, N. Y.

FIG 5.3. Tobacco label featuring Giuseppe Garibaldi in a red shirt, 1864. Library of Congress, Print and Photograph Division, Tobacco Label Collection, LOT 10618–15.

villain: anticlerical, a pirate, an anarchist.[177] At his death, the bishop of Montevideo took revenge, denying permission to hold honorary funeral services in the cathedral.[178] Perhaps fittingly, this slap engendered new demands for the separation of church and state in Uruguay, in the hope that the Church's "insipid and retrograde fanaticism" would be destroyed by "the incessant progress of ideas."[179]

Across the Americas, Garibaldi had become the symbol of American republican modernity. There is no irony in a European filling this role, for in spite of the rancorous rhetoric contrasting America and Europe, most committed republicans saw the struggle against monarchy as uniting peoples around the Atlantic, physically embodied by the Hero of Two Worlds. Despite Garibaldi's begrudging acquiescence to monarchy in Europe, in the Americas he remained a champion of the "republican idea."[180] Not surprisingly, the Garibaldi of the American imagination was a much purer, uncompromised champion of the republic, liberty, and equality than the complex real man and politician. Long after the power of radical republican ideas had faded in Latin America, when Joseph Conrad created his old Garibaldino as an isolated expatriate, seeing no connection between his struggle and local affairs, Garibaldi's memory would still linger among real Latin Americans.[181] Soldiers in a federalist revolt in southern Brazil took the name Legión Garibaldina in 1893.[182] Garibaldi's grandson fought in the Mexican Revolution.[183] The photographer and activist Tina Modotti worked for the Giuseppe Garibaldi Anti-Fascist Alliance in the early 1940s after her return to Mexico.[184] Avenues and squares and statues across the Americas bear his name, from Buenos Aires's Garibaldi Street to his monument in Washington Square Park in New York City. These echoes remind us that although largely erased from historical memory, American republican modernity's remnants still bear witness to the powerful emancipatory struggle of a previous age, and they may not be as lost as those opposing a liberating universalism might wish.

CHAPTER 6

David Peña and Black Liberalism

After the death of David Peña in 1878, thousands of Caleños gathered to mourn the man who had provided a living link between the elite leadership of the Colombian Liberal Party and its popular followers. Peña was a teacher, librarian, newspaper essayist, soldier, politician, and public official, but he was perhaps best known for his bravery on the battlefield and his inspiring oratory in local Democratic Societies, where he preached the gospel of liberty, equality, and fraternity. He also had skin darker than that of those Europeans and North Americans who were increasingly employing modern science to fetishize the value of whiteness. While in the North Atlantic world race was increasingly becoming a marker of modernity, Peña's career illustrates the possibilities opened up by American republican modernity in Spanish America. Peña, most likely of some African descent and certainly famous as a representative of Afro-Colombians, embodied what we might call "black liberalism." This tight connection in Spanish America between Liberals and people of African descent was so obvious in the nineteenth century that Joseph Conrad employed it as a key feature in Nostromo.[1] Peña fought with both rifle and pen throughout his life to realize the promises of democratic republicanism that Liberals espoused. His career and words reveal the challenge—however incomplete—that American republican modernity posed to racial hierarchy's hegemony.

American republican modernity placed at least a rhetorical value on racial universalism. For many, especially Indians, this was a double-edged sword, promising equality but only at the cost of dispossessing communities from their racially defined culture, local governance, and communal land rights. For others, especially those of African descent, universalism promised possibilities of liberty and equality never before experienced in the Americas. Peña's life, and the commitment of thousands of Afro–Latin Americans to defend liberalism and universalism across the hemisphere, demonstrates the power of this often ignored or derided rhetoric. In Latin America—as in the English Atlantic world of the eighteenth, but not the nineteenth, century—race was a powerful force, although it was overcome at certain moments to unite citizens in a universal project of liberty and equality.[2] Since such a project had faded so memorably and devastatingly in the North Atlantic, the assumption has been that it did not exist elsewhere. Yet Afro–Latin Americans' triumphs in abolishing slavery and securing citizenship speak eloquently of the importance of American republican modernity. Conversely, the repression and marginalization that would accompany Western modernity's scientific racism reveal race's centrality in the project to debilitate the vitality of republicanism and citizenship for Latin America's lower classes.

An Armed Citizen in Defense of Liberty

David Peña was born in 1826 to Nicolás Peña and María de Jesús Bustamente in the town of Cali, in the Cauca region of southwestern Colombia. Peña's family lived modestly, but independently, due to their production of liquors.[3] The young Peña managed to secure an education at the Colegio de Santa Librada. Interested in both classical and scientific knowledge, he would eventually obtain a professorship, often teaching mathematics.[4] As a student, he also developed the oratorical skills that would serve him so well throughout his life.[5] Peña would always struggle financially, but wealth alone, or lack thereof, was not the only difference between him and most of Colombia's powerful. A Conservative detractor, Pedro José Piedrahíta, in a private letter to the powerful politician Tomás Mosquera, described Peña as "belonging to the African race, he is a *mulato claro*." Piedrahíta conflated his racial description of Peña with other supposed character flaws; he mocked Peña as an intellectual dilettante, morally weak, an atheist, and from a questionable family, claiming his father had died of insanity. However, even an elite enemy such as Piedrahíta admitted that Peña had an enviable library (due to Cali's "modern booksellers") and enjoyed an impressive, even frightening, ability to inspire the masses with his passion and eloquence.[6] Belisario Zamorano, Peña's Liberal colleague and contemporary biographer, painted a much different picture; Peña was a brilliant polymath, intensely courageous, eloquent, charitable, and selfless. Zamorano was too much of a republican to ever mention Peña's race directly, but he made allusions to Africa in his sketch of Peña.[7] Whether Peña actually had ancestors from Africa is of much less importance than the reality that many thought he did and that he became the most vibrant leader of southwestern Colombia's black and *mulato* popular liberals. Peña may or may not have been black, but he certainly embodied a popular liberalism, which—with its focus on radical liberty and social equality and its appeal to many Afro-Colombians—became synonymous with blackness.

Peña's public life began in 1851 when he enlisted, at the lowest rank, in the Liberal army that was defending the government from a Conservative rebellion. Conservatives had revolted to seize power, but also to protest the Liberals' abolition of slavery; Peña joined those, including many former slaves, who fought to prevent the return of the chain and whip.[8] Colombia's recurring civil wars provided ample opportunity for those willing to defend their cause in battle. Peña quickly climbed through the ranks, fighting in 1854 for the Constitutionalists, if with severe reservations, and joining the 1860 rebellion against Conservative rule with the rank of sergeant major.[9] By the end of the war, in 1862, his meteoric rise culminated with the rank of general.[10] His ascent was not without controversy. Peña was notorious for fraternizing with his men, taking meals with them, discussing the meanings of republican thought with them, and calling his troops "armed citizens in defense of liberty."[11] In 1861, during the siege of Bogota, he was arrested for intoxication and insulting a superior officer. However, when Liberals faced entrenched Conservative forces barricaded in the San Diego church, they released Peña, who rewarded their faith by storming the building. Mosquera, the former Conservative who was now leader of the rebellion against Conservative rule, immediately bestowed on Peña a battlefield promotion to the rank of colonel.[12] In 1865 Peña helped lead a mission to Panama in an attempt to overthrow the Conservative government there.[13] The mission ended poorly, and Peña was arrested and put in jail in Cali. However, a Conservative rebellion necessitated that the state release him so that he could once again rouse the people to the Liberals' defense.[14] More than once, military service allowed Peña to escape punishment. He would use his bravery and eloquence to propel himself to the top of the Cauca region's political society. It took him only a decade to become a respected and much feared general; he ascended the political ranks equally quickly, although he never rose quite so high there. He served on Cali's town council, as municipal judge, and as Jefe Municipal of Palmira and Cali. He was elected to the State Constitutional Convention, to the National Congress, and to the State Legislature numerous times, even serving as president of the legislature. After the 1876–77 war, Peña was considered as influential in regional politics as Colombian President Julián Trujillo.[15]

Peña drew his power not through the traditional channels of patron-client relations but because so many of Cali's lower classes saw him as a loyal representative of their interests. He enjoyed enviable success in recruiting volunteers to follow him in war.[16] Caudillos are often imagined as conscripting peons by force, or as using their economic power to coerce military service. In contrast, Peña's success resulted from convincing his followers that he represented them both ideologically and in the halls of republican government.[17] Peña was able to establish such a deep connection with his followers, as well as to understand their visions, due to his leadership of Cali's Democratic Society, in which Afro-Colombians made up a large portion of the membership.[18] As one Conservative commented, "The blacks are those who make up the Democratic Societies of Buga, Palmira and Cali."[19] Some scholars assume that Latin America's associational democratic culture was heavily segregated, but this was not always the case in Colombia, where universalism held much weight.[20] These Democratic Societies also gave Peña a potent body of organized and armed men that he could lead when politics turned to war, as it so often did in Colombia.[21] In the societies' meetings, Peña established a shared discourse of popular republicanism and secured a power base. During the 1876–77 civil war, a newspaper noted that "Cali's battalions, five in all, are the Democratic Societies in arms and they bring to the battle not only their physical force, but the profound conviction and courage obtained from the voices of passionate orators during the club's tumultuous weekly meetings."[22]

Peña, a professor, certainly saw the Democratic Societies as a way to educate the masses. An 1850 petition signed by Peña and over three hundred members of Cali's Democratic Society requested further aid for popular education, noting this was a duty of a "republican government." Such education would prevent the success of those who "always have abused the pueblo's ignorance." Primary education would create "useful citizens" for the nation out of "that poor majority" whose members "are unjustly called ignorant, barbarous and corrupt."[23] In an 1867 report on education, Peña warned that progress was not inevitable and people could fall "under the weight of new chains," if they were not educated in their rights and duties.[24] Certainly, men such as Peña saw themselves as leading the poor. They might still share elitist notions of a cultured civilization defined by education, but they rejected the exclusivity of such notions, presuming that the poor could participate in the republican project of modernity. However, although Peña imagined himself a leader and tutor of the lower classes, his status among Cali's subalterns was not due to a unilateral leadership but to a sustained mutual relationship in which Peña regularly responded to the poor's demands.

Peña made his career by championing the practical application of liberty, equality, and fraternity. In general, he believed in a radical equality and was the avowed enemy of any "social hierarchy" that was not based strictly on merit.[25] In addition to the all-important question of land rights, he regularly supported lower-class concerns, arguing for expanded public education, free access to water for poor barrios, the right of the poor to distill and sell cane liquor (in the face of official monopolies or high taxes), access to suffrage, and lower taxes on the cockfighting pit where the Democratic Society would meet.[26] As we saw in chapter 4, it was Peña, as president of Cali's Democratic Society, who demanded that the state president revoke a law taxing cane liquor, in the name of the free and sovereign pueblo.[27] Peña explicitly warned his Liberal colleagues that if they did not respect the popular will, the pueblo would abandon them and perhaps join the Conservative Party.[28]

In the Cauca River Valley, dominated by massive haciendas, questions of land ownership obsessed the imagination of the landless poor. Peña, in the press, as head of various Democratic Societies, and as a state official, regularly promoted popular access to land. As Palmira's Jefe Municipal, he supported the local Democratic Society in its attempts to allow the poor access to common lands to gather wood and to resist local hacendados' efforts to enclose such lands as private property.[29] Peña's vision of citizenship and the nation reflected not European classical liberalism but instead a popular liberalism (which scholars of nineteenth-century nation formation have traced).[30] He did not imagine just a liberalism of atomistic economic actors, but a popular republicanism whose members were united as a community in defense of political and social rights. In 1863, after his success in the civil war, he coauthored a reply to an article criticizing the disorder in the Cauca Valley. The solution to disorder could be found by aligning economic and social rights with political rights: "We would like the liberty and independence of the individual complemented with the recognition of their right to the land." Peña argued that the poor would not defend the nation (and the Liberal Party) simply because of grand but abstract ideas: "What interest in the nation can someone have who does not have a secure home for himself or for his children?" He questioned: "What good are rights that do not protect you against the avarice of the propertied on whose lands you live and exercise your labor?" The poor had to either submit to the capriciousness of landlords or die of hunger: "either of these choices is a death." He demanded that laws favoring landlords be reformed. While certainly the poor had fought for liberal ideas, they also had sacrificed so much to improve their lives. Peña closed his missive by demanding that republicanism serve the poor, echoing the calls we saw in chapter 4: "The pueblo . . . has the perfect right to be protected against usurpation and iniquity."[31]

Peña's steadfast support of expanded rights and a radical vision of democratic republicanism earned him a loyal following in Cali and its environs. In 1859, as State President Tomás Mosquera plotted a revolt against the Conservative national government, over 750 Caleños wrote to Mosquera, urging him to appoint Peña as provincial governor. The petitioners praised Peña's intelligence, loyalty, and popularity with the people, describing him as a supporter of "ideas of progress and social well-being." Finally, the petitioners promised Mosquera: "We will accompany him [Peña] in danger and when you, Citizen Governor, need the residents of Cali Province, you will find more than two thousand soldiers resolved to sacrifice themselves in defense of the state."[32] Mosquera named Peña an alternate provincial governor, causing Mosquera's old Conservative allies to decry the appointment of a man supported by the Democratic Societies, the hero of "ignorant" and "stupid" masses.[33] Similarly, in 1877 the Democratic Societies of Vijes, Yumbo, and Cali (whose petition boasted over 450 signatories) wrote to urge Peña's appointment to the post of Jefe Municipal, describing him as a teacher, a great solider, and a "democrat" who enjoyed the "voluntary collaboration of the citizens."[34] After Peña's installation in office, Cali's Democratic Society thanked the state president, noting that Peña would enjoy tremendous support since he was such a "loyal servant of the popular cause."[35] Cali's residents in 1859 had described Peña as a promoter of "progress" and social betterment, which they and he clearly saw not as a capital-oriented modernity of order but as a republican utopia of independent and equal yeomen.[36]

The 1876–77 civil war was the culmination of Peña's career. Conservatives in the Cauca and neighboring Antioquia rebelled against the Liberal government once again, this time with a focus on religion: they claimed that the Liberals' support of secular public education would destroy Colombian society. And once again, Peña, with his fellows in the Democratic Societies, took up arms to defend the Liberal Party. Peña fought in numerous battles, including the critical engagement at Los Chancos that ensured the Liberals' triumph. However, for his enemies, it was the 1876 sacking of Cali that defined Peña and his followers as dangerous agents of chaos, black barbarians defiling civilization's temples. Conservatives had initiated the battle for Cali. The lines of combat had moved well to the north when Conservatives remaining behind secretly rose up and seized Cali. Conservatives also attacked Peña's wife, Dolores Carvajal de Peña, during their coup.[37] When news reached Liberal forces, Peña raced back from the northern front lines, gathering two thousand men along the way—considered an astounding feat in such a short period of time.[38] Peña, after attempting to parlay, stormed the city with his volunteer army, routing the enemy forces. His troops then proceeded to loot Conservative property and attack and insult prominent Conservatives. Conservative commentators explicitly blamed Peña for the sack of Cali, claiming that he had promised his soldiers "four hours of slaughter and three days of looting." One contemporary claimed that Peña actively participated in the orgy of looting and violence, decrying how he had charged into the San Pedro church on horseback, gunning down the Conservative rebels cowering in the confessionals inside.[39] Another reported three hundred bodies in the streets, with more inside of homes, writing that "Peña could not contain his people."[40]

The sack of Cali became a lens that magnified and distorted race. Conservatives saw it as the opening of the inevitable race war that the rise of men like Peña foreordained. The grandee Manuel María Mosquera described the sack as "a bloody catastrophe," committed by "multitudes of blacks and mulatos armed with Remingtons, screaming 'down with the godos' [Conservatives]."[41] These same mobs would later call on Peña to run for state president, which Mosquera thought was the prelude to a "race war," with uprisings of the "African race" in the hot country and "the Indians" in the uplands. However, Mosquera also fretted that even the "white people are showing a spirit of communism," which was first manifested as a disregard for social rules but would soon mean the redistribution of property.[42] For all of his hysterical racism, Mosquera sensed the growing demand for equality, moving from social to material, that the soldiers thought defined democracy. These twin obsessions—elite Conservatives' mania that the racially degenerate poor would seize their property in the name of democracy and popular liberals' demands that true democracy necessitated social equality and economic justice—would push many elites, both Conservative and Liberal, to abandon American republican modernity in favor of a civilization defined by whiteness, order, and capitalist economic development.

Conservatives had perceptively observed that subalterns were requesting that democratic republicanism's promises be fulfilled. In return for their service during the war, Cali's poor now demanded a revolution in land rights in the Cauca Valley. Just as Peña had made his career through military service, subalterns regularly cited their sacrifices in war as justification for both political demands, especially citizenship, and more concrete economic demands. Cali's popular liberal soldiers partook of this long tradition in an extraordinary petition they crafted after the 1876–77 civil war, a document on which, after the club's officers, Peña's name appears first among the signatories of Cali's Democratic Society. They demanded, as a reward for all the blood they had shed, the abolition of all land rents, the "perfect right" to settle on any uncultivated land and claim it as their own, and the right to gather wood and other forest products throughout the state. The soldiers questioned if as "citizens" they would enjoy both social as well as political rights.[43] These men had fought in a grueling civil war, inspired by the oratory of American republican modernity. The elite and middle-class producers of this oratory may have never intended to challenge private property rights, but they had constantly elevated political rights over economic concerns. The poor simply understood the logic of such rhetoric better than the politicians and essayists who had preached it. Cali's soldiers now demanded that republicanism be made meaningful to them. Hearing rumors that he might be assassinated, more than a hundred of Peña's followers accompanied him on a trip to Popayán to meet with the state president, where they hoped to ask for land seized from Conservative hacendados during the war.[44] Peña himself wrote the proposed law that, had it been enacted, would have profoundly altered capitalist development in the Cauca Valley (although it was still not nearly as radical as the Democratic Society's proposal). His law exempted the poor from paying any land rents for five years and allowed those without land to farm—also without rent for five years—up to three hectares of any uncultivated land in haciendas' vast reserves.[45] Peña sought to make real the liberty and equality that his soldiers had fought and died for, even at the expense of capitalist modernity.

Peña succeeded in having the old rents owed by soldiers on their leased properties forgiven for the duration of the war, but the Cauca's elites united to defeat his expansive land law. Conservatives and many Liberals with less popular sensibilities had long hated Peña.[46] Peña frightened many elite Liberals, who tracked his movements from as far away as Boyacá. In 1867 Manuel Vernaza wrote from Cali that Peña was once again stirring up trouble in the Democratic Society among "those who do not want work" with his "soaring speeches."[47] The 1877 direct attacks on property rights and the rule of the hacienda only confirmed the antipathy of these Liberals and Conservatives to Peña: one Caucano described Peña's land bill as "disguised communism."[48] A legislative commission to study the law was more careful, given that the Democratic Societies had saved the Liberal Party from a Conservative triumph, but still urged the law's defeat, arguing that it would destroy the right to property while accustoming the poor to assert their own rights to land ownership.[49] Moderates and Conservatives denounced Peña for his solicitude for the lower classes, urging that he be removed from power and his followers punished—a demand that prefigured the alliance of Conservatives and Independent Liberals (a order-and-progress-oriented Liberal Party faction) that would lead to Colombia's Regeneration (see chapter 7).[50] The law was not enacted, and its failure (as well as the demands it represented) marked the end of American republican modernity's dominance in not just the Cauca region, but in Colombia as whole. Peña and his popular liberal allies had demanded that economic property rights be set aside in favor of fostering a political modernity of equal citizens. The united elites who defeated the law would transform the language of modernity in the Colombian public sphere over the next decade, so that economic modernity would not suffer from democratic demands.

After the law's failure, Peña was under immense pressure to restrain his allies.[51] However, Peña—by then on his deathbed—sent a telegram to the Liberal state president, urging him to maintain a "sacred respect for popular rights" and the "democratic Republic."[52] He continually urged his party to imagine a different, better world than one limited by capital's exigencies—a world defined around the rights of citizens. Zamorano explicitly linked Peña's career with the pursuit of political modernity, noting that Peña came of age when the Cauca was dominated by immense haciendas that acted as "feudal castles, where in spite of being in the middle of the nineteenth century, they wielded the tyranny of the middle ages."[53] One of his last acts in office was to warn a Caleño not to enclose and fence off some land that belonged to the city as commons.[54] Peña championed a democratic modernity over a retrograde, feudal past until his very end.

David Peña died on 26 May 1878. Between three thousand and six thousand "citizens" gathered to mourn his passing.[55] Even the editors of El Ferrocarril, a newspaper devoted to economic development and hostile to popular demands, noted that they had never seen so many people gather for a funeral. The paper eulogized Peña as "always concerned with the fate of the poor."[56] Our sensibilities urge a cynical detachment from historical figures such as Peña, and we tend to look for such easily understandable motivations as power and greed. Yet Peña lived and died a man of modest means, so poor that the city paid for his funeral; his children soon requested payment of their dead father's pension from the state, describing themselves as hungry, sick, and "sunk in misery."[57] Zamorano added the Peñas had always lived modestly, refusing to employ servants and citing the Bible: "The mother of God never had maids."[58] More eloquent yet are Peña's own words and deeds, and the determination he inspired in his followers to imagine a present and future defined by democratic republicanism and a popular vision of liberty, equality, and fraternity. American republican modernity is an analytical description I invented to make sense of the past. Yet the ideas behind it—of a political and social equality that would create a better future—were very real to Peña and his fellow citizens in the Democratic Societies. For Peña these ideas were not abstractions but organizing dreams for which he lived and died.

Black Liberals and the Particular Appeal of Universalism

The debate over Peña's "race" only obscures that in the nineteenth century, in a very real sense, his physical appearance did not matter. For Colombian Conservatives, Peña represented the blackness of the Liberal Party, a party that represented the interests of blacks and mulatos, regardless of whether or not he was of any African descent. For radical Liberals, race did not matter or even exist, given the commitment to universalism that many Afro-Colombians also eagerly embraced. As we saw in the introduction, and as scholars like Marixa Lasso and Reid Andrews have shown, Afro–Latin Americans across Spanish America eagerly embraced racial equality after independence.[59] From the wars of independence onward, a strong bond developed between Afro-Americans and Liberal parties.

In Peña's Colombia, the Liberal Party made a concerted and coordinated effort to recruit Afro-Colombians as allies, trading policies of abolition, racial equality, and expanded citizenship rights for votes and volunteer soldiers. By the 1860s this bond was so well established that Conservatives regularly referred to Liberal armies, and even the party itself, as black, although of course the membership was multiracial. Conservatives contemptuously derided Liberal armies as "composed of blacks, zambos and mulatos, assassins and thieves of the Cauca Valley" or as "ferocious gangs of blacks."[60] A Conservative paper warned in 1861 that if Tomás Mosquera won the civil war, Bogota would be invaded by "an army of blacks, half-naked with ferocious visages," to sack the houses of Liberals and Conservatives alike.[61] Liberals only won elections, according to their critics, thanks to "black votes."[62] The Conservative Manuel González averred that his party could triumph over "the blacks and all who call themselves Liberals."[63] A member of the powerful Arboleda family described the Liberal legislature as a "crowd of blacks," even if almost all of the representatives were white.[64] By the late 1870s not just Conservatives, but also their Independent Liberal allies (who were wary of popular democracy), were referring to Liberal troops as "bands of armed blacks."[65]

If not quite to the same extent as in midcentury Colombia, in 1840s Uruguay a close relation existed among liberalism, republicanism, and blackness. During the abolitionary fervor of 1842, a newspaper argued that former slaves should be able to denounce masters who did not allow them to join the National Guard and fight for their freedom. By fighting, the freed slaves would gain "the honor of enlisting in the ranks of their comrades, in order to immortalize themselves, just like all those *morenos* and *pardos* [blacks and browns, roughly, or simply people of African descent] who fought with such admirable valor in the Wars of Independence achieved immortality."[66] While later erased from memory, in the mid-nineteenth century Liberals knew that Afro-Latin Americans had played an irreplaceable role in securing independence.

Across the Americas, Conservative forces often denigrated Liberal leaders as blacks or *mulatos*, as we saw earlier in Uruguay. The Conservative paper *La Sociedad* joked that Benito Juárez would take the part of "El Negro Sensible" in an upcoming play.[67] Even in Mexico, with its much smaller Afro–Latin American population, the association of blackness with liberalism existed, solidifying with support for the Liberal leader Juan Alvarez in the 1850s.[68] The liberal paper *La Chinaca* accused Conservatives of describing Liberal armies as nothing more than a "mob of *mulatos*."[69] In Mexico City, the pro-business English-language *Two Republics* reported a rumor in 1879 that Juárez and Sebastián Lerdo would rely on "North American troops, mostly negroes," to assist them in case of a rebellion.[70]

As we explored in an earlier chapter, antiracism and universalism were central, if often unfulfilled, tenets of American republican modernity. Scholars such as David Goldberg have long recognized how central race is to the project of European or Western modernity. In Goldberg's words: "This is a central paradox, the irony perhaps, of modernity: The more explicitly universal modernity's commitments, the more open it is to and the more determined it is by the likes of racial specificity and racist exclusivity."[71] He argues that "modernity comes increasingly to be defined by and through race."[72]

Race allows boundaries to be drawn, separating white, male, European, rational subjects from colonial others, separating those who could enjoy liberty and equality from those outside their reach.[73] Of course, Goldberg is correct for Europe, but he does not consider how modernity could be formulated elsewhere in reaction to this paradox. From the beginning of Mexico's and Colombia's struggle for independence, the caste system's destruction and the promotion of racial equality—pushed by soldiers and mulato leaders such as José Padilla, José María Morelos, and Vicente Guerrero—became crucial elements in the countries' political culture and eventually in the conception of modernity.[74] In an Independence Day speech in 1868, Manuel Merino celebrated Mexico's racial diversity, "the heterogeneous elements of races that the European politicians believe incapable of amalgamation and purification," while proclaiming that in the Americas there would eventually be a "fusion" of all races: "the day will come when these distinctions of caste will completely disappear."[75] La República even questioned the privileging of whiteness, mocking Maximilian for attempting to rule Mexico as the Spanish had before and for presuming that Mexicans would think the invading "whites were gods."[76] In the Americas, another writer noted, there was no difference between the blood of Charlemagne and Montezuma.[77] American republican modernity's proponents took great pride in their commitment to emancipation, racial equality, and universalism, which together formed the bedrock on which their relations with Afro-Americans rested. Carlos Gómez, governor of Cauca Province, argued that "true democracy" meant slavery's abolition and effective citizenship rights for former slaves.[78] When Francisco Bilbao defended American republics' accomplishments, the first item he listed was emancipation. Following this titanic achievement was the abolition of racial distinctions and inequality before the law.[79]

Universalism held great appeal to Afro–Latin Americans, who had an inherited colonial identity based on slavery and caste discrimination; this is not to say they did not have or value a particular cultural identity, but that they did not see this as incompatible with pursuing equality as citizens within the nation-state. They did not need, at least in Colombia, to demand a particular black citizenship.[80] Indians were much less sanguine about universalism's benefits, and with good reason. Indigenous identity—a legal, cultural, and racial construct from the colonial period—was explicitly nonuniversal. Indigenous people also suffered under the stigma of caste discrimination and a virulent racism, but unlike African identity, indigenous identity provided tangible, material benefits, especially rights of communal landholding and local self-governance. Those coveting indigenous lands, which were protected by communal ownership, used universalism and equality to argue that such local identities were incompatible with a modern, civilized nation. The residents of one Colombian town, hoping to divide nearby Indians' *resguardos* (communal lands), claimed that maintaining such lands violated the principle of equality, arguing that after independence laws had been passed demanding "that the Indians become citizens and property holders." The petitioners protested that the entire identity of "Indian" should disappear and that maintaining such an identity, and the customary rights of local governance and communal landholding, only kept Indians tied to the "post of barbarism." As long as indigenous peoples were legally "Indians," they would never "advance on the road to civilization."[81] Of course, in Mexico, elite Liberals' 1856 Ley Lerdo struck at the heart of indigenous landholding by ordering the disentailment of communal property, although popular liberal Indians created their own interpretations of the law.[82] As discussed in chapter 4, in a civilization defined by universal citizenship in the nation, many Liberals saw no place for the category of Indian.

In economic and political matters Liberals tended to promote the dissolution of indigenous identity as a legal category. However, rhetorically they had a more ambiguous relation to Indians, both promoting the indigenous past as part of an essential American identity while nonetheless condemning their actual contemporary Indian neighbors as backward and benighted, if settled, or as dangerous savages, if still at war with the state, as was the case in northern Mexico.[83] Liberals often embraced a mythic indigenous past, which had the added benefit of criticizing Spanish and European colonialism; the Peruvian Federico Flores celebrated the Inca as forerunners of American resistance to European oppression.[84] Higinio Muñoz orated that the Aztecs had been a "civilized people, who cultivated the arts," were "governed by good institutions," and enjoyed their "liberty" until degraded by the "long night" of Spanish colonialism.[85] Some Liberals sought to establish closer relations with Indians, arguing that "indigenous blood runs in our veins" and again blaming Spanish colonialism for Indians' poverty (a result of colonial landholding traditions), religiosity, and laziness.[86] Indians themselves, although often defending communal landholdings from the colonial era, would still condemn the Conquest. Indians from the village of Coconuco, Colombia, declared that "the conquest was most usurping, most cruel, most barbarous." However, they expected better of the nations that had newly become independent.[87]

Liberals seemed to want to expand their conception of universalism to include Indians, but only if Indians abandoned their culture, legal prerogatives, and traditions. During the French Intervention, a liberal paper castigated Indians for their laziness and religiosity but declared they could redeem themselves in defense of the *patria* and, by doing so, could be included in the nation: "The warriors will turn into citizens."[88] The appeal reveals Liberals' immense condescension toward Indians and shows that even while promoting universalism, Liberals pointedly excluded Indians, unless they earned their way into the citizen body. The intense contradictions of liberalism and republicanism could often be papered over, but the issue of race and culture forced the issue time and again. Less so in Colombia but especially in Mexico, many indigenous peoples eagerly embraced the emancipatory possibilities of liberalism and citizenship in the nation, aided by American republican modernity's political culture. Indians forged their own popular republicanism—focused on the fraternity of their villages, local independence and liberty, equitable and just access to landholding, and equality within the nation—while maintaining an indigenous identity, rights, and privileges.[89] For Liberals, the disconnect between universalism, Indian identity, and classical liberal individualism was an untenable position that many would resolve by rejecting universalism and inclusive citizenship under Western modernity, a stance much more compatible with liberalism, if less so with republicanism. Indeed, in the same issue of Chihuahua's *La Alianza de la Frontera* that celebrated the universalism of humanity—"we are all brothers"—and Mexico's leading role in promoting "the fraternity of the human race," the editors compared their Conservative enemies to "barbarous Indians."[90]

Modernity, Race, Democracy

Eric Hobsbawm notes that before the spread of electoral democracy in late nineteenth-century Europe, it was very easy for large states to ignore minority peoples.[91] In Spanish America, I argue that the existence of democracy (not just electoral) forced many states to wrestle with the inclusion of their Afro-American and indigenous peoples, if often in an incomplete and halting fashion. The reason this inclusionary struggle has not been obvious is the general dismissal of nineteenth-century Spanish American democracy. For contemporary observers, both elite and plebian, the problems and opportunities of democracy were very real, as were the consequences for national inclusion. A wave of studies of nation and state formation have shown how subalterns, including people of indigenous and African ancestry, appropriated the nation and used democratic and republican political cultures to bargain for social, political, and economic rights—even if they did so unevenly and distinctly throughout Spanish America. In Colombia, Afro–Latin Americans were very successful in using the Liberal Party to advance their own interests. Black liberalism was, of course, not confined to Colombia. Andrews's *Afro-Latin America* shows the breadth of Afro–Latin Americans' political engagement in both civil wars and electoral contests to secure abolition, citizenship rights, social respect, and economic resources.[92] In (at least) Colombia, Cuba, Brazil, Uruguay, Venezuela, Ecuador, Peru, and Mexico, Afro–Latin Americans supported popular liberal or republican movements (as, of course, did African Americans in the United States).[93] Meanwhile, elite Liberals, with a commitment to a modernity marked by racial equality and even a denial of race's existence, abandoned to a remarkable degree liberalism's historic tendency for exclusion. In Mexico, Indians—needing to embrace universalism's emancipatory possibility while resisting its destruction of local identities—faced a tougher path but still found ways to bargain with the nation-state.

Universalism is easily condemned for its totalizing principles that seek to subdue minorities and those less powerful to a homogeneous narrative of progress. However, in the nineteenth century, universalism was also a powerful tool of emancipation that could be seized to challenge racism and imperialism, as well as to make the nation and citizenship more inclusive. Latin American universalism also imagined a modernity that challenged a Eurocentric civilization based on racial subordination.[94] Latin America was universalism's greatest champion, despite Anglophone historians' insistence on U.S. exceptionalism.[95] Likewise, nineteenth-century democracy is easily mocked for its corruption and collapse into civil wars, but the necessity of rallying popular support to a political movement afforded subalterns extensive opportunities. The collapse of American republican modernity's commitment to universalism and of democracy late in the century would make the links between democratic republicanism, race, and effective citizenship obvious. David Peña's life and his championing of Cali's racially mixed lower classes demonstrate the possibilities of a democratic republicanism not totally limited by white racial privilege. His death in 1877 occurred at a moment when the commitment to both democracy and universalism in Mexico and Colombia would begin to waver and fail, when American republican modernity's political promise would cede pride of place to visions of civilization explicitly white, European, and premised on limited citizenship.

CHAPTER 7

The Collapse of American Republican Modernity

A s Justo Sierra surveyed the Porfirio Díaz regime's transformative accomplishments at the turn of the century, he employed what had already become a clichéd metaphor for progress: the locomotive. In defending his patron from charges of kowtowing to foreigners, Sierra argued that Díaz had realized that Mexico must "hook itself to the powerful Yankee locomotive and set off to the future."[1] In a phrase, Sierra captured the new vision of modernity that had come to dominate the public sphere by the 1880s. Industry, economy, and technology defined civilization now, and modernity's locus was no longer in Latin America but in the United States and Europe. For Sierra, modernity was the U.S. economy, which he envisioned as the preeminent symbol of technological and economic progress, and Mexicans must accede to capital's demand for order or be reduced to the status of barbarians, waiting to be absorbed by greater powers. American republican modernity had assumed that political liberties would lead to economic progress. However, by the 1870s this promise seemed to have failed. Indeed, some began to argue that the political modernity of democratic republicanism, including the disorder and popular demands that expanded citizenship often entailed, hindered economic growth. In 1884 La Libertad criticized old attempts to create a model democracy in Mexico: "The disrepute of the old revolutionary utopias increases daily. Those who still pursue an unrealizable democracy fight with arms whose point has been broken by the iron-plated armor of reality. The worn-out hot air of speeches that could seduce in a moment the gullible now does not exercise any sway over people's feelings."[2] This rhetoric was not accidental. Reality was now iron-plated, the undeniable advance of industry in the North Atlantic. Spanish Americans' proud claims to have achieved modernity were now dismissed as nothing but hot air that dissipated in the face of the economic, military, and scientific power of a new entity: the West.

Western industrial modernity, as I call it, had eclipsed American republican modernity by the 1880s in both Mexico and Colombia, but in the 1870s the two mentalités still vied with one another for supremacy.[3] American republican modernity's collapse coincided with the rise of elite political projects to remake both Mexico's and Colombia's political cultures. At times both projects were called the Regeneration, but the one in Mexico was more commonly called the Porfiriato.[4] Mexico's Porfiriato began formally with Porfirio Díaz's seizure of power in 1876; he would rule as president until 1911, save for the interregnum of 1880–84. The beginning of Colombia's Regeneration might be marked in 1880 with the election of the Independent Liberal Rafael Núñez, who was president in 1880–82, 1884–86, and 1887–88 (and was elected again in 1892, although he left his vice president in charge). However, in many ways both projects began earlier. Many of Díaz's and Núñez's preoccupations were shared by Sebastián Lerdo (president of Mexico in 1872–76) and Julián Trujillo (president of Colombia in 1878–80), both of whom promoted efforts to restrict popular influence on the state and public sphere. Liberals disenchanted with the promises of American republican modernity initiated both projects of regeneration (the Porfiriato was more successful). These regenerators made peace with the Church and Conservatives (and adopted many of their policies), hoped to foster peace and order, sought to inculcate economic development, and wanted to attract foreign capital. Critically, via constitutional reform, outright electoral fraud, and increased state power, both programs weakened democratic republicanism and restricted popular political participation.

Sierra, followed by most historians, would argue that Mexico's Regeneration began with Benito Juárez after the French Intervention.[5] Certainly, in many ways it did, as both Juárez and especially Lerdo moved from emphasizing a popular republicanism to preferring a more classically elite liberalism. Juárez, Lerdo, and Díaz all shared with the conservative monarchical project a desire to strengthen the Mexican state.[6] Although historians have rightly noted the continuities between the Restored Republic and the Porfiriato, especially regarding economics, the divide in terms of visions of modernity is large and stark.[7] The shifting of the dominant vision of modernity in the public sphere away from American republicanism did not gather force until Díaz seized power in Mexico and a rift erupted in Colombia between radical Liberals and their Independent Liberal foes, who would eventually ally themselves with Conservatives. As shown in chapter 5, American republican modernity's opponents had long promoted their own visions of modernity, continually challenging American republicanism. The Mexican and Colombian Regenerations absorbed and repackaged many of the conservative visions of civilization and modernity that had vied, unsuccessfully, with republican visions after midcentury.[8] By the 1880s, elite letrado visions, older conservative notions, and new ideas coming from the North Atlantic would coalesce into a recognizable Western industrial modernity.

Western industrial modernity's triumph displaced yet again the locus and meaning of modernity. As we did with our analysis of American republican modernity in chapter 4, here we will explore how Latin Americans imagined modernity: its geography, its essential defining characteristics, its conceptions of the nation and state power, and its relation to subalterns. We will first examine the reimagination of modernity's center and periphery. While Americans, both North and South, had previously thought themselves the cradle of modernity and envisioned Europe as increasingly backward, after 1880 they turned to Europe for their visions of social progress.[9] Spanish Americans often reacted to the ascension of the United States by embracing a Hispanophile culture, rejecting the republican fraternity of earlier years. The elevation of the North Atlantic, combined with hispanismo (the celebration and promotion of Spanish culture as defining Latin American cultural and spiritual life) and powerful ideas of scientific racism, worked to debilitate American republicanism's antiracist and universal politics. Second, we will turn to modernity's new meanings, increasingly defined by industrial, technological, and scientific accomplishments, often presided over by a newly empowered imperial state. Latin America seemed to be lagging behind in this race to civilization and could hope to catch up only by imitating the North. However, this focus on economic progress directly clashed with the rich but chaotic political life celebrated by American republicanism. Therefore, third, we must consider how obtaining Western modernity necessitated a restructuring of state power under the projects of Regeneration in both Mexico and Colombia. For economic development to happen and for Western capital to be attracted in order to work its modernizing magic, order must be paramount, even at the cost of political liberties. Fourth, this institutional transformation impelled a concomitant evaluation of the meanings of democracy, state, and nation. The desire for democracy and a nation of citizens evaporated due to the necessity of creating a more powerful state, which would couple Spanish America's faltering economies to the locomotive of Western industrial capitalism. Fifth, for subalterns, this would be a decisive shift. Instead of being citizens in a republic, whose freedoms defined modernity, they would become workers for capital, at best a tool for economic progress and at worst an anarchic threat whose political demands undermined civilization. Finally, we will review subalterns' response, which vacillated between defending cherished republican citizenship and adapting to the new regime's economic rhetoric.

To Imitate the Civilized World

Latin America would cease to be the vanguard of the future. Once again, Spanish Americans would turn their eyes outward in search of the path to civilization. The 1870s was a time of transition in the competition among various discourses of modernity, but in that decade Europe began to reclaim its old place as the center of the Atlantic world, and the United States emerged as essentially different from Latin America instead of a sister republic with a shared destiny, due to its "colossal industry, its extensive commerce and its marvelous prosperity."[10] By the 1880s American republican modernity's boundless confidence was waning fast. In 1884 El Siglo Diez y Nueve surveyed Mexican history and lamented the long struggle "to enter fully on the road of progress."[11] The paper thought that Mexico was now on that path under Díaz, but more telling is the rewriting of the previous decades, erasing Mexico's political triumphs and vanguardism and its confidence in its own indigenous modernity, while casting Mexico as a failure, only now beginning to compete in the race to civilization. Although some were optimistic about Mexico's movement on the path to progress, a new pessimism about modernity had solidified. An anonymous contributor to La Libertad argued that humanity progressed with "distressing slowness" and many setbacks.[12] José Gaibrois, editor of the new Colombia Ilustrada, surveyed the state of "the modern age," arguing that "the inexorable law of progress" would touch even the most remote parts of the globe. His paper would cover science, art, and industry, the last being the most important, but never politics: "it will remain dead to questions of this class." Industry and science now defined modernity, not questions of rights and citizenship. This, of course, strongly affected Colombia's place in the race to be modern: "The Republic of Colombia . . . certainly cannot boast anymore of marching at the vanguard of its sisters in Hispanic America, concerning the distinct aspects of material progress."[13] Gaibrois's memory was not quite accurate: Colombia had boasted of being at the vanguard not of Hispanic America, but of the whole world. Now that material progress had replaced political progress, Colombia was no longer in the lead but struggling to catch up.

Modernity had not arrived in Mexico or Colombia; instead, it was something to be strived for, something occurring in distant lands, something always just out of reach. El Porvenir Nacional celebrated Díaz's upcoming electoral victory in 1884 by opining that it would lead to further material gains and secure the future for a Mexico "eager to fully enter the current of progress."[14] El Pabellón Nacional praised Díaz's 1887 speech to Congress, sure that true prosperity and modernity awaited "in a future not far away."[15] A theatergoer complained about the poor seating in Mexico City, noting that the capital's ambitions "demand that its theaters be as modern as possible."[16] Modernity seemed within reach, but clearly the yardstick no longer was internal but belonged to the North Atlantic. As Mexico City's La República surveyed Mexico in 1890, it remarked with satisfaction how far the country had advanced in a little over a decade (the timing, of course, coincided with Díaz's ascension). Mexico now enjoyed railroads, telegraphs, electric lights, and "all the other modern inventions," and "the mercantile and industrial activity visibly grows." Mexico now advanced along the "path of progress," following the North Atlantic's more powerful economies.[17] In spite of the paper's economic boosterism, the locus of modernity had clearly shifted. Even if many across Spanish America were confident in the bright future that electric lights, railroads, and international commerce would bring, this technology would now be imported from elsewhere. La República examined the state of both railroads and urban trolleys and noted that although Mexico was currently behind in trolleys, it was sure to adopt, "with time, all that is useful, great and modern that in other countries already has been conquered."[18] Observers could be optimistic that Mexico would one day enjoy modernity, but they had no doubts that Mexico was pursuing a future that had already arrived elsewhere.[19]

Once again, as under Europhile modernity, civilization equaled imitation. Cali's El Ferrocarril baldly stated that Colombia's maladies were due to the long history of accustoming the pueblo to life in the armed camps during civil wars: "We must break this custom, abandon old habits, and imitate the civilized world." The paper warned that although Colombians were consumed with being a "heroic pueblo," this did not even slightly impress foreign powers.[20] Past political accomplishments no longer mattered; indeed, they inhibited progress, which could be obtained only by aping Europe and the United States. In 1889 Bogota's El Heraldo also readily acknowledged civilization's foreign locus. Discussing the project to link Bogota to the sea by railroad, the paper cited geographers who noted that Colombia's capital should be on the coast, like Venezuela's: "Venezuela is in greater contact with the civilized countries and enjoys more plentiful commerce" than we do. The paper accepted this reality but argued that "progress will arrive one day to those rocky peaks," with the railroad's arrival.[21] Modernity, understood as commerce and technological prowess, might one day come, but that day had not yet dawned in Bogota. Mexico City's La Libertad could casually state that "Europe is the cradle of science and civilization," claiming both a new locus and definition of modernity.[22]

La Libertad opined that the Liberal Party had made a great error by isolating the country internationally after Maximilian's empire. Such isolation could lead only to "a simply vegetative existence, without aspirations of progress." If Mexico wanted to participate in "the benefits of civilization," then it must not separate itself from "the civilized countries." Otherwise, Mexico risked being treated like a "savage," as had happened to Asian and African societies. The paper applauded Presidents Díaz and Manuel González for restoring diplomatic relations with Europe.[23] In this vision, Europe again possessed the civilizing gaze, and only by its recognition could Mexico be brought, as a junior member, into the family of nations, instead of being judged a savage and condemned to imperial conquest, as had happened in Africa and Asia. In the course of two decades, Mexico had gone from being the leading voice in condemning imperialism as barbaric to accepting the rules of the imperial powers for determining modernity.

As opposed to under Europhile modernity, imitation alone could no longer instigate industrial modernity. Capital was essential. In 1888 El Porvenir de México expressed dissatisfaction with Díaz for his arbitrariness and personalistic rule and for "having bastardized democratic institutions." However, in spite of all this, the paper's editor stated that although he might prefer a better government, he would settle for Díaz's, because of the foreign press's admiration for Mexico, due to the country's improved financial situation.[24] Thus, although lack of democracy was a problem, it paled next to foreigners' judgment, a judgment largely based on the security of and opportunities for capital. By the turn of the century, Sierra could state unequivocally that progress was due to foreign influence assimilated into Mexican life; Mexico had to look to the United States as its "perpetual reference" to measure its level of modernity.[25] The journalist and politician Francisco Cosmes declared that Mexico should not imitate the United States politically, as political culture varied among peoples, but it should do so economically, since economic laws were "based on immutable nature."[26] A political universalism of sister republics and fraternal citizens no longer existed; now only the laws of capital transcended nation-states.

Europeans would increasingly be the judge of this modernity. Bogota's *El Taller* commented on the shame felt by Colombian travelers in Europe, "the embarrassment for the anarchy that we have reached due to the excesses of a misunderstood liberty."[27] *La República*, using the most delicate language so as not to offend its readers' sensibilities, demanded that the police act to stop the poor from using the streets as a toilet, in full view of decent, moral residents. Worse, the editors imagined that "a foreigner who views these deeds could not help but think a capital, in which such attacks on morality are still committed, very crude."[28] The civilizing gaze now bore down on Mexico, and the public sphere feared its judgment. Similarly, Bogota's *El Correo Nacional* applauded the removal of beggars from the city's streets, claiming that with so many mendicants, Bogota made a poor impression on foreign travelers.[29] Foreign expatriates' judgments of Latin America's civilization took on critical importance, though they had only been mocked before.

Even more critical was the impression that traveling Mexicans and Colombians made in modernity's undisputed heartland, the North Atlantic. *El Pabellón Nacional* expressed fury with a young Mexican who had staged a show in New York called "Aztec Fair and Mexican Village," which had women making tortillas, tamales, and chocolates; a shrine to the Virgin of Guadalupe; and a band with dancers. There were also panoramas, "ugly vistas" of Mexico—the only one that met the paper's approval was of the Veracruz railroad. The paper fulminated that the spectacle was an insult to Mexico's new industriousness.[30] *El Pabellón Nacional*'s screed reflected the deep-seated fear of the foreign gaze: would Mexico be seen as a place of industry, and thus judged to be civilized and modern, or would it be seen as a premodern and semibarbarous curiosity, an other of lazy markets, dancers, exotic peoples, and vistas submitted for imperial enjoyment?

As Mauricio Tenorio-Trillo has argued, the nineteenth century's universal exhibitions were the definitive markers of societies' achievements in the race to civilization.[31] In Mexico, exhibitions like that of New Orleans in 1884 were celebrated as a "modern invention, and truly one of the most beautiful that civilization offers."[32] However, Mexicans approached the exhibitions with much trepidation; under Western industrial modernity, the ruling elites knew their society's level of civilization could easily be found wanting. El Siglo Diez y Nueve questioned whether Mexico should even participate in Belgium's universal exhibition, unless the resources to guarantee a good showing in the world's eyes could be ensured.[33] The powerful Catholic prelate Eulogio Guillow praised President Díaz on his birthday for his attention to Mexico's participation in the New Orleans Universal Exhibition. Guillow cast Mexico, however, almost as an anthropological exhibit, as the other that would submit to foreigners' gaze, allowing "the study of our culture, the peculiar habits of our Indians and the immense elements of natural wealth stored in our land."[34] Not to participate, however, was to acknowledge defeat. El Heraldo lamented that Colombia had been unable to contribute to any of the Parisian exhibitions: "We always have been so poor, and so involved in our lamentable internal affairs, that we have not been able to even think about taking part in those contests of civilization."[35] The exhibitions were both the measure of modernity and pathway to modernity, particularly because exhibiting might entice foreign capital, with its salubrious effects.[36] El Heraldo urged Colombia to participate in the 1892 Washington Exposition, as that would encourage "foreign capitalists" to invest.[37]

Although state builders and capitalists courted foreign investment, they also faced the increased threat of another critical aspect of Western modernity: states' ability to exert their imperial presence across the globe. The Europe to which Latin America turned for lessons in modernity was certainly not that of the 1848 French Revolution; instead, it was increasingly militaristic and racist and had renewed imperial ambitions. In the public sphere, admiration of imperial state power—the ability of states to project force—became more common.[38] For letrados, this had long been the case. Juan Bautista Alberdi claimed that the use of power was not a sign of barbarism, since no one would call France barbaric for conquering Africa.[39] Of course, across the Americas, accusing France of barbarism for its imperialism had been a staple of the public sphere under American republican modernity. There was also a strong sense that nothing could stop an imperial modernity of world commerce; not pirates or bandits or recalcitrant states, such as China, could stop trade: "All civilized nations understand this."[40] In 1900, La Gaceta Comercial celebrated U.S. and European imperial efforts to force open the China market, which had resulted in "the entrance of the civilization and commerce of the West" into the Orient.[41] The Spanish-born Anselmo de la Portilla, who had moved to Mexico in 1840, played a part in redefining imperialism in the public sphere and promoting the hispanismo that would reject North American imperialism while often embracing Spanish imperialism. Writing about the land of his birth, he noted that Spain had made great progress of late in improving its agriculture, industry, navy, infrastructure, and commerce (all hallmarks of Western modernity, of course). De la Portilla focused on one marker of progress, however: Spain's ability to crush rebellion in colonial Cuba: "Of the things that most palpably demonstrate its [Spain's] vitality and wealth of resources is the facility with which it annually sends twelve or fifteen thousand men across the ocean to the island of Cuba."[42] Thus imperialism, especially as it revealed state power, became a sign not of barbarous force but of the force of modernity.

U.S. imperialism played both the suspected role in this process (as an encourager of export capitalism, a model of neocolonial ideologies, a promoter of scientific racism, and an example of a new vision of modernity) and, perhaps, an unexpected one as well.[43] Late in the nineteenth century, anti-imperial rhetoric replaced the ideology of sister republics that had shaped thinking on U.S.–Latin American relations for much of the century. However, this anti-imperial rhetoric did not always benefit democracy or the working class. Mexican state builders used U.S. imperial designs as justifications for the necessity to construct a stronger state. One paper argued that while after the U.S invasion of 1846 the United States and Mexico had been friendly sister republics, this was no longer possible given increased U.S. aggression. Indeed, the need to defend themselves against a possible U.S. intervention made democracy and republicanism unaffordable luxuries: "We have to make the national territory not a theater of democracy, but an armed camp." Under Juárez, republicanism had been seen as providing the moral force necessary to defeat an imperial enemy, but "at the head of our government we do not need today men of the toga, but, rather, soldiers, like the current President."[44] The prestige of republicanism had withered. As we will see below, the rise of the state (and the dismissal of republicanism) was quite detrimental to the ability of the working class to appropriate the nation for its own ends.

Another reaction to the late nineteenth-century North Atlantic imperial offensive was *hispanismo*.[45] Since industry defined modernity, Latin American *letrados* and state builders acknowledged that their region was now behind in the race to civilization. However, although generally recognizing the North Atlantic's mastery of modernity, slavish imitation in all things would not have been palatable. *Letrados*, both Liberals and Conservatives, reacted to the North Atlantic's dominance by asserting a new love of *hispanidad*, turning back to the Spain that their more radical Liberal predecessors had rejected as backward.[46] As Erika Pani notes, Liberals had often excoriated Spain, but many traditional sectors of society had long embraced Spain and Spanish culture.[47] The embrace of *hispanismo* by the upper and middle classes began to replace ideas of universalism (long rejected by Conservatives) in which Latin America had been a leader of a shared Atlantic republican tradition.[48] In 1860 the Conservative paper *La Sociedad* had imagined an international movement of "demagogic revolution," blaming Juárez (for his links to the United States) and the Italian unifiers for ignoring "the principle of nationalism, that had always been the first and most sacred principle." Both Giuseppe Garibaldi and Juárez wanted to topple the Church and see "established the empire of the scum of the earth over virtue, education, property and true patriotism."[49] *La Sociedad* spelled out clearly the link between nationalism, as a conservative, religious project, and the concomitant repression of the popular classes in order to protect property and the elite.

One of *hispanismo*'s most important promoters was the Colombian author and politician Miguel Antonio Caro. Caro urged an embrace of Spain, rejecting the denunciations of the Spanish conquest that were common in nineteenth-century essays. Caro's contemporaries did not have any illusions about *hispanismo*'s deeply conservative nature or the tight connection between what has been seen as a literary project and politics: "Mr. Caro is, in politics, in religion and in literature a type [best described] as conservative."[50] Although *hispanismo* is often seen as a cultural reaction to U.S. imperialism, its origins lay in political developments internal to Latin America. The Spaniard José Ramón Leal, writing in *El Siglo Diez y Nueve*, urged Mexico to embrace its Spanish past and even to adopt "a moderate monarchy" as in Spain to secure its future. He noted that Mexico and Spain were natural allies, as they shared "interests due to reasons of race, of family, of victories and defeats, of Christian names and surnames, of language and literature."[51] Of course, this summary established an alliance on the basis of high culture and Spanish blood, which many Mexicans could not claim. *Hispanismo* would be the cultural truss used to justify the banning, both literal and figurative, of Indians and Afro–Latin Americans from political, public life. *Hispanismo* also was linked to state power, as Colombian regenerators looked with nostalgia to colonial state and religious institutions, around which "civilization" had grown, especially in comparison to the weak state of the Liberal era.[52] Sierra certainly understood the elite nature of *hispanismo* and its ties to politics and economics. When he attended the Hispanic-American Congress in Barcelona in 1900 and wrote to Secretary of the Treasury José Yves Limantour about the gathering, he marveled over the company, composed of the best people "of literature, of politics, of the aristocracy of titles and money."[53] The other attendees greeted him warmly, sighing: "Oh, if only we had a Porfirio Díaz!"[54] *Hispanismo* was an elite project with deep roots in the conservative vision of society.

Hispanismo also sought to rewrite Mexican history, its proponents arguing that Mexicans should not celebrate independence on the anniversary of Hidalgo's Grito de Dolores, which represented anarchy and bloodshed, but instead on the date when Viceroy Juan O'Donojú abdicated. Thus a date that represented a movement of the pueblo (here reinterpreted as a civil war between Conservatives and those "demagogues" interested in looting) was replaced with a date that gave agency to a Spanish foreigner, excluded the pueblo, and signified a phase in the "evolution of human civilization" that had begun with the Spanish conquest.[55] De la Portilla sensed this shift in Mexican historiography, noting that even Liberals were reconsidering their vilification of Spain. He argued that the conquest was not nearly as brutal as it had been portrayed, noting that the U.S. Pilgrims acted just as the Conquistadors had, yet the Pilgrims were celebrated in the United States, while the Conquistadors were shunned in Mexico.[56] *Hispanismo* merged with Western modernity to once again insist that the origin of democracy lay not in the New World, but in the Latin countries (especially France) of the Old.[57] Although perhaps opposed to imperialism or the United States, *hispanismo* created a subject that was of European descent and culture.

Critiques of imperialism also reveal *hispanismo*'s conservative roots. *La Gaceta Comercial* might issue stinging indictments of British and U.S. imperialism, but this was not part of a general denunciation of imperialism, as had been common during the French Intervention. Instead, the paper celebrated Spanish colonialism, noting that Spanish American cities were "filled with true monuments of culture" and that New Spain had created "many rich and well-to-do Mexican families."[58] This idea that colonialism had produced wealth and high culture allowed the writer to ignore hunger in Mexico and the repression of Mexican laborers. What is missing in intellectual histories—like that of Jorge Cañizares-Esguerra for the colonial period—is the relation of abstract theories that celebrate Spain to the realities of what they justified or covered up on the ground: namely, the Porfiriato's violence.[59] *La Gaceta Comercial* closed by wishing that Spain and Mexico could control colonies, as "the facts prove that for extending civilization in the world, there is not in the modern age a race superior or even equal to ours."[60] Imperialism had previously been rejected as antidemocratic and antirepublican, but by the late nineteenth century it was a problem only if the wrong type of high culture—gringo greed versus Spanish munificence—possessed colonies.

Cuba's anticolonial rebellions (1868–78, 1879–80, and 1895–98) also revealed how imperial racism generated an internal racist, albeit national-ist, reaction in Latin America. During Cuba's first failed independence war (1868–78), loyalists openly warned that due to Cuba's racially mixed pop-ulation, the revolt could lead to "nothing but extermination."[61] The Liberal and pro-Díaz La República applauded the anti-insurgency campaign of Gen-eral Camilo de Polavieja in Cuba against "the bandits" who were commit-ting "acts of savagery."[62] La Gaceta Comercial lamented the support that some had shown for the Cuban patriots because such support was anti-Spanish: "We were working against our own race in Cuba, and, attacking here, as they have attacked, the Spanish element, we are also working against our-selves and our patria."[63] The paper mocked those who supported Cuba (and the United States) as thinking that "the ideal of liberty should be placed above all things."[64] Instead of criticizing Spain, Mexico needed to encour-age Spanish immigration in order to "strengthen our national character."[65] Thus we see the abandonment of any idea of sister republics, the rejection of liberty as a marker of civilization, and the embrace of racism. The paper lashed out at U.S. racism, for demanding Cubans prove themselves capable of government, celebrating the Spanish state's granting Cubans "Spanish citizenship." In critiques of imperialism so furious over humiliations to "our race," the reality that many Afro-Cubans had not enjoyed equal citizenship under Spain and that antiracism was a central part of the patriot struggle was elided.[66]

Imperialism abroad served both as a model for and to mitigate criticisms of internal imperialism at home. La Gaceta Comercial dismissed criticism of the conduct of the "Yaqui rebellion" by pointing out that this war—just a revolt of "half-civilized Indians"—was nothing like U.S. imperialism in the Philippines.[67] Colombia's Regenerators looked to France's imperial effort in Algiers—in which the Church, army, and colonial institutions worked together—to shape their own state-building efforts.[68] Mark Thurner notes that by the 1890s, Peruvians had accepted French imperialist justifications for colonialism as a "scientific discourse" (and indeed used them to justify internal colonial projects in the Amazon), although earlier in the century they had rejected such notions.[69] Of course, the U.S. imperial threat was real. Latin Americans' profound disappointment in the United States arose because U.S. actions had destroyed the hope for a community of sister re-publics in which nationalism would not reign supreme. Eric Hobsbawm, in contrasting revolutionary-democratic views of the nation versus nation-alist ones, described the latter as more focused on defining the nation by some sort of shared culture, language, and history and as marked by an emphasis on state power.[70] The new nationalism of the post-1880s Americas embraced these trends, emphasizing a shared culture (antigringo and pro-Spanish) and the efficacy of state power. Both of these trends worked to delegitimize and remove popular groups from the public sphere of national political life. The rise of the idea of the West, which tended to exclude Latin America, may have doomed American republicanism's universalism. However, Spanish American state builders also rejected universalism, eager to exclude subalterns from the political sphere. Hispanismo and anti–North Americanism have generally been seen as positive by historians and cultural theorists, representing the start of a search for an "authentic" identity and an end to imitating the United States or northern Europe (a view that also misreads Latin America's past imagination of itself as the vanguard).[71] However, hispanismo was also a cultural project that was conservative, antidemocratic, and procolonial (at least for Spanish colonialism) and one that had no place for uncivilized workers, Indians, or Afro–Latin Americans—indeed, its political project actively repressed them.[72] This ultranationalist response to U.S. imperialism did lead to gains in elite, letrado self-actualization, but at the expense of subaltern interests.

The most deleterious link between Western industrial modernity, patriotic nationalism, and hispanismo was the resurgence of racism and racial thinking, as American republican modernity's universalism fell to the wayside. Hispanismo's anti-African and anti-Indian racism combined, if at times uncomfortably, with the scientific racism that was gaining hegemony in the North Atlantic (and its celebration of Anglo-Saxons).[73] The powerful conservative letrado and politician Sergio Arboleda embraced scientific racism, classifying Colombia's races by the "facial angle" they exhibited, with blacks having more sloping foreheads.[74] El Pabellón Nacional was equally direct: "We have the two great vices of the Spanish race, vanity and arrogance, which united with the Aztec characteristic, laziness, forms a mixture that make us a pueblo of little vigor, hostile to labor, and therefore, a poor people in spite of our infinite elements of wealth." The paper attributed the wealth of the United States to its people's laboring habits. However, as was common during this period, the paper rejected scientific racism's harshest judgment and suggested that practical education might be the answer.[75] This vision of race tried to incorporate scientific racism—accepting the idea that races existed and that they had certain propensities—but still maintained an optimism that racial cultures could change. After all, elites worried that they too might be judged racially suspect by the North. A subscriber to La Gaceta Comerical—a loud proponent of hispanismo—wrote to protest an article in the paper, "Latinos y sajones," which the reader felt drew too prominent division between these two groups. According to the reader, "DECENT men across the world have understood one another and continue understanding one another, no matter what blood that runs through their veins." The subscriber then criticized those who would arm people who were not decent—as when the British armed the Zulus or allowed Indian attacks on the North American colonists.[76] The editors of the paper agreed, noting that even Juárez had rejected arming "barbarous Indians."[77] Hispanismo might question Anglos' racism, but it embraced its own rejection of Afro–Latin Americans and Indians as part of the nation, which it reserved for decent men of the right race and class.

Other elites, no longer limited by American republicanism's universalism and antiracist values, could more openly blame their societies' problems on Afro–Latin Americans and Indians. Colombian regenerators referred to their popular liberal opponents as "barbarous blacks."[78] Colombian President Núñez lamented the weakness of his nation, which had only three million inhabitants, "the majority hardly civilized."[79] Quibdó's El Atratense reviewed the state of the Pacific coastal region in 1880, taking special note of the area's racial composition. It dismissed the Indians as having no "political interests" and not consuming anything but what nature provided. Concerning "the black race," the paper lamented their fecundity and castigated them for being lazy, ignorant, and superstitious. However, if they could be made to work and forced to abandon their small plots of land, the paper believed that they might eventually live like "civilized man."[80] The paper argued that "the privileged class" was composed of "the white race," which in Colombia's northwest was a minority. However, this minority must direct society because it was the only class "that has intellectual life."[81] Conservatives and now even Liberals began to blame Colombia's problems on the character of its races.[82]

El Pabellón Nacional lamented the state of Mexico's three million Indians, denigrating them as ignorant, unproductive, lazy, uninterested in national life, and "more than living, only vegetating." The paper warned that they were a great drag on the country's progress, and a comparison with the United States proved that Mexico must "invigorate our nationality."[83] In 1894 El Estado de Guanajuato did not hesitate to cite "the race weakness" of Mexico's Indians to explain their conquest by Europeans.[84] Many still thought that the Indians could be reformed through education. However, for El Siglo Diez y Nueve the Indian problem was no longer that they might not be good citizens, but that they did not consume enough clothing and food, thus inhibiting Mexican industry. The paper proposed Foucauldian discipline administered by the priest, schoolteacher, and state and also, if necessary to make the Indians work, "perhaps a little violence, the restrained and paternal violence that fathers exercise over their children."[85]

As in earlier Liberal regimes, immigration seemed to be the answer, the only difference being that such plans were now more openly racist. Earlier proponents of immigration did not always link it to race, and some openly rejected claims that certain immigrants—French or Italian, for example—were better than others—such as Spanish or Canary Islanders.[86] By the 1880s race was more clearly linked to civilization. For El Heraldo in Colombia, due to European immigration, Argentina seemed to combine the best of "European civilization" with the material progress of the "Colossus of the North" and was making many advances in agriculture, commerce, and industry.[87] Leal lamented the state of Mexican laborers but assured his readers that Spanish immigrants would solve this problem.[88] Sierra was more blunt: Mexico must "attract the immigrant of European blood" to improve the race; otherwise, Mexico would move backward on the path to "civilization."[89] Racial thinking, lionizing the North Atlantic, and embracing a Spanish identity, only confirmed what had become dogma in the public sphere: modernity now existed elsewhere, in more northern, more industrial, and whiter climes.

The Urgent Necessity of Modern Life: Defining Modernity Anew

Spatially, modernity—once so powerfully imagined as eagles springing forth from the Americas to liberate Europe—had become transmogrified into a machine that was firmly located in the North, but whose rumblings would be felt around the world. Yet even more important than Latin Americans' ceding the vanguard to the West was the reconfigured meaning that modernity assumed in the public, political sphere. Instead of a political emphasis on democracy, republicanism, universalism, rights, and citizenship, Western industrial modernity championed production, trade, economics, technologies, scientific advances, order, patriotic nationalism, and military force. In short, the shift was from liberty to power.

The paramount measure of modernity was now industrial might. The Colombian Luis Umaña argued in 1888 that "one of a country's best measures of progress is, without a doubt, the greater or lesser development of industry." Without industry, nations "remain in their primitive and rudimentary state." Yet Umaña urged Colombia to develop its mining and agriculture, which could be broadly understood as industrial but was also clearly different than English or U.S. factories.[90] Thus, according to this vision not only was Colombia behind, but it also needed to enter into a neocolonial relation with modernity's true heartlands if it ever wanted to advance. In the Cauca, one regenerator wrote to Tomás Mosquera, the former president, that a railroad was the "way to civilize" the region.[91] The mantle of civilization that Colombia had ceded must be imported from elsewhere. Guanajuato's La Aurora warned that unless Mexico abandoned politics and dedicated itself to developing its commerce, agriculture, and industry, the country risked "disappearing from the list of civilized nations."[92]

Commerce, not abstract liberty, mattered now. El Cosmopolita praised Nicaragua for cultivating "modern ideas and principles," which included promoting industry, agriculture, commerce, respect for the law, and guarantees for foreigners.[93] In 1894 a paper could describe Díaz as "the personification of Peace, Order, Liberty and National Credit," thus elevating capital to the level of liberty.[94] Even in a small frontier town such as Lampazos de Naranjo, the latest technologies of banking and capital flows were understood as central to Western modernity's project.[95] Mixing hispanismo with commerce, La Gaceta Comercial welcomed Spanish shopkeepers to Mexico, as their industriousness and success would be a model for Mexican youth on how to succeed in "modern civilization."[96] Celebrating the New Orleans Universal Exhibition, La Libertad marveled at the commercial spirit of England, Scotland, the United States, and Australia, which through links of trade would "civilize the world."[97]

American republican modernity had rejected economic and technological power as the sole markers of modernity, but by the 1870s the obvious potency of the North Atlantic's economic growth could not be ignored. In 1878 a Colombian newspaper—significantly titled El Ferrocarril (The Railroad)—argued that "true civilization" was impossible without railroads and steamships.[98] Indeed, modern transport "brings riches and civilization."[99] Constitutions, rights, and republicanism no longer held center stage in descriptions of modern accomplishments but were pushed aside by railroads, telegraphs, and electric lights.[100] In Mexico modernity was now completely redefined around economic development: "The time has arrived to leave behind all other concerns in order to unite ourselves in a reciprocal and common interest, of relations of industry, contract and commerce, that is the urgent necessity of modern life."[101] Now politics would not create the conditions for economic progress; instead commerce would redefine Mexican political and social life: "That an economic revolution which changes completely our mode of individual and social life is coming is indisputable, and any efforts that are made to contain it will be in vain."[102] Nothing could stop the transformative locomotive of Western industrial progress.

Under Europhile modernity, industry had still borne the taint of vulgar strivers unconcerned with the lettered life of the city, but such concerns now bothered only the most effete letrados. Mexico City's El Cosmopolita argued that although people had previously believed that a dedication to industry degraded men, in "modern civilization," everyone agreed that industry and labor formed the "law of progress."[103] Capitalists, meanwhile, confidently adopted a language of material progress and "the future"—opposed to past economic stagnation.[104] Cotton producers on Mexico's Gulf Coast, requesting aid in adopting North American methods and machinery, claimed that by encouraging foreign immigration, attracting capital, putting fallow fields under production, and exporting cotton they were serving "the cause of civilization."[105] In 1902, Rafael Reyes, soon to be the president of Colombia, condensed the past century's struggles over modernity down to a transition from cultural to economic civilization, largely eliding the political interlude: "In times past it was the Cross or the Koran, the sword or the book that accomplished the conquests of civilization; today it is the powerful locomotive, flying over the shining rail, breathing like a volcano, that awakens peoples to progress, well-being, and liberty . . . and those who do not conform to that progress it crushes beneath its wheels."[106]

This power to destroy a society's sense of itself and its future sprang from the undeniable technological prowess of the United States and Europe. Papers such as Bogota's El Heraldo were filled with news of the latest technological and scientific marvels from the North Atlantic: French archeological work in Pompeii, new English maritime steam power, North American steelworks, Edison's electrical inventions, gas lighting in Paris, the electric chair in Sing Sing—with one mention of work on arsenic in Mexico.[107] Constant conflations of civilization and modernity with telegraphs, railroads, institutions of credit (itself a form of technology—Leal called it "the motor force of modern life"), steamships, canals, and dynamite abounded.[108] El Heraldo sadly commented in 1889 that Bogota did not have the "luxuries" of a "European city," lamenting how slow progress had been, due to the horrible political struggles of yore. However, the paper pointed to recent elements of growth, noting that although previously the only things the city could boast in terms of civilization were churches, the museum, the library, and the observatory, now it had a telephone network, an aqueduct, gas lines, and, of course, the railroad.[109] Politics was simply dismissed as a problem, and although older high-cultural markers of civilization were still something of

FIG 7.1. Masthead of El Siglo Diez y Nueve. El Siglo Diez y Nueve (Mexico City), 17 July 1875.

which to be proud, clearly technological and commercial development were what now defined a city as belonging to the civilized world. El Heraldo further opined that railroad entrepreneurs should be honored the way triumphant generals had been feted in previous years.[110] Similarly, Revista Telegráfica de México declared that instead of honoring its military heroes, Mexico should erect a statue to Juan de la Granja, who had introduced the telegraph locally. The paper noted that statues to Samuel Morse and André-Marie Ampère had been erected in New York and Lyon, concluding that, after all, telegraphs were the messengers of "modern society."[111] El Siglo Diez y Nueve's masthead from 1875 (see figure 7.1) emphasized the importance of technology (depicting telegraphs, railroads, and gears), commerce (a busy port and tobacco plants), and connections to the rest of the world (the globe).

A critical factor in reshaping the debate on technology and consumption in the public sphere was the changing nature and importance of newspaper advertisements. Ads had become more and more prominent as the nineteenth century progressed, both in their number and graphical elaboration; of even greater import were the types of goods and services advertised. As late as 1867, ads in Mexico City's El Globo had very few graphics and most ads were for luxury consumer goods—such as coaches, furniture, and clothing, many with no foreign reference—hotels, legal services, tobacco, medicine, literature, and education, with some for foreign manufactured goods such as sewing machines.[112] Less than a decade later, the graphical style of ads, the products advertised (the emergence of ads for large capital-intensive machinery) and especially the importance of their foreign provenance had certainly changed. On the last day of 1875, Mexico City's El Siglo Diez y Nueve's front and back pages contained ads for steam engines, gas works, printing presses (two competing firms) and ink, ironworks, furniture, adjustable chairs, lamps, windows, doors, carriages, tools, drills, hair dye, and oilcloths, all from companies based in New York. Other ads promoted ink from

Philadelphia, Smith and Wesson revolvers, Babcock fire extinguishers, Kearney's gout potion, Dr. Zed's codeine syrup from Paris, Dr. Humphry's homeopathic cures, and British dynamite. There were also railroad schedules and a mercantile company's offer to serve as an agent in New York for locals hoping to sell coffee, hides, chocolate, and rubber. The only cultural advertisements were for copies of Emilio Castelar's speeches, a book on business math, and a translation of Harriet Beecher Stowe. Aside from these books, almost nothing was of local provenance, except for a wine shop (no doubt selling imported wines), the Hotel Español in Puebla boasting a French and Spanish restaurant, another restaurant, and one local machine shop. The ads, many of which were at least partially in English, all boasted of fabulous goods from U.S. and British companies, built and imported from abroad, providing intricate details about the machinery.[113] The front page no longer bore political news, presenting instead images of a modernity that one could participate in via consumption but one that came from somewhere else, that represented itself proudly—even necessarily—as foreign.

The *Revista Telegráfica de México* reflected both the interest in technology and the sense that it was advancing faster elsewhere, that Mexico needed to rush to keep up with the latest inventions.[114] Mexico's success in establishing a telegraphic network, which the paper dated not to the introduction of the technology but to 1876 and Díaz's guarantees of order, also caused great optimism that Mexico could share the technology, and thus the modernity, of the "best nations of the globe."[115] However, it was clear who was imitating whom: a visitor to the national telegraph office in Mexico City "could think he were in a European office. There, everything breathes order, efficiency, activity and work."[116]

Technology, science, and industry were not just modernity's markers, they were also its agents. Sierra asserted that science was what led man to civilization.[117] The locomotive, above all, civilized the barbarous masses with its approach. When a short railroad line opened in Bogota, essayists were enraptured, one of them exclaiming that the train's whistle sounded "the first call to battle" in the quest for industrial progress.[118] El *Ferrocarril* argued that railroads would encourage commerce, agriculture, and foreign immigrants—which would improve society, as these new domestic and foreign businessmen, "being property holders and educated, will come to constitute one of the best elements of order." The paper smugly noted: "In this manner, pueblos become civilized."[119] For almost everyone, save perhaps Francisco Bilbao, railroads were a marker of modernity.

A sense of lagging behind, instead of marching at the vanguard, began

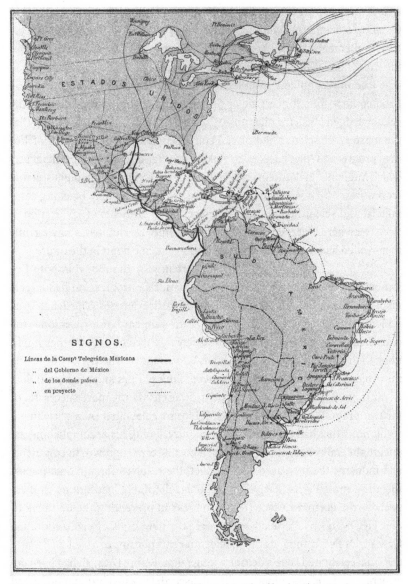

FIG 7.2. Map of American telegraph lines, 1889. *Revista Telegráfica de México* (Mexico City), 15 November 1889.

to permeate the public sphere. Mexico City's *La República* lamented that although hundreds of thousands of patents had been issued in the United States in the nineteenth century, Mexico could boast of but a few.[120] At the turn of the century, *La Gaceta Comercial* lashed out at Starr Jordan, a eugenicist and the president of Stanford University, for criticizing Mexico's inertia and lack of progress. However, the paper sought to prove Mexico's civilization by citing statistics showing that the country was importing more agricultural implements, books, geographic tools, and scientific instruments from the United States than was any other "Latin country." The paper demanded that Jordan recognize, "whether he wants to or not, the capacity of this Latin country for a high grade of progress and civilization."[121] Sierra sadly acknowledged Mexico's dilemma of scientific backwardness, asserting that the mastery of science had placed some peoples at the "vanguard of human progress." Others needed to "take advantage of every foreign element," which might not make them equal to those at the forefront but might still foster progress.[122] Thus, Mexico could prove its modernity only by citing commercial and scientific imports—the recognized elements of civilization—from elsewhere. But even this claim to modernity was limited, showing only that Mexico had the capacity for civilization at some point in the future.

Perhaps as early as the 1870s, and certainly by the 1880s, in both Colombia and Mexico the sense of Latin America's retrogression had largely displaced the optimism and confidence of earlier decades. The debate was no longer if Mexico or Colombia was at the vanguard of civilization—the consensus was "no"—but how each society might catch up, how they might hook their caboose to Western industry's locomotive. The answer would be the projects of Regeneration, designed to limit politics and promote industrialization. By 1900 Mexico's Porfiriato was clearly the more successful of the two programs. As early as 1888, El Progreso celebrated Díaz's "civilizing revolution" that had regenerated the country, listing his accomplishments: telegraphs, railroads, roads, bridges, a postal service, growth in commerce and industry, the increased state budget, the resolved foreign debt issues, the army (notably its discipline), schools, charitable institutions, and especially the Porfirian Peace (Díaz's success in preventing the outbreak of new civil wars).[123] These advances were the new signs of civilization. On New Year's Eve in 1900, as the nineteenth century came to an end, La Gaceta Comercial celebrated Díaz's decades-long reign. Before Díaz, all had been destruction and endless, bloody political discord. Díaz had brought order and peace, which had allowed industry to grow and, crucially, had attracted foreign capital. Due to Mexico's "noble and correct conduct," all nations of the globe esteemed the country.[124] Foreign respect and foreign capital were now earned by a disciplined comportment, not through democratic republicanism's political innovations. Western modernity's locus and meaning clearly lay elsewhere, but Mexico had found a place in this system, under the foreign capitalist's admiring gaze. We must now turn to how Mexico, and to a lesser extent Colombia, achieved this admiring foreign gaze (which a generation before would have been insulting to even consider) through a complete reorganization of political life, especially the working classes' role in the nation.

A Healthy Dictatorship: Regenerations

In both Mexico and Colombia the 1870s and 1880s witnessed projects of national regeneration. Liberals, upset with the radical or populist cast of elements of their parties, began both projects, allying themselves with their old Conservative enemies.[125] Both projects (and the protagonists in both societies certainly considered their efforts programs to remake society) sought to make their societies modern by linking their economies to those of the North Atlantic via exporting primary resources. The resulting earnings would allow the importation of machinery to modernize infrastructure and would create the capital for an eventual internal industrialization. Critically, to achieve this capitalist modernity required a transfiguration of political life, to create the order necessary for economic development and to attract nervous foreign capital. Order could be obtained, the regenerators imagined, only by both suppressing the idea of revolution as leading to modernity and institutionally (and discursively) removing upstart subalterns, and their constant demands, from the political system. Finally, a newly empowered state would act as the guarantor of order, operating independently of and above the troublesome democratic imagined community of the nation. For those who see modernity's rise as linked to that of the nation-state, the Latin American experience provides a corrective.[126] Modernity is tied not so much to the nation-state as it is to the nation and the state, distinct entities that are often in opposition. Although American republican modernity favored the nation, Western industrial modernity needed and fetishized the state.

While in Mexico this Regeneration would become synonymous with Porfirio Díaz, his *cientfficos* (technocratic advisors), and the rise of positivism, the tensions in liberalism between a procapitalist economic liberalism and a popular republicanism were long-standing—extending to Juárez's Restored Republic, but especially to Lerdo's presidency.[127] After the triumphs against the French, some Mexican Liberals began to reorient civilization's meaning from political to economic. The misnamed *El Amigo del Pueblo* declared that free trade was the best ensurer of "progress," without which "we would retrogress to a savage state."[128] A paper supporting Lerdo rather than more radical Liberals in 1871 warned that only Lerdo could prevent "the hydra of revolution" from destroying Mexico.[129] Revolution had changed from the seed from which modernity would sprout to the poison that would destroy it. (The "revolutionary hydra" was also used by the French to justify their intervention in Mexico only a few years earlier.)[130] We see the switch in the Guanajuatense paper El Aguijón, which in 1871 had followed a standard American republican line of optimism and political progress but in 1872 suddenly darkened its outlook, perhaps reflecting the broader changes in Liberal politics with Lerdo's ascension. The paper lamented recent uprisings and the lack of industrial progress, which threatened Mexico's very existence as an independent nation.[131] The paper that had boasted of Mexico's political potency now looked elsewhere for modernity:

> "What says God?" asked the people of Israel.
> "What says the telegraph?" asks modern pueblos.

The paper argued that "the domination of science"—here defined as physics, mechanics, chemistry, industry, and mathematics—was what marked a pueblo as "civilized."[132]

Industry must subsume revolution. In 1871 El Aguijón had mocked the French for their slavish monarchism and backwardness, but in 1872 the same paper approvingly translated an article from the French-language Mexican paper Trait d'Union. The Francophone paper hoped an upcoming universal exhibition would expose Mexico not to men of "the sabre and cannon, who only come to destroy and impoverish her," but to "peaceful and hard-working men who come to animate and enrich her, carrying with them the conquests of science, industry and arts."[133] Instead of exporting political modernity to France, Mexico now hoped to import economic and technological modernity from Europe. El Siglo Diez y Nueve declared that railroads, the "powerful element of civilization," would transform Mexico's "social, political, industrial and commercial organization." With the spread of commerce following the steam engine's tracks, "the agitated spirit of political contests will direct and apply its activity to other enterprises and labors."[134] Peace and order, necessary to inculcate work habits, mattered more than politics.[135] El Aguijón celebrated the increased commercial ties with the United States that railroads would foster; after all, the northern colossus would not invade if it risked destroying its own investments.[136] Previously, the United States and Mexico had shared a sense of being sister republics, which had supposedly—but not in fact—guaranteed peace; now commerce would prevent war. Indeed, the paper was quite perceptive; in coming decades the talk would be less of sister republics than of trading partners and foreign creditors.[137]

In Colombia regional movements presaged the formal, national Regeneration of Núñez. In the Cauca, Independent Liberals turned away from radical Liberals, eventually seizing local power in a coup in 1879. Their program focused on order and material progress—directly echoing the markers of Western modernity—achieved by disciplining an unruly pueblo. Cali's municipal president wrote to State President Ezequial Hurtado to celebrate his administration's efforts to create "a cultured and civilized nation," defined by "moral and material progress." The railroad then being constructed exemplified material progress, while moral progress—which involved education to remove "any thoughts of barbarism" from the pueblo by inculcating feelings of peace, order, and respect—allowed material advancement to proceed.[138]

However, for many elites in Latin America and across the Atlantic world, order seemed less secure with each passing year. While historians center the Age of Revolution around the beginning of the nineteenth century and consider that it ended in 1848, such temporal delineations were not clear at the time. The Paris Commune terrified elite Latin Americans of all political stripes, and they imagined their own uncontrollable plebeians' rebellions, especially the 1876 sack of Cali discussed in chapter 6, as part of an Atlantic-wide assault on civilization from below.[139] A telegram reported the sack of Cali, describing scenes of looting, destruction, and massacred bodies strewing the city's streets, all signs of "barbarism in this cursed land."[140] Manuel María Mosquera warned of the coming complete destruction of the elite class: "The first victims . . . are the Conservatives, but later they will also be the Liberals of order."[141] Alberdi worried that socialist masses would destroy European civilization.[142] In Colombia elites feared that the general poverty would lead to more popular uprisings, a "republican plague," comparable to locusts.[143] In Mexico U.S. observers feared the growth of "agrarianism" after the French Intervention and worried about large haciendas' fate.[144] Sierra argued that all the civil wars had turned the rural populace into a "savage horde."[145]

Revolution was no longer creative destruction, but just destruction. Indeed, Regenerators rewrote their countries' histories, erasing republican triumphs; revolutionary advances now signified only meaningless conflict. In an 1888 speech to Congress Colombian President Núñez looked back on the history of Colombia, from independence until the Regeneration, and saw only stagnation: "After Independence, Honorable Legislators, we had not really advanced even one step until now." Due to meaningless but bloody political obsessions, Colombia, "forgetting God," had become "the

anarchic Republic."[146] Núñez was more concise in 1891: "Civil war is barbarism."[147] Revolutions had been markers of Latin America's modernity
compared to that of monarchical Europe, but by the late nineteenth century civil wars again became the impediments to progress that *letrados* had
imagined doomed Latin America to barbarism in the era immediately after
independence.

Both Mexican and Colombian regenerators thought that order was the
paramount necessity in any attempt to catch up to the locomotive of civilization, now speeding away from their societies. As Eustaquio Palacios noted
in a letter printed in *El Ferrocarril*, political rancor in Colombia had led only
to "misery, immorality and barbarism."[148] Peace was the "indispensable element for any step forward."[149] *Colombia Ilustrada* argued that if war might be
needed to win "civil liberty," peace was certainly needed to win "industrial
liberty."[150] Of course, after so many decades of anarchy, such order was elusive. *El Correo Nacional* expressed how disappointed many Conservatives were
by the slow progress of the Regeneration, since "the virus of anarchy" had
infected society so severely under Liberal rule.[151] Mexico City's *La República*
stated succinctly: "If we want to progress, we must avoid anything that
could disturb the public order." The editors clearly linked progress with
"material improvements," and just as certainly understood that Mexico was
at best only moving toward modernity, a journey that a revolution might derail at any moment.[152] In 1885 international and civil wars, lack of industry,
a population incapable of participating in the nation, and a tropical climate
all led Lima's *El Comercio* to describe Peru as basically doomed: "A pueblo in
these conditions must renounce any promising future" and await absorption
by a "more robust" state.[153] American republican modernity's optimism had
faded, with additional pessimism provided by the dictates of geography and
scientific racism.

The demands of order now superseded the republicanism that had previously defined the future. A Colombian paper directly disparaged Atlantic
republicanism's political path to modernity, arguing that "the presumption
of being the most free nation in the world" had reduced Colombia "almost
to the level of barbarians."[154] While revolutions had been celebrated as creating the political systems that marked modernity, now "the worst government
is better than the most perfect revolution."[155] One Independent Liberal wrote
in 1878 about the need for a government that would "only attend to the sal-
vation of order, even at the cost of a dictatorship."[156] The Caucano politician
Eliseo Payán, a former progressive Liberal, declared in 1880 that disorder
had reached such extremes, that capital had fled, that economic prostration

had sunk to such depths, and that property suffered such attacks "that the path of the dictator is considered justifiable as the way to obtain order and peace."[157] By 1899, the Venezuelan Laureano Vallenilla Lanz, who would eventually pen one of the most complete and wide-ranging justifications for dictatorial rule in *Cesarismo democrático* (1919), had already become convinced that a society beset by anarchy and lawlessness could be redeemed only by "the protection of despotism."[158] Similarly, Leal urged his neighbors to abandon their republican experiments, "where everyone leads and no one obeys." If necessary to secure order and develop the economy, "a healthy dictatorship" would suit Mexico fine.[159] A discourse of order necessary for economic growth became a way to justify the restriction of citizenship as well as the control of popular political action. A healthy dictatorship was now a legitimate path to the future, while disorderly republicanism only doomed Latin America to barbarism.

To achieve this order, revolts and banditry must be quickly crushed and property respected. In Colombia properties that popular liberals had seized were returned to their previous owners after the regenerators took power, one declaring this would ensure that everyone understood that "property is inviolable."[160] Regenerators stressed that the most important right was the "sacred right of property."[161] Crime must be punished to the full extent of the law; one Colombian legislator argued that it "was not civilization, but barbarism," when criminals were able to laugh at the state's authority.[162] However, such plans would evaporate into thin air, until a stronger state emerged in Mexico with the rhetorical and physical resources to discipline the pueblo.

In Colombia the Regeneration would largely fail to secure the order for which some elites so ardently pined (although it would succeed, as shown below, in remaking the public sphere's content and character to delegitimize democracy and exclude subalterns). However, in Mexico, the project succeeded spectacularly. El Siglo Diez y Nueve reviewed Mexico's situation on New Year's Day 1884, noting the increase in telegraphs, railroads, steamships, banks, property values, and employment—the new and undisputed measures on the "road of material progress." Of course, there were a few dark spots, but the paper was sanguine: "After all, a nation like ours is not regenerated in a day."[163] Endorsing Díaz for president in 1884, the paper praised him for extinguishing the political passions that had plagued the country.[164] Guillow feted Díaz in the same year for having shaped the Mexican pueblo by fostering "order and peace," which had drawn the admiration of "the most cultured nations."[165] Now order and peace, not democratic innovation, were the path to the future, a future in which Mexico had to earn more civilized nations' admiring gaze.

The key to obtaining this order, and the justification for order's paramount status, was the denigration of politics, especially democratic politics. Regenerators in Colombia understood that turning middle-class public opinion away from revolutionary disorder and to favoring economic progress was central to the project's survival (this was accomplished in part via new newspapers).[166] P. P. Cervantes declared that only those most loyal to the Democratic Societies "do not tremble upon hearing the word 'Democracy.'"[167] Democracy had become synonymous with popular disorder. Eliseo Payán, on assuming the Cauca state presidency in 1883, said: "We need to have more peace, more industry, more labor and less politics."[168]

The editors of La Libertad—which included Francisco Cosmes, Eduardo Garay, Telesforo Garcia, and Justo and Santiago Sierra—inaugurated their paper with an editorial praising Díaz, dispelling concerns over unpleasantnesses in his rise to power that may have violated republican norms. They casually dismissed the history of republican modernity, arguing that it mattered little whether society had a "beautiful ideal" or whether it had mastered the "conquests of the century," if there were no practical results. The most important goal now was the maintenance of order, central to "the true conservative base" of society, so that Mexico might progress.[169] In a speech to the Preparatory School, Justo Sierra redefined politics' goal in Mexico— no longer was it ensuring "the happiness of the pueblo," now mattered the creation of a state that would only "administer justice."[170] The broad hopes of a democratic republicanism—the pursuit of happiness—had been replaced by a narrowly defined classical liberalism. The question of whether Mexico had already made meaningful progress seemed settled, answered with a resounding no.

The pueblo should no longer concern themselves with politics as citizens of the nation but should turn their efforts to productive labor instead. Guanajuato's El Quincenal argued that "the productive classes" must unite in a "powerful phalanx of work" against society's parasites, the unproductive and the professional revolutionaries.[171] Labor, not politics, was the new watchword. El Estado de Guanajuato agreed, arguing that the masses "who lack economic knowledge" expected the state to solve their problems and their poverty. The paper chided them for their ignorance, arguing that the state's main role was to maintain order, and that if it tried to interfere in society, it might disrupt the "social machine."[172] Thus, the invisible hand came to Mexico, and the public sphere rejected what the pueblo firmly believed, as evidenced by hundreds of petitions: that the state had a duty to serve them and try to improve their lives.

Excluding plebeians now trumped reforming the masses. El Ferrocarril lamented that the electoral season had become a "tempest that threatens every enterprise."[173] Worse, the season seemed to never end: "Citizens have accustomed themselves to live in the public plazas, engaging in nothing but politics . . . and abandoning their work." Frequent elections just created disorder that "completely impedes the country's progress."[174] El Ferrocarril praised the English and the French, who—although obsessed with politics in the past—had now turned their attention to industry, "and politics remained the charge of a limited portion of individuals that had made a special study of that subject." The paper demanded that subalterns "devote themselves to useful occupations" and leave governing to the elite.[175] Classical liberals under republican modernity had jousted with radical republicans over whether politics or economics created the citizen.[176] However, under Western modernity Liberals and Conservatives went much further, not just privileging economics over politics, but dropping any pretense that economic change would soon create a citizen body. Now the concern was creating economic growth for capital's sake, with the desire to limit citizenship (both in its extension and its meaning) to create propitious conditions for development.

Regenerators hoped labor would absorb subalterns' political energies, but they also sought a rapprochement with the Catholic Church in both Mexico and Colombia, seeing it as a guarantor of social order. Although some Liberals still viewed the Church's obscurantism as incompatible with "modern ideas" in an age "of the undersea cable, of the railroads and the telephone," others saw the Church as a useful ally.[177] Payán lamented that Colombia's educational system prepared students only for politics and war; instead, a Catholic-based system would inculcate morals and respect for authority.[178] Many Conservatives had always insisted that moralizing religion's influence defined civilization.[179] El Correo Nacional applauded the Regeneration for recognizing that the Church was a powerful element for "social order."[180] In a meeting of Cali's artisans to honor Bishop Carlos Bermúdez, one speaker, after praising the artisans for their honest labor, claimed that the Catholic religion taught the limits of "human liberty so that such liberty would be rational and civilized."[181] Western modernity envisioned its own global struggle, not now between republicanism and monarchy but between socialism and capitalism. Religion would be a bulwark against socialist barbarism, especially necessary in a society with a weak state, by inculcating "order and subordination" in the pueblo.[182]

Colombia would enshrine the antidemocratic nature of its Regeneration in a new constitution. Arboleda had proposed a new constitution in 1885 that would not imitate that of the United States but would instead appropriate some of the advantages of Great Britain's "monarchical system."[183] He suggested a "permanent Senate" composed of "the most distinguished men of the country" and more stringent requirements for citizenship.[184] Conservatives, and an increasing number of Liberals, equated the participation of the poor in politics with "savage democracy."[185] In Colombia, a key element of the Regeneration was eliminating democratic republicanism at the local level, as municipal councils had too often represented radical interests.[186] The constitution that was enacted in 1886 rolled back many of the rights of previous constitutions, most notably establishing literacy and property requirements for citizenship (surpassing even Arboleda's hopes) but also reducing the frequency of elections, reinstating the death penalty, and outlawing "popular political organizations."[187] Anselmo Soto Arana, speaking in Cartago, celebrated the new constitution, ridiculing Colombia's 1863 charter as full of "absurd theories and utopian idealism." He praised the constitution for abandoning such ideals, noting that instead it controlled the press, protected religion, established a strong army, and restricted the popular clubs that had stirred up so much trouble.[188] El Taller celebrated restrictions on the "revolutionary" press, arguing that "it is now time that we live the life of civilized pueblos."[189]

In Mexico the break with the past was never as starkly marked institutionally as with Colombia's 1886 constitution. Mexico instead relied more on ignoring or repressing democratic elements, while vitiating republican institutions.[190] As Justo Sierra admitted, the 1876 revolution of Tuxtepec (which brought Díaz to power) was a democratic and popular movement that wanted to disband the Senate, not allow the president to be reelected, and lower taxes.[191] Tuxtepec was a reaction against Lerdo's increasingly formal liberalism, but—in a betrayal that would take many subalterns years to recognize—vastly strengthened and accelerated the elite liberal project. Sierra justified Tuxtepec's false democratic promises as only a "momentary passion" necessary to secure victory.[192] Sierra plainly stated that Díaz's project represented "the Mexican bourgeoisie."[193] Democratic politics would be cast aside, in favor of economic development.

Therefore, to achieve economic modernity demanded the sacrifice of political modernity, which would now have to wait until some unspecified time in the future. Sierra approvingly noted that under Díaz, "Mexico's political evolution has been sacrificed to other phases of its social evolution."[194] While republican rule and expanded citizenship rights still existed on paper, Díaz served the same purpose as a "moderate monarch" in reforming European states, which the Regeneration's writers so admired. Cosmes argued that economics should replace politics: "Today political questions have become of secondary importance. Mexicans have spent too many years of the current century looking in constitutions and political rights for a remedy for the economic malaise that we suffer." He further declared that Mexicans, in spite of their numerous rights and freedoms, did not feel more free or happier, due to their economic impoverishment. Indeed, this "general poverty" was the direct result of these ill-conceived rights and liberties. Economics, not politics, would provide "practical solutions" to the country's problems. Cosmes cited a French paper—now a standard for authority—to claim that the solution was strengthening the state and increasing its budget.[195] For classical liberal capitalism to flourish, a conservative political system must replace the active republicanism of earlier years. The *científicos'* obsessions—a rational, scientific state that managed the economy without the influence of plebeians or even elite partisans—had deep roots in the failed imperial project.[196] However, the pueblo, after decades of paeans to its sovereignty, expected to have a place at the nation's table. Only a strong state, insulated from democratic pressure, would be able to discipline the masses in order to make the regenerators' economic dreams a reality.

The Knife of the State

The Colombian and Mexican states, as well as most other Latin American states, were decidedly weak throughout most of the nineteenth century. However, while oft lamented, some American republicans recognized the dangers of a strong state. Bilbao thought state power, "the knife of the state," was antithetical to popular sovereignty; he argued that it was European despots who prided themselves on powerful states, which only suppressed popular aspirations and weakened citizenship.[197] With the abandonment of American republican modernity, a stronger state became both the means to achieve modernity and one of the best evidences of modernity. Diaz's state of the union addresses were odes to the power of the state that he had mastered, filled with updates on the rural and federal police, postal services, census projects, crime statistics, the Army's artillery, schools, hospitals, and the National Library; of course, he also bragged about the development of telegraphs, canals, steamships, railroads, mines, agriculture, and the national credit.[198] Meanwhile, Colombia's Regenerators realized that they suffered from the weakness and poverty of their state, whose institutions were almost completely absent throughout most of the country.[199]

La Libertad (so critical for transforming Mexican liberalism into positivism, as noted by Pablo Piccato and Charles Hale) performed the intellectual labor of justifying a stronger state, directly attacking American republican modernity's presumptions.[200] The state was the "head of the nation" and must recover "its rights and its dignity."[201] Now it was the state's rights that mattered, not those of the nation's citizens. The paper argued that a strong state was critical to less developed societies, including "countries like ours, where the level of intellectual and moral culture is still extremely low." Indeed, democracy could not be trusted, as clergy and caciques dominated the countryside. Therefore, the central state had a duty to intervene in elections. Although in the United States the state might play less of a role, this was not possible in Mexico, where authority must be stronger "than in other more advanced nations."[202] La Libertad applauded the speech of President González, whose interregnum of 1880–84 interrupted Díaz's personal rule (although not his program), for its two great ideas: the "strengthening of the State" and the focus on economic progress. In Mexico "the work of material and moral progress" could be completed only by the state, which would then work to increase national sentiment.[203] Previously, the nation had been stronger than the weak state; now the inverse was held to be true. La Libertad admitted that Mexico was behind and that it therefore must be governed with a strong hand, even overturning elections if necessary. According to this logic, Mexico's form of government must reflect its backward character. Mexico could not have democracy because it was not modern—a view that inverted the old republican argument that Mexico was modern because it had democracy.

A stronger and well-funded state, according to Cosmes, could more adequately fulfill its duties: "These duties are greater while the country directed by it [the state] finds itself less advanced in civilization, because then the State is not only the tutor of society, but also the initiator of all works of progress."[204] Cosmes admitted that Mexico was not as advanced as other societies, and that therefore the state must play a greater role in disciplining its populace in order to create civilization. Now Mexico and other Latin American nation-states were not at the vanguard of the Atlantic world but simply untutored, barely civilized nations in need of strong states, imitative of Europe, to guide them away from barbarism. Political scientists, and to a lesser extent some historians, lament the weakness of the nineteenth-century Latin American state.[205] However, the strength of the state seemed to grow inversely to subalterns' inclusion as meaningful citizens in new nations.

A professional, disciplined army and effective penitentiaries were central to the modern state's power. Guanajuato's El Ferrocarril celebrated the nearby Salamanca penitentiary for promoting the "social regeneration" of the country. The paper praised the quotes from Jeremy Bentham on the walls, the work routines of the 708 prisoners, and the sense of order throughout the institution.[206] As in Colombia, in Mexico proposals for prison islands were popular.[207] The legal scholar Miguel Macedo approvingly noted the 1901 constitutional reform that fully reinstated the death penalty, which he saw as a vital "weapon" to reform society.[208] Adolfo M. de Obregón, an engineer, argued that the army was "the first and more powerful factor in this epoch of miraculous regeneration.[209] He cited Morelia's El Demócrata, which argued: "The great powers of the Old World pay special attention to the army, not only for international politics but, rather, for interior peace."[210] In Mexico the National Guard was demobilized in 1888, further removing subalterns from the status of citizen soldiers.[211] Prussia became particularly admired for its military prowess, rejecting American republican modernity's insistence that such force defined only European ambition.[212] Independent Liberals in the Cauca demanded the national state station in their region a "permanent force, as a powerful element for the conservation of public order."[213] If the Regeneration were to succeed, state power must increase dramatically. Bilbao was remarkably prescient in his warning to those who saw modernity in railroads, telegraphs, and steamships. He noted despairingly how tyrants and despots loved modern technology: "Don't you see that by using telegraphs and railroads insurrections can be suffocated more quickly?"[214] This, of course, is a capsule history of the Porfiriato.

Central to the state's goals was control over the public sphere, which entailed mastery of the press. In Mexico the press was urged to support "authority" in order to help the economy advance.[215] Colombia's press law of 1888 banned any "subversive publications," which included anything that attacked the Church, offended civil or ecclesiastical authority, or insulted the military; information that might depreciate money; obscenity; and anything "attacking the legitimate organization of property," "inciting some social classes against others, or organizing coalitions with the same object," or "taking the name and representation of the pueblo."[216] The last two points were key in separating the pueblo from the press and thus the public sphere, an important step in removing subalterns from political life.

Although prisons, bureaucracies, and armies, supported by telegraphs and railroads, were the most tangible material proof of a more potent state, equally if not more important was the state's independence from the nation and from democratic republicanism. The editors of *La Gaceta Comercial* argued: "The truth is that certain words are losing their magic. Men of experience care little or nothing if governments are republican or monarchical; what is important is that, under one name or the other, in this or that form, they *realize the ends of the State—security and justice, progress through order.*"[217] *La Libertad* argued that the state had to take precedence over the nation and its citizens. The paper rejected the idea that the state was "a collection of individuals united together by an arbitrary pact," instead arguing that it was an independent organism.[218] Thus the imagined community of citizens now had no claim on the state, which should govern autonomously as it saw fit. While republican modernity had rhetorically celebrated the people and the nation, Mexican regenerators sought to elevate the state above the nation: "The State is not a servant of the nation to which it owes services in exchange for taxes. The State does not offer services, but, rather, exercises its own functions, since it is a special body within society and superior to society." The state, according to this vision, was independent of society and thus of republican or democratic constraints, and it exercised "functions that its nature imposed," rather than functions chosen by the pueblo.[219] This must be the case, for if the state were beholden to the pueblo, it would lose its "right" to legislate, judge, and "punish."[220] The rise of state power was closely tied to the decline of democratic and republican pressures from both subalterns and the larger public sphere.

The Pueblo Excluded

There is very little in this vision of Western modernity and the nature of the state that workers could appropriate, since citizens and even the nation as a whole had no claim on the state. In general, the public sphere's embrace of the dominant European and North American vision of modernity profoundly affected the state's relation to the lower classes. In Colombia a politician exhorted that to implement the Regeneration "there is much work to be done in order to make the masses understand what real and true liberty and democracy are."[221] The pueblo would no longer be sovereign but subject to the state, a state increasingly able (at least in Mexico) to adopt the disciplinary projects of which many elite Liberals had long dreamt. If democracy and republicanism did not really matter for determining modernity, then it certainly no longer mattered if the pueblo enjoyed status as rights-bearing citizens—indeed, such a status was a hindrance to progress. In general, the pueblo were no longer the bearers of modernity as citizens but an obstacle, due to their lack of education, questionable race, propensity for disorder, and constant demands that might undermine a society's appeal to capital.

If the pueblo fit anywhere in the new understanding of civilization, it was as workers who propelled economic development forward. Mexican newspapers declared that the poor must turn aside from politics and utopian dreams and instead pin their hopes to labor.[222] Modern civilization was no longer a product of the political life of citizens—indeed, this hindered progress—but was produced in the "workshop."[223] El Taller quoted a speech by the foreign traveler Gaspar Bodmer, who declared that "without work there is neither education in individuals nor civilization in nations" and that "the great nations" are the result of the "gradual accumulation of industrialization."[224] Popayan's La Regeneración exclaimed, "Work! This is the principal contribution of the pueblo in the noble task of strengthening the patria. We will prove that we are not just a pueblo of heroes in massacres, but also in the bloodless fight of work."[225] The diplomat Francisco Marulanda hoped that labor would calm the poor, "distracting them from sterile political discussions."[226] Oaxaca's governor echoed Marulanda, warning his state that people must abandon "once and for all sterile political questions" and dedicate themselves only to labor.[227] Labor was the cure for politics. Subalterns no longer needed to be, or even should be, citizens in order to achieve modernity; only their labor, discipline, and order mattered now.

If subalterns mattered as workers, they contributed to Western modernity only if they were pliant ones. Leal argued that civilized societies must look to work as the future, now that "civilization, like Hercules, has strangled the serpents."[228] As Peter Linebaugh and Marcus Rediker have noted, the image of Hercules defeating the hydra was one used throughout the Atlantic world to represent capital subduing labor.[229] Of course, the Díaz regime was notorious for suppressing labor organizing and for breaking strikes. Discussing a textile factory workers' strike in Puebla (mostly over being paid by the piece instead of with daily wages), La Libertad—citing the English economist Stanley Jevons as its authority—argued that the state should actively suppress strikes to protect capital.[230] Puebla's workers had been on strike for four weeks and had dared to petition the national government for aid, arguing that they had a right to assemble peacefully. La Libertad rejected such rights, instead arguing that other weavers had a "right to work" and that the state could not interfere in what industrialists paid their workers. However, this did not mean the state should not become involved; the paper reminded Puebla's governor that "the supreme law is public security, and therefore you should punish the strike's promoters." The state was not beholden to rights but to a higher call for order, necessary for industrial progress. The workers had pleaded their case to Díaz, whom the paper advised to tell the strikers to go back to their labors, as only by working could they improve their lives. The political sphere had shrunk.[231]

Carlos Gris took labor's centrality for modernity to terrible extremes: "The criminal is a man, or woman, who does bad work and he should be shot or put in an insane asylum; but the idler, man or woman, is a terrible parasite that consumes social vitality and kills nations." He described those who loved laziness as "savages."[232] The new barbarians were not Conservative despots, European tyrants, or wild Indians but the poor who refused to submit to labor. They should be given no quarter. By 1890 the Porfiriato's repression seemed to have worked. La República, after lamenting the high number of strikes in the United States and England, approvingly noted: "Strikes are not popular in Mexico."[233]

Strikes were a concern, of course, but most laborers were not industrial or transport workers in position to engage in labor strikes. However, all subalterns could pose a great danger to public order due to their presumption to have claims on the state. American republicanism had a long history of fearing the state's abuse of power; now, though, the limitation of the pueblos' liberty was exactly what a strong state must accomplish. Yet American republican modernity had legitimized a deep political repertoire on which the pueblo could draw. The Mexican and Colombian Regenerations would work to delegitimize protests, petitions, and demonstrations; repress them directly with force; and strengthen the state so much that it could confidently ignore them.

In 1884 demonstrations erupted over the acceptance as legitimate by González's government of the debts incurred by past governments to Great Britain, presenting a major popular challenge to the Regeneration. The protests were violently repressed, with some papers lamenting the resulting deaths and violence. However, La Libertad dismissed such concerns: "We lament that the merchant loses money, that the passer-by his watch." The paper stressed that it was the duty of the state to guard "the lives and interests of honorable citizens," even at the cost of the protestors' lives. In response to those who said the demonstrators had a right to march, the paper claimed that although this might be the case in the United States, Mexicans could not be trusted with such rights: "The Saxon worker is able to march very seriously with his banner or with the instruments of his job; our worker wrestles with the desire to break, at least, a streetlight." The paper reproachfully noted that such violent demonstrations, with stone throwing and window breaking, would not be tolerated elsewhere in the world.[234] No longer insisting that Mexicans enjoyed more rights than anyone else in the Atlantic world, elites now embraced an idea of limited rights, which they saw as necessary due to differences (including racial differences) between Mexico and the United States. This celebration of difference was not only an embrace of spiritual values over U.S. materialism; it also involved a rejection of rights and political practices seen as alien and imported (if in times past celebrated as intrinsically Mexican).

The protests over the English debt helped Cosmes reconfigure the meanings of republicanism and sovereignty. He lamented that Congress had suspended debate on the matter due to the tumult, claiming this had destroyed the principle of authority. When the "ignorant mob," by shouting in the galleries of the legislature and protesting in the streets, succeeded in placing its will over the elected representatives, then Congress had collapsed. Now, instead of a constitution and representative government, Mexico had submitted to the "law of the riot."[235] An unsigned essay on public opinion went further, mocking those public figures who claimed that the pueblo was on their side. The essay said that the pueblo could never understand the foreign debt's complexities, and therefore their opinions had no value and "signify nothing." If even many journalists did not understand the debt crisis, how could "Indians who do not even know how to read?"[236] Popular influence and opinion, which under American republican modernity had defined a democratic republican system, now delegitimized republicanism and destroyed the state's authority.

Politically, subalterns were no longer fit to be citizens. La Libertad lamented that "in the most advanced nations in social evolution," political parties followed their leaders, and protests such as those over the English debt would not have happened.[237] Less important than the paper's erroneous reading of international politics was its insistence that Mexico was no longer part of modernity's vanguard due to its inability to control plebeians. In Colombia Conservatives equated popular liberals' political power and their subsequent political and economic demands as barbarism triumphant, while "morality and civilization" meant a return to a political order with limited popular influence.[238] El Lampacense argued: "The middle class is everywhere that which best observes, without violence, the principles of order, morality and compliance with the law, those elements of civilization that give the most pride to modern pueblos."[239]

Therefore, if the pueblo was too ignorant and barbarous to participate responsibly in political life, Colombian and Mexican regenerators must move to restrict subalterns' political repertoires. *La Libertad* complained of the ignorant masses that shouted and yelled in the galleries during Congress's sessions, which had converted the chamber into nothing more than a "cockfighting pit." Worse, this behavior scandalized foreign observers (the ever-present worry about the imperial gaze). The paper approvingly noted that in England one could attend sessions of Parliament only by invitation.[240] *El Pabellón Nacional* condemned the "Club Melchor Ocampo" for holding a meeting, also attended by various workers' clubs, to discuss the reform to allow the president to be reelected. The police intervened after there were verbal attacks on the president, and the paper lamented that such conduct showed that Mexicans were not ready to exercise their citizenship rights.[241] Colombia's regenerators particularly targeted popular liberal clubs—the Democratic Societies.[242] These societies had united the pueblo and allowed them to bargain with the state (and demand the redistribution of land); moreover, since the clubs had so often served as hubs of recruitment in civil wars, they threatened the state's monopoly on power.[243] Similarly, Justo Sierra argued that after the French Intervention, the decommissioned militiamen had developed a taste for adventure, combat, and pillaging: "They disdained industrial or agricultural work, so poorly paid that it seemed a joke."[244] Of course, the solution would not be to raise wages, but to eliminate the armed citizenry as part of subalterns' repertoire.

Citizenship itself must be restricted. Electoral laws needed to be reformed so election days were what "they should be in a civilized country," instead of bloody battles and embarrassing scandals.[245] The Colombian diplomat Enrique Cortés noted that Liberals had abandoned their former admiration of universal suffrage when they realized that most people were too ignorant or religious to participate in governance. Moreover, rights of suffrage, association, religion, and the press simply did not apply to a population of Catholic, uneducated, and illiterate peasants. Other liberties, such as the right to bear arms and the lack of a professional army, had led only to civil wars. Liberty would not work until the poor were educated and, critically, disciplined.[246] The former radical Liberal José María Samper agreed. Becoming increasingly conservative as he aged, he had dismissed his former faith in democracy by the 1880s, writing that universal suffrage had only led to rule by the "masses incapable of understanding" good government. As did other *letrados*, he rewrote the past, claiming that Colombia's political history from the 1850s until the Regeneration was nothing but a failed utopian experiment.[247] Cortés and Samper show Liberals' disenchantment with rights and with a universal democratic republicanism. Regenerators relentlessly attacked—both rhetorically and institutionally—subalterns' repertoire of politics, working to delegitimize citizen soldiers, political clubs, petitions, demonstrations, and even voting.

If the pueblo would ever be allowed to influence public life again, it would be only after its members had submitted to the state's disciplinary fist. El Ferrocarril lamented that much of Colombia's poor never worked, always striking or treating every day as a fiesta.[248] For the regenerators and especially letrado social scientists, "the pueblo bajo (the bottom of society)" was best characterized by laziness, drunkenness, dirtiness, nudity, polygamy, and complete lack of hygiene, which threatened the public at large. The vision of the pueblo as the embodiment of the nation had long passed. In spite of all this, the poor did not take advantage of charity hospitals, for they thought of going to them "as if they were in prison."[249] Long before Foucault, subalterns understood the disciplinary function of supposedly beneficent state institutions. Indeed, La República often read like a Foucauldian treatise. In just one issue, of 16 August 1890, the editors expressed their desire for more police in the city, praised the increase in census taking in Mexico, condemned lotteries and assured its readers that such gambling was generally forbidden in the United States, complained that the streetlights had been out the previous night ("darkness and crime go hand in hand"), applauded the scarcity of labor strikes, and finally noted smugly that political disorder in Central America opened up new opportunities for Mexican exports to the United States.[250] The paper sensed the opportunities for a disciplinary project provided by both technology and augmented state power: electric lights, censuses, police officers, industrial order, and political quietude. Elite Liberals—now shedding their concerns about rights—and Conservatives could unite over their shared need to discipline the pueblo. Prison construction grew; the death penalty was accepted as necessary for discipline; and politicians turned their attention to controlling gambling, unruly public festivals, cockfights, drunkenness, and prostitution.[251] El Heraldo demanded improvements to Colombia's police forces and cited a report noting that in Europe and the United States the police were the advance guard for maintaining social order.[252]

Concerns over discipline neatly merged with ideas about the modern state's power and authority: the pueblo must submit to the state, not negotiate with or make claims on it. In Colombia, Cauca State President Ezequial Hurtado rejected an amnesty for soldiers who had supported his faction in a civil war. Such amnesties only weakened authority's prestige and emboldened criminals, which in turn served to detain the "forward march of any civilized society."[253] El Estado de Guanajuato argued it was not the state that repressed people, but the people themselves when they riled themselves up politically, often incited by a corrupt press, instead of dedicating themselves to labor.[254] Thus, the pueblo caused its own repression. Of course, always behind the disciplinary project was the threat of brute force. Justo Sierra applauded Díaz's dictatorship—although not calling it that—for ending rural revolts via "fear, the ultimate resort of government."[255] In Jalisco, Governor Francisco Tolentino revealed in a confidential letter to Díaz his plan for dealing with residents of Tepic (many of whom were indigenous) who were opposed to the "expropriation of lands." Tolentino believed this was only a pretext for their rebellion, which was really about winning concessions from the government; the pueblo's demands reflected a past experience of negotiation, which must not continue. He had first tried to crush the rebels militarily, but this had failed due to their knowledge of the terrain and local villagers' support. His new plan was to seize the families of several known rebels and send them to the Marías islands off San Blas as hostages. He was confident that such a brutal punishment would lead to "absolute and unconditional submission," establishing the order necessary for progress.[256] Even Díaz worried that such a plan would, unfairly in his opinion, lead to public condemnation for its cruelty, but he allowed Tolentino to proceed if no other options worked.[257] The state had no need to negotiate with the nation.

When Latin American state builders looked north for guidance in regulating their unruly pueblos, they saw an increasingly undemocratic and unrepublican Atlantic world. Indeed, the repression of popular forces was a shared project. Soon after the French Intervention and the U.S. Civil War, Mexico City's English-language The Two Republics urged a conservative reaction against radicals' excesses in both Mexico and United States. In the United States, this involved overturning Reconstruction, which had established nefarious "ideas of political and social equality between the educated, the enlightened, the moral and highly bred; and the ignorant, coarse, immoral, brutal barbarian."[258] For both countries, the paper urged that Conservatives overcome the efforts of "Liberals" who "have more unfortunately adopted the pernicious error of considering all votes as of equal value," not distinguishing between the educated and the ignorant, between the wealthy taxpayer and the dissolute.[259] In 1868 these were minority views in both the United States and Mexico, but by the 1880s and 1890s they would be the norm. In the 1870s many intellectual and patrician U.S. Northerners had begun to reconsider their support for universal manhood suffrage, especially in the face of organized labor and widespread immigration. Of course, after 1890 southern U.S. states legally codified previously extralegal exclusions of African Americans from citizenship, enacting a broad range of suffrage requirements based on class to circumvent the Fifteenth Amendment. States enacted literacy requirements, poll taxes, and residency requirements to exclude blacks; voting rates that had been as high as 85 percent during Reconstruction fell to the single digits in most states.[260] These laws, somewhat intentionally, pushed many poor whites off the voting rolls as well; in 1899, the Washington Post urged that white "sansculottes" be disenfranchised.[261] Europe, meanwhile, had never been particularly democratic on the whole. Even after the reform act of 1884, which supposedly gave the suffrage to male householders and brought "democracy" to Great Britain, 40 percent of adult males still were excluded, unimpressive compared to republicanism's zenith in the Americas.[262] The U.S. historian H. W. Brands also sees the second half of the nineteenth century as a momentous struggle between capitalism and democracy, with capitalism triumphant after the Civil War. He traces the enormous economic and technological advances in American life but notes that they came at the cost of eroding any sense of equality and democratic institutions' efficaciousness: "By the century's end the imperatives of capitalism mattered more to the daily existence of most Americans than the principles of democracy."[263]

Elites and the middle class had never lacked a sense of the need to discipline the lower classes, discipline being one of the most powerful tropes of modern liberalism. However, in the period of American republican modernity, discipline was not the main or only goal for the lower class; instead, it had gone hand in hand with the idea that the pueblo's inclusion was a hallmark of the modern project. Given the demands for order under Western modernity, discipline became the central concern of the powerful and the state with regard to the lower classes. The removal of subalterns from participation in politics as citizens was not limited to Mexico and Colombia but occurred across Spanish America in the last quarter of the nineteenth century.[264] As we have seen, in Colombia this took place through constitutional reform that restricted popular rights and citizenship. More commonly, states removed subalterns by vitiating democratic electoral practices and political cultures. This could occur, as in Mexico and Argentina (under President Julio Roca after 1880), within an older, democratic legal framework if the public sphere devalued civic engagement and the state, with the support of the oligarchy, faced little electoral competition.[265] Argentina and Chile best epitomized "oligarchic democracy," or the rule by elites invested in the export sector, with little real competition and almost no popular influence.[266] Of course, under the Porfiriato (and under Antonio Guzmán Blanco in Venezuela and Justo Rufino Barrios in Guatemala), elections could be manipulated and rivals either co-opted or eliminated, creating an effective dictatorship.[267] New visions of the meaning of modernity and the nation allowed for subalterns' exclusion—republican politics were no longer the path to the future or national development—and for citizenship to be reimagined from a contested arena of social and national meaning to an increasingly formalized and empty legal terrain. The diplomat Francisco de la Fuente Ruiz praised Díaz for establishing the peace that was necessary for all progress, marveling at how the "popular masses" were no longer interested in politics—indeed, "they seem to have spontaneously renounced" the political life.[268]

Subaltern Response: The Defense of True Republican Institutions

Of course, subalterns did not renounce political life, except in moments of extreme fear. Indeed, it was remarkable that even as many elites abandoned American republicanism's values, subalterns continued to insist on them. After all, as Justo Sierra himself had noted, Díaz came to power on a platform (the 1876 Plan de Tuxtepec) that was in line with popular notions of republicanism, liberty, and justice. Subalterns hoped Díaz would administer justice, especially in regard to local authorities' abuses and unfair and corrupt divisions of lands, and petitions to the new government poured in.[269] Gregorio Padilla and Manuel Mendoza, writing in 1877 from San Martín de los Canseco, Oaxaca, requested a return of their land, seized by a nearby hacienda. The "capitalist *hacendado*" had taken their land, forcing them to pay rent, even though their village had enjoyed use of the land since "the time of the King." They suffered much, "their rights usurped," but they had great hope now that a government with "true republican institutions and justice" ruled. This government would "guarantee popular rights," especially since it was well known that their village had fought against "every tyrant" since the War of the Reform.[270] The language and lived experience of republicanism was strong, having long ago been appropriated by subalterns as their own. A group of men from Guanajuato state, who had fought under Juan Medina for Díaz's Plan de Tuxtepec, wrote Díaz to ask that their old leader be freed from jail. They claimed that a local official interested in their land had jailed Medina because he had been helping them try to recover their property. The petitioners argued that they had fought in the recent revolution "believing that the newly established government would look after the rights" of the pueblos.[271] After Díaz's triumph, subalterns expected a reinvigoration of the values of republican modernity—the reign of "true republican institutions"—not the abandonment of political liberties in pursuit of a distant industrial modernity.

As Díaz moved to implement Lerdo's land laws and to push for surveying of land and registration of titles that would eventually dispossess many indigenous villages and owners of small properties, subalterns were unsure of such measures' intent. Given Díaz's early embrace of popular republicanism, many seemed unable or unwilling to believe the betrayal they faced. Indigenous residents of a small village near Zitácuaro, Michoacán, asked the new president for help in a land dispute with local *hacendados*. They argued that they had embraced the Plan de Tuxtepec to put an end to the violence they had experienced at the *hacendados'* hands. These local *hacendados* had joined together "to extort and harass those Indian pueblos that try to exercise any of their rights." The governor in Morelia had sided with the *hacendados*, in spite of the fact that his public office required him to act with "impartiality." The villagers demanded that Díaz act, threatening that "we believe we have equal right" to responded to force with force.[272] Similarly, Indians from a small village near Celaya, Guanajuato, wrote Díaz, confident in their "right to petition" if hesitant due to their inability to afford a lawyer. As had happened to many others, their property had been usurped by *hacendados*, who forced them "to live in a humiliating slavery, contrary to our democratic institutions." They were sure that Díaz would help them since they had backed the Tuxtepec plan. They applauded the new president for carrying "the standard of Liberty and Justice," but they implicitly warned that the "sovereign pueblo" was "the guardian of our institutions that watches over the fulfillment of our rights."[273] Rights, direct action, democracy, and demands that the state perform its duties all reflected American republican modernity's discourse. Subalterns had seized that as their own and hoped to employ it to ensure that the new president followed the will of the people. The petitioners believed they still faced a state that sought to justify itself in terms of popular sovereignty.

Subalterns demanded that the Díaz regime fulfill the president's promises. A coalition of indigenous villages from Hidalgo State wrote to Díaz in 1879, noting that they had been "inspired by your proclamation of liberty" and Díaz's defense of the constitution; they had supported him in the hope of recovering "our sacred rights." They urged him to fulfill his promises and asked for his support to recover land seized by *hacendados*. Instead of being on the "path of justice," they found themselves sunk in misery due to the machinations of "the *hacendados* united with the rich," who tried to deny that the Indians were citizens: the wealthy laughed at the "unforgettable sacrifice that the indigenous pueblos" had made. The Indians lamented that, "above all, there is not a government to whom we can complain, because we believe that in our Republic nothing surpasses the monopolist ambition." They closed their petitions by demanding that "your promises be fulfilled."[274] The Indians of Hidalgo thus combined central tropes of American republican modernity: the embrace of liberty, a demand for the government to respond to its citizens, an emphasis on rights, a condemnation of Spain and its imperialism (they traced their suffering back to Columbus), and a suspicion of the rich.

This language had resonated powerfully in the 1850s and 1860s, but by the late 1870s its efficacy was being called into question by Western modernity's values. Residents of San Miguel Tesechoacán, Veracruz, petitioned Díaz in 1877 for help in a dispute with foreign *hacendados*, who had violently evicted the petitioners from their land. They argued that this violated the constitution and that their village deserved better, due to the sacrifices it had made defending the nation.[275] In an attached letter, two residents, Juan de la Rosa Bravo and Cosario Rangel, added that Lerdo's Supreme Court had overturned previous judicial rulings that had been favorable to the village, but the petitioners argued that after Díaz's victory, all the judicial rulings of Lerdo's officials should be null and void.[276] They clearly hoped Díaz would reverse Lerdo's land policies; indeed, they imagined that popular sovereignty and respect of the pueblo's rights were central to Díaz's revolution. They were wrong. Their petition was dismissed with a curt "it does not have the appropriate stamps."[277] As Díaz and his *científicos* took charge, elite Liberals and Conservatives united to reframe the meaning of civilization, and *letrados* poured their efforts into writings legitimizing Western modernity, much of the pueblo held fast to the values of a popular democratic republicanism.

Most subalterns, in spite of a long-standing erroneous assumption that they are mostly concerned with local affairs, know from long experience that it is very dangerous to be ignorant of the powerful's political maneuverings, even those in faraway statehouses and counting rooms. Many sensed—and would have heard in taverns, worksites, and the street—the new language of politics, the new rhetoric of modernity, gaining traction in the public sphere. Subalterns attempted to incorporate some of this new discourse, but many, at least in the Porfiriato's early years, refused to abandon their own popular republicanism. Certainly some of Díaz's supporters believed his popular rhetoric and hoped that the proposed division of lands would benefit them. They tried as best they could to adapt the new language of Western modernity to their situations. A group of partners from Rosales, Chihuahua, claiming to represent over three hundred "honorable and hardworking residents," wrote to support the division of lands, which they hoped would mean making available to them land from a nearby hacienda. They argued that as long as their region was dominated by these "old feudal lords" who call themselves "masters of lives and haciendas," there was no land for "the laborer, the artisan, the *campesino*." This was unproductive, a drain on the economy, and it violated "the sacred rights of man." They were renters now, but they hoped to buy land from the hacienda after it was divided. Previously, the masses had been inert, "but now they are not lambs that innocently are led to the slaughter. Today they are industrial laborers and honorable artisans who know their position." They were confident that Díaz would act, "because among us the precious 1857 Constitution still reigns."[278] These renters tried their best to incorporate a new language of labor, landholding, and productivity—the new hallmarks of modernity—yet constantly fell back on the powerful language of rights.

Indians from Ahuacatlán, Jalisco (present-day Nayarit), petitioned Díaz's new government in 1877 to request that land that had once belonged to their local church's Indian-founded *cofradía* (popular religious confraternity)—land that had been divided in 1856 and sold to private citizens—be returned to them, but as private property. The Indians combined numerous discourses: a colonial discourse stressing their ancient use of the land; a republican discourse of rights; and a new discourse stressing order, law, and progress. They argued that they should get their land back because that would follow the law; lead to "the consolidation of public peace," because "Indians" would see that they could obtain their lands through legal means; and encourage "prosperity and growth."[279] However, the local priest urged that the petition be rejected, since the buyers of the land had given it back to the Church.[280] Residents of Santa María Peñamiller, Querétaro, involved in a violent dispute with local authorities, combined the new and old discourses as well. They claimed that they wanted to secure "peace" and declared "our obedience," in contrast to officials who promoted "anarchy." However, they also asserted that since their rights and properties had been violated, they could employ "the right to rebellion" if justice were not done and their rights not respected.[281]

As the Porfirian state rejected petition after petition containing land claims and moved to unify the political elite behind its program, popular republicans took note and were furious. Former Liberal opponents of Lerdo fulminated when Díaz considered allowing a lerdista general, Ignacio Mejía, to return to Mexico. A petition originating from a number of clubs—such as Club 2 de Abril de 1867, and the Club Melchor Ocampo—accused Mejía of assassinating Lerdo's opponents and being the enemy of "the unhappy and suffering working class." The petitioners were confident that Díaz, as a "liberal and independent man who knows how to appreciate the sacrifices of the entire nation," would accede to their wishes. They closed with some confidence that Díaz would listen, "because the will of the pueblo is sovereign."[282] They too were wrong. Their petition was dismissed abruptly, with a short note explaining that although the right to petition was indeed guaranteed, such petitions must be written "in a respectful manner," a requirement this petition failed to meet.[283]

The disappointment was almost palpable. Members of Tampico's Club Constitucionalista, representing veterans from the town, wrote in 1878 to express their dismay that greater changes had not occurred after Díaz's victory. They opened by emphasizing that they had voluntarily "spilled our blood" many times in order to defend "the sacred cause of Liberty." They had enlisted to support the Plan de Tuxtepec, fighting against all the "enemies of the pueblo's well-being." However, their "hope that the new order of things" would improve their lives had already disappeared, and now their hunger and misery were worse than ever. The soldiers bitterly complained about the garrison's current officers, who were "monopolizing all the trades," seemingly interfering with the soldiers' gathering of firewood and transporting of water. They asked that these officers be removed and replaced with decent men who would never interfere with the people's "means of subsistence."[284] The citizen soldier had been the agent of modernity in decades past, but he was now only a hindrance, a potential source of disorder.

Many subalterns still tried to emphasize their right to bargain with the state, and even to rebel in the face of gross violations of their rights. Juan Santiago, claiming to represent five thousand Indian heads of households around Tamazunchale, San Luis Potosí, wrote to Díaz to protest the continued seizure of indigenous lands by hacendados, as well as the murderous violence the hacendados utilized. Santiago claimed that the Indians had tried the courts, but the judges were all corrupt. He also wrote about his people's violated rights and how the hacendados wanted the Indians to submit like slaves, but his most powerful bargaining chip was the implied threat of those five thousand men who obeyed his orders.[285] Díaz's government certainly recognized the threat, but an official advised Santiago that "any violence, however insignificant, will irredeemably harm the interests that you represent." Instead, Díaz's office told Santiago to put his faith in the court system, ignoring the petitioner's complaint about the inefficacy and corruption of the courts.[286] Bargaining had been closed down.

Of course, many subalterns would eventually adapt to the new regime's demands; their powerful allies certainly did. In 1885 Mazatlán's artisans wrote Díaz, asking for charitable contributions to help the families of sailors who had been lost in the previous year's hurricanes. They pleaded for "public charity," promising the "admiration and obedience of your humble cociti-zens."[287] Although a little of the former proud republicanism was present— the talk of citizenship—the focus was squarely on charity, obedience, and authority. Pueblos fell back on the ancient colonial model of declaiming their misery and abjection while begging for mercy.[288] In the 1880s lawyers (if not their more humble clients) and local politicians certainly understood the Mexican Regeneration's changing public discourse. Colima's governor, Esteban García, to whom Díaz referred as "my esteemed friend," wrote to help some indigenous villages in his state who were facing the loss of their lands to a hacendado who had the concession to survey public lands. The hacendado was claiming as public numerous indigenous lands that bordered his own hacienda. Governor García noted that such actions were "dangerous to the peace and public order of the state," echoing the Porfiriato's most powerful rhetorical justification. He did not speak of the Indians' rights, except for the critical "right of property," which was being violated.[289] Díaz promised to have his ministers look into the matter.[290] Manuel Zamora, representing the village of San Miguel Achiutla, Oaxaca, in a land dispute with a local judge, employed a similar tactic. He did not rely on a language of rights or popular sovereignty. Instead, after slavishly praising the president, Zamora stressed that a favorable ruling would result in the "peace and tranquility of the pueblos" and would lead to "progress and growth."[291]

Although Zamora clearly understood the new regime, his clients, in an attached letter to the local political boss, still could not relinquish the language of rights, of the nefarious rich versus the deserving poor, and of the popular expectation the state would serve them.[292] Many subalterns understood the appeal and power of rights, citizenship, and popular sovereignty—the language of American republican modernity—even if their lawyers might prefer a language of order and deference appealing to the state. Without this republican language, subalterns' position was weak, essentially that of beggars. José Rosas, representing the village of Santa Ana Jilotzingo, Mexico State, wrote Díaz to ask for aid in a dispute with General Eulalio Núñez, who had attacked their village, assassinating some people and hunting others "like animals." Rosas emphasized how the villagers had tried to resolve the manner peacefully and argued that the violence prevented them from farming. They hoped for relief so that "we would be able to dedicate ourselves tranquilly to our labors."[293] Without the security that a discourse of citizenship provided, the *campesinos* could offer only a promise of labor.

A common critique of those who examine subaltern discourse is that such language is meaningless, because subalterns simply parrot what the powerful want to hear: if they wrote of liberty, rights, and citizenship, the language was just instrumental and strategic; subalterns could as easily talk of corporate bonds, noblesse oblige, and humble subjecthood. However, if we follow such a thesis, subalterns under the Porfiriato should have been employing a language of labor, productivity, authority, and national wealth to justify their claims. Instead, we see a desperate rearguard action, with subalterns unwilling to abandon a discourse of citizenship and rights. Certainly certain subalterns, at certain times, did strategically employ a language with the goal of flattering rulers and reflecting their values (especially if they had no other options), but the insistence on citizenship and rights, even when the public sphere had decidedly rejected such talk as inimical to modernity, shows that subalterns placed a value beyond the strategic on popular republicanism. Citizenship and rights were appealing for the power and inclusion they promised, which many subalterns refused to abandon. These petitions also help explain why the Mexican and Colombian regenerators could not just maintain a public discourse of American republican modernity while pursuing their developmentalist and antidemocratic agenda. The pueblo would make demands on the state and nation, which if ignored would raise questions about the legitimacy of the regenerators to rule. Since fulfilling the demands, especially for land, was antithetical to the state project, the only option was to create a new legitimacy. Western modernity provided this legitimacy. *Letrados*, politicians, and state makers did not weaken American republican modernity and champion Western modernity on a whim; they had no choice but to do so if they wanted their projects of Regeneration to succeed. The equation of modernity with economic and technological power not only delegitimized subaltern demands (what did rights matter now?) but also allowed the ruling class to argue that only their leadership could propel Mexico or Colombia from barbarism to civilization.

The Ruin of the Republic

Referring to China's authoritarian capitalism in the twenty-first century, Slavoj Žižek asked: "What if democracy is no longer the necessary and natural accompaniment of economic development, but its impediment?"[294] One can argue that capitalism has always coexisted uneasily with democracy, but certainly in the late nineteenth-century Atlantic world, democracy was not conducive to capital's needs, at least as the holders of capital saw it. Democracy was an impediment to capitalist development in Mexico and Colombia, and thus the regenerators undermined and restricted democracy. To triumph, economic modernity had to destroy political (and moral) modernity.[295] Democracy, as often as not, has served as a counterbalance to capitalism. At times, democracy has facilitated capitalism's advance by allowing the free flow of ideas, goods, and peoples from which capitalism can draw much vitality and profit. Just as often, the rights that democrats assert have acted as a brake on capital's demands for cheap labor and unrestricted market access to resources. Žižek is wrong about democracy and capitalism's historic relation but prescient in worrying that capitalism in the twenty-first century may undermine democracy. For Latin America, that is a story oft foretold.

Real and discursive violence against subalterns accomplished modernity's reorientation around capitalism. The regenerators' project reduced subalterns' ability to influence the state via republican efforts; often greatly impoverished them in the name of capitalist development; and robbed them of their status as citizens, and citizenship itself of meaningful power. The adoption of Western industrial modernity as the ruling ethos meant that Latin America made itself the periphery of a northern Atlantic center. More important, Spanish America abandoned its pride and experience in being democracy's incubator in the Atlantic world, with clear effects on subalterns and less-studied effects on the world history of democracy. Within Latin America, this retreat also intensely affected the historiography of the nineteenth century, as both regenerators and nationalist letrados effaced the successes of American republican modernity.

The time of being at the vanguard of modernity, at the center of the world's future, had passed. What mattered to the Mexican and Colombian regenerators was not that the international community saw Mexico or Colombia as an examplar of liberty and democratic politics, but rather that it saw those countries as a safe place to make investments. The future was no longer in Mexico or Colombia but was only something that Mexico and Colombia would move toward—namely, the economic development already achieved in other places. In Mexico progressives and radicals looked on Mexican politics with despair, especially compared to the country's past glories. The republic—at least in fact, if not in name—was dying: "You see that the government contemplates, with a stoical indifference, the ruin of the Republic."[296] Colombians opposed to the antidemocratic politics of the 1880s and 1890s lamented that the Regeneration had removed their nation from its leading role in modernity by destroying "the institutions that had placed us at the *vanguard of American and European democracy.*"[297] In the garden of forking paths, a new way had been chosen. Modernity now happened elsewhere, in the "West," and "modernization" pursued by state planners (as well as modernization theory pursued by academics) would be the way that Latin Americans tried to catch up with the North.[298] No longer the proud bearers of modernity in the Atlantic world, Mexicans and Colombians cast themselves as less civilized, waiting to be tutored by the state to work for an economic modernity that would become increasingly elusive in the next century.

A "Gift That the New World Has Sent Us"

D id American republican modernity matter? Certainly, I would argue we cannot understand nineteenth-century Latin American history without taking into account the political and cultural moment that American republican modernity represented. However, I contend that American republican modernity affected more than the decades in which it was dominant. Although the most obvious site of subalterns' struggles to improve their lives would shift from citizenship to labor activism, the power of citizenship would continually reemerge throughout the twentieth century and into the twenty-first. Indeed, much of the inclusionary impulses of early twentieth-century populist movements—anti-imperial national histories, celebrations of the popular over the elite, and formulations of mestizaje and antiracism—echoed currents of the nineteenth century.[1] Beyond Latin America, American republican modernity demands a reconsideration of the general history of world democracy. Latin America is usually consigned to just a footnote in this story, but nineteenth-century experiences call into doubt the claims of the West to have invented democracy. Finally, considering Latin Americans' wrestling with modernity in the past allows us to understand our own contemporary preoccupations with the relationship of modernity, democracy, and capitalism.

Cuba and Costaguana

By the 1890s Western modernity had come to rule the public sphere across Latin America, challenged more by new socialist and worker-oriented politics than by the concerns over citizenship and rights that subalterns had deployed under American republican modernity. However, the timing of this shift varied in each society. For example, Cuba came late to this transition. In the 1890s Cuba was still a colony of Spain, and the Cuban patriots challenging Spanish rule justified their rebellion with a language startlingly similar to American republican modernity. Cuban patriots' celebration of their struggle for "moral republicanism in America" echoed republicanism's earlier centrality in defining a more just and hopeful modernity.[2] José Martí's insistence on using American models, instead of slavish imitation, mirrored the confidence in an American vanguard.[3] Likewise, patriots' condemnation of "the corrupt and provincial monarchy of Spain" read just like past denunciations of foreign enemies.[4] The notion that "Cuban citizenship" would create a fraternal nation out of warring parties reflected the long-standing exaltation of citizenship's role in creating the new American nations.[5] The celebration of fighting for the "rights of man" was a battle cry befitting the 1850s.[6] The claim that Cuban independence would be "for the good of America and of the world" recalled the powerful sense of an Atlantic-wide struggle between republicanism and monarchy, between popular sovereignty and colonialism, between American civilization and imperial barbarism.[7] Most powerfully, of course, the Cuban patriots' insistence in denying race (however incompletely) and embracing universalism echoed American republican modernity.[8]

Many scholars still assume that Martí's formulations in "Our America"—concerning race, the locus of civilization, pan-Americanism, and alternative modernities—were unique and ahead of their time. The cultural theorists of *Reframing Latin America* declare that "'Our America' is obviously a very progressive work. It challenged many essentialisms of the day, and it would be decades before its propositions became more commonplace."[9] Of course, many of Martí's ideas were commonplace in the public sphere of the mid–nineteenth century. This is not to slight Martí, who gave these concepts a poetical beauty and literary power, and he certainly embraced these ideas when they had faded elsewhere. However, Martí was not always ahead of his time; indeed, in some ways he was behind it. (A half-century later, another great anti-imperialist, Frantz Fanon, would also make exhortations similar to those of American republican modernity: "Let us decide not to imitate

Europe" and "No, we do not want to catch up with anyone.")[10] While the Cuban revolutionary movement is often seen as foreshadowing the struggles over racism and imperialism that would define the twentieth century, the Cuban patriots' cause looked back as much to the republican struggles of the nineteenth. The Cuban war for independence was, in some ways, the last hope for creating the fraternal republics of equality about which so many mid-nineteenth-century writers and orators had dreamt.

It was not to be. The U.S. intervention cut short and detoured Cuban experiments in creating this new republic. Martí, rightly suspicious of U.S. designs, largely excluded the United States from his fraternity of American nations (although he remained hopeful that Cuba's northern neighbor would come to know and respect the southern republics and thus rejoin the American community), marking one critical difference with American republican modernity.[11] The U.S. intervention definitively killed the ideal of sister republics: the disappointment felt throughout Latin America with the U.S. failure to live up to its own republican heritage was now complete. José Enrique Rodó's *Ariel*, published in 1900, attacked the materialism of the United States, embracing the value of Latin spiritual culture.[12] Roberto González Echevarría has observed that "Rodó's call to be different from the United States by reaching back to the European tradition nearly became a cult."[13] Eventually, as González Echevarría notes, Rodó's elitism would become "odious."[14] However, both the elitism and the embrace of spiritual culture promoted by Rodó were not new, but part of a long-standing elite, conservative tradition of modernity. Rodó's contribution was to give it the patina of emancipatory potential. By fetishizing the cultural sphere over the political sphere, and especially turning to Europe, Rodó not only reserved agency for the educated elite, but he also effaced the contributions of both elite and popular Spanish Americans in creating and maintaining republicanism and democracy.[15] By 1900, of course, a generation of writers in the public sphere had worked diligently to ensure that earlier, more progressive conceptions of modernity had been forgotten or dismissed as failures.

Rodó and many of his disciples were and are searching for an authentic "American self," whether found in pre-Columbian indigenous cultures or in an Americanized spiritual *hispanismo*.[16] However, decades earlier the public sphere across Spanish America embraced an "American self" built on republican rights and citizenship. Edward Said bravely critiques nativist movements for accepting the terms of imperialism—European versus native—while simply reversing the valuation of the group that was formerly oppressed and denigrated.[17] He sees moving beyond such nativism as a major challenge for the twentieth-century postcolonial world, but as we have seen, this was a challenge already met in nineteenth-century postcolonial Latin America, where a more sophisticated and emancipatory vision of universalism had matured. American republican modernity had already discovered "a universalism that is not limited or coercive" that seems so elusive in today's world.[18] By the end of the nineteenth century, however, universalism had been completely abandoned.

The neocolonial project did not just affect perceptions of U.S. and Latin American relations; instead, it shaped visions of modernity in general. As Ada Ferrer eloquently observes, when Máximo Gómez accepted the measurement of his skull by a foreign phrenologist, this marked a movement from the racial universalism of the Cuban patriots' mission during the war to a grudging (or, in some white Cubans' case, welcoming) acceptance of U.S. power and science as defining modernity.[19] From "a nation for all," Martí's great sentiment that echoed the words and voices of hundreds if not thousands of nineteenth-century orators, we descended into the racial technology of Western modernity. As Alejandro de la Fuente has shown, this was of course not the end of Cuban efforts to create a more just society and a more racially inclusive one, but it did explicitly seem to mark the end of Latin Americans' long nineteenth-century struggle to define a democratic future on their own terms, at least for some time.[20]

By 1904 the Cubans' bright hopes had dimmed considerably under the heel of U.S. imperialism and the retrenchment of racialism. In that same year, Joseph Conrad published his canonical novel of Latin America, Nostromo. Set in a fictional Costaguana, which strongly resembles Colombia, the novel is both a reaction to and a reflection of imperialism and its encounter with native others. Nostromo tells the story of the Goulds, English investors, and their encounters with republicanism in Latin America, which entails a civil war between Liberals (Monteristas) and Conservatives (Blancos). In the novel, Latin American republicanism is a joke for both the narrator and the characters. Conrad sees Costaguana's republican politics as depraved and ultimately childish: politics are a "degradation," "parody," "farcical," "screamingly funny," "comic," and ultimately only a cynical scramble to loot the state.[21] Mr. Gould mocks the "Liberals, as they call themselves. Liberals! The words one knows so well have a nightmarish meaning in this country. Liberty, democracy, patriotism, government—all of them have a flavour of folly and murder."[22] Another European character is the old Garibaldino, Giorgio Viola, who chastises the political infancy of Costaguana's rioting subalterns: "He had immense scorn for this outbreak of scoundrels and leperos, who did not know the meaning of the word 'liberty'."[23] Viola had fought in the New World with Giuseppe Garibaldi, but in Costaguana he only despises the masses and their actions, lamenting "the non-political nature of the riot."[24] On a surface level, Conrad captured much of the nineteenth-century Latin American experience—black liberalism, local revolts, Garibaldinos, elite aristocrats, imperial investors, and the boom and bust of mines—but he interpreted everything in the fashion of the ruling elites, although he was critical of them. Describing the Liberal revolution at the center of the novel, Conrad (as narrator, not any single character) presents the motivation of the revolts as "rooted in the political immaturity of the people, in the indolence of the upper classes and the mental darkness of the lower."[25] Politics is farce, and the poor are horribly exploited but have no true or valuable (European) political response.

As we have seen, however, Conrad missed the real Garibaldinos, who were not disaffected old Europeans, cursing the political immaturity of their neighbors, but Spanish Americans who castigated Europe for its political backwardness. Black liberals were not atavistic savages, attacking without reason, but—like David Peña—skilled politicians and orators, who fought to make liberty and equality meaningful for themselves and their comrades. Conrad could criticize European imperialism as exploitative, but he could not imagine that Latin American peoples had formulated their own response to it. For Conrad, democracy and republicanism are European, as fundamentally alien to the Latin American landscape as the disgruntled Goulds. Europe is the only motor force of history—indeed, the only place with a meaningful history, be it for ill (imperialism) or good (democracy).[26] If the U.S. colonial project clearly marked the end of American republican modernity, then Nostromo capped (and reflects) a long process of eradicating the memory of that project. American republican modernity had been successfully effaced.

Christopher GoGwilt has proposed that Conrad played an important role in "inventing" the West, a term that was not used much until the very end of the nineteenth century.[27] The configuration of the West not only excluded Latin America geographically but also rewrote history. Most curiously, historians regularly employ the anachronistic term—the West—to refer to pre-twentieth-century ideas and identities.[28] For our study, more important is the West's assumption of itself as democracy's mother, a view shared at times by critics of the West. In discussing modernity and the West, Richard Wolin argues: "One must resist the temptations of cultural relativism: the assumption that just because an idea or notion happens to emanate from the West, it is inherently defective."²⁹ Wolin is certainly correct to warn against pernicious cultural nationalism that uses the bugbear of Western imposition to justify gross abuses of political and social rights. However, this formulation seems to assume that ideas—such as rights and democracy, one supposes—emanate from the West. This is both ahistoric, because the West is such a recent invention, and inaccurate, because many of modernity's ideas—especially democracy and republicanism—matured not just in what would become the West but in Latin America as well.

"Your Thunderclap, Emanating from the Andes, Has Shaken the World"

Yet before Conrad's time, some in Europe and the United States did not think that Europe best represented the values of republicanism and democracy. Instead, they believed that these ideals flourished in the New World. This proposition is often ignored, even by critics of the West's monopolization of political subjecthood. Said notes that Stendhal does not mention colonies in *The Red and the Black*, in a section primarily devoted to establishing the power and integrity of the "fundamental ontological distinction between the West and the rest of the world."³⁰ However, Stendhal does talk about the Americas, about waiting for the Americas to take up the ideas abandoned in France. Describing the liberal aristocrat Altamira, Stendhal writes: "Despairing of Europe, poor Altamira had been reduced to the hope that when the nations of South America became strong and powerful, they might restore to Europe the liberty Mirabeau had sent them."³¹ Since Said assumes European domination and that this distinction between the West and natives held everywhere (at least throughout the nineteenth century), he could not see that not everyone in the world (or even in Europe) assumed European hegemony. The power of Europe's self-absorption, a power that Said traced eloquently, is intimidating, but we need not believe it to be true—especially in the Americas, but also for many Europeans. Of course, the idea of "the West and the rest" won in the end, but that does not mean it was always dominant or that others did not promote, successfully for decades, more fraternal alternatives.

If we return to our starting point of Maximilian's execution and Mexico's republican triumph, we can see that even in Europe and the United States some democrats assumed that the Americas, not Europe, led the way toward a new civilization.³² In a letter addressed to "The Republican French Workers," the French revolutionary writer Féliz Pyat saluted Benito Juárez for joining the pantheon of republican heroes. Pyat celebrated Juárez's execution of Maximilian as avenging the lost republics of France and Rome. He mocked Europeans' gasping at Juárez's supposed barbarism, declaring that the Mexican president had given a "lesson in justice" to degenerate European civilization, an example Europeans would do well to follow in revolting against their own monarchs and oppression: "Your thunderclap, emanating from the Andes, has shaken the world." Pyat concluded that, perhaps "in a France regenerated by Mexico, there might also be justice."[33] The radical French adventurer Gustave Cluseret rebuked his countrymen for invading Mexico and praised the Americas as "the living and universal protestation of the free human species against crowned oppressors." In America, he believed, there would be a "fusion" of races to create "the future type of humanity, the FREE MAN," while Europe would only stagnate in its decrepitude.[34] Mexico had been subjected to "the invasion of the Russians of the west, of a new Attila coming to destroy republican civilization in the name of monarchical barbarity."[35] Cluseret urged Mexicans to resist the French, for he thought "the European system" could not survive alongside the American system: "It must kill us or die itself."[36] Once again, progressive Europeans saw the Americas, in this case explicitly including Mexico, as ultimately redeeming Europe and showing it the path to the future.

Similarly, Italian workers from Genoa (where the Uruguayan Garibaldinos had sent their battle flags decades before) also hoped to imitate the Mexicans. They saluted Mexico for Maximilian's defeat: "One more gift that the New World has sent us." They only hoped that "in our Italy just one ray of that splendid light that shines over the peoples of the American continent would appear."[37] The Association of Militant Democracy of Brussels declared that Mexico was the star that would guide other peoples and assured Juárez that, when the moment was right, they would not hesitate to act against their own tyrants, "imitating your valor."[38]

The war between Mexico and France illuminated the stark political difference between the Old and New Worlds and the progress that the New World had made in creating a distinct civilization. The Spanish republican Emilio Castelar credited the Americas with destroying retrograde ecclesiastical privileges, promoting equality, abolishing slavery, and promoting the freedom of thought: "American democracy, so assailed, had lent great services to liberty and civilization." Castelar clearly thought that Americans represented modernity and that their "progress" would overwhelm any European attempts to impose a monarchy.[39] Castelar, as did American republicans, saw modernity as marked by democratic republicanism and independent nations, which the Americas had achieved, while monarchical Europe—with its internal colonies of Poland, Hungary, and Venice—had not.[40] By the end of the war, radical Europeans knew that the true home of civilization lay across the sea. Because they opposed the death penalty, Victor Hugo and Garibaldi wrote Juárez, asking him to spare Maximilian. Praising Juárez's success, Hugo admitted that it was the Americas that would show barbarous Europe the true meaning of both democracy and civilization: "You have just interred monarchies underneath democracy. You have shown them its power; now show them its beauty! . . . Show the barbarians civilization."[41] Garibaldi praised Juárez and Mexico as a whole for being the "Illustrious Champion of world liberty and human dignity." Mexico's defeat of "European despotism" served not just the New World, but also all of "humanity."[42]

In the United States exceptionalism, isolationism, and racism often led to a disparaging view of Latin American sister republics. However, some in the United States recognized the progress made to the south. The Florida planter Zephaniah Kingsley declared in 1835 that "this government of Haiti approaches nearer to pure republicanism than any other, now in use or on record."[43] He based his claim on his travels to the island; he saw that Haiti had no "privileged grades of society" and that, since everyone enjoyed equal protection under the law, it had achieved what other republics (including the United States) had not.[44] Kingsley was a strange man: a slave owner and slave trader, he married and manumitted one of his slaves, Anna Madgigine Jai Kingsley, and legally recognized their children. Although he supported slavery, he thought it should be only a legal condition, not based on race. Indeed, he came to know Haiti as he sought a refuge for his mixed-race family, when their status as free people came under attack in an increasingly racist Florida.[45] Kingsley found Haiti a bastion of racial equality compared to Florida and praised the way "all seemed to mix together equally in society."[46] He concluded that he had never found "any civilized country now known to us, where substantial freedom and happiness, unalloyed by licentiousness, or any dread of injury to persons or property, are enjoyed to the same extent as in Haïti."[47] In his will, Kingsley lamented the racism that would so limit U.S. claims to modernity in Latin Americans' eyes. He urged his children to "remove themselves and properties to some land of liberty and equal rights, where the conditions of society are governed by some law less absurd than that of color." He warned that "the illiberal and inequitable laws of this Territory [Florida] will not afford to them and to their children the protection and justice, which is due in a civilized society to every human being."[48] Kingsley looked south to Latin America to discover a true republicanism not tainted by the racism of the United States, seeing in Haiti—so often dismissed as barbarous—a superior civilization based on racial equality.[49]

Kingsley was an exception among white North Americans, but his views of equality as defining civilization were more common among African Americans, who would look to Latin America to find the "land of liberty and equal rights" for which Kingsley pined.[50] In 1852 the abolitionist and physician Martin Delany urged African Americans to emigrate to Central and South America, in order to escape U.S. slavery and racism in a "land of liberty."[51] Delany approvingly noted that the independent nations of South America had no policies of racial prejudice.[52] He, as did Bilbao, saw a great contest between tyrannical societies (like the United States) and free ones (such as Colombia), and he urged African Americans to "go forward and take their position, and do battle in the struggle now being made for the redemption of the world."[53] Delany argued that African Americans who defined civilization largely by economic standards were wrong. He declared that they must first enjoy liberty, must become "worthy citizens" of either Colombia or Nicaragua—material comforts would come later.[54] Political modernity must precede economic modernity: "All we ask is Liberty—the rest follows as a matter of course."[55] As with other African Americans considering emigration who thought the Colombian constitution "the most just and liberal that exists anywhere in the world," Delany saw Spanish American republics as these nations saw themselves: at the vanguard of free civilization, a civilization defined by liberty and equality.[56]

The struggle for abolition, the U.S. Civil War, and the French Intervention for a moment made an appreciation of Spanish American progress and the sense of a shared destiny as sister republics much more common in the United States. A manifesto from "Radical Germans in the United States" sent to Juárez celebrated his defeat of the French and the progress this entailed for universal republicanism. These Germans saw Mexico as a key battleground in the Atlantic war between republics and monarchies. If Napoleon III, whom they called the destroyer of republics, had succeeded in Mexico, he would have used his regime to support the Confederacy, as part of a plot to extend slavery and monarchy across the Americas. Moreover, the Germans claimed that the French had invaded because kings and aristocrats feared that if there appeared—even across the ocean—"only one Republic, in the form of a community with equal rights," this would be a "terrible and threatening phantasm" to European despots. Therefore, according to the manifesto, European tyrants, in league with the Vatican, hoped to destroy "American liberty, the ultimate obstacle that restrains their power, the only force that threatens their existence." Juárez and the Mexican Republic represented liberty, while Europe, for all its industrial successes, was still ruled by oppressive aristocrats. In spite of dominating half the world, Europe was a land of "savages in the middle of civilization." These Germans respected European technical accomplishments, but they recognized American superiority and hoped American influence would spread from their new to their old homeland.[57] Juárez had taught all the world's nations that it was possible to defeat "crowned criminals" and institute a republic that would ensure "true human happiness."[58] Again, Latin America is the teacher of democracy and Europe the balky pupil.

Such rhetoric even reached, if infrequently, the floor of the U.S. Capitol. The radical reformer Gerrit Smith delivered a speech in Congress on 6 April 1854 in which he denounced the failures of the United States to abolish slavery, and lamented that the support for the peculiar institution had led his government "to oppose popular movements, in behalf of liberty and republicanism." Instead of supporting sister republics, the United States had opposed the progress already made in Mexico, Colombia, and, of course, Haiti.[59] In 1863 U.S. Senator J. A. McDougall observed that the "sister republic" of Mexico was critical to the success of world democracy, arguing that France's invasion was designed to weaken republicanism in general across the New World in order to protect the monarchical tradition. To safeguard princes' interests, European powers schemed so that "the experiment of free government on this continent shall prove a failure."[60]

Of course, we need not rely only on the perceptions of Europeans or North Americans (or Latin Americans), even if uncovering their contemporary understanding of the world has been the focus of this book. We can investigate the real, lived experience of republicanism and democracy throughout the nineteenth-century Atlantic world. Indeed, although the North Americans and the French struck the first blows against aristocracy, only in the Americas, both North and South, was aristocracy consistently eliminated from public life.[61] The citizenship revolution would eventually proceed much further in Spanish America than it had in North America, especially in regard to its universal applicability and appeal. The United States faltered since it was the states—not the nation-state—that determined citizenship, and especially because U.S. citizenship had such strong racial limits.[62] Furthermore, the vast literature on nation and state formation produced by Latin Americanist historians during the last two decades has revealed the intense engagement of subalterns with democracy and republicanism and the important role played by this engagement in shaping political and social life.[63]

I am not trying to make a new essentialist argument, that it was really Latin America that defined republicanism, rights, and democracy, influencing Europe and the United States (although nineteenth-century Spanish Americans argued that exact point). By the nineteenth century, cultures were not isolated one from another but were complexly interdependent.[64] Instead, I am arguing that the dependence of Europe and the United States on Latin America for the survival and maturation of democratic political culture in the nineteenth century has not been sufficiently acknowledged. Present-day scholars, especially political scientists and public intellectuals, seem loath to recognize this, believing instead that positive influence can only flow in one direction: from Europe to other parts of the world.[65] In a recent volume, John Headley has argued that it was Europe (and the United States) that truly created democracy and ideas of universal rights; he dismisses non-European efforts as not sustained and noninstitutional.[66] Yet we have tantalizing hints that such a chauvinistic vision was not the case for at least some Europeans in the nineteenth century. While I argue that Latin America kept republicanism, rights, and democracy alive and practiced in a nineteenth-century world largely hostile to republics, the confines of this study (and my own limitations) do not allow me to trace this influence in Europe and the United States. However, until the political and intellectual history of nineteenth-century Spanish American democracy and modernity is taken seriously by historians (as it was by many in the nineteenth century), no such studies would ever need to be done.[67] A wide-ranging discussion by nine authors in the *American Historical Review* on "Historians and the Question of 'Modernity,'" included no Latin Americanist, and Latin America merited scant mention in any of the articles—an unfortunately common pattern in general histories of modernity, democracy, and republicanism.[68] Of course, just adding Latin America into the mix would accomplish little. American republican modernity was not just an "alternative modernity" that I present "in order to arrive at some 'equal opportunity' view of modernization," a practice that Dipesh Chakrabarty has criticized as a presentist historiographical preference.[69] Instead, I am arguing that Latin American politics were critically central to the development of universalism, rights, equality, and democracy in world history, not just a sideshow to the history of the West.

Where Those Rights Lived

Establishing the West as world history's all-powerful hero or villain has stakes far beyond the sphere of historiography. Edward Said critiques an imperial historiography that claims "Western ideas of freedom led the fight against colonial rule," while ignoring long-standing indigenous Asian and African resistance.[70] The limitations of the postcolonial formulation, such as that of Said or Walter Mignolo, is that while rightly critiquing those who ignore non-European ideas and practices, these authors still accept that certain ideas of freedom or rights or democracy are somehow Western.[71] Similarly, Chakrabarty decries the limits of a European politics that denies the communal and spiritual ethos of the non-European world, but he seriously errs in ascribing such institutions and concepts as democracy, equality, and human rights to Europe.[72] Of course, this book argues that such ideas are not of the West at all: they developed before the idea of the West existed, and—more important—they matured in Latin America, in reaction against European politics, culture, and, critically, imperialism. Frederick Cooper argues that "critics award 'modernity' to the most West-centered version of the story and look away from the importance of debate and struggle in shaping what reason, liberalism, equality and rights can be claimed to mean."[73] This book has labored to undermine assumptions of what modernity was in its heyday, while struggling to reclaim republicanism, equality, citizenship, rights, and even modernity from both their appropriation by the West and their limited and restricted uses today.

This point is not simply academic. Allowing concepts such as liberty or equality or fraternity to be classified as Western both undercuts their historic meaning and contemporary resonance while allowing conservative nationalists to claim that such ideas are foreign importations into their own self-defined essentialist cultures.[74] Similarly, those on the Left often dismiss popular republicanism as either too Western or simply a distraction from class-based organizing. However, I cannot help wondering if popular, democratic republicanism and its handmaidens—liberty, equality, and fraternity—could do any worse, and perhaps might fare better, at reinvigorating a Left mired in despair, nihilism, infatuation with all violence as resistance, and cultural particularism. American popular republicanism transformed the colonial, aristocratic, and slaveholding world of the eighteenth century in profound ways that no observer in 1750 would have predicted as possible. Its collapse certainly opened up new progressive possibilities, especially the labor movement (which also became the site of murderous repression by states and elites), but also decisively established a world order based on imperialism, capitalism, and racism.[75] The destruction of nineteenth-century Spanish American republican experiments makes it clear that democracy and capitalism were not harmonious; indeed, they were antithetical. Debates on capitalism, democracy, and modernity continue today, as we struggle to define a future based either on economic productivity and imperial power or on faltering notions of human rights and inclusive citizenship. Perhaps looking to the past might reveal that Western assumptions of modernity are, of course, not natural but simply the political manifestation of a certain historical project. As with all history, looking backward to tell this story of democracy reveals as much about our own times as it does about the past.

As in so much else, Francisco Bilbao looked forward as well as back; he was remarkably prescient in predicting the future scholarship on democracy's history. He rejected those who only saw democracy as synonymous with the history of France and its revolutions. After all, he noted, the French Revolution had failed, so it could hardly be "the ideal for the liberty of man."[76] He also rejected elevating the French Revolution for chronological reasons, arguing that it hardly mattered that the French were the first to put the Rights of Man down on paper. What mattered was where "those rights lived," which was of course in the Americas.[77] I simply follow Bilbao. Establishing a genealogy of democracy that emphasizes who was first in promoting certain ideas profoundly misreads the history and development of democracy and republicanism. What mattered then, and what matters today, is where those ideas of freedom and equality are practiced, where they form the lived experience of not just intellectuals, but peoples.

Notes

PROLOGUE

1. Speech of Maximilian at Veracruz, 28 May 1864, reprinted as a broadside, de Villar y Bocanegra, El prefecto in AHMRG-FBPCM, #510. All translations are mine, unless otherwise noted.

2. New York Times, 16 July 1867; at least this is the account of the execution by Maximilian's valet, published in Le Mémorial Diplomatique (Paris), 10 October 1867, translated by Anna Swinbourne, in Elderfield, Manet and the Execution of Maximilian, 191. See also Quirarte, Historiografía sobre el imperio de Maximiliano.

3. Arias, Reseña histórica de la formación y operaciones del cuerpo de Ejército del Norte, 267, 718–19.

4. Diario de la Marina, 21 July 1867.

5. Elderfield, Manet and the Execution of Maximilian, 11, 47, 86, 120.

6. F. Bilbao, "El evangelio americano," 419.

7. F. Bilbao, "El evangelio americano," 425.

8. Muñiz, Protesta, broadside in AHMRG-FII, #530.

9. D. Landes, The Wealth and Poverty of Nations; Huntington, "Political Modernization."

INTRODUCTION. AMERICAN REPUBLICAN MODERNITY

1. Hilda Sabato, in an excellent essay, has also argued that Spanish Americans thought republicanism put them at the center of modernity ("La reacción

de América"). Guy Thomson describes a period of "democratic optimism" in mid-nineteenth-century Spain and Mexico during which Liberal middle classes also assumed the mantle of modernity ("Mid-Nineteenth-Century Modernities," 75). With a more institutional focus, Fernando López-Alves also argues that Latin America created its own modernity based on republicanism ("Modernization Theory Revisited," 248). For a unique vision of mid-century modernities, see Dunkerley, Americana.

2. El Siglo Diez y Nueve, reprinted in La Alianza de la Frontera, 8 January 1863.

3. Emilio Castelar, "Política de Napoleón en América," La Bandera Nacional, 14 May 1864.

4. "El voto del pueblo," La Libertad (Durango), reprinted in La Alianza de la Frontera, 28 August 1862.

5. El Caucano, 3 November 1864.

6. F. Bilbao, "Emancipación del espíritu en América," 2:551.

7. Many theorists have noted that non-European societies appropriated so-called Western concepts—such as rights—to suit their own, often anticolonial, ends. See, for example, Winichakul, "The Quest for 'Siwilai'"; Bayly, The Birth of the Modern World, 3. However, I am arguing that Latin Americans are not appropriating modernity from Europe, but creating their own modernity (which, they argued, would spread to Europe). For alternative modernities, see Pratt, "Modernity and Periphery," 28–39.

8. Even scholars critiquing modernity tend to fall back on "Western ideas" as a product of European modernity. See, for example, Ben-Dor Benite, "Modernity," 649.

9. Dubois, A Colony of Citizens, 4–5, 28, 167–68; Nesbitt, Universal Emancipation. See also Cooper, Colonialism in Question, 21; Ferrer, "Haiti, Free Soil, and Anti-slavery."

10. Said, Culture and Imperialism, 41. See also Ben-Dor Benite, "Modernity," 638–39, 642–43.

11. Dallmayr, G. W. F. Hegel.

12. Giddens, The Consequences of Modernity, 174. See also Iparraguirre and Campos Goenaga, "Presentación," 5–6. For a more complex vision, see Coronil, The Magical State, 69–75. For Charles Taylor, Western modernity might be just one form of modernity, but he still holds that it was the first model (Modern Social Imaginaries). See also Bonnett, The Idea of the West, 163.

13. Bayly, The Birth of the Modern World, 12. See also Eisenstadt, "Multiple Modernities."

14. Berman, All That Is Solid, 17.

15. P. Johnson, The Birth of the Modern, 701.

16. Domingues, Latin America and Contemporary Modernity, ix.

17. Dussel, "Eurocentrism and Modernity," 67. See also Mignolo, The Idea of Latin America, 57–58. I am not dealing with modernism, of course, but many schol-

ars of modernism in Latin America also assume that Latin America had not experienced modernity when it adopted modernism. See, for example, Guillén, "Modernism without Modernity," 6–7.

18. Bailyn, Atlantic History, 110.

19. Landes, The Wealth and Poverty of Nations, 313. See also Huntington, "Political Modernization."

20. Wiarda, The Soul of Latin America, 8. See also Duncan, Latin American Politics, 17–18; Dealy, "Prolegomena"; Schneider, Comparative Latin American Politics, 16–21; Worcester, "The Spanish-American Past."

21. Harrison, The Pan-American Dream, 2. See also Fernández-Armesto, The Americas, 133–34. Paul Drake takes a more balanced view, but still sees democracy as having "largely failed" in nineteenth-century Latin America. Drake, Between Tyranny and Anarchy, 124.

22. For the nineteenth-century United States and the quotation, see Bradburn, The Citizenship Revolution, 303.

23. Mark Thurner makes a similar point ("After Spanish Rule," 21–22). For independence, see Anderson, Imagined Communities. For folk, see Burns, The Poverty of Progress, 1. For patron-client relations, see Chasteen, Heroes on Horseback. For prepolitical, see Bushnell and Macaulay, The Emergence of Latin America; Lynch, The Spanish American Revolutions; Wiarda, The Soul of Latin America, 143. For the postcolonialist critique of nations as elite, see Klor de Alva, "The Postcolonization," 251.

24. Morse, "Claims of Political Tradition," 84. See also Vargas Llosa, Liberty for Latin America, 28–33.

25. Latin American Subaltern Studies Group, "Founding Statement," 117.

26. Halperín Donghi, The Contemporary History of Latin America, 74. See also Duncan, Latin American Politics, 17–18.

27. Hobsbawm, The Age of Revolution, 142–43. See also Mignolo, Local Histories/Global Designs, 137–38; Quijano, "Coloniality of Power," 214–18.

28. Hobsbawm, The Age of Capital, 312.

29. For promoting the West, see Headley, The Europeanization of the World; McNeill, The Rise of the West, 731. For the use of the West, see Bailyn, Atlantic History, preface, 8, 9, 12, 13, 17, 24, 27, 55, 104, 107, 109; Mignolo, The Darker Side; Domingues, Latin America and Contemporary Modernity, ix–xvii; Alonso, The Burden of Modernity, 15. For the West as including but distinct from Latin America, see Carmagnani, The Other West. For the West as an anachronism, see Bonnett, The Idea of the West, 5.

30. Samuel Huntington has been most vociferous in excluding Latin America from the West (Who Are We?).

31. Thurner, "After Spanish Rule," 29. For letrados' views on modernity, see Alonso, The Burden of Modernity; Arciniegas, Latin America, 314–77; Arias Vanegas, Nación y diferencia; Cancino, Los intelectuales latinoamericanos; Martínez, El

nacionalismo cosmopolita; Melgarejo Acosta, *El lenguaje;* A. Rama, *La ciudad letrada;* C. Rojas, *Civilization and Violence.*

32. Alberdi, *La monarquía,* 87, 305.

33. Sarmiento, *Facundo,* 1:17.

34. Brading, *The First America,* 628; Ortiz, "From Incomplete Modernity"; Véliz, *The Centralist Tradition,* 163–83; Alonso, *The Burden of Modernity,* 20–23, 50–65; Mignolo, *The Idea of Latin America,* 57–58; Ching, Buckley, and Lozano-Alonso, *Reframing Latin America,* 190.

35. Braudel, *A History of Civilizations,* 454.

36. Burns, *The Poverty of Progress,* 18, 20.

37. Roldán Vera and Caruso, "Introduction," 9. See also Iparraguirre and Campos Goenaga, "Presentación," 5–6; Pratt, "Modernity and Periphery," 30–31.

38. Larrain, *Identity and Modernity,* 90. See also Franco, *The Modern Culture;* Morse, "Claims of Political Tradition," 85, 99. Even those scholars interested in different conceptions of modernity have focused mostly on the writings of dissident elite intellectuals, especially those of José Martí; see, for example, Ramos, *Divergent Modernities.*

39. Quijano, "Coloniality and Modernity/Rationality," 176. See also Alonso, *The Burden of Modernity,* 32; Mignolo, *The Idea of Latin America,* 66.

40. Eakin, *The History of Latin America,* 253; see also Quijano and Wallerstein, "Americanity as a Concept," 556; C. Rojas, *Civilization and Violence,* xxvi, 5, 105; Carmagnani, *The Other West,* 179; Ortiz, "From Incomplete Modernity," 251.

41. Mejías-López, *The Inverted Conquest,* 9, 15–33; Quijano, "Coloniality of Power," 190–91; Pratt, "Modernity and Periphery"; Guillén, "Modernism without Modernity," 6–7; N. Miller, *In the Shadow.*

42. For Western modernity, see Taylor, *Modern Social Imaginaries,* 195–96. Mignolo sees Western modernity as having much deeper chronological roots (*The Darker Side*).

43. For the West as an imported, invented, and often exclusionary creation, see Cañizares-Esguerra, *Puritan Conquistadors,* 224–26.

44. For critiques of the use of literary sources without considering their class bias, see Beverley, *Against Literature;* A. Rama, *La ciudad letrada;* Thurner, *From Two Republics,* 13.

45. Piccato, *The Tyranny of Opinion,* 105–8. One difficulty in working with nineteenth-century newspapers is that most articles bore no byline. Many were simply unacknowledged reprints from other newspapers. Of course, there was also little if any separation between "editorial" and "news." If available and of interest, I will provide the author and title (also lacking quite often) of newspaper articles; generally, however, I will only provide the paper and date, following the standard precedent. For newspaper and oratorical culture, see Piccato, *The Tyranny of Opinion,* 52; Forment, *Democracy in Latin*

America, 192–200; Acree and González Espitia, *Building Nineteenth-Century Latin America*; Jaksic, *The Political Power*.

46. A. Rama, *La ciudad letrada*; Martínez, *El nacionalismo cosmopolita*.

47. *La Guerra*, 20 December 1861.

48. González Montes, *Prefecto Municipal*, broadside in AHMRG-FII, #530.

49. *El Siglo Diez y Nueve*, 13 June 1848.

50. Sarmiento, *Facundo*, 1:108–9. See also Piccato, *The Tyranny of Opinion*, 51, 60; Guardino, *The Time of Liberty*, 164.

51. *El Montañés*, 1 February 1876.

52. "Conmoción," *La Alianza de la Frontera*, 11 July 1861.

53. This somewhat mirrors Habermas's own denomination of a public sphere of letters and a political public sphere, except that for Habermas both of these are largely the world of the bourgeoisie, while in Latin America the public sphere of the street reflected not a society of bourgeois capitalism, but a re-publicanism struggling with capitalism and liberalism. See Habermas, *The Structural Transformation*. See also Cohen and Arato, *Civil Society*, 201–54. For Latin America, see Uribe-Uran, "The Birth of the Public Sphere"; Forment, *Democracy in Latin America*.

54. Waters, "General Commentary," xii–xiii. Even S. N. Eisenstadt, studying "alternative modernities," has a similar formation ("Multiple Modernities").

55. Even scholars highly critical of modernity as a process and theoretical approach still fall back on it as something that actually exists, even if the exact definition and its effects could be endlessly debated. See Adams, Clemens, and Orloff, *Remaking Modernity*.

56. Berman, *All That Is Solid*, 16–19.

57. Bayly, *The Birth of the Modern World*, 10; see also 11. See also Pratt, "Modernity and Periphery."

58. Cooper rightly stresses the importance of exploring how historical actors used terms versus accepting modernity as a useful analytical category; however, he is suspicious of alternative modernities (*Colonialism in Question*, 3–32, 113–49). I am, too, if by that we mean alternative conditions of modernity, not alternative representations. I am not trying to impose an analytical category of alternative modernity, but to understand the consequences of a discourse and practice of politics developed by nineteenth-century Latin Americans. See also Thomas, "Modernity's Failings," 734, 739; Tenorio-Trillo, *Mexico at the World's Fairs*, 1. My approach differs from that of the great François-Xavier Guerra (*Modernidad e independencias*), who also promoted Latin America as a site of modernity in the Atlantic world, but as a marker of a real transformative moment, the independence era—when, for him, Latin America became modern. As I don't think modernity is a useful historical analytical category (as opposed to an endogenous category used by societies, which I think is supremely important), I am less concerned with marking when Latin America

became modern. In addition, unlike Guerra, I ascribe much more importance to the role of subalterns in affecting concepts of modernity and being affected by them. Alan Knight argues that an "emic" vision of modernity was not important in nineteenth-century Mexico, and that modernity is an "etic" construct ("When Was Latin America Modern?"). Hopefully, the evidence in this book shows that was not the case. Focusing on emic (endogenous) constructions of modernity also allows one to circumvent the increasingly sterile debates on when and how modernity "really" happened. For such debates, see Chakrabarty, "The Muddle of Modernity"; Symes, "When We Talk about Modernity."

59. Thus my approach is different, I think, from that of most scholars who have proposed "alternative modernities" as ways the primary European modernity has been redefined or appropriated (Eisenstadt, "Multiple Modernities"; Gluck, "The End of Elsewhere"). For a critique of alternative modernity, see Cooper, *Colonialism in Question*, 113–49; Bhambra, "Historical Sociology," 653–56.

60. Similar innovations were also occurring in Asia, although they were largely unrecognized by nineteenth-century Latin Americans. See S. Conrad, "Enlightenment in Global History," 1022.

61. Hobsbawm, *The Age of Capital*, 4.

62. Alberdi, *La monarquía*, 123, 165, 437. See also *La Alianza de la Frontera*, 4 September 1862; *Los Amigos del Pueblo* (Mexico City), 23 June 1832; *El Genio de la Libertad*, 9 October 1832; *El Monitor Republicano*, 8 January 1848; *El Siglo Diez y Nueve*, 15 August 1848; Francisco de la Fuente Ruiz, "La época moderna," *El Cosmopolita*, 26 February 1884; *La Gaceta Comercial*, 15 January 1900. And see also Bayly, *The Birth of the Modern World*, 12; Mignolo, *The Idea of Latin America*, 70.

63. *El Monitor Republicano*, 20 June 1848; Douglass, *Lecture on Haiti*, 20.

64. *Diario de la Marina*, 14 July 1867.

65. Bayly, *The Birth of the Modern World*, 106; N. Miller, *In the Shadow*, 3.

66. Holt, "Marking," 11–12.

67. See Thomas, "Modernity's Failings," 734; Méndez, *The Plebeian Republic*.

68. For Creole nation builders, see Anderson, *Imagined Communities*.

69. Letter to Emperor Agustín de Iturbide from "the female slaves" of Don Isidro González, San Juan, 14 November 1822, AGNM-IG-FG, caja 54, expediente 15, foja 4.

70. Hobsbawm, *Nations and Nationalism*, 10. See also Gellner, *Nations and Nationalism*. Partha Chatterjee also notes that for postcolonial Africa and Asia, nations preceded states (*The Nation and Its Fragments*, 6).

71. See López-Alves, "Modernization Theory Revisited," 248.

72. See Quijada Mauriño, "From Spain to New Spain"; Palti, *El momento romántico*, 13–28.

73. Thompson, *Customs in Common*, 55.

74. Moore, *Forty Miles from the Sea*.
75. McGuinness, "Searching for 'Latin America'"; Gobat, "The Invention of Latin America."
76. For a model of connected history instead of comparative history, see Scott, *Degrees of Freedom*.
77. Knight, "The Peculiarities of Mexican History." See also Thomson with La-France, *Patriotism, Politics, and Popular Liberalism*, xiii; Safford, "The Problem of Political Order"; Melgarejo Acosta, *El lenguaje*.
78. For Argentina, see Sabato, "La reacción de América."
79. For the comparative weakness of republicanism in Andean states, see Larson, *Trials of Nation Making*; Mallon, *Peasant and Nation*; Thurner, *From Two Republics*; Jacobsen, *Mirages of Transition*; Walker, *Smoldering Ashes*; Henderson, *Gabriel García Moreno*. However, we should not overestimate the difference: see Gootenberg, "Order[s]"; Méndez, *The Plebeian Republic*, 241.

CHAPTER ONE. GARIBALDI, THE GARIBALDINOS, AND THE GUERRA GRANDE

1. *El Nacional*, 20 September 1853.
2. See Maiztegui Casas, *Orientales*; López-Alves, *State Formation and Democracy*, 49–95.
3. Although I have no space to treat this here, the Blancos and Manuel Rosas prefigured some aspects of the patriotic nationalism that would eventually replace American republican modernity.
4. Valero, *Anita Garibaldi*.
5. C. Rama, *Garibaldi y el Uruguay*.
6. Garibaldi, *Autobiography of Giuseppe Garibaldi*, 63.
7. Garibaldi, *Autobiography of Giuseppe Garibaldi*, 110–11.
8. *El Nacional*, 13 April 1843. See also *El Conservador* (Montevideo), 10 February 1848; Scirocco, *Garibaldi*, 75.
9. *El Nacional*, 4 February and 5 May 1843; Scirocco, *Garibaldi*, 87.
10. *El Constitucional*, 13 June 1843.
11. Servando Gomez to President Rosas, Daymén, 14 February 1846, in *El Nacional*, 4 March 1846; *El Defensor de la Independencia Americana*, 2 January 1847, 22 April 1848; *Comercio del Plata*, 9 February 1849; McLean, "Garibaldi in Uruguay."
12. *El Conservador* (Montevideo), 8 February 1848; *El Nacional*, 25 February 1846.
13. *El Montevideano*, 5 March 1846.
14. Pacheco y Obes, Decree of 23 February 1846, *El Nacional*, 25 February 1846.
15. José Garibaldi to Ministro, Salto, no date, in *Comercio del Plata*, 9 May 1846; *El Conservador* (Montevideo), 8 February 1848; Scirocco, *Garibaldi*, 88–89.
16. *El Montevideano*, 25 February 1846. For a dissenting view, see Machado, *Historia de los Orientales*, 39–51.

17. El *Conservador* (Montevideo), 10 February 1848.

18. *Comercio del Plata*, 26 June and 8 July 1847; Scirocco, *Garibaldi*, 107–9.

19. El *Conservador* (Montevideo), 14 April 1848.

20. José Garibaldi to Ministro, Salto, no date, in *Comercio del Plata* (Montevideo), 9 May 1846.

21. Bartolomé Mitre, "Un episodio Troyano," *El Siglo*, 7 June 1882.

22. Riall, *Garibaldi*, 39.

23. *El Constitucional*, 2 June 1843; Oribe, *Circular de D. Manuel Oribe*; *El Nacional*, 6 April 1843.

24. Wright, *Montevideo*, appendix.

25. "Legión Italiana," MHN-CMHN, tomo 1283; Wright, *Montevideo*, appendix.

26. *El Nacional*, 16 February 1843. See also, *El Constitucional*, 1 April 1843, 9 June 1843, 12 June 1843.

27. *El Nacional*, 8 May 1843. See also *El Nacional*, 27 September 1853.

28. *El Nacional*, 29 May 1843.

29. *El Constitucional*, 4 and 5 April 1843.

30. *El Constitucional*, 5 April 1843.

31. Speech of Coronel Anchel Mancini to the French Legion, Montevideo, 13 June 1843, in *El Constitucional*, 16 June 1843.

32. *El Nacional*, 2 May 1843.

33. *El Nacional*, 6 April and 2 May 1843; *El Constitucional*, 4 April 1843.

34. Petition of officers and soldiers of the Legión de Voluntarios, Montevideo, 11 April 1844, in *El Nacional*, 17 April 1844. See also *Mensaje del Poder Ejecutivo a las Cámaras sobre la desnacionalización*.

35. Oribe, *Circular de D. Manuel Oribe*, 3; *El Constitucional*, 12 December 1842, 8 February 1845; *El Nacional*, 18 February, 7 April, and 5 May 1843.

36. *El Constitucional*, 14 June 1843; *Comercio del Plata*, 26 October 1846; *El Nacional*, 6 April 1843.

37. Wright, *Montevideo*, 247; *El Nacional*, 8 May 1843, 24 May 1845, 20 September 1853; *El Constitucional*, 19 and 20 May 1843.

38. Decree of Ministerio de Gobierno, 14 March 1846, in *Comercio del Plata*, 16 March 1846; *El Nacional*, 10 April 1843; *Comercio del Plata*, 25 November 1847; Sergeant Luis Lanzani to Ministerio de Gobierno, Montevideo, 11 March 1846, AGNU-AGA, caja 967.

39. *El Nacional*, 2 March 1846.

40. *El Nacional*, 12 April 1844.

41. *El Nacional*, 20 September 1853.

42. "A Militiaman," to the editor, in *El Constitucional*, 28 July 1845.

43. See Borucki, "From Shipmates to Soldiers"; Borucki, Chagas, and Stalla, *Esclavitud y trabajo*.

44. Decree of 12 December 1842, in *El Nacional*, 13 December 1842.

45. *El Nacional*, 16 December 1842; Andrews, *Blackness in the White Nation*, 32–36.

46. Decree of 12 December 1842, in El Nacional (Montevideo), 13 December 1842.

47. El Nacional, 13 December 1842.

48. El Nacional, 13 December 1842.

49. El Nacional, 14 December 1842.

50. El Nacional, 14 December 1842.

51. El Nacional, 14 December 1842.

52. El Constitucional, 12 May 1845.

53. El Nacional, 16 December 1842.

54. "El Soldado Juan Uriarte solicitando casarse con Rita Mendez," 2 March 1846, AGNU-AGA, caja 967.

55. "El Cabo José Antonio Masambique solicitando la libertad de su hija, Juana Masambique," Montevideo, 25 January 1846, AGNU-AGA, caja 967. There are other similar cases in the same caja.

56. El Nacional, 14 December 1842.

57. El Nacional, 14 December 1842.

58. El Nacional, 21 February 1843.

59. El Nacional, 14 December 1842.

60. El Nacional, 20 January 1845.

61. El Nacional, 17 December 1842.

62. Melchor Pacheco y Obes, Ministerio de Guerra y Marina, to the editor, El Constitucional, 11 March 1843.

63. Comercio del Plata, 27 February 1846.

64. Comisario de la 7.a sección de la Policia to Ministerio de Gobierno, Cerro, 13 December 1842, AGNU-AGA, caja 941.

65. Melchor Pacheco to Manuel Herrera y Obes, Mercedes, 15 December 1842, AGNU-EAM, caja 39.

66. El Constitucional, 3 July 1843.

67. El Constitucional, 22 December 1842.

68. Garibaldi, Autobiography of Giuseppe Garibaldi, 165.

69. El Constitucional, 17 December 1842.

70. The letter is written in dialect: among other changes, most of the rs and ds are replaced with ls, and many letters are omitted. I suspect it might be by someone trying to imitate Africans' Spanish accent instead of a real product of the freedmen. If so, this letter would be further evidence of Colorados' desires to claim credit for abolition. See El Constitucional, 15 December 1842. However, a similar written approximation of the dialect does occur in other accounts. See El Tambor de la Linea, 1843 (no month or date).

71. El Nacional, 8 February 1843.

72. El Constitucional, 27 February 1845.

73. El Defensor de la Independencia Americana, 2 January 1847, 14 April 1848.

74. El Constitucional, 14 June 1843.

75. El Constitucional, 5 April 1843. See also Riall, Garibaldi, 41.

76. "Unos ciudadanos" to the editor, El Constitucional, 17 December 1842.
77. Melchor Pacheco y Obes, Ministerio de Guerra y Marina , to the editor, Montevideo, 10 March 1843, in El Constitucional, 11 March 1843.
78. Petition of officers and soldiers of the Legión de Voluntarios, Montevideo, 11 April 1844, in El Nacional, 17 April 1844. See also El Nacional, 27 September 1853.
79. El Nacional, 2 May 1845.
80. Comercio del Plata, 1 October 1845.
81. El Nacional, 5 and 7 April 1843.
82. Speech of Melchor Pacheco y Obes to "Voluntarios Franceses," Montevideo, 25 May 1853, in El Constitucional, 26 May 1843.
83. El Hijo de la Revolución, 2 August 1846.
84. Comercio del Plata, 21 January 1848.
85. Comercio del Plata, 28 February 1846.
86. El Nacional, 16 December 1842.
87. Comercio del Plata, 18 May 1846.
88. Comercio del Plata, 20 May 1846.
89. Comercio del Plata, 20 May 1846.
90. El Compás, 5 December 1840.
91. El Compás, 12 May 1841.
92. Comercio del Plata, 2 January 1849.
93. Comercio del Plata, 7 December 1847; Scirocco, Garibaldi, 121–4.
94. Manini Ríos, Garibaldi, 25.
95. El Conservador (Montevideo), 19 April 1848.
96. Scirocco, Garibaldi, 125–37; Riall, Garibaldi, 46–58.
97. Comercio del Plata, 8 February 1849. Most biographies of Garibaldi downplay his New World adventures; see, for example, Trevelan, Garibaldi; Riall, Garibaldi; Hibbert, Garibaldi. For more balance, see Scirocco, Garibaldi.
98. Comercio del Plata, 3 February 1847. See also Riall, Garibaldi, 45–56.
99. El Conservador (Montevideo), 19 April 1848.
100. Draft of letter from members of the Italian Legion to the Uruguayan national government, [1852], MHN-CMHN, tomo 1283.
101. El Nacional, 19 February 1845.

CHAPTER TWO. "A PUEBLO UNFIT TO
LIVE AMONG CIVILIZED NATIONS"

1. Bolívar, "Letter to General Juan José Flores,"146.
2. For the independence era, see Adelman, Sovereignty and Revolution; Aguilar Rivera, En pos de la quimera; Annino, "The Ballot, Land and Sovereignty"; Breña, El primer liberalismo español; Colom González, Relatos de nación; Connaughton, Illades, and Pérez Toledo, Construcción de la legitimidad; Guerra, Las revoluciones hispánicas; Halperín Donghi, The Aftermath of Revolution; L. Johnson, Workshop of Revolution; Lasso, Myths of Harmony; Múnera, El fracaso de la nación; Quijada

Mauriño, "From Spain to New Spain;" Rodríguez O., "The Emancipation of America"; Staples, "La modernidad decimonónica"; Thibaud, *Repúblicas en armas*; Van Young, *The Other Rebellion*; Warren, *Vagrants and Citizens*.

3. *El Farol*, 4 October 1821.
4. *La Minerva Guanajuatense*, 24 September 1829.
5. *La Minerva Guanajuatense*, 28 May 1829.
6. *Rasgo patriótico*, broadside in AHMRG-FEM, #417.
7. Bolívar, "A Glance at Spanish America," 98.
8. Bolívar, "A Glance at Spanish America," 99.
9. Bolívar, "A Glance at Spanish America," 101.
10. Bolívar, "A Glance at Spanish America," 102. See also Aguilar Rivera, *En pos de la quimera*, 167–201.
11. Bolívar, "Letter to Colonel Patrick Campbell,"173. See also Bushnell, introduction, xlii; R. Rojas, *Las repúblicas de aire*, 334–49; Racine, "'This England and This Now.'"
12. Bolívar, "Letter to General Juan José Flores," 146.
13. For this period, see Di Tella, *National Popular Politics*; Rodríguez O., *Mexico*; R. Rojas, *Las repúblicas de aire*; Stevens, *Origins of Instability*; Van Young, *Writing Mexican History*; Wasserman, *Everyday Life and Politics*.
14. *El Observador de la República Mexicana*, 6 June 1827.
15. *El Observador de la República Mexicana*, 6 June 1827.
16. *El Observador de la República Mexicana*, 5 September 1827.
17. *Los Amigos del Pueblo*, 8 February 1832. See also *El Genio de la Libertad*, 8 June 1832.
18. *El Observador de la República Mexicana*, 7 November 1827.
19. *Diario de la Marina*, reprinted in *El Constitucional*, 8 May 1845.
20. *El Constitucional*, 9 May 1845.
21. Halperín Donghi, Jaksic, Kirkpatrick, and Masiello, *Sarmiento*; Villavicencio, "Republicanismo y americanismo"; Goodrich, "*Facundo*"; Shumway, *The Invention of Argentina*; Katra, *The Argentine Generation of 1837*.
22. Sarmiento, *Facundo*, 1:14.
23. Sarmiento, *Facundo*, 1:12.
24. Sarmiento, *Facundo*, 1:57. See also Vázquez, "Europa desde América."
25. Sarmiento, *Facundo*, 1:100.
26. Sarmiento, *Facundo*, 1:51–54. See also Alamán, *Historia de Méjico*, 1:27; Halperín Donghi, "Sarmiento's Place in Postrevolutionary Argentina."
27. Sarmiento, *Facundo*, 1:11. See also *El Siglo Diez y Nueve*, 27 September 1848.
28. Sarmiento, *Facundo*, 3:31.
29. Sarmiento, *Facundo*, 3:26–31. After traveling to Europe and the United States, Sarmiento became convinced that it was in the latter that civilization had diffused to the pueblo. See Palti, *El momento romántico*, 70–75; Halperín Donghi, "Sarmiento's Place in Postrevolutionary Argentina."

30. Alonso, *The Burden of Modernity*, 50.

31. *Registro Oficial*, 19 October 1830, quoted in Warren, *Vagrants and Citizens*, 100. See also Shumway, *The Invention of Argentina*, 90.

32. *El Farol*, 11 November 1821. See also *El Compás*, 27 March and 3 April 1841.

33. *El Siglo Diez y Nueve*, 27 September 1848. See also *La Palanca*, 1 May 1849.

34. *El Observador de la República Mexicana*, 6 June 1827.

35. Halperín Donghi, *The Aftermath of Revolution*, 82–88.

36. *El Observador de la República Mexicana*, 13 June 1827.

37. *Comercio del Plata*, 21 January 1848. See also *El Siglo Diez y Nueve*, 27 September 1848. For similiar discussions in the United States, see G. Wood, *The Radicalism*, 194.

38. For the public sphere, see F. Guerra and Lempérière, *Los espacios públicos*; Forment, *Democracy in Latin America*; Rodríguez O., "Introduction," 1–10. For public opinion, see Piccato, *The Tyranny of Opinion*, 15–18; Villavicencio, "Republicanismo y americanismo."

39. *El Observador de la República Mexicana*, 2 January 1828.

40. *El Observador de la República Mexicana*, 2 January 1828.

41. *El Siglo Diez y Nueve*, 23 June 1848.

42. *La Salud del Pueblo*, 13 December 1848.

43. Ramos, *Divergent Modernities*; Habermas, *The Structural Transformation*, 51–56.

44. *El Genio de la Libertad*, 9 October 1832.

45. *El Genio de la Libertad*, 9 October 1832.

46. *El Farol*, 30 December 1821.

47. de Castillo y Lanzas, *Arenga cívica*, 15–16.

48. *El Procurador de Pueblo* (Matamoros), reprinted in *Los Amigos del Pueblo*, 15 February 1832.

49. *El Siglo Diez y Nueve*, 5 June 1848. See also *La Salud del Pueblo*, 13 December 1848.

50. *El Monitor Republicano*, 20 June 1848.

51. *El Observador de la República Mexicana*, 20 June and 12 December 1827.

52. *Los Amigos del Pueblo*, 30 May 1832; *El Genio de la Libertad*, 8 June 1832; *La Salud del Pueblo*, 13 December 1848.

53. For the obsession with order, see Halperín Donghi, *The Aftermath of Revolution*, 113–15; Posada-Carbó, *In Search of a New Order*; Safford, "The Problem of Political Order"; Brading, *The First America*, 646–47; Warren, *Vagrants and Citizens*, 100.

54. *Los Amigos del Pueblo*, 20 June 1832.

55. *El Imperio de la Ley* (Durango), reprinted in *El Genio de la Libertad*, 8 June 1832.

56. *Los Amigos del Pueblo*, 23 June 1832.

57. *El Genio de la Libertad*, 4 September 1832.

58. *El Siglo Diez y Nueve*, 7 June 1848.

59. de Castillo y Lanzas, *Arenga cívica*, 5, 13.

60. El Observador de la República Mexicana, 12 December 1827.
61. El Siglo Diez y Nueve, 18 July 1848.
62. Los Amigos del Pueblo, 9 and 16 June 1832.
63. El Farol, 28 October 1821.
64. El Farol, 4 November 1821.
65. El Sol, 15 May 1822.
66. El Sol, 29 December 1821.
67. El Sol, 15 May 1822.
68. El Observador de la República Mexicana, 25 July 1827.
69. El Condor de Bolivia, 22 October 1825.
70. El Condor de Bolivia, 11, 17, and 21 December 1825.
71. El Condor de Bolivia, 6 July 1826.
72. Quoted in El Observador de la República Mexicana, 28 November 1827.
73. Quoted in El Observador de la República Mexicana, 12 December 1827.
74. El Genio de la Libertad, 28 August 1832.
75. El Genio de la Libertad, 21 August 1832.
76. Juan Bautista Alberdi to Juan María Gutiérrez, Valparaíso, 15 August 1852, in Alberdi, Cartas inéditas, 55.
77. El Genio de la Libertad, 28 September 1832.
78. "Varios Guatemaltecos," letter to the editor, El Siglo Diez y Nueve, 21 June 1848.
79. Alamán, Historia de Méjico, 5:905. See also Brading, The First America, 642–46.
80. El Hijo de la Revolución, 16 August 1846.
81. El Compás, 3 March 1842.
82. Echeverría, Cartas a D. Pedro de Angelis, 43.
83. Echeverría, Cartas a D. Pedro de Angelis, 43.
84. José Fernando Ramírez to Francisco Elorriaga, Mexico City, 16 September 1846, in Ramírez, Mexico, 75.
85. Adelman, "Between Order and Liberty," 90–93. See also Comercio del Plata, 11 March 1847.
86. Comercio del Plata, 18 May 1846.
87. Gutiérrez Estrada, Carta dirigida al excelentísimo Señor Presidente, 31–32.
88. Gaceta de Guatemala (Guatemala City), reprinted in El Monitor Republicano, 31 May 1848.
89. Alamán, Historia de Méjico, 5:885–86.
90. El Observador de la República Mexicana, 1 August 1827. See also El Observador de la República Mexicana, 5 December 1827.
91. Echeverría, Cartas a D. Pedro de Angelis, 37.
92. Warren, Vagrants and Citizens, 91.
93. Bolívar, "A Glance at Spanish America," 96.
94. Bolívar, "Letter to General Juan José Flores," 147.
95. Bolívar, "A Glance at Spanish America," 98.
96. Bolívar, "A Glance at Spanish America," 101.

97. Bolívar, "Letter to General Juan José Flores,"146.

98. *Comercio del Plata*, 2 January 1849.

99. *Comercio del Plata*, 2 January 1849.

100. *El Siglo Diez y Nueve*, 3 June 1848. See also González Undurraga, "De la casta a la raza"; Sarmiento, *North and South America*, 7.

101. *El Farol*, 4 October 1821.

102. *El Farol*, 28 October 1821.

103. *El Sol*, 15 May 1822.

104. Alamán, *Historia de Méjico*, 5:928–29.

105. *El Sol*, 15 May 1822.

106. *El Siglo Diez y Nueve*, 13 June 1848.

107. *El Condor de Bolivia*, 11 December 1825.

108. *El Condor de Bolivia*, 11 December 1825.

109. *El Condor de Bolivia*, 17 December 1825.

110. *El Siglo Diez y Nueve*, 6 June 1848. See also Ávila Quijas, "La transición." Clément Thibaud has a fascinating essay on how caudillos navigated changing notions of sovereignty in the early republics ("Entre les cités").

111. Echeverría, *Cartas a D. Pedro de Angelis*, 49, 52.

112. *El Observador de la República Mexicana*, 20 June 1827. See also *El Genio de la Libertad*, 8 June 1832; Urías Horcasitas, "Ideas de modernidad"; Brading, *The First America*, 634–47.

113. *El Observador de la República Mexicana*, 20 June 1827.

114. *Los Amigos del Pueblo*, 16 June 1832.

115. *El Genio de la Libertad*, 9 October 1832.

116. *El Observador de la República Mexicana*, 25 July 1827.

117. *El Observador de la República Mexicana*, 21 November 1827. See also Halperín Donghi, "Sarmiento's Place in Postrevolutionary Argentina"; Warren, *Vagrants and Citizens*, 99–100.

118. *El Siglo Diez y Nueve*, 18 December 1848.

119. *El Genio de la Libertad*, 2 October 1832.

120. Lasso, *Myths of Harmony*, 2–3.

121. Gibson, *The Constitutions of Colombia*, 43, 82–83, 119–20, 162. For Venezuela, see Hebrard, "Ciudadanía y participación política."

122. Warren, *Vagrants and Citizens*, 125–26; Wasserman, *Everyday Life and Politics*, 50.

123. Escorcia, *Sociedad y economía en el Valle del Cauca*, 3:101.

124. Alamán, *Historia de Méjico*, 5:936.

125. Maiguashca, "The Electoral Reforms," 88–89.

126. P. Alonso, "Voting in Buenos Aires," 182.

127. Valenzuela, "Building Aspects of Democracy," 223–28.

128. *El Siglo Diez y Nueve*, 20 June 1848.

129. Aminzade, *Ballots and Barricades*, 22.

130. Aminzade, *Ballots and Barricades*, 290, note 10.

131. Bentley, *Politics without Democracy*, 55.

132. Foucault, *Discipline and Punish*, 15.

133. G. Wood, *The Radicalism*, 261.

134. Baker, "The Domestication of Politics," 626; Formisano, "Deferential-Participant Politics."

135. Keyssar, *The Right to Vote*, 348, 354.

136. Noah Webster to William Stone, 29 August 1837 in Webster, *Letters*, 504–5. See also Lepore, *The Story of America*, 120. Thanks to Dan McInerney for helping me track this down.

137. M.N., "Retrograde Movement of National Character," *The Panoplist, and Missionary Herald* 14 (May 1818), 212 cited in G. Wood, *The Radicalism*, 311.

138. José Trinidad Martínez to Señor [Emperor Iturbide], received in Mexico City, 16 January 1823, AGN M-IG-FJJ, vol. 22, expediente 3, 8.

139. José Trinidad Martínez to Señor [Emperor Iturbide], received in Mexico City, 10 September 1822, AGN M-IG-FJJ, vol. 22, expediente 3, 10.

140. Desiderio Antonio de Meza to Señor [Emperor Iturbide], Tehuacán, 8 December 1822, AGN M-IG-FJJ, vol. 21, expediente 26, 255.

141. "Indians and others who compose the pueblo of Tlaltenango," Zacatecas, to Señor [Emperor Iturbide], [1822], AGN M-IG-FJJ, vol. 14, expediente 21, 182.

142. Report on petition of "El Común de Naturales" of Maravatío, Maravatío, 28 February 1822, and attached report of Jefe Político Mariana Quevedo, undated, AGN M-IG-FG, caja 40/7, expediente 40, 1. See also Guardino, *The Time of Liberty*, 272.

143. Pablo Ramires, Alcalde del Ayuntamiento del Pueblo de Santa Marta Chichihualtepec [signed by another] to Señor [Emperor Iturbide], [1822 or 1823], AGN M-IG-FJJ, vol. 14, expediente 29, 275.

144. Chiaramonte, "The 'Ancient Constitution.'"

145. Representatives of the Villa de San Miguel el Grande, Oaxaca, to V.M.I. [Emperor Iturbide], Mexico City, 12 January 1823, AGN M-IG-FJJ, vol. 14, expediente 31, 290.

146. Francisco Reyes, Pascual de la Cruz, and Francisco de la Cruz [all names signed by another] to Congress, Tlalnelhuayocan, received 26 February 1825, AGN M-IG-FJJ, vol. 17, expediente 24, 293; the priest and residents of San Miguel de Coneto to Señor [Emperor Iturbide], Coneto, Durango, 12 February 1823, AGN M-IG-FG, caja 48, expediente 2, 3.

147. All the individuals that belong to the parcialidad of Santiago Tlatelolco to Don Luis Velasquez de la Cadena, Mexico City, 4 February 1843, AGN M-IG-FG, caja 259, expediente 6, 1.

148. Response to the petition of Francisco Reyes and Pascual de la Cruz, 3 October 1825, AGN M-IG-FJJ, vol. 17, expediente 24, 293.

149. Domingo Ramos and nine others of San Damián to V.S. [Emperor Iturbide], received by 3 November 1824, AGN M-IG-FG, caja 80, expediente 4, 5.

150. El Ayuntamiento del Real de San Francisco de los Pozos to Exmo. Señor [Emperor Iturbide], Real de San Francisco de los Pozos, 24 August 1822, AGNM-IG-FG, caja 48, expediente 8, 2. See also representatives of the Villa de San Miguel el Grande, Oaxaca, to V.M.I. [Emperor Iturbide], Mexico City, 12 January 1823, AGNM-IG-FJJ, vol. 14, expediente 31, 290.

151. José de los Santos Contreras for the común de Santa Gertrudis, Oaxaca to Señor [Emperor Iturbide], [1822], AGNM-IG-FG, caja 18, expediente 1, 24.

152. Andres Alcantarra and José Carmona to judge, Tampico, 14 August 1822, AGNM-IG-FJJ, vol. 15, expediente 7, 63.

153. For popular political language, see Caplan, *Indigenous Citizens*; Di Tella, *National Popular Politics*; Garrido, *Reclamos y representaciones*; Guardino, *The Time of Liberty*; Lasso, *Myths of Harmony*; Méndez, *The Plebeian Republic*; Reina, *La reindianización de América*; Stevens, "Lo revelado y lo oscurecido"; Thurner, *From Two Republics*.

154. Ducey, *A Nation of Villages*; Méndez, *The Plebeian Republic*.

155. Speech of Luis Gonzaga Solana, president of the Chamber of Deputies, 31 December 1844, in *El Siglo Diez y Nueve*, 1 January 1845.

156. *El Tiempo* quoted in *El Republicano*, 28 March 1846.

157. *La Hesperia*, 28 March 1846.

158. *El Siglo Diez y Nueve*, 24 November 1848.

159. Palti, *La política del disenso*, 20–58.

160. José Fernando Ramírez to Francisco Elorriaga, Mexico City, 25 April 1847 in Ramírez, *Mexico*, 121.

161. Fernando Ramírez to "my dear friend" [Francisco Elorriaga], Mexico City, 8 May 1847, in Ramírez, *Mexico*, 141–42.

162. Fernando Ramírez to "my dear friend" [Francisco Elorriaga], Mexico City, 8 May 1847, in Ramírez, *Mexico*, 141–42. See also J. Wood, *The Society of Equality*, 82–83.

163. *El Siglo Diez y Nueve*, special issue, May 1848.

164. *El Siglo Diez y Nueve*, 1 June 1848.

165. *El Siglo Diez y Nueve*, 2 June 1848.

166. Alamán, *Historia de Méjico*, 5:903.

167. *El Siglo Diez y Nueve*, 20 June 1848.

168. *El Siglo Diez y Nueve*, 23 June 1848.

169. *El Siglo Diez y Nueve*, 19 November 1848.

170. Varios Mexicanos, "Consideraciones sobre la situación política y social de la república Mexicana en el año de 1847," *El Monitor Republicano*, 23 and 24 June 1848.

171. See Alamán, *Historia de Méjico*, 5:904.

172. For critiques of relying on letrados, see Beverley, *Against Literature*; A. Rama, *La ciudad letrada*.

CHAPTER THREE. THE SAN PATRICIO BATTALION

1. For a thorough account of the batallion, see R. Miller, *Shamrock and Sword*, 3, 9, 29–32.

2. Roa Bárcena, *Recuerdos de la invasión norteamericana*, 304.

3. Peskin, *Volunteers*, 146–47; Brooks, *A Complete History*, 381.

4. Brooks, *A Complete History*, 400. See also Chamberlain, *My Confession*, 226.

5. R. Miller, *Shamrock and Sword*, 89.

6. José Fernando Ramírez to Francisco Elorriaga, Mexico City, 21 August 1847 in Ramírez, *Mexico*, 152.

7. R. Miller, *Shamrock and Sword*, 150.

8. *New Hampshire Sentinel*, 5 August 1847.

9. José Fernando Ramírez to Francisco Elorriaga, Mexico City, 28 April 1847 in Ramírez, *Mexico*, 127; *El Monitor Republicano*, 22 January and 11 April 1847.

10. *El Monitor Republicano*, 21 March 1847.

11. *El Monitor Republicano*, 21 March 1847.

12. *El Monitor Republicano*, 22 January 1847. See also *El Indicador*, 23 September 1846; Hogan, *The Irish Soldiers of Mexico*, 17, 97–99.

13. *El Monitor Republicano*, 22 January 1847.

14. Quoted in R. Miller, *Shamrock and Sword*, 142.

15. Quoted in R. Miller, *Shamrock and Sword*, 79.

16. *Mexico Illustrated*, 30. See also Brooks, *A Complete History*, 381.

17. Chamberlain, *My Confession*, 226–27; R. Miller, *Shamrock and Sword*, 107.

18. Roa Bárcena, *Recuerdos de la invasión norteamericana*, 58.

19. *El Siglo Diez y Nueve*, 1, 3, 6, and 21 June 1848.

20. Roa Bárcena, *Recuerdos de la invasión norteamericana*, 58.

21. Alcaraz, *The Other Side*, 295.

22. Alcaraz, *The Other Side*, 295.

23. Roa Bárcena, *Recuerdos de la invasión norteamericana*, 58–59.

24. Brooks, *A Complete History*, 401; McCornack, "The San Patricio Deserters."

25. Peskin, *Volunteers*, 158, note 26. For historians, see Merry, *A Country of Vast Designs*.

26. Brooks, *A Complete History*, 540. See also O'Brien, *Making the Americas*, 35–44.

27. Peskin, *Volunteers*, 181. See also Horsman, *Race and Manifest Destiny*, 208–28.

28. *Daily Picayune* (New Orleans), 7 November 1847, in Kendall, *Dispatches from the Mexican War*, 402.

29. *El Monitor Republicano*, 13 October 1847.

30. *El Diario del Gobierno* (Mexico City) reprinted in *El Indicador*, 3 October 1846.

31. For racism, see González Undurraga, "De la casta a la raza."

32. *Spirit of the Times*, 2 January 1847.

33. Ignatiev, *How the Irish Became White*.

34. Horsman, *Race and Manifest Destiny*, 6. See also Bradburn, *The Citizenship Revolution*, 297–308.

35. Johannsen, *To the Halls*, 290–91.

36. Chamberlain, *My Confession*, 52, 63, 65, 66, 82, 87, 96, 116.

37. Quoted in Zinn, *A People's History*, 118.

38. Quoted in Johannsen, *To the Halls*, 22.

39. Brooks, *A Complete History*, 400–401.

40. *El Monitor Republicano*, 3 October 1847.

41. *El Monitor Republicano*, 4 October 1847.

42. *El Monitor Republicano*, 4 October 1847.

43. *El Monitor Republicano*, 13 October 1847.

44. See Horsman, *Race and Manifest Destiny*.

45. Linebaugh and Rediker, *The Many-Headed Hydra*, 104–42, 174–210.

46. *Brooklyn Daily Eagle*, 27 October 1847.

47. *El Corresponsal del Ejército*, 10 April 1847; *El Monitor Republicano*, 16 April 1847; *El Diario del Gobierno* (Mexico City), reprinted in *El Indicador*, 12 October 1846.

48. Proclamation of the state of México's Legislature to its inhabitants, Toluca, 26 April 1847, in *El Monitor Republicano*, 2 May 1847.

49. *El Monitor Republicano*, 30 April 1847; *El Corresponsal del Ejército*, 12 June 1847.

50. *El Monitor Republicano*, 30 April 1847.

51. *El Monitor Republicano*, 23 September 1846.

52. Alcaraz, *The Other Side*, 308.

53. For a contrary view, see Pani, *Para mexicanizar el Segundo Imperio*, 58.

54. Alberdi, *La monarquía*, 520.

55. *El Nacional*, 7 March 1846; *Comercio del Plata*, 11 March 1847 and 12 February 1848; López, *Mensaje del Poder Ejecutivo*; *La Alianza de la Frontera*, 13 November 1862; *La Chinaca*, 16 June 1862; Alberdi, *El imperio del Brasil*, lix; *Gaceta Oficial del Cauca*, 10 August 1867; *El Pensamiento Público*, 31 March 1872.

56. *Comercio del Plata*, 18 May 1846.

57. *El Observador de la República Mexicana*, 19 December 1827; *El Genio de la Libertad*, 28 August 1832; *Comercio del Plata*, 1 October 1845 and 18 May 1846; *Ariete*, 29 September 1849.

58. T. C. de Mosquera, "Mensaje del Gobernador de Estado a la Lejislatura de 1859," Popayán, Colombia, 11 August 1859, ACC-AM, paquete 74, legajo 48.

59. T. C. de Mosquera, "Discursos pronunciados en la recepción del Gobernador del Estado del Cauca," *Gaceta del Cauca*, 23 August 1859.

60. Sarmiento, *North and South America*, 44.

61. Julián Trujillo, Eliseo Payán, and Manuel del Quijano to Constitutional Convention, Popayán, 14 July 1872, ACC-AM, paquete 116, legajo 16.

62. For sister republics, see *El Constitucional*, 9 May 1845; *El Monitor Republicano*, 8 January 1848 and 2 May 1847; *Los Verdaderos Constitucionalistas, A los liberales*, broadside, in AGNC-SC-FEOR, caja 114, carpeta 426.

63. *El Republicano*, 28 March 1846.

64. *Comercio del Plata*, 12 February 1848.

65. *Boletín de la División del Norte*, reprinted in *El Republicano*, 15 May 1846.
66. Los Nuevo-Leoneses, letter to the editor, *El Monitor Republicano*, 21 April 1847.
67. "Cuestión extranjera," Morelia, 14 May 1847, in *El Monitor Republicano*, 20 May 1847.
68. Speech of José María Godoy, Mexico City, 27 September 1846, in *El Monitor Republicano*, 30 September 1846.
69. *El Corresponsal del Ejército*, 17 April 1847.
70. *El Monitor Republicano*, 2 February 1847.
71. *El Monitor Republicano*, 28 January 1848.
72. *El Conservador* (Montevideo), 22 January 1848; *El Hijo de la Revolución*, 16 August 1846; *Comercio del Plata*, 13 November 1847.
73. *El Nacional*, 7 March 1846.
74. Quoted in *El Monitor Republicano*, 26 June 1847.
75. *El Diario del Gobierno* (Mexico City), reprinted in *El Indicador*, 12 October 1846; *El Monitor Republicano*, 2 February 1847.
76. McGuinness, "Searching for 'Latin America.'"
77. *El Monitor Republicano*, 16 January 1848.
78. *La Opinión Nacional*, reprinted in *El Monitor Republicano*, 12 April 1847.
79. *El Monitor Republicano*, 23 and 27 January 1848.
80. *El Nacional*, 10 February 1843; *Comercio del Plata*, 12 February 1848.
81. *El Corresponsal del Ejército*, 12 June 1847; *El Monitor Republicano*, 25 May 1847; Johannsen, *To the Halls*, 302–3.
82. Grant, *Personal Memoirs*, 22–23.
83. Grant, *Personal Memoirs*, 24.
84. Alberdi, *La monarquía*, 112.
85. Adelman, "Between Order and Liberty," 99–101, 105–6.
86. *El Monitor Republicano*, 7 January 1847.
87. *El Monitor Republicano*, 7 July 1848.
88. *El Monitor Republicano*, 8 January 1848.
89. F. Bilbao, "Iniciativa de la América," 292–93.
90. Francisco Vela, "La suerte de las Americas," *La Guerra*, 31 January 1862.
91. Francisco G. Palacio, "Los Estados-Unidos en la cuestión presente," *La Independencia* (Durango), reprinted in *La Alianza de la Frontera*, 17 April 1862. See also Grandin, "The Liberal Traditions," 84.
92. Ignacio Manuel Altamirano, "Algunas palabras acerca de Mr. Wagner, ministro de Prusia en México," Mexico City, 5 August 1862, *La Alianza de la Frontera*, 4 September 1862.
93. Ignacio Manuel Altamirano, "La nota de Campbell," in *La República* (Chihuahua), 12 July 1867.
94. "Los Estados Unidos hácia México un tributo al Sr. Juárez por medio del Sr. Romero," Washington, D.C., 26 July 1867, in *La República* (Chihuahua), 13 September 1867.

95. Juan González Urueña, "El verdadero objeto de la intervención," *La Guerra*, 7 February 1862.

96. La doctrina de Monroe," *La Bandera Nacional*, 18 June 1864.

97. *La Bandera Nacional*, 14 May 1864.

98. Los Pisqueños, "Pisco: Unión Americana," Pisco, 6 July 1864, *El Comercio*, 13 July 1864.

99. Sarmiento, *North and South America*, 16.

100. The standard view is to see only hostility. See O'Brien, *Making the Americas*, 15–49. For a more nuanced view, see Dunkerley, *Americana*.

101. McGuinness, *Path of Empire*, 152–83.

102. Quoted in Alamán, *Historia de Méjico*, 5:924–25.

103. Proclamation of the state of México's Legislature to its inhabitants, Toluca, 26 April 1847, in *El Monitor Republicano*, 2 May 1847.

104. *El Diario del Gobierno* (Mexico City), reprinted in *El Indicador*, 3 and 12 October 1846.

105. President Pedro María Anaya to Army, México, 3 April 1847, *El Corresponsal del Ejército*, 10 April 1847. See also Gobat, "The Invention of Latin America."

106. For more on the conservative press, see Suárez Argüello, "Una punzante visión," 95–104.

107. Alamán, *Historia de Méjico*, 5:877, 924–25.

108. Alamán, *Historia de Méjico*, 1:26–28.

109. Quoted in McGuinness, *Path of Empire*, 160; see also 159–70.

110. Mignolo, *The Idea of Latin America*, 63–64, 89.

111. Grandin, "The Liberal Traditions," 80; McGuinness, *Path of Empire*, 160–61.

CHAPTER FOUR. EAGLES OF AMERICAN DEMOCRACY

1. *El Ferrocarril* (Santiago), reprinted in *La Nación*, 19 December 1860.

2. Speech of Manuel Ojinaga, Chihuahua, 16 September 1861, in *La Alianza de la Frontera*, supplement, 5 October 1861.

3. For Mexican political history, see Cosío Villegas, *Historia moderna*; Quirarte, *Historiografía*. For Colombia, see Bushnell, *The Making of Modern Colombia*. For intellectual histories, see Jaramillo Uribe, *El pensamiento colombiano*; Hale, *Mexican Liberalism*; Hale, *The Transformation of Liberalism*; Connaughton, Illades, and Pérez Toledo, *Construcción de la legitimidad política*; Palacios, *Ensayos*. For La Reforma, see Mallon, *Peasant and Nation*; McNamara, *Sons of the Sierra*; Guerrero Mendoza, *La impasibilidad cuestionada de Juárez*; Merino, "La formación"; Wasserman, *Everyday Life and Politics*; Sinkin, *The Mexican Reform*; Thomson with LaFrance, *Patriotism, Politics, and Popular Liberalism*; Hernández Chávez, "Monarquía-República-Nación-Pueblo."

4. Tomás Mosquera, "A sus conciudadanos miembros del Senado y Cámara de Representantes," Popayán, 24 March 1873, ACON-C-1873, Correspondencia Oficial IX, 275.

5. Speech of Manuel Merino, Chihuahua, 15 September 1868, in *La República* (Chihuahua), 18 September 1868.

6. *La Guerra*, 3 January 1862.

7. Federico Flores, "La América se salvará," *El Comercio*, 13 July 1864.

8. Speech of Avelino Vela, Ipiales, Colombia, 15 February 1864, ACC-AM, paquete 85, legajo 85.

9. Speech of Benito Juárez, Mexico City, 10 January 1861, in *La Alianza de la Frontera*, supplement, 9 March 1861.

10. Speech of Gabino Ortiz to National Guard, Morelia, 5 January 1862, in *La Guerra*, 10 January 1862.

11. Speech of Gabino Ortiz to National Guard, Morelia, 5 January 1862, in *La Guerra*, 10 January 1862. See also López-Alves, "Modernization Theory Revisited," 256.

12. Speech of Juan Cervin de la Mora to the Battalion of Artisans, Morelia, 5 January 1862, in *La Guerra*, 24 January 1862.

13. *La Guerra*, 27 December 1861.

14. Speech of Gabino Ortiz to National Guard, Morelia, 5 January 1862, in *La Guerra*, 10 January 1862.

15. *La Bandera Nacional*, 13 July 1864. See also Galeana, "Encuentros y desencuentros," 96.

16. *La Opinión Nacional*, 1 April 1868.

17. *El Voto del Pueblo* (Guadalajara), reprinted in *La Alianza de la Frontera*, supplement, 29 July 1862.

18. *La Chinaca*, 30 June 1862.

19. *El Monitor Republicano*, 1 July 1867.

20. Federico Flores, "La América se salvará," *El Comercio*, 13 July 1864.

21. Héctor F. Varela, "El Americano: Sus prospectos y su misión," *El Americano*, 7 March 1872.

22. Speech of Jesús Escobar y Armendáriz, Villa del Paso del Norte, 16 September 1867, in *La República* (Chihuahua), 8 November 1867.

23. Chakrabarty, "Postcoloniality," 17. See also, C. Alonso, *The Burden of Modernity*, 32; Mignolo, *The Idea of Latin America*, 57–58. For a critique of Chakrabarty, see Coronil, *The Magical State*, 13–14.

24. F. Bilbao, "El evangelio americano," 2:419.

25. F. Bilbao, "Emancipación del espíritu en América."

26. Alejandro Mejías-López argues that the *modernismo* movement of the 1880s was the "first instance" in which the direction of influence between Europe and America was reversed (*The Inverted Conquest*, 9). It was not; moreover, republican modernity was more influential since it involved not just elite *letrados*, but also the broader public sphere.

27. *El Republicano*, 28 March 1846.

28. López, *Mensaje del Poder Ejecutivo*, 1, broadside in BN-R.

29. El Voto del Pueblo (Guadalajara), reprinted in La Alianza de la Frontera, supplement, 29 July 1862. See also La Chinaca, 5 June 1862; El Aguijón, 8 October 1871.
30. See also Dubois, A Colony of Citizens, 4–5; Cooper, Colonialism in Question, 21.
31. El Aguijón, 8 October 1871.
32. El Grito de Guerra, 1 February 1863.
33. Ben-Dor Benite, "Modernity," 638–46.
34. Chakrabarty, Provincializing Europe.
35. Juan González Urueña, "El verdadero objeto de la intervención," La Guerra, 31 January 1862.
36. Juan González Urueña, "El verdadero objeto de la intervención," La Guerra, 31 January 1862.
37. La Guerra, 27 December 1861. See also Thomson, "Mid-Nineteenth-Century Modernities," 77.
38. Juan González Urueña, "El verdadero objeto de la intervención," La Guerra, 7 February 1862.
39. "Las repúblicas americanas," El Independiente (Santiago), reprinted in El Globo, 1 July 1867.
40. F. Bilbao, "El evangelio americano," 2:424–25.
41. See Jaramillo Uribe, El pensamiento colombiano.
42. La Unión, 23 October 1864. See also, Julián Trujillo, Eliseo Payán, and Manuel del Quijano to deputies of the Constitutional Convention, Popayán, 15 July 1872, ACC-AM, paquete 116, legajo 16.
43. El Neogranadino (Bogotá), 23 December 1848, quoted in König, En el camino, 453.
44. La Unión, 23 October 1864.
45. La Unión, 18 October 1863, 31 January 1864; El Caucano, 21 January 1864.
46. Zamorano, Bosquejo biográfico, 4–5.
47. Emiro Kastos [Juan de Dios Restrepo], "La Guerra," Buga, 13 January 1864, El Caucano, 21 January 1864. See also El Ciudadano, 17 June 1848.
48. F. Bilbao, "El evangelio americano," 2:420.
49. F. Bilbao, "El evangelio americano," 2:421–22.
50. F. Bilbao, "El evangelio americano," 2:420.
51. F. Bilbao, "Movimiento social de los pueblos," 1:169, 171.
52. El Nacional, 5 April 1843.
53. Speech of Carlos Pachecho, Chihuahua, 5 May 1864, in La Alianza de la Frontera, 7 May 1864.
54. La Chinaca, 1 May 1862.
55. T. C. Mosquera to National Congress, 17 December 1863, ACON-S, 1864, Expedientes del Poder Ejecutivo IV, 31.
56. Carlos Santa María, "Ultimas noticias de México," La Independiente (Durango), reprinted in La Alianza de la Frontera, 17 April 1862.
57. S. Cosío, La República (Zacatecas), reprinted in La República (Chihuahua), 10 May 1867.

58. S. Cosío, *La República* (Zacatecas), reprinted in *La República* (Chihuahua), 10 May 1867.

59. *El Constitucional* (México), reprinted in *La República* (Chihuahua), 8 November 1867.

60. S. Cosío, *La República* (Zacatecas), reprinted in *La República* (Chihuahua), 10 May 1867.

61. *El Globo*, 5 July 1867. Guy Thomson finds some similar ideas in Mexico but tends to see this vision of modernity emerging from rising consumption and technological progress as much as from political change ("Mid-Nineteenth-Century Modernities").

62. "La guerra de Europa," *El Siglo Diez y Nueve*, reprinted in *La Cuestión Social*, 2 March 1861.

63. *La Unión*, 31 January 1864.

64. For the fascination with railroads, see Gómez Pérez, "Ceremonias cívicas."

65. Máximo Castañeda, "Presidente de la Junta Patriótica," Paso del Norte, 19 September 1867, in *La República* (Chihuahua), 8 November 1867.

66. *El Nacional*, 7 March 1846.

67. Mercado, *Memorias*, xci–xciii.

68. Luis G. Bossero, "Introducción," *El Estandarte Nacional*, 16 November 1856.

69. Speech of Manuel Ojinaga, Chihuahua, 16 September 1861, in *La Alianza de la Frontera*, supplement, 5 October 1861.

70. José M. Obando, "Mensaje del Presidente," Bogota, 1 February 1854, ACON-C, 1854, Correspondencia Oficial IV, 2

71. F. Bilbao, "El Presidente Obando," 1:187.

72. Barbacoas's Municipal Council to senators and representatives, Barbacoas, 13 January 1855, ACON-S, 1855, Informes de Comisiones VI, 317.

73. Cosío Villegas, *Historia moderna*.

74. León Guzmán, Isidoro Olvera, and José Antonio Gamboa, "El Congreso Constituyente á la Nación," 5 February 1857, in *Constitución*, 16.

75. León Guzmán, Isidoro Olvera, and José Antonio Gamboa, "El Congreso Constituyente á la Nación," 5 February 1857, in *Constitución*, 21, 22.

76. León Guzmán, Isidoro Olvera, and José Antonio Gamboa, "El Congreso Constituyente á la Nación," 5 February 1857, in *Constitución*, 19.

77. León Guzmán, Isidoro Olvera, and José Antonio Gamboa, "El Congreso Constituyente á la Nación," 5 February 1857, in *Constitución*, 19, 22.

78. Federico Flores, "La América se salvará," *El Comercio*, 13 July 1864.

79. Mercado, *Memorias*, xviii.

80. Mercado, *Memorias*, liii.

81. Mercado, *Memorias*, liii.

82. Mercado, *Memorias*, lxv.

83. Arias, *Reseña histórica*, 238–40; *La República* (Chihuahua), 9 August 1867.

84. *La Nación*, 25, 26 December 1860.

85. Speech of Manuel Ojinaga, Chihuahua, 16 September 1861, in *La Alianza de la Frontera*, supplement, 5 October 1861.
86. *La República* (Chihuahua), 18 September 1868.
87. Speech of President Benito Juárez to Congress, Mexico City, 13 June 1861, in *La Alianza de la Frontera*, 13 June 1861.
88. Speech of Gabino Ortiz to National Guard, Morelia, 5 January 1862, in *La Guerra*, 10 January 1862.
89. Speech of Mariano Samaniego, Villa del Paso, 16 September 1862, in *La Alianza de la Frontera*, 13 November 1862.
90. Speech of Jesús Escobar y Armendáriz, Villa del Paso del Norte, 16 September 1867, *La República* (Chihuahua), 8 November 1867.
91. *El Estandarte Nacional*, 14 April 1857.
92. *La Opinión Nacional*, 1 April 1868.
93. *La Chinaca*, 30 June 1862.
94. Speech of José María Camarena, Hidalgo de Parral, no date, in *La Alianza de la Frontera*, supplement, 20 April 1861.
95. *La Guerra* (Morelia), 27 December 1861; Máximo Castañeda, "Presidente de la Junta Patriótica," Paso del Norte, 19 September 1867, *La República* (Chihuahua), 8 November 1867; speech of Jesús Escobar y Armendáriz, Villa del Paso del Norte, 16 September 1867, in *La República* (Chihuahua), 8 November 1867; Juan González Urueña, "El verdadero objeto de la intervención," *La Guerra*, 7 February 1862.
96. *La Chinaca*, 19 May 1862.
97. *La Chinaca*, 1 May 1862.
98. *La República* (Chihuahua), 2 February 1867.
99. *La República* (Chihuahua), 15 February 1867. See also *La República* (Chihuahua), 12 July 1867 and 23 August 1867.
100. Presidente Lucas Aguilar and 45 others, "Protesta de la Junta Municipal y vecindario del Norte," Norte, 12 August 1862, in *La Alianza de la Frontera*, 4 September 1862.
101. Varios Mexicanos, "La Europa y la prisión de Maximiliano," reprint of a broadsheet, in *El Globo*, 30 June 1867.
102. Speech of Jesús Escobar y Armendáriz, Villa del Paso del Norte, 16 September 1867, in *La República* (Chihuahua), 8 November 1867.
103. *La Guerra*, 27 December 1861.
104. Hall, "The West and the Rest"; Quijano, "Coloniality of Power."
105. For postcolonialism, see Mignolo, *The Darker Side*, xx–xxiii.
106. F. Bilbao, "Emancipación del espíritu en América," 2:549. For Hegel, see Buck-Morss, *Hegel, Haiti, and University History*.
107. Speech of Mariano Murillo, Chihuahua, 15 September 1862, in *La Alianza de la Frontera*, supplement, 23 September 1862. For debates on Spanish colonialism and nationalism, see Schmidt-Nowara, *The Conquest of History*.

108. Governor of Pasto to the secretary of Hacienda, Pasto, 18 December 1852, AGNC-SR, Fondo Gobernaciones—Pasto, tomo 8, 539.

109. Speech of Juan Cervin de la Mora to the Battalion of Artisans, Morelia, 5 January 1862, in *La Guerra*, 24 January 1862.

110. Earle, *The Return of the Native*, 19. See also Ortega y Medina, "Indigenismo e hispanismo."

111. *El Compás*, 8 May 1841.

112. Mercado, *Memorias*, vii.

113. Mercado, *Memorias*, xviii, xcv.

114. López, *Mensaje del Presidente*, 1, broadside in BN-R.

115. *La Bandera Nacional*, 13 July 1864.

116. *La Bandera Nacional*, 13 July 1864.

117. Mignolo, *Local Histories/Global Designs*, 133. For the sense of possibilities in the mid-century Americas, see Dunkerley, *Americana*.

118. For *letrados*, see Brading, *The First America*, 648–74.

119. López-Alves, "Modernization Theory Revisited," 268.

120. *La Guerra*, 3 January 1862.

121. Captain Cayetano Justiniani to Volunteers, Chihuahua, 9 January 1861, in *La Alianza de la Frontera*, 17 January 1861.

122. José María Jaurrieta, "Protesta del Congreso del Estado," Chihuahua, 31 May 1862, in *La Alianza de la Frontera*, 5 June 1862.

123. Speech of Gabino Ortiz to National Guard, Morelia, 5 January 1862, in *La Guerra*, 10 January 1862.

124. Hobsbawm, *Nations and Nationalism since 1780*, 22; Sewell, "The French Revolution." For studies of Latin American nationalism, see Colom González, *Relatos de nación*; Castro Klarén and Chasteen, *Beyond Imagined Communities*; Dunkerley, ed., *Studies in the Formation*.

125. Speech of Manuel Muñoz, Villa de Allende, 16 September 1863, in *La Alianza de la Frontera*, 14 November 1863.

126. Speech of Mariano Murillo, Chihuahua 15 September 1862, in *La Alianza de la Frontera*, supplement, 23 September 1862. See also Palti, *La nación como problema*.

127. Speech of Joaquín H. Domínguez, Villa de Allende, 16 September 1862, in *La Alianza de la Frontera*, 20 November 1862. Domínguez, however, would defect to serve Maximilian's Empire.

128. Speech of Higinio Muñoz, Santa Rita, 8 August 1867, in *La República* (Chihuahua), 23 August 1867.

129. See Thurner, *From Two Republics*, 10; Florescano, *Historia de las historias*.

130. Estrada, *El catolicismo y la democracia*, 123.

131. Speech of Mariano Murillo, Chihuahua, 15 September 1862, in *La Alianza de la Frontera*, supplement, 23 September 1862.

132. *El Montañes*, 15 February 1876.

133. [José Hilario López] to José de Obaldía [Ibagué, 1854], AGNC-SACH-FJHL, caja 9, carpeta 8, 217.

134. El Nacional, 15 December 1842.

135. Comercio del Plata, 20 May 1846.

136. Manuel Ibáñez to Tomás Mosquera, Cali, 12 October 1850, ACC-SM, #27,586.

137. Speech of Vicente Camilo Fontal, Almaguer, 1 January 1852, ACC-AM, paquete 53, legajo 77.

138. Speech of J.N. Núñez, Cali, 6 February 1850, in Ariete, 2 March 1850.

139. La Chinaca, 8 May 1862.

140. La Chinaca, 12 May 1862.

141. La Chinaca, 12 May 1862.

142. La Unión, 23 October 1864. See also Lasso, Myths of Harmony.

143. El Globo, 5 July 1867. See also McGuinness, Path of Empire, 181.

144. La Voz Nacional, 14 April 1862.

145. For sovereignty, see Forment, Democracy in Latin America; Casaús Arzú, El lenguaje de los ismos. For the pueblo, see Palti, El momento romántico.

146. See Thomson, "Mid-Nineteenth-Century Modernities," 77.

147. El Sentimiento Democrático, 17 May 1849.

148. El Pensamiento Popular, 1 July 1852.

149. Hobsbawm, Nations and Nationalism since 1780, 20.

150. El Monitor Republicano, 19 September 1846.

151. "El llamado partido conservador en Durango," La Libertad (Durango) reprinted in La Alianza de la Frontera, 13 December 1860.

152. La Chinaca, 1 May 1862.

153. The contrast with Habermas's notion of the nineteenth-century bourgeois public sphere is striking. See Habermas, The Structural Transformation, 51–56.

154. López, Mensaje del Presidente, 1, broadside in BN-R.

155. Juan Antonio Delgado to José Hilario López, Cali, 14 February 1852, AGNC-SACH-FJHL, caja 7, carpeta 2, 75.

156. C. T. E., "La independencia de México,"El Siglo Diez y Nueve reprinted in La Alianza de la Frontera, 24 July 1862.

157. For public opinion, see Piccato, The Tyranny of Opinion; Sabato, "La reacción de América."

158. El Nacional, 7 April 1843.

159. The Democratic Society of Roldanillo to President, Roldanillo, 31 December 1853, ACON-C, 1854, Informes de Comisiones V, 68.

160. Los Verdaderos Constitucionalistas, A los liberals, 1, broadside in AGNC-SC-FEOR, caja 114, carpeta 426.

161. El Caucano, 6 August 1863.

162. Protest of Ayuntamiento de Distrito Bravos, Villa del Paso, 21 July 1862, in La Alianza de la Frontera, 14 August 1862.

163. General José López Uraga and others, San Marcos, 26 March 1864, in *La Bandera Nacional*, 22 June 1864.

164. *El Calavera*, 25 June 1871.

165. *La Bandera Nacional*, 14 May 1864.

166. *La Bandera Nacional*, 18 June 1864.

167. Speech of Manuel Ojinaga, Chihuahua, 16 September 1861, in *La Alianza de la Frontera*, supplement, 5 October 1861.

168. de la Luz Rosas, *La Junta*, 1, broadside in AHMRG-FBPCM, n. 510; Hernández, *El C. José M. P. Hernández*, 1, broadside in AHMRG-FBPCM, n. 510.

169. Speech of Governor Luis Terrazas, 1 May 1862, in *La Alianza de la Frontera*, 1 May 1862.

170. *Ariete*, 19 January 1850.

171. *La Unión*, 20 May 1852.

172. *El Imperio*, 20 August 1863.

173. *La Chinaca*, 23 June 1862.

174. *La Guerra*, 17 January 1862.

175. *Observaciones*, 1, broadside in AGNC-SC-FEOR, caja 73, carpeta 265. See also Urías Horcasitas, "Ideas de modernidad."

176. Comonfort, *El ciudadano*, 1, broadside in AHMRG-FBPCM, n. 510.

177. *La Opinión Nacional*, 3 April 1868.

178. *El Calavera*, 30 July 1871. For independence-era debates, see Adelman, *Sovereignty and Revolution*. For municipal sovereignty, see Dym, *From Sovereign Villages*.

179. *El Monitor Republicano*, 1 July 1867.

180. Quijada Mauriño, "Los confines del pueblo soberano."

181. Palti, *La política del disenso*, 23–24.

182. *El Ciudadano*, 22 July 1848.

183. *Ariete*, 10 August 1850.

184. *El Obrero del Porvenir*, 11 June 1871.

185. For repertoires, see Tilly, "Contentious Repertoires in Great Britain." For a bibliography, see Sanders, "Popular Movements."

186. The Democratic Society of Roldanillo to President, Roldanillo, 31 December 1853, ACON-C, 1854, Informes de Comisiones V, 68.

187. *El Pensamiento Popular*, 1 July 1852.

188. Sabato, *The Many and the Few*, 4. Hilda Sabato uses the constitution for dating universal male suffrage, while Paula Alonso focuses on the electoral law of 1856 ("Voting in Buenos Aires," 182).

189. *Constitución*, 37. The 1863 Colombian constitution allowed states to determine citizenship requirements. For citizenship, see Sabato, *Ciudadanía política*.

190. Keyssar, *The Right to Vote*, 348, 354.

191. Aminzade, *Ballots and Barricades*, 159.

192. Posada-Carbó, "Elections before Democracy," 1.

193. Jorge J. Hoyos to Mariano Ospina, Buenaventura, 25 March 1859, BN-FM, libro 189, 363.

194. Pedro José Piedrahíta to T. C. de Mosquera, Cali, 12 March 1859, ACC-SM, #36,922.

195. Simón Arboleda to T. C. de Mosquera, Coconuco, 14 February 1859, ACC-SM, #36,041; El Montañes, 1 February 1876.

196. Tomás M. Mosquera to Tomás C. de Mosquera, Buenosaires, 17 February 1859, ACC-SM, #36,666; El Ferrocarril (Cali), 13 September 1878.

197. Guardino, The Time of Liberty; Sanders, Contentious Republicans.

198. Forment, Democracy in Latin America, xvii. See also Thomson, "Mid-Nineteenth-Century Modernities," 80; J. Wood, The Society of Equality, 187–223.

199. González Bernaldo, "Los clubes electorales."

200. McEvoy, "La experiencia republicana," 261.

201. Sociedad Democrática de Palmira, Estatuto, 9, 12, 15, 16; El Sentimiento Democrático, 6 December 1849; La Voz del Pueblo (Cali), 20 February 1879; El Boyacense, 26 June 1867; Sanders, Contentious Republicans.

202. La Alianza de la Frontera, 29 August 1861.

203. Máximo Castañeda, "Presidente de la Junta Patriótica," Paso del Norte, 19 September 1867, in La República (Chihuahua), 8 November 1867.

204. La Alianza de la Frontera, 29 August 1861, See also Beezley, Martin, and French, Rituals of Rule; Pérez Martínez, "Hacia una tópica"; Lempérière, "De la república," 336–43.

205. Judge Luis Pastor to Minister of Justice, México, 29 October 1868, AGNM-IG-FJJ, vol. 601, exp. 31, 169; Report of General José Calderón, Poncitlán, 1 April 1857, AGNM-IG-FJJ, vol. 592, exp. 13, 107; Becker, "In Search of Tinterillos."

206. For patria chica, see Van Young, The Other Rebellion.

207. El Cronista de México, 23 August 1862; El Monitor Republicano, 4 June 1848; La Libertad, 22 November 1884; Las Máscaras, 21 November 1850; Gaceta Oficial del Cauca, 22 December 1866; Los Principios, 20 February 1874; Ariete, 18 May 1850; La Voz del Pueblo (Cali), 21 November 1878.

208. La Libertad, 19 November 1884; El Guaitara, 20 September 1864.

209. Bautista Feijoo to the provincial governor, Caloto, 6 May 1849, ACC-AM, paquete 47, legajo 84.

210. See the petitions in this chapter. In general, the ACC-AM; ACON, AGNM-FJJ; and UI are rich sources of petitions.

211. Mercado, Memorias, xc. See also Ferrer, Insurgent Cuba, 37–42.

212. Thomson with LaFrance, Patriotism Politics, and Popular Liberalism; Mallon, Peasant and Nation.

213. Mallon, Peasant and Nation, 31; Sanders, Contentious Republicans, 18–57.

214. Ramón Mercado, El Núcleo (Bogotá), n.d.

215. El Hombre, 10 July 1852.

216. El Pensamiento Popular, 22 July 1852.

217. El *Pensamiento Popular*, 22 July 1852.

218. F. Bilbao, "Sociabilidad chilena," 1:22, 23.

219. Manuel [Luna] to Sergio Arboleda, Popayán, 1 November 1854, ACC-FA, #1518.

220. *La Bandera Nacional*, 3 August 1864.

221. Decree of 15 April 1845, in *El Constitucional*, 17 April 1845.

222. *El Hijo de la Revolución*, 2 August 1846; *El Nacional*, 20 September 1853; *El Constitucional*, 8 February 1845, 3 April 1845, and 17 April 1845; *Comercio del Plata*, 16 March 1846.

223. Miguel Burbano to Túquerres Legislature, Túquerres, 22 November 1853, ACC-AM, paquete 54, legajo 53.

224. "El alto clero," *Diario de Gobierno* (San Luis Potosí), reprinted in *La Alianza de la Frontera*, 19 September 1863. See also Iparraguirre, "Modernidad y religiosidad."

225. See Guardino, *The Time of Liberty*, 281; Posada-Carbó, "Elections before Democracy," 11–12; Carmagnani, *The Other West*, 182–87.

226. For claims making and modernity, see Cooper, *Colonialism in Question*, 131, 146; Falcón, *Culturas de pobreza y resistencia*.

227. Guha, "Preface," 35; Guha, "On Some Aspects," 44.

228. Sanders, *Contentious Republicans*.

229. Muñiz, *Protesta*, 1, broadside in AHMRG-FII, #530.

230. Muñiz, *Protesta*, 1, broadside in AHMRG-FII, #530. See also Mallon, *Peasant and Nation*. For the preconquest indigenous past, see Earle, *The Return of the Native*.

231. For Europe, see Weber, *Peasants into Frenchmen*; Connor, "When Is a Nation?"

232. See Mallon, *Peasant and Nation*; Thurner, *From Two Republics*; Sabato, *Ciudadanía política*.

233. The undersigned, residents of Guadalupe y Calvo, "Protesta en contra de la intervención francesa," Guadalupe y Calvo, 28 August 1863, *La Alianza de la Frontera*, 12 September 1863.

234. Speech of Sr. Portugal to La Nueva Sociedad, 31 July 1848, in *El Siglo Diez y Nueve*, 7 August 1848.

235. The undersigned members of the Democratic Society to "Citizen President of the State," Cali, 1 June 1877, ACC-AM, paquete 137, legajo 7. For land claims, see LeGrand, *Frontier Expansion*.

236. Juan Ascención Pérez and others to the minister of justice, Trinidad, 7 July 1856, AGNM-IG-FJJ, vol. 547, expediente 3, 14; Village of Santiago Tlaltelolco to Luis Velázquez de la Cadena, Mexico City, 4 February 1843, AGNM-IG-FG, caja 259, expediente 6, 1; the governor and officials of Indians of Pitayó to the state governor, Popayán, 24 November 1858, ACC-AM, paquete 67, legajo 19.

237. Sanders, *Contentious Republicans*, 18–57. See also Falcón, "El arte de la petición."

238. See Valentín Gómez to the minister of justice, Toluca, 8 November 1867, AGNM-IG-FJS, vol. 3, expediente 667.5.

239. Santiago Avila and eleven others to the president, San Andrés Aparco, 7 June 1856, AGNM-IG-FJJ, vol. 546, expediente 42, 417; See also Caplan, *Indigenous Citizens*.

240. For popular sovereignty, see Sabato, "La reacción de América."

241. Undersigned members of the Democratic Society to the state president, Cali, 14 October 1866, ACC-AM, paquete 65, legajo 67.

242. Trinidad García and five others to "Ecsmo. Señor," Mexico City, 30 August 1856, AGNM-IG-FJJ, vol. 547, expediente 13, 106.

243. Indigenous residents of the Aldea of Cajamarca to Cauca state president, Cajamarca, 30 July 1871, ACC-AM, paquete 112, legajo 29.

244. "El pequeño cabildo de Indíjenas de Mocondino" to the state president, Pasto, Colombia, 18 February 1866, ACC-AM, paquete 94, legajo 54.

245. El *Compás*, 19 March 1842.

246. José Joaquín Reies to Cabildo president, Cali, 20 June 1853, AHMC-ACM, tomo 124, 517.

247. Undersigned residents of Cartago [four and a half pages of names] to senators and representatives, Cartago, 28 February 1855, AC-S, 1858, Asuntos Varios XII, 196.

248. Report of Jefe of Veracruz Department, 2 September 1848, AGNM-IG-FG, caja 350, expediente 14, 6.

249. Governor Juan Soto to the minister of the interior and foreign relations, Jalapa, 4 September 1848, AGNM-IG-FG, caja 350, expediente 14, 6.

250. Angel Camas to the president, Chiapa, 29 December 1855, in *La Voz del Pueblo* (San Cristóbal), 5 January 1856.

251. Manuel López to Ayuntamiento, no place, 5 January 1856, in *La Voz del Pueblo* (San Cristóbal), supplement, 5 January 1856.

252. J. Nicolás Domínguez and ten others to the governor, Ciudad de Comitán, 9 January 1856, AGNM-IG-FJJ, vol. 585, expediente 1, 24.

253. Angel Corzo to the minister of justice, Chiapa, 28 December 1855, AGNM-IG-FJJ, vol. 585, expediente 1, 15.

254. Francisco Zapata and others of the Municipal Corporation of Huimanguillo to the president, Huimanguillo, 9 October 1856, AGNM-IG-FJJ, vol. 547, expediente 36, 268.

255. José María Mata, representing el Chico, to the president, Mexico City, 5 August 1856, AGNM-IG-FJJ, vol. 547, expediente 40, 298.

256. Rafael Cataño to the president, Veracruz, 20 October 1859, AGNM-IG-FJJ, vol. 621, expediente 3, 17.

257. For state legitimacy, see Annino, "El paradigma y la disputa"; Connaughton, Illades, and Pérez Toledo, *Construcción de la legitimidad política*; Guerra, "Mexico from Independence to Revolution," 136; Wolfe, *The Everyday Nation-State*.

258. Undersigned residents of Paso del Bobo to [the president], Paso del Bobo, 1 October 1859, AGNM-IG-FJJ, vol. 621, expediente 24, 155.

259. Wright, *Montevideo*, appendix.

260. "Those who wait and see," letter to *El Constitucional*, 17 April 1845.

261. "The Loyal Ones," letter to *El Constitucional*, 7 May 1845.

262. "Ten employees of the Republic," letter to *Comercio del Plata*, 3 March 1846.

263. Decrees of Ministerio de Gobierno, 14 March 1846, in *Comercio del Plata*, 16 March 1846; *Comercio del Plata*, 23 April 1846.

264. "Santos Gutiérrez á los Colombianos," on board *El Danuvio*, 7 August 1867; *El Boyacense*, 7 September 1867; Mercado, *Memorias*, xc.

265. See Mallon, *Peasant and Nation*; McNamara, *Sons of the Sierra*. For origins, see Thibaud, *Repúblicas en armas*; Lasso, *Myths of Harmony*.

266. Bonifacio Loria, representing the community of Indians of Teremendo, Mexico City, 4 December 1867, AGNM-IG-FJS, vol. 3, expediente 668.

267. Mallon, *Peasant and Nation*, 114.

268. Residents of Quilcacé Aldea to municipal vocales, Quilcacé, Colombia, 14 February 1864, ACC-AM, paquete 88, legajo 54.

269. Democratic Society of Palmira to the president, Palmira, 21 June 1868, INCORA-B, tomo 7, 492.

270. Petition of officers and soldiers of the Legion de Voluntarios, Montevideo, 11 April 1844, in *El Nacional*, 17 April 1844.

271. José del Carmen Castillo and others to the president, Tumaco, 12 December 1875, INCORA-B, tomo 10, 49.

272. Alcalde Marcelino Peña and twenty-five others to [the minister of justice], Amoles, 30 March 1857, AGNM-IG-FJJ, vol. 547, expediente 4, 23.

273. Sebastiana Silva to jefe municipal, Popayán, 13 October 1874, ACC-AM, paquete 129, legajo 39.

274. Juan José Baz to President Comonfort, Mexico City, 25 July 1856, AGNM-IG-FJJ vol. 547, expediente 38, 287.

275. Democratic Society of San Pedro to President José Hilario López, San Pedro, 21 March 1852, ACON-C, 1852, Proyectos de Ley Negados I, 47.

276. This literature has grown too vast for each item in it to be cited. For a review of the literature, see Sanders, "Popular Movements."

277. For liberalism versus republicanism, see Brading, *The First America*, 663; Ávila, "Liberalismos decimonónicos."

278. Speech of Roque J. Morón, Chihuahua, 16 September 1862, in *La Alianza de la Frontera*, 25 September 1862.

279. *La República* (Chihuahua), 9 August 1867.

280. *Comercio del Plata*, 29 September 1847.

281. *El Amigo del Pueblo* (Mexico City), 15 August 1869.

282. Popayán Legislature to National Congress, Popayán, 20 September 1854, ACON-S, 1855, Informes de Comisiones VI, 525. See also McGuinness, *Path of Empire*, 159–70; Earle, *The Return of the Native*, 161–83.

283. Lerdo de Tejada, *Cuadro sinóptico*, 28.

284. Alberdi, La monarquía, 91.

285. Alberdi, La monarquía, 451.

286. Samper, Ensayo sobre las revoluciones, 90–91. See also C. Rojas, Civilization and Violence, 29–30.

287. Samper, Ensayo sobre las revoluciones, 95.

288. Samper, Ensayo sobre las revoluciones, 299.

289. Samper, Ensayo sobre las revoluciones, 299–300.

290. Múnera, Fronteras imaginadas, 22–31.

291. See Mehta, Liberalism and Empire; Foucault, Discipline and Punish.

292. La Cuestión Social, 13 March 1861.

293. El Pensamiento Público, 21 March 1872.

294. Pinzón, Catecismo republicano; El Sentimiento Democrático, 3 May 1849; Fabián Mestas, "Historia y educación."

295. Registro Oficial, 23 February 1874.

296. Luis Sánchez to the judge, Popayán, 6 April 1848, ACC-ACSR, #2708. See also Caplan, Indigenous Citizens; Thurner, From Two Republics.

297. Citizens and residents of Silvia Parish to senators and representatives, Silvia, 19 March 1852, ACON-S, 1852, Informes de Comisiones IV, 137.

298. Las Máscaras, 26 September 1850.

299. López-Alves, "Modernization Theory Revisited," 250–56. See also Quijada Mauriño, "Los confines del pueblo soberano," and other essays in Colom González, ed., Relatos de nación; Urías Horcasitas, "Ideas de modernidad."

300. Jesus Camarena, interim governor of Jalisco, to the minister of justice, Guadalajara, 23 October 1856, AGNM-IG-FJJ, vol. 573, expediente 23, 74.

301. Registro Oficial, 8 December 1877.

302. See Larson, Trials of Nation Making.

303. La Alianza de la Frontera, supplement, 9 March 1861.

304. Pesqueira, Ignacio Pesqueira, 1, broadside in AGNM-IG-FJJ, vol. 600, expediente 21, 184.

305. J. Landes, Women, 7. See also Chambers, From Subjects to Citizens; Dore, "One Step Forward"; Earle, "Rape and the Anxious Republic"; Murray, "Mujeres género, y política."

306. El Ferrocarril (Cali), 28 February 1879.

307. El Aguijón, 1 April 1872.

308. La Guerra, 3 January 1862.

309. La Bandera Nacional, 13 July 1864.

310. El Cernícalo, 8 September 1850.

311. Chambers, From Subjects to Citizens.

312. Petra Hinojosa de Gutiérrez and three others to General Epitacio Huerta, Tacámbaro de Codallos, 14 January 1862, in La Guerra, 24 January 1862.

313. Benjamín Pereira, "Informe del Secretario de Gobierno del Estado Soberano del Cauca á la Legislatura de 1871," ACC-AM, paquete 112, legajo 10.

314. Estrada, El catolicismo y la democracia, 102; Kerber, "'I Have Don,'" 250–51; Zahler, Ambitious Rebels, 150–85.

315. La República (Chihuahua), 20 September 1867; Herrera Olarte, La administración Trujillo, 147–49. See also Martínez, El nacionalismo cosmopolita, 309, 312–16, 329.

316. Tomás Cuenca, El Boyacense, 28 March 1866.

317. Tomás Cuenca, El Boyacense, 4 April 1866.

318. El Nacional, 16 March 1846.

319. El Constitucional, 3 July 1843. See also El Constitucional, 12 May 1845.

320. El Constitucional, 3 April 1845.

321. Comercio del Plata, 25 November 1847.

322. El Hombre, 26 June 1852.

323. El Hombre, 26 June 1852.

324. Alvino Carvallo Ortega to the president, Veracruz, 8 November 1859, AGNM-IG-FJJ, vol. 621, expediente 24, 147.

325. La Cuestión Social, 2 March 1861.

326. Francisco Zarco, "El discurso del Presidente de la República," El Siglo Diez y Nueve, reprinted in La República (Chihuahua), 10 January 1868. See also, Mallon, Peasant and Nation.

327. Manuel María de Zamacona, El Globo, 2 July 1867.

328. For forms of liberalism, see Ávila, "Liberalismos decimonónicos."

329. Speech of Gabino Ortiz to National Guard, Morelia, 5 January 1862, in La Guerra, 10 January 1862.

330. Adelman, "Between Order and Liberty," 100–108.

331. El Ferrocarril (Santiago), reprinted in La Nación, 19 December 1860.

332. M. M. Mallarino, "Mensaje del Poder Ejecutivo al Congreso," Bogotá, 1 February 1857, ACON-C, 1857, Mensajes y Correspondencia IV, 30.

CHAPTER FIVE. FRANCISCO BILBAO
AND THE ATLANTIC IMAGINATION

1. For biographies, see M. Bilbao, "Vida de Francisco Bilbao"; Figueroa, Historia de Francisco Bilbao; Varona, Francisco Bilbao. For intellectual histories, see Jalif de Bertranou, Francisco Bilbao; Ugarte Figueroa, Francisco Bilbao; J. Wood, "The Republic Regenerated"; J. Wood, The Society of Equality.

2. For modernism, see Mejías-López, The Inverted Conquest, 9–33.

3. M. Bilbao, "Vida de Francisco Bilbao," 1:xiv.

4. Varona, Francisco Bilbao, 42–43.

5. M. Bilbao, "Vida de Francisco Bilbao," 1:xxxxiii–xlii; Varona, Francisco Bilbao, 52–59; Ugarte Figueroa, Francisco Bilbao, 9, 64–65.

6. M. Bilbao, "Vida de Francisco Bilbao," 1:xxv–xxvi; Varona, Francisco Bilbao, 75–77.

7. M. Bilbao, "Vida de Francisco Bilbao," 1:xxvii.

8. M. Bilbao, "Vida de Francisco Bilbao," 1:xxxi. See also 1:xxix.

9. Varona, *Francisco Bilbao*, 85–86.

10. Varona, *Francisco Bilbao*, 83–90; M. Bilbao, "Vida de Francisco Bilbao," 1:xxxi–xxxii.

11. M. Bilbao, "Vida de Francisco Bilbao," 1:xlv.

12. M. Bilbao, "Vida de Francisco Bilbao," 1:lvi–lxxi.

13. Varona, *Francisco Bilbao*, 110.

14. Varona, *Francisco Bilbao*, 102–36; M. Bilbao, "Vida de Francisco Bilbao," 1:lxxxi–xcii. See also J. Wood, "The Republic Regenerated."

15. Ugarte Figueroa, *Francisco Bilbao*, 36–50; Varona, *Francisco Bilbao*, 136–38.

16. M. Bilbao, "Vida de Francisco Bilbao," 1:cxxxiii–cxxxv; Varona, *Francisco Bilbao*, 138–53.

17. M. Bilbao, "Vida de Francisco Bilbao," 1:cxliii. See also Ugarte Figueroa, *Francisco Bilbao*, 56.

18. M. Bilbao, "Vida de Francisco Bilbao," 1:clvii–clxviii.

19. *La Alianza de la Frontera*, 7 February 1863.

20. M. Bilbao, "Vida de Francisco Bilbao," 1:clxix. See also Ugarte Figueroa, *Francisco Bilbao*, 59.

21. Donoso, *El pensamiento vivo*, 45; Ugarte Figueroa, *Francisco Bilbao*, 64. Alberto Varona argues that "Bilbao was not an original thinker" (*Francisco Bilbao*, 396).

22. F. Bilbao, "La América en peligro," 2:180–81.

23. F. Bilbao, "La América en peligro," 2:242; see also 188–89, 235–36.

24. F. Bilbao, "El evangelio americano," 2:419. For colonial-era visions, see O'Gorman, *The Invention of America*.

25. F. Bilbao, "Sobre la revelación del porvenir," 2:529.

26. *La Chinaca*, 5 June 1862.

27. F. Bilbao, "La América en peligro," 2:175–76. See also Varona, *Francisco Bilbao*, 392.

28. F. Bilbao, "Sociabilidad chilena," 1:10.

29. *Liberal* (Bogota), reprinted in *El Aguijón*, 17 September 1871.

30. *La Opinión Nacional*, 11 April 1868.

31. Hernández, *El C. José M. P. Hernández*, broadside in AHMRG-FBPCM, n. 510.

32. Speech of Juan Cervín de la Mora to the Battalion of Artisans, Morelia, 5 January 1862, in *La Guerra*, 24 January 1862.

33. Hernández, *El C. José M. P. Hernández*, broadside in AHMRG-FBPCM, n. 510.

34. T. C. de Mosquera to César Conto, Popayán, 2 December [1874], BLAA-M, #113; *La Frontera*, 12 March 1882; *Boletín Republicano*, 28 June 1867.

35. *El Garibaldi*, reprinted in *La Alianza de la Frontera*, 2 May 1861.

36. Estrada, *El catolicismo y la democracia*, 20. See also *El Estandarte Nacional*, 14 April 1857.

37. *El Amigo del Pueblo* (Mexico City), 16 December 1845.

38. César Conto, "Mensaje del Presidente del Estado Soberano del Cauca," Popayán, 1 July 1877, ACC-AM, paquete 137, legajo 27.

39. President of the Democratic Society to the state president, Cali, 14 September 1877, ACC-AM paquete 137, legajo 7.
40. El Juicio Público, 9 March 1858.
41. La Guerra, 20 December 1861. See also La Sombra, 31 July 1866.
42. La Chinaca, 16 June 1862. See also May, Slavery, Race, and Conquest.
43. Speech of Eduardo Urueta, Santa Rita, 8 August 1867, in La República (Chihuahua), 16 August 1867.
44. Emiro Kastos [Juan de Dios Restrepo], "La Guerra," Buga, 13 January 1864, El Caucano, 21 January 1864.
45. El Aguijón, 1 October 1871.
46. "El Año de 1866," La República (Zacatecas), reprinted in La República (Chihuahua), 15 February 1867.
47. Speech of Matías Romero, 16 December 1863, reprinted as Romero, The Situation of Mexico, broadside in LC-JSP, Box 77, folder "French Occupation of Mexico: Printed Matter, 1863–1866." See also La Chinaca, 16 June 1862.
48. Fernández-Armesto, The Americas, 117, 132; Bailyn, Atlantic History.
49. El Comercio, 13 July 1864.
50. La Voz Nacional, 14 April 1862.
51. La Voz Nacional, 1 April 1862.
52. L'Estafette (Mexico City), reprinted in El Ultimo Mohicano, 27 February 1865.
53. La Voz Nacional, 1 April 1862; La Chinaca, 22 May 1862; El Caucano, 21 January 1864.
54. Emiro Kastos [Juan de Dios Restrepo], "La Guerra," Buga, 13 January 1864, El Caucano, 21 January 1864.
55. La Chinaca, 7 August 1862.
56. La Guerra, 20 December 1861.
57. El Siglo Diez y Nueve, 25 May 1861.
58. Report from New Orleans, 4 September 1863, La Patria, 27 September 1863.
59. La Bandera Nacional, 18 June 1864. See also El Globo, 30 July 1867; Arias, Reseña histórica, 68.
60. Speech of Brigadier General A. J. Hamilton, 29 January 1864, in La Alianza de la Frontera, 19 March 1864.
61. F. Bilbao, "La América en peligro," 2:187.
62. Speech of Eduardo Urueta, Santa Rita, 8 August 1867, in La República (Chihuahua), 16 August 1867.
63. F. Bilbao, "Emancipación del espíritu en América," 2:551.
64. "El Año de 1866," La República (Zacatecas), reprinted in La República (Chihuahua), 15 February 1867.
65. Speech of Jesús Escobar y Armendáriz, Villa del Paso del Norte, 16 September 1867, in La República (Chihuahua), 8 November 1867.
66. Mariano Yañes, "El Congreso á la Nación," Mexico City, 8 January 1868, in La República (Chihuahua), 7 February 1868.

67. Speech of Mr. La Reintrie, Baltimore, 26 July 1867, in *Diario Oficial del Gobierno Supremo de la República*, 27 August 1867.

68. Speech of Matías Romero, Baltimore, 26 July 1867, in *Diario Oficial del Gobierno Supremo de la República*, 27 August 1867.

69. Alamán, *Historia de Méjico*; Alberdi, *La monarquía*; Sarmiento, *North and South America*. For *letrados* in general, see Martínez, *El nacionalismo cosmopolita*; C. Rojas, *Civilization and Violence*.

70. Proclamation of Manuel G. Aguirre, Prefecto Político de México, 13 July 1863, in *El Noticioso Diligente*, 1 August 1863.

71. Almonte and de Salas, *Mexicanos*, broadside in AHMRG, Fondo Gobierno, #511.

72. *La Sociedad*, 6 July 1860. See also Galeana, "Encuentros y desencuentros," 96–98.

73. *Diario de la Marina*, 12 July 1867.

74. Pani, "Dreaming of a Mexican Empire"; Pani, *Para mexicanizar el Segundo Imperio*.

75. *Diario de la Marina*, 14 July 1867.

76. Comisión especial de Asamblea de Notables, "Dictamen acerca de la forma de gobierno," in *Documentos relativos*, 42; see also 29–31.

77. Comisión especial de Asamblea de Notables, "Dictamen acerca de la forma de gobierno," in *Documentos relativos*, 44–45.

78. *Correio Mercantil*, 5 August 1867.

79. Juan Bautista Alberdi to Juan María Gutiérrez, Paris, 6 January 1863, in Alberdi, *Cartas inéditas*, 193.

80. Sarmiento, *North and South America*, 14.

81. Vergara y Vergara, "La Política," 100.

82. Alberdi, *La monarquía*, 119.

83. Alberdi, *La monarquía*, 61, 87.

84. Alamán, *Historia de Méjico*, 5:928–29.

85. *La Sociedad*, 6 July 1860.

86. Vicente Cárdenas to Sergio Arboleda, Quito, 1 April 1879, ACC-FA, #1,506.

87. Protest of the pueblo of Ipiales to State Convention, Ipiales, 1 August 1872, ACC-AM, paquete 116, legajo 17.

88. *El Telégrafo*, 24 August 1865.

89. Francisco González to the governor, Santander, 20 March 1855, ACC-AM, paquete 60, legajo 60.

90. *Ariete*, 27 July 1850.

91. Arboleda, *El clero*, 15–16.

92. Comisión especial de Asamblea de Notables, "Dictamen acerca de la forma de gobierno," in *Documentos relativos*, 37.

93. Comisión especial de Asamblea de Notables, "Dictamen acerca de la forma de gobierno," in *Documentos relativos*, 37.

94. Speech of Ignacio Gutiérrez, Bogotá, 1 January 1868, in *El Boyacense*, 22 January 1868.

95. Speech of Ignacio Gutiérrez, Bogotá, 1 January 1868, in *El Boyacense*, 22 January 1868.

96. Speech of Ignacio del Campo, Coronado, 16 September 1861, in *La Alianza de la Frontera*, supplement, 28 September 1861. See also Holden, "Priorities of the State."

97. *El Globo*, 2 July 1867.

98. Alamán, *Historia de Méjico*, 5:884.

99. *La Cruz*, 1 October 1857. See also Pani, "Dreaming of a Mexican Empire," 15.

100. José V. López to Mariano Ospina, Cali, 3 June 1859, BN-FM, libro 210, 132.

101. Pedro José Piedrahíta to T. C. de Mosquera, Cali, 12 March 1859, ACC-SM, #36,922.

102. *El Clamor Nacional*, 22 March 1851.

103. *El Porvenir*, 26 February 1861.

104. Antonio José Chaves, "Mensajes del Gobernador," Pasto, 15 September 1856, ACC-AM, paquete 61, legajo 10.

105. Arcesio Escobar, "La Confederación Granadina," *El Espectador*, 3 April 1862.

106. *El Espectador*, 2 October [1862].

107. Thomson, "Mid-Nineteenth-Century Modernities," 75.

108. Speech of Juan de Dios Burgos, Querétaro, 28 May 1867, in *La República* (Chihuahua), 31 May 1867; *La Alianza de la Frontera*, supplement, 29 July 1862.

109. López, *Mensaje del Poder Ejecutivo*, broadside in BN-R; *La Unión*, 12 March 1864; *La República* (Chihuahua), 7 February 1868; Hostos, *A Carlos Holguín*, broadside in LC-RB, portfolio 316, #33.

110. F. Bilbao, "El Presidente Obando," 1:187.

111. *La Voz Nacional*, 1 April 1862; Muller, "Latin America."

112. Jorge Isaacs to the secretary of the interior and foreign relations, Bogota, 15 June 1870, AGNC-SR-FC, legajo 5, 553; See also *Gaceta Oficial*, 31 July 1869.

113. *El Imparcial*, 18 July 1871.

114. Governor J. N. Montero to secretary of foreign relations, Barbacoas, 7 January 1852, AGN-SR, Fondo Gobernaciones Varias, tomo 179, 171.

115. *La Alianza de la Frontera*, 5 June 1862; Santiago Arcos Arlegui, "Carta á Francisco Bilbao," Cárcel de Santiago, 29 October 1852, in C. Rama, *Utopismo*, 162.

116. F. Bilbao, "Iniciativa de la América," 1:293; F. Bilbao, *La Revista del Nuevo Mundo*, 18–21, 323–28; Samper, *Ensayo aproximado sobre la jeografía*, 36–37; McGuinness, *Path of Empire*; Varona, *Francisco Bilbao*, 226, 258–59, 261–62.

117. López, *Mensaje del Poder Ejecutivo*, broadside in BN-R. See also *Gaceta Oficial del Cauca*, 10 August 1867.

118. "Las repúblicas americanas," *El Independiente* (Santiago), reprinted in *El Globo*, 1 July 1867.

119. *La Unión*, 12 March 1864; Scarpetta, *El grito*, broadside in BN-R; *El Compás*,

11 November 1840; speech of Guadalupe Galván, Hidalgo de Parral, 16 September 1862, in *La Alianza de la Frontera*, 6 November 1862; *La Guerra*, 3 January 1862; F. Bilbao, "La América en peligro," 2:186; *La Alianza de la Frontera*, supplement, 29 July 1862; *La República* (Chihuahua), 8 November 1867.

120. *La Guerra*, 27 December 1861; F. Bilbao, "El evangelio americano," 2:385.

121. "Elecciones," *El Voto del Pueblo* (Guadalajara), reprinted in *La Alianza de la Frontera*, supplement, 29 July 1862.

122. *La Unión*, 30 October 1864.

123. *El Caucano*, 3 November 1864.

124. Speech of Alejo Morales, Bogota, 27 February 1865, translated and reprinted in House of Representatives, *President Juárez of Mexico*, 39th Congress, 1st session, document #31, 5, found in LC-JSP, box 77, folder "French Occupation of Mexico: Printed Matter, 1863–1866"; *El Monitor Republicano*, 23 September 1846; *La Alianza de la Frontera*, 12 June 1862 and 29 July 1862; *El Compás*, 11 November 1840; Scarpetta, *El grito*, broadside in BN-R; speech of Guadalupe Galván, Hidalgo de Parral, 16 September 1862, in *La Alianza de la Frontera*, 6 November 1862.

125. Bilbao, "La América en peligro," 2:186.

126. *Diario de la Marina*, 15 June 1867 and 9 July 1867.

127. Speech of Juan de Dios Burgos, Querétaro, 28 May 1867, in *La República* (Chihuahua), 31 May 1867.

128. F. Bilbao, "La América en peligro," 2:186.

129. Speech of Mariano Samaniego, Villa del Paso, 16 September 1862, in *La Alianza de la Frontera*, 13 November 1862; commission report by Ramon E. Paláu and others, Popayán, 24 August 1875, ACC-AM, paquete 130, legajo 17.

130. *El Compás*, 12 May 1841.

131. *La Restauración Liberal* (Durango), reprinted in *La República* (Chihuahua), 22 November 1867.

132. *El Aguijón*, 8 October 1871; *La Chinaca*, 1 May 1862 and 19 May 1862.

133. *El Patriota*, 15 May 1848; J. Wood, "The Republic Regenerated."

134. *El Sentimiento Democrático*, 10 January 1850.

135. *Comercio del Plata*, 20 May 1846; speech of Antonio Ochoa, Guadalupe y Calvo, 16 September 1862, in *La Alianza de la Frontera*, 16 October 1862.

136. D. Landes, *The Wealth*, 313. For more nuanced views, see Lynch, *Argentine Caudillo*; Chasteen, *Heroes on Horseback*.

137. *El Ferrocarril* (Santiago), reprinted in *La Nación*, 19 December 1860.

138. F. Bilbao, "Sociabilidad chilena," 1:17.

139. F. Bilbao, "Emancipación del espíritu en América," 2:546.

140. *El Grito de Guerra*, 1 February 1863. See also *La Patria*, 27 September 1863.

141. F. Bilbao, "El evangelio americano," 2:338.

142. F. Bilbao, "El evangelio americano," 2:377. See also F. Bilbao, "Sociabilidad chilena," 1:5.

143. Speech of Jesús Escobar y Armendáriz, Villa del Paso del Norte, 16 September 1867, in La República (Chihuahua), 8 November 1867. See also Muñiz, Protesta, broadside in AHMRG-FII, #530; La Alianza de la Frontera, supplement, 20 April 1861.

144. F. Bilbao, "Movimiento," 178. See also Jorge Quijano and thirty-seven others to Julián Trujillo, Popayán, 30 April 1877, AGNC-SR-FLM, tomo 155, 330.

145. Mariano Yañes, "El Congreso á la nación," México, 8 January 1868, in La República (Chihuahua), 7 February 1868.

146. F. Bilbao, "La América en peligro," 2:187.

147. F. Bilbao, "El evangelio americano," 2:334, 385; F. Bilbao, "Emancipación del espíritu en América," 2:550; F. Bilbao, La Revista del Nuevo Mundo, 342.

148. Speech of Jesús Escobar y Armendáriz, Villa del Paso del Norte, 16 September 1867, in La República (Chihuahua), 8 November 1867; Varios Mexicanos, "La Europa y la prisión de Maximiliano," in El Globo, 30 June 1867.

149. El Monitor Republicano, 1 July 1867; La Fraternidad, 7 July 1871.

150. Said, Culture and Imperialism. See also El Comercio, 13 July 1864.

151. Diario Oficial del Gobierno Supremo de la República, 25 August 1867.

152. La Alianza de la Frontera, 11 July 1861.

153. F. Bilbao, "La América en peligro," 2:235–36, 240–41; F. Bilbao, "Sociabilidad chilena," 1:33; F. Bilbao, "Movimiento," 1:177; El Constitucional, 5 April 1843; La República (Chihuahua), 8 November 1867; La Alianza de la Frontera, 16 October 1862; López, Mensaje del Poder Ejecutivo, broadside in BN-R; El Globo, 6 July 1867.

154. El Compás, 11 November 1840; F. Bilbao, "Sociabilidad chilena," 22; La Alianza de la Frontera, 8 January 1863.

155. El Compás, 12 May 1841.

156. F. Bilbao, "Iniciativa de la América," 1:297; McGuinness, Path of Empire.

157. T. C. de Mosquera to César Conto, Popayán, 2 December [1874], BLAA-M, #113; La República (Chihuahua), 16 August 1867; La Alianza de la Frontera, 12 June 1862.

158. Gaceta Oficial del Cauca, 23 July 1867; Arias, Reseña histórica.

159. "Elecciones," El Voto del Pueblo (Guadalajara) reprinted in La Alianza de la Frontera, supplement, 29 July 1862. See also Diario Oficial del Gobierno Supremo de la República, 21 August 1867; La Alianza de la Frontera, 5 June 1862; speech of Juan de Dios Burgos, Querétaro, 28 May 1867 in La República (Chihuahua), 31 May 1867.

160. F. Bilbao, "El evangelio americano," 2:414.

161. La Alianza de la Frontera, 8 January 1863; El Globo, 28 June 1867.

162. Muñiz, Protesta, broadside in AHMRG-FII, #530; Un Mexicano, "Agustín de Iturbide," El Constitucional (Mexico City), reprinted in La República (Chihuahua), 8 November 1867; La República (Chihuahua), 20 September 1867 and 8 November 1867.

163. Speech of Roque Morón, 10 December 1866, in *La República* (Chihuahua), 15 March 1867. See also McNamara, *Sons of the Sierra*, 83–87.

164. Manuel de Silva to Benito Juárez, Sevilla, 12 July 1867, in *Diario Oficial del Gobierno Supremo de la República*, 24 August 1867; *Sacramento Union* (Sacramento), reprinted in *La República* (Chihuahua), 19 July 1867; speech of Alejo Morales, Bogota, 27 February 1865, translated and reprinted in House of Representatives, *President Juárez of Mexico*, 39th Congress, 1st session, document #31, 5, found in LC-JSP, box 77, folder "French Occupation of Mexico: Printed Matter, 1863–1866."

165. F. Bilbao, "La América en peligro," 2:187; speech of Jesús Escobar y Armendáriz, Villa del Paso del Norte, 16 September 1867, in *La República* (Chihuahua), 8 November 1867; J. Wood, "The Republic Regenerated," 10; Hale, "Emilio Castelar and Mexico."

166. F. Bilbao, "Ecce homo," 2:492.

167. R. M. Arana to T. C. de Mosquera, María, 13 September 1859, ACC-SM, #36,026.

168. *El Grito de Guerra*, 1 February 1863.

169. *La Chinaca*, 5 June 1862.

170. *Liberal* (Bogota), reprinted in *El Aguijón*, 17 September 1871.

171. *El Garibaldi*; *El Globo*, 8 August 1867; *La Frontera*, 17 September 1882.

172. "La guerra de Europe," *El Siglo Diez y Nueve*, reprinted in *La Cuestión Social*, 2 March 1861.

173. *La Nación*, 4 June 1882.

174. *El Siglo*, 4 June 1882. For Colombia, see Benjamín Pereira to Secretario de Gobierno, Bogota, 8 July 1882, AGNC-SR-FC, legajo 33, 565.

175. *Honores fúnebres*, 10.

176. Angel Floro Costa to Los Presidentes de las Sociedades Italianas, Montevideo, 6 June 1882, in *El Siglo*, 7 June 1882.

177. Peña, *Oda al triunfo obtenido*; *La Sociedad*, 3 July 1860; *Diario de la Marina*, 10 August 1867.

178. *La Democracia*, 7 June 1882.

179. *La Nación*, 7 June 1882.

180. *El Siglo*, 4 June 1882.

181. J. Conrad, *Nostromo*.

182. Leoni, *Gumersindo Saraiva*.

183. Knight, *The Mexican Revolution*, 1:229.

184. Poniatowska, *Tinisima*, 317.

CHAPTER SIX. DAVID PEÑA AND BLACK LIBERALISM

1. J. Conrad, *Nostromo*, 59, 104, 174, 239, 338.

2. For the English Atlantic, see Linebaugh and Rediker, *The Many-Headed Hydra*.

3. Ramírez, *General David Peña*, 36. Gustavo Arboleda gives the year of Peña's birth as 1825 (*Diccionario biográfico y genealógico*, 343).

4. Ramírez, *General David Peña*, 38.

5. Zamorano, *Bosquejo biográfico*, 1–4. See also Buenaventura, *Del Cali que se fue*, 63–78.

6. Pedro José Piedrahíta to T. C. de Mosquera, Cali, 14 May 1859, ACC-SM, #36,933.

7. Zamorano, *Bosquejo biográfico*, 26. Francisco Ramírez, working from notes from Peña's grandson, Luis David Peña, claimed that David Peña's mother was not a *mulata* (*General David Peña*, 36).

8. Zamorano, *Bosquejo biográfico*, 5; Mercado, *Memorias*, lxxvi.

9. Zamorano, *Bosquejo biográfico*, 8; Ramírez, *General David Peña*, 43.

10. David Peña to the secretary of government, Cali, 29 March 1863, ACC-AM, paquete 65, legajo 67.

11. Zamorano, *Bosquejo biográfico*, 9–10.

12. Zamorano, *Bosquejo biográfico*, 11–12.

13. Report of Barbacoas's Jefe Municipal, 11 August 1865, ACC-AM, paquete 90, legajo 49.

14. Buenaventura's Jefe Municipal to General Santos Gutiérrez, [Buenaventura, 1865], ACC-AM, paquete 92, legajo 73.

15. Belisario Zamorano to Salvador Camacho Roldán, Cali, 5 July 1878, AGNC-SACH-FSCR, caja 13, carpeta 175, 40.

16. Of course, he took conscripts as well, when the need arose. *Los criminales*, broadside in BN-R.

17. For bargaining and recruitment elsewhere, see *El Garibaldi*, 11 January 1862; *El Boyacense*, 7 September 1867.

18. Ramírez, *General David Peña*, 40. See also, Manuel Vernaza to Nemecio Colmenares, Cali, 7 June 1867, in *El Boyacense*, 26 June 1867.

19. Manuel José González to Mariano Ospina, Cali, 21 December 1859, BN-FM, libro 210, 127.

20. Forment, *Democracy in Latin America*, 435.

21. Rafael [Arboleda] to T. C. de Mosquera, Popayán, 14 June 1876, ACC-SM, #56,924.

22. *El Estado de Guerra*, 9 January 1877.

23. The members of the Democratic Society to Buenaventura's Provincial Legislature, Cali, 1 September 1850, AHMC-ACM, tomo 109, 303.

24. David Peña, "Informe de una comisión," Popayán, 5 August 1867, in *Gaceta Oficial del Cauca*, 10 August 1867.

25. Zamorano, *Bosquejo biográfico*, 26.

26. Denuncio of Rafael Caicedo Cuero, David Peña, and Narciso Riascos, Cali, 12 July 1856, AHMC-ACM, tomo 134, 747; David Peña, "Ordenanza 62 sobre rentas," Cali, 12 May 1867, AHMC-ACM, tomo 153, 350; David Peña to the president of the municipality, Cali, 18 February 1878, AHMC-ACM, Tomo 162, 42; *Gaceta Oficial del Cauca*, 10 November 1866; David Peña to National Congress, Cali, 1 March 1867, AC-C, 1867, Antecedentes de Decretos I, 86.

27. The undersigned members of the Democratic Society to the state president, Cali, 14 October 1866, ACC-AM, paquete 65, legajo 67.
28. David Peña, "Informe de una comisión," Popayán, 10 July 1867, *Gaceta Oficial del Cauca*, 21 September 1867.
29. The undersigned Colombian citizens, members of the state and Democratic Society (over sixty names) to the president of Colombia, Palmira, 21 June 1868, INCORA-B, tomo 7, 492.
30. Mallon, *Peasant and Nation*; Sanders, *Contentious Republicans*; Guardino, *The Time of Liberty*; McNamara, *Sons of the Sierra*.
31. Manuel María Villaquirán Espada and David Peña, "Contestación," Cali, 13 May 1864, in *El Caucano*, 21 May 1863.
32. Residents of Cali Province to the state governor, Cali, 30 July 1859, ACC-AM, paquete 71, legajo 15.
33. Manuel Joaquín Otero to T. C. de Mosquera, Cali, 19 August 1859, ACC-SM, #36,809.
34. Vijes's Democratic Society to the state president, Vijes, 24 June 1877, ACC-AM, paquete 137, legajo 7. See also, Cali's Democratic Society to the state president, Cali, 19 July 1877, ACC-AM, paquete 137, legajo 7; Yumbo's Democratic Society to the state president (undated fragment), ACC-AM, paquete 137, legajo 7.
35. Cali's Democratic Society to the state president, Cali, 3 November 1877, ACC-AM, paquete 137, legajo 21.
36. Residents of Cali Province to the state governor, Cali, 30 July 1859, ACC-AM, paquete 71, legajo 15.
37. Ramírez, *General David Peña*, 10.
38. Marco A. Lasprilla to Tomás C. de Mosquera, Cartago, 2 January 1877, ACC-SM, #57,506. See also *El Estado de Guerra*, 9 January 1877; Ramírez, *General David Peña*, 12–13.
39. Anonymous, "Relación de los sucesos de Cali," 30 December 1876, ACC-FA, #440, 1. See also Sinisterra, *El 24 de diciembre*.
40. Marco A. Lasprilla to Tomás C. de Mosquera, Cartago, 2 January 1877, ACC-SM, #57,506.
41. Manuel María [Mosquera] to Tomás [Mosquera], Popayán, 15 May 1877, ACC-SM, #57,555.
42. Manuel María [Mosquera] to Tomás [Mosquera], Popayán, 15 May 1877, ACC-SM, #57,555.
43. The undersigned members of the Democratic Society to the "Citizen President of the State," Cali, 1 June 1877, ACC-AM, paquete 137, legajo 7.
44. [Tomás Mosquera] to Aquileo Parra, Cali, 28 September 1877, ACC-SM, #57,579.
45. David Peña, "Proyecto de lei por la cual se fomenta la agricultura," Popayán, 9 August 1877, ACC-AM, paquete 137, legajo 30.

46. Los Miembros de la Sociedad Republicana de Artesanos, *Una representación*, broadside in BN-R.

47. Manuel Vernaza to Nemecio Colmenares, Bogotá, 7 June 1867, in *El Boyacense*, 26 June 1867.

48. B. González to Julián Trujillo, Popayán, 2 August 1877, AGNC-SC-FEOR, Serie Generales y Civiles, caja 94, carpeta 346, 18,565.

49. Ramón Cerón, Report of Legislative Commission, Popayán, 14 August 1877, ACC-AM, paquete 137, legajo 30.

50. Modesto Garcés to Tomás C. de Mosquera, Popayán, 2 November 1876 [1877], ACC-SM, #57,036.

51. Juan de. D. Ulloa to Tomás C. de Mosquera, Cali, 23 November 1877, ACC-SM, #57,711.

52. David Peña to the state president, Cali, 15 May 1878, ACC-AM, paquete 144, legajo 61.

53. Zamorano, *Bosquejo biográfico*, 4–5.

54. *El Estandarte Liberal*, 5 June 1878.

55. *El Estandarte Liberal*, 5 June 1878; *Registro Oficial*, 1 June 1878; Zamorano, *Bosquejo biográfico*, 24.

56. *El Ferrocarril* (Cali), 31 May 1878.

57. María, Vicente, Ramona, Dolores, and David Peña to the state president, Cali, 4 October 1878, ACC-AM, paquete 141, legajo 38. See also *El Estandarte Liberal*, 10 July 1878.

58. Quoted in Zamorano, *Bosquejo biográfico*, 25.

59. Andrews, *Afro-Latin America*; Lasso, *Myths of Harmony*. See also Blanchard, "The Language of Liberation"; Landers, *Atlantic Creoles*; Scott and Hébrard, *Freedom Papers*.

60. Anonymous, "Diario Histórico del Ejército Unido de Antioquia y Cauca" [1861], ACC-FA, #63,235. A *zambo* was a person of both African and Indian descent. See also *El Espectador*, 2 October 1852 [1862].

61. *El Porvenir*, 1 March 1861.

62. Pedro José Piedrahíta to T. C. de Mosquera, Cali, 12 March 1859, ACC-SM, #36,922.

63. Manuel González to Mariano Ospina, Cali, 21 December 1859, BN-FM, libro 210, 127.

64. Alfonso [Arboleda] to Sergio Arboleda, Popayán, 3 September 1879, ACC-FA, #447, 71.

65. Juan E. Ulloa to Eliseo Payán, Palmira, 29 January 1885, ACC-AM, paquete 168, legajo 15.

66. *El Constitucional*, 17 December 1842.

67. *La Sociedad*, 5 July 1860.

68. Andrews, *Afro-Latin America*, 97.

69. *La Chinaca*, 12 May 1862.

70. The Two Republics, 15 January 1870. For Chile, see J. Wood, The Society of Equality, 203.

71. Goldberg, Racist Culture, 4.

72. Goldberg, Racist Culture, 24.

73. Goldberg, Racist Culture, 28.

74. Andrews, Afro-Latin America, 87; Lasso, Myths of Harmony.

75. Speech of Manuel Merino, Chihuahua, 15 September 1868, in La República (Chihuahua), 18 September 1868.

76. La República (Chihuahua), 8 March 1867.

77. La República (Chihuahua), 22 November 1867.

78. Carlos Gómez to the secretary of foreign relations, Buga, 10 February 1851, AGNC-SR-FMAN, tomo I, 588.

79. F. Bilbao, "El evangelio americano," 2: 428.

80. Sanders, "'Citizens of a Free People.'"

81. Citizens and residents of Silvia Parish to senators and representatives, Silvia, 19 March 1852, ACON-S, 1852, Informes de Comisión IV, 137.

82. Mallon, Peasant and Nation, 98–104.

83. Rebecca Earle sees this embrace of the pre-Columbian indigenous past fading by midcentury (The Return of the Native).

84. Federico Flores, "La América se salvará," El Comercio, 13 July 1864.

85. Speech of Higinio Muñoz, Chihuahua, 15 September 1867, in La República (Chihuahua), 20 September 1867. See also El Aguijón, 7 January 1872.

86. La Guerra, 20 December 1861.

87. Indíjenas de Coconuco to [the state president], Popayán, 22 July 1870, ACC-AM, paquete 112, legajo 18.

88. La Guerra, 7 February 1862.

89. Mallon, Peasant and Nation; McNamara, Sons of the Sierra; Guardino, The Time of Liberty; Thomson with LaFrance, Patriotism, Politics, and Popular Liberalism; Sanders, "'Belonging to the Great Granadan Family'"; Reeves, Ladinos with Ladinos; Wolfe, The Everyday Nation-State; Alda Mejías, La participación indígena; Grandin, The Blood of Guatemala; Appelbaum, Muddied Waters; Gotkowitz, A Revolution for Our Rights; Méndez, The Plebeian Republic; Thurner, From Two Republics; Hylton, "Reverberations of Insurgency."

90. La Alianza de la Frontera, 26 September 1861.

91. Hobsbawm, Nations and Nationalism since 1780, 43.

92. Andrews, Afro-Latin America, 92–100.

93. Scott, Degrees of Freedom; Kraay, Race, State, and Armed Forces; Lasso, Myths of Harmony; Aguirre, Agentes de su propia libertad; McGuinness, Path of Empire; Guardino, Peasants, Politics; Ferrer, Insurgent Cuba; Foner, Reconstruction; Landers, Atlantic Creoles; Beattie, The Tribute of Blood; Castilho, "Abolitionism Matters"; Schmidt-Nowara, Slavery, Freedom, and Abolition; Sartorius, Ever Faithful; Leal, "Recordando a Saturio." For a bibliography, see Andrews, Afro-Latin America.

94. For Eurocentric modernity and race, see Fischer, *Modernity Disavowed*.

95. Davis, *Inhuman Bondage*, 328; Foner, *Reconstruction*, 279.

CHAPTER SEVEN. THE COLLAPSE OF
AMERICAN REPUBLICAN MODERNITY

1. Sierra, *Obras completas*, 12:389.

2. *La Libertad*, 27 December 1884.

3. An obsession with material progress crystallized around the world in the 1880s. See S. Conrad, "Enlightenment in Global History," 1017.

4. The idea of regeneration had a long history in both countries, linked to social control. See Melgarejo Acosta, *El lenguaje político*.

5. Sierra, *Obras completas*, 12:375.

6. Pani, *Para mexicanizar el Segundo Imperio*, 356.

7. See Vaughan and Lewis, introduction; Ávila, "Liberalismos decimonónicos." For the importance of changing patterns of political thought and claims making as marking historical epochs, see Armitage and Subrahmanyam, *The Age of Revolutions*.

8. Pani, *Para mexicanizar el Segundo Imperio*, 357–58.

9. For the U.S. turn to Europe, see Rodgers, *Atlantic Crossings*.

10. Anselmo de la Portilla, "Lo que pienso y me propongo," *El Siglo Diez y Nueve*, 2 January 1877. For this period, see Tenorio-Trillo, *Mexico at the World's Fairs*.

11. *El Siglo Diez y Nueve*, 16 April 1884.

12. *La Libertad*, 13 September 1884.

13. José T. Gaibrois, "Prospecto," *Colombia Ilustrada*, 2 April 1889.

14. "El triunfo es seguro," *El Porvenir Nacional*, 30 June 1884.

15. "El discurso del Presidente en la apertura de las sesiones del Congreso," *El Pabellón Nacional*, 13 April 1887.

16. *La República* (Mexico City), 17 August 1890.

17. *La República* (Mexico City), 10 August 1890.

18. *La República* (Mexico City), 3 September 1890. See also Beezley, *Judas at the Jockey Club*.

19. Tenorio-Trillo, *Mexico at the World's Fairs*, 19.

20. *El Ferrocarril* (Cali), 6 February 1880.

21. *El Heraldo*, 25 July 1889.

22. *La Libertad*, 22 August 1884.

23. *La Libertad*, 23 September 1884.

24. *El Porvenir de México*, 26 February 1888.

25. Sierra, *Obras completas*, 12:398.

26. F. G. Cosmes, "La revolución económica III," *La Libertad*, 18 October 1884.

27. *El Taller*, 24 May 1888.

28. *La República* (Mexico City), 27 August 1890. See also Tenenbaum, "Streetwise History," 143; Overmyer-Velázquez, *Visions of the Emerald City*.

29. *El Correo Nacional*, 8 April 1891.

30. *El Pabellón Nacional*, 23 March 1887.

31. Tenorio-Trillo, *Mexico at the World's Fairs*.

32. *El Cosmopolita*, 1 April 1884.

33. *El Siglo Diez y Nueve*, 9 September 1884.

34. Speech of Mgr. E. Guillow, México, 11 September 1884, in *El Siglo Diez y Nueve*, 12 September 1884.

35. *El Heraldo*, 29 August 1889.

36. *El Correo Nacional*, 14 April 1891.

37. *El Heraldo*, 4 July 1889.

38. *La Voz del Comercio*, 21 October 1894.

39. Alberdi, *La barbarie histórica de Sarmiento*, 60.

40. José Ramón Leal, "Cartas íntimas á mi amigo Don Emilio Castelar: Séptima," *El Siglo Diez y Nueve*, 15 September 1884.

41. *La Gaceta Comercial*, 8 January 1900.

42. Anselmo de la Portilla, "Lo de España," *El Siglo Diez y Nueve*, 4 January 1877.

43. For racism, see Andrews, *Afro-Latin America*, 117–51; Graham, *The Idea of Race*; Appelbaum, Macpherson, and Rosemblatt, *Race and Nation*; Thurner, *From Two Republics*; Wade, *Race and Ethnnicity*. For imperialism, see Thurner, "After Spanish Rule."

44. *La Gaceta Comercial*, 3 March 1900.

45. Rafael Altamira referred to the "tendencia hispanista" (*España y el programa americanista*, 9). See also Martínez, *El nacionalismo cosmopolita*, 188; Arias Vanegas, *Nación y diferencia*. For use of *hispanismo* in the nineteenth century, see Faber, "'La hora ha llegado,'" 66–67. See also Moraña, *Ideologies of Hispanism*. For *hispanismo* around midcentury, see Gobat, "The Invention of Latin America."

46. Anselmo de la Portilla, "Lo de España," *El Siglo Diez y Nueve*, 4 January 1877.

47. Pani, *Para mexicanizar el Segundo Imperio*, 89.

48. Sepúlveda Muñoz, *Comunidad cultural*; Pike, "Making the Hispanic World."

49. *La Sociedad*, 3 July 1860.

50. *La Libertad*, 11 October 1884. See also Martínez, *El nacionalismo cosmopolita*, 458–59.

51. José Ramón Leal, "Cartas íntimas á mi amigo Don Emilio Castelar: Séptima," *El Siglo Diez y Nueve*, 15 September 1884.

52. *El Correo Nacional*, 24 October 1890.

53. Sierra, *Obras completas*, 17:28–29.

54. Sierra, *Obras completas*, 17:31.

55. *La Libertad*, 24 September 1884. For similar debates in Colombia, see Appelbaum, "Reading the Past," 369–73.

56. Anselmo de la Portilla, *El Siglo Diez y Nueve*, 6 July 1877. See also *El Heraldo*, 1 August 1889.

57. *La Gaceta Comercial*, 7 March 1900.
58. *La Gaceta Comercial*, 1 March 1900.
59. Cañizares-Esguerra, *How to Write the History*.
60. *La Gaceta Comercial*, 1 March 1900.
61. Arango, *The Cuban Revolution*, broadside in LC-RB, portfolio 256, #12.
62. *La República* (Mexico City), 26 September 1890.
63. *La Gaceta Comercial*, 21 March 1900.
64. *La Gaceta Comercial*, 21 March 1900.
65. *La Gaceta Comercial*, 21 March 1900.
66. *La Gaceta Comercial*, 24 March 1900.
67. *La Gaceta Comercial*, 6 March 1900. Tracy Guzmán refers to this tradition in the twentieth century as "anti-imperialist imperialism" ("Our Indians in Our America," 39).
68. *El Correo Nacional*, 17 January 1891.
69. Thurner, "After Spanish Rule," 44–45.
70. Hobsbawm, *Nations and Nationalism since 1780*, 22–23.
71. Larrain, *Identity and Modernity*.
72. Mignolo, *The Idea of Latin America*, xv; Shumway, "Hispanism Is an Imperfect Past," 284–89.
73. *La Gaceta Comercial*, 2 January 1900.
74. Arboleda, *Rudimentos de geografía*, 18.
75. *El Pabellón Nacional*, 12 March 1887.
76. "Carta de un suscritor sobre latinos y sajones," *La Gaceta Comercial*, 9 March 1900.
77. "Nota de la Redacción," *La Gaceta Comercial*, 9 March 1900.
78. *El Demócrata*, 13 March 1879.
79. Speech of Rafael Núñez to Congress, Bogotá, 8 April 1880, in *Rejistro Oficial*, 1 May 1880.
80. *El Atratense*, 9 September 1880.
81. *El Atratense*, 26 October 1880.
82. Vicente Cárdenas to Sergio Arboleda, Quito, 2 September 1878, ACC-FA, #1506.
83. *El Pabellón Nacional*, 26 March 1887.
84. *El Estado de Guanajuato*, 15 September 1894. See also Overmyer-Velázquez, *Visions of the Emerald City*.
85. *El Siglo Diez y Nueve*, 30 June 1877.
86. *El Compás*, 29 September 1841.
87. *El Heraldo*, 8 August 1889.
88. José Ramón Leal, "Cartas íntimas á mi amigo Don Emilio Castelar: Séptima," *El Siglo Diez y Nueve*, 15 September 1884.
89. Sierra, *Obras completas*, 12:398. See also Quijada Mauriño, "Los confines del pueblo soberano."

90. Luis Umaña L., "La industria," *El Taller*, 5 October 1888.
91. Juan de D. Ulloa to Tomás C. de Mosquera, Cali, 25 October 1877, ACC-SM, #57,710.
92. *La Aurora*, 31 March 1880.
93. *El Cosmopolita*, 1 May 1884.
94. *El Estado de Guanajuato*, 15 September 1894.
95. *El Lampacense*, 17 January 1892.
96. *La Gaceta Comercial*, 15 January 1900.
97. *La Libertad*, 22 August 1884.
98. *El Ferrocarril* (Cali), 14 February 1878.
99. *El Ferrocarril* (Cali), 25 June 1880.
100. *La República* (Mexico City), 10 August 1890; *Revista Telegráfica de México*, 16 March 1889.
101. José Ramón Leal, "Cartas íntimas a mi amigo Don Emilio Castelar: Séptima," *El Siglo Diez y Nueve*, 15 September 1884. See also Pérez-Rayón Elizundia, *México 1900*, 275–323; Rodríguez Morales, "La modernidad."
102. F. G. Cosmes, "La revolución económica," *La Libertad*, 15 October 1884.
103. *El Cosmopolita*, 26 February 1884.
104. Manuel María Alegre to the president, Mexico City, 7 May 1885, UI-CPD, legajo 10, caja 10, #4,670.
105. Manuel María Alegre to the minster of development [no place given; 1885], UI-CPD, legajo 10, caja 10, #4,671; see also Montero García, "La modernización."
106. Quoted in Bergquist, *Coffee and Conflict in Colombia*, 221 (Bergquist's translation). See also Bushnell, *The Making of Modern Colombia*, 156.
107. *El Heraldo*, 1 August 1889.
108. José Ramón Leal, "Cartas íntimas á mi amigo Don Emilio Castelar: Undécima," *El Siglo Diez y Nueve*, 13 October 1884.
109. *El Heraldo*, 8 August 1889.
110. *El Heraldo*, 25 July 1889.
111. *Revista Telegráfica de México*, 16 September 1889.
112. *El Globo*, 8 August 1867.
113. *El Siglo Diez y Nueve*, 31 December 1875.
114. *Revista Telegráfica de México*, 1 January 1889.
115. *Revista Telegráfica de México*, 16 March 1889.
116. *Revista Telegráfica de México*, 16 March 1889. See also Pérez-Rayón Elizundia, *México 1900*, 325–43.
117. Speech of Justo Sierra, México, 8 September 1877, in *La Libertad*, 6 January 1878.
118. *Colombia Ilustrada*, 2 April 1889.
119. *El Ferrocarril* (Cali), 1 March 1878.

120. La República (Mexico City), 13 August 1890.

121. La Gaceta Comercial, 12 March 1900.

122. Sierra, Obras completas, 12:362.

123. El Progreso, 20 May 1888.

124. La Gaceta Comercial, 31 December 1900.

125. Tenorio-Trillo, Mexico at the World's Fairs; Hale, Emilio Rabasa; Wasserman, Everyday Life and Politics; McNamara, Sons of the Sierra; Chassen-López, From Liberal to Revolutionary Oaxaca; Thomson with LaFrance, Patriotism, Politics, and Popular Liberalism; Valencia Llano, Estado Soberano del Cauca; Bergquist, Coffee and Conflict in Colombia; Martínez, El nacionalismo cosmopolita; Melgarejo Acosta, El lenguaje político.

126. Van Der Veer, "The Global History of 'Modernity.'"

127. Cosío Villegas, Historia moderna, 1: 363–505. For positivism, see Hale, The Transformation of Liberalism, although he does not discuss modernity much; Roig, "El positivismo en Hispanoamérica."

128. El Amigo del Pueblo (Mexico City), 28 August 1869.

129. El Escolar, 25 June 1871.

130. Mathis de Dalmstad to General Escobedo, Querétaro, 26 April 1867, in Arias, Reseña histórica, 723.

131. El Aguijón, 7 January 1872.

132. El Aguijón, 21 January 1872.

133. Trait d'Union (Mexico City), reprinted in El Aguijón, 11 February 1872.

134. El Siglo Diez y Nueve reprinted in El Aguijón, 10 June 1872.

135. El Aguijón, 26 February 1872.

136. El Siglo Diez y Nueve, reprinted in El Aguijón, 10 June 1872.

137. La República (Mexico City), 10 August 1890.

138. Municipal president to State President Ezequial Hurtado, Cali, 29 October 1882, ACC-AM, paquete 161, legajo 25.

139. El Ferrocarril (Cali), 14 February 1878; El Amigo del Pueblo (Guanajuato), 23 June 1871; Los Principios, 18 February 1876.

140. M. D. Martínez to the secretary of the treasury, Palmira, 25 December 1876, AGNC-SR-FLM, tomo 194, 410.

141. Manuel María [Mosquera] to Tomás [Mosquera], Popayán, 15 May 1877, ACC-SM, #57,555.

142. Adelman, "Between Order and Liberty," 99.

143. Guillermo [Pereira] to Salvador Camacho Roldán, Popayán, 29 May 1878, AGNC-SACH-FSCR, caja 10, carpeta 129, 1.

144. The Two Republics, 17 February 1869.

145. Sierra, Obras completas, 12:383.

146. Speech of Rafael Núñez to Congress, Bogotá, 20 July 1888, in El Taller, 26 July 1888.

147. Quoted in Posada-Carbó, preface, 6 (Posada-Carbó's translation).
148. Eustaquio Palacios to J. M. Correa, Cali, 11 October 1879, in El Ferrocarril (Cali), 17 October 1879.
149. El Ferrocarril (Cali), 21 February 1879.
150. Colombia Ilustrada, 20 July 1889.
151. El Correo Nacional, 7 January 1891.
152. La República (Mexico City), 29 August 1890. See also Cosío Villegas, Historia moderna, 1:363–505.
153. El Comercio, 2 January 1885.
154. El Conservador (Bogota), 21 March 1882.
155. El Ferrocarril (Cali), 31 October 1879.
156. Foción Mantilla to Salvador Camacho Roldán, Popayán, 4 December 1878, AGNC-SACH-FSCR, caja 9, carpeta 104, 1.
157. Speech of Eliseo Payán to Congress, Bogotá, 8 April 1880, in Rejistro Oficial, 1 May 1880. See also Martínez, El nacionalismo cosmopolita, 434–37, 493–94.
158. Quoted in Vallenilla Lanz, Cesarismo democrático y otros textos, xiii.
159. José Ramón Leal, "Cartas íntimas a mi amigo Don Emilio Castelar: Séptima," El Siglo Diez y Nueve, 15 September 1884.
160. Alejandro Micolta to the deputies, Popayán, 7 September 1879, ACC-AM, paquete 146, legajo 3.
161. Mantilla, Informe del Secretario de Hacienda, 3.
162. Enrique Muñoz to the deputies, Popayán, 26 August 1881, ACC-AM, paquete 157, legajo 62. See also El 21 de Abril, 18 May 1879.
163. El Siglo Diez y Nueve, 1 January 1884.
164. El Siglo Diez y Nueve, 16 April 1884.
165. Speech of Mgr. E. Guillow, México, 11 September 1884, in El Siglo Diez y Nueve, 12 September 1884. See also El Campeón de la Fe, 19 May 1895.
166. Carlos Dorronsoro to Sergio Arboleda, Buga, 24 September 1875, ACC-FA, #1511.
167. Cervantes, Observaciones, 1.
168. Speech of Eliseo Payán to State Legislature, 1 August 1883, in El Cauca, 6 August 1883.
169. Editors, "Programa," La Libertad, 5 January 1878.
170. Speech of Justo Sierra, México, 8 September 1877, in La Libertad, 6 January 1878.
171. El Quincenal, 15 March 1879.
172. El Estado de Guanajuato, 15 September 1894.
173. El Ferrocarril (Cali), 24 January 1879.
174. El Ferrocarril (Cali), 16 May 1879.
175. El Ferrocarril (Cali), 7 November 1879.
176. Adelman, "Between Order and Liberty," 99–101.
177. El Progreso, 17 June 1888.

178. Address of Eliseo Payán to Congress, Bogotá, 8 April 1880, in *Rejistro Oficial*, 1 May 1880.

179. *El Cruzado*, 9 September 1894.

180. *El Correo Nacional*, 1 October 1890.

181. Speech of Miguel Guerrero, Cali, 24 November 1880, in *El Ferrocarril* (Cali), 1 December 1880.

182. Anonymous [probably Sergio Arboleda], "Un paso adelante," *Los Principios*, 9 March 1873. See also Overmyer-Velázquez, *Visions of the Emerald City*.

183. Sergio Arboleda, "Plan de reorganización política de los Estados Unidos de Colombia," [1885], ACC-FA, # 464, 1.

184. Sergio Arboleda, "Plan de reorganización política de los Estados Unidos de Colombia," [1885], ACC-FA, # 464, 1.

185. Vicente Cárdenas to Sergio Arboleda, Quito, 19 November 1878, ACC-FA, #1506.

186. Bautista Feijoo to Sergio Arboleda, Caloto, 7 March 1883, ACC-FA, #1513.

187. Quoted in Gibson, *The Constitutions of Colombia*, 321 (Gibson's translation).

188. Speech of Anselmo Soto Arana, Cartago, in *El Cauca*, 16 October 1886.

189. *El Taller*, 11 February 1890.

190. Piccato, *The Tyranny of Opinion*, 244.

191. Sierra, *Obras Completas*, 12:394.

192. Sierra, *Obras Completas*, 12:394.

193. Sierra, *Obras Completas*, 12:388.

194. Sierra, *Obras Completas*, 12:396. See also F. Guerra, "Mexico from Independence to Revolution,"139.

195. F. G. Cosmes, "La revolución económica," *La Libertad*, 15 October 1884. See also Forment, *Democracy in Latin America*, 355–59.

196. Pani, *Para mexicanizar el Segundo Imperio*, 363.

197. F. Bilbao, "El evangelio americano," 2:334.

198. Speech of President Díaz, México, 16 September 1884, in *El Siglo Diez y Nueve*, 30 September 1884; speech of President Díaz, México, 16 September 1890, in *La República* (Mexico City), 18 September 1890.

199. *El Correo Nacional*, 24 October 1890.

200. Piccato, *The Tyranny of Opinion*, 84; Hale, *The Transformation of Liberalism*.

201. *La Libertad*, 2 October 1884.

202. *La Libertad*, 5 September 1884.

203. *La Libertad*, 18 September 1884.

204. F. G. Cosmes, "La enfermedad de México—11," *La Libertad*, 23 October 1884.

205. Schneider, *Comparative Latin American Politics*, 20; Wiarda with Skelley, *Dilemmas of Democracy*, 8; Flores-Quiroga, "Legitimacy, Sequencing, and Credibility"; Duncan, *Latin American Politics*, 17–18; Véliz, *The Centralist Tradition*; Stevens, *Origins of Instability*. See also Novak, "The Myth."

206. *El Ferrocarril* (Guanajuato), 22 April 1878. See also Salvatore and Aguirre, *The Birth of the Penitentiary*.

207. El Transcendental, 14 July 1895; La Gaceta Comercial, 23 March 1900.
208. Macedo, "Parte octava," 2:705. For Colombia, see "Pena de muerte," El Heraldo, 18 September 1889.
209. Adolfo M. de Obregón, "Importancia del ejército," La Gaceta Comercial, 14 March 1900.
210. El Demócrata (Morelia) reprinted in La Gaceta Comercial, 14 March 1900.
211. Thomson, "Mid-Nineteenth-Century Modernities," 84.
212. P. Santacoloma, military inspector, to the secretary of government, Popayán, 27 May 1873, ACC-AM, paquete 119, legajo 72.
213. El Cauca, 9 June 1883.
214. F. Bilbao, "El evangelio americano," 2:421.
215. La República (Mexico City), 10 August 1890.
216. Law of 17 February 1888 (#151), in El Heraldo, 4 July 1889.
217. La Gaceta Comercial, 2 March 1900.
218. La Libertad, 3 September 1884.
219. La Libertad, 2 October 1884.
220. La Libertad, 3 September 1884.
221. Juan E. Ulloa to Salvador Camacho Roldán, Palmira, 19 June 1879, AGNC-SACH-FSCR, caja 13, carpeta 166, 6.
222. La Libertad, 27 December 1884; El Taller, 21 July 1888; French, "Progreso Forzado."
223. El Siglo Diez y Nueve, 15 September 1884.
224. Quoted in El Taller, 21 July 1888.
225. "Sociedades anónimas," La Regeneración (Popayán), reprinted in El Taller, 11 February 1890.
226. Francisco Marulanda to Julián Trujillo, Popayán, 20 November 1880, AGNC-SC-FEOR, Serie Generales y Civiles, caja 93, carpeta 342, 18,184.
227. Quoted in La Libertad, 8 November 1884.
228. José Ramón Leal, "Cartas íntimas á mi amigo Don Emilio Castelar: Séptima," El Siglo Diez y Nueve, 15 September 1884.
229. Linebaugh and Rediker, The Many-Headed Hydra.
230. La Libertad, 1 October 1884.
231. La Libertad, 2 October 1884.
232. Carlos Gris, "Los inútiles," El Lampacense, 28 February 1892.
233. La República (Mexico City), 16 August 1890.
234. La Libertad, 22 November 1884. See also Piccato, The Tyranny of Opinion, 160–61, 225.
235. Francisco G. Cosmes, "La ley motín," La Libertad, 22 November 1884.
236. La Libertad, 27 November 1884.
237. La Libertad, 23 December 1884.
238. Vicente Cárdenas to Sergio Arboleda, Quito, 8 July 1878, ACC-FA, #1506.
239. El Lampacense, 20 December 1891.
240. La Libertad, 19 November 1884.

241. El *Pabellón Nacional*, 27 April 1887.

242. *Los Principios*, 17 April 1874.

243. [Tomás Mosquera] to Aquileo Parra, Cali, 28 September 1877, ACC-SM, #57,579.

244. Sierra, *Obras Completas*, 12:370.

245. *El Heraldo*, 12 March 1890.

246. Ignotus, *La lección del pasado*, 13–32.

247. Quoted in Jaramillo Uribe, *El pensamiento colombiano*, 242. See also Clark, "The Good."

248. *El Ferrocarril* (Cali), 12 March 1880.

249. Macedo, "Parte octava," 2:721–22. See also Ross, "Mexico's Superior Health Council"; Falcón, "Rituals, Rules."

250. *La República* (Mexico City), 16 August 1890.

251. Beezley, *Judas at the Jockey Club*; Beezley, "The Porfirian Smart Set"; French, "*Progreso Forzado*."

252. *El Heraldo*, 25 September 1889.

253. Ezequial Hurtado to the deputies, Popayán, 19 September 1879, ACC-AM, paquete 146, legajo 1.

254. *El Estado de Guanajuato*, 15 September 1894.

255. Sierra, *Obras Completas*, 12:386.

256. Governor Francisco Tolentino to Porfirio Díaz, Guadalajara, 13 March 1885, UI-CPD, legajo 10, caja 7, #3269.

257. Porfirio Díaz to Francisco Tolentino, 21 March 1885, UI-CPD, legajo 10, caja 7, #3275.

258. *The Two Republics*, 30 May 1868.

259. *The Two Republics*, 1 July 1868.

260. Keyssar, *The Right to Vote*, 110–16; Scott, *Degrees of Freedom*, 160–61.

261. Quoted in Keyssar, *The Right to Vote*, 120.

262. Bentley, *Politics without Democracy*, 177.

263. Brands, *American Colossus*, 7.

264. Mallon, "Subalterns and the Nation," 162.

265. Sabato, *The Many and the Few*, 180–81.

266. Skidmore and Smith, *Modern Latin America*, 46.

267. Bushnell and Macaulay, *The Emergence of Latin America*, 286–87; Wasserman, *Everyday Life and Politics*, 209–28.

268. Francisco de la Fuente Ruiz, "La situación política," *El Cosmopolita*, 8 May 1884.

269. Mallon, *Peasant and Nation*, 247–75; M. León, representing the pueblo of San Jerónimo Araceo to the minister of justice, Mexico City, 26 November 1877, AGNM-IG-FJS, vol. 69A, expediente 1270; Felipe López B. to the president, Mexico City, 8 May 1877, UI-CPD, legajo 2, caja 2, #734. See also Falcón, ed., *Culturas de pobreza y resistencia*; McNamara, *Sons of the Sierra*.

270. Gregorio Padilla and Manuel Mendoza to the president, San Martín de los Canseco, 8 September 1877, AGNM-IG-FJS, vol. 69B, expediente 1383.

271. The undersigned residents of Guanajuato State to the president, Mexico City, 19 March 1877, AGNM-IG-FJS, vol. 69C, expediente 1431.

272. The undersigned residents of San Mateo del Rincón to the president, Mexico City, 30 November 1877, AGNM-IG-FJS, vol. 69B, expediente 1316.

273. C. D. Rodríguez for Antonio Medrano and fifteen others to the president, Pueblo de Santa María del Monte del Puente de la Concepción, 19 May 1877, AGNM-IG-FJS, vol. 69B, expediente 1402.

274. Francisco Vega and over fifteen others representing villages of Hidalgo State to the president, Huichapan, 16 June 1879, and Francisco Vega and over fifteen others representing villages of Hidalgo State to the president, Mexico City, 28 October 1879, UI-CPD, legajo 4, caja 1, #165.

275. Undersigned residents of San Miguel Tesechoacán to the president, Mexico City, 18 December 1877, UI-CPD, legajo 2, caja 3, #1280.

276. Juan de la Rosa Bravo and Cosario Rangel to the president, Mexico City, 18 December 1877, UI-CPD, legajo 2, caja 3, #1280.

277. Note written on petition 18 December 1877, UI-CPD, legajo 2, caja 3, #1280.

278. Undersigned residents of Canton Rosales to the president, Rosales, Meoqui, and Camargo, 4 May 1878, AGNM-IG-FJS, vol. 77, exp. 376.

279. Undersigned Indians of Ahuacatlán to the Jefe Político and the military commander, Tepic, 22 April 1877, AGNM-IG-FJS, vol. 69A, expediente 1255.

280. Report of J. M. Alfaro, Tepic, 25 April 1877, AGNM-IG-FJS, vol. 69A, exp. 1255.

281. Undersigned residents of Santa María Peñamiller to the president, Jalpan, 12 March 1880, UI-CPD, legajo 5, caja 2, #507.

282. Presidents and members of ten clubs to the president, Mexico City, 18 June 1878, AGNM-IG-FJS, vol. 77, exp. 353.

283. Marginal notations of 17 July 1878, AGNM-IG-FJS, vol. 77, expediente 353.

284. Jesús Reyna, president of the Club Constitucionalista, and 170 others to the president, Tampico, 10 November 1878, UI-CPD, legajo 3, caja 1, #345; see also Beezley, "Kaleidoscopic Views of Liberalism Triumphant," 172–73.

285. Juan Santiago to Porfirio Díaz, Tamazunchale, 22 July 1880, UI-CPD, legajo 5, caja 6, #2872.

286. Response of 2 August 1880, UI-CPD, legajo 5, caja 6, #2873.

287. La Sociedad de Artesanos Unidos de Mazatlán to the president, Mazatlán, 11 January 1885, UI-CPD, legajo 10, caja 2, #863.

288. Francisco Anaya, representing Nexquipayac, to the president, San Juan de Aragón, 22 April 1885, UI-CPD, legajo 10, caja 8, #3659.

289. Esteban García to the president, Colima, 28 January 1885, UI-CPD, legajo 10, caja 4, #1538.

290. Porfirio Díaz to Esteban García, 7 February 1885, UI-CPD, legajo 10, caja 4, #1539.

291. Manuel Zamora to the president, Tlaxiaco, 29 December 1884, UI-CPD, legajo 10, caja 3, #1101.

292. Felix Montes, representing San Miguel Achiutla, to Jefe Político, Tlaxiaco, 1 December 1884, UI-CPD, legajo 10, caja 3, #1102.

293. José Reyes and three others to the president, Mexico City, 27 January 1885, UI-CPD, legajo 10, caja 4, #1967.

294. Slavoj Žižek, "20 Years of Collapse," New York Times, 9 November 2009.

295. In "Modernity versus Postmodernity," Habermas seems to suggest that modernity's economic, moral, and cultural aspects have a unity, but the nineteenth-century experience in Latin America suggests otherwise.

296. El Socialista, 6 January 1878.

297. Diario de Cundinamarca, 16 October 1891.

298. For the link between conceptions of modernity and modernization theory, see Knight, "When Was Latin America Modern?," 94–95.

CONCLUSION. A "GIFT THAT THE NEW WORLD HAS SENT US"

1. On the twentieth century, see Vaughan and Lewis, introduction; N. Miller, In the Shadow.

2. Martí and Gómez, "The Montecristo Manifesto," 344. See also Martí, "Our America," 291.

3. Martí, "Our America."

4. Martí and Gómez, "The Montecristo Manifesto," 344.

5. Martí and Gómez, "The Montecristo Manifesto," 343.

6. Martí and Gómez, "The Montecristo Manifesto," 345.

7. Martí and Gómez, "The Montecristo Manifesto," 337. See also Martí, "Our America," 291.

8. Martí, "Our America," 295–96; Martí, "My Race." See also Ferrer, Insurgent Cuba; de la Fuente, A Nation for All; L. Guerra, The Myth of José Martí; Scott, Degrees of Freedom.

9. Ching, Buckley, and Lozano-Alonso, Reframing Latin America, 222.

10. Fanon, The Wretched of the Earth, 313, 314.

11. Martí, "Our America," 288–96. See also Ramos, Divergent Modernities; Abel and Torrents, José Martí; Belnap and Fernández, José Martí's "Our America."

12. Rodó, Ariel.

13. González Echevarría, The Voice of the Masters, 17. See also Shumway, "Hispanism Is an Imperfect Past," 292–93.

14. González Echevarría, The Voice of the Masters, 19.

15. On Europe, see Faber, "'La hora ha llegado,'" 67.

16. González Echevarría, The Voice of the Masters, 30. See also Ramos, Divergent Modernities, xxxix–xl.

17. Said, *Culture and Imperialism*, 228–29.

18. Said, *Culture and Imperialism*, 299.

19. Ferrer, *Insurgent Cuba*, 201–2.

20. de la Fuente, *A Nation for All*.

21. J. Conrad, *Nostromo*, 103, 119, 124, 152, 175, 273.

22. J. Conrad, *Nostromo*, 344.

23. J. Conrad, *Nostromo*, 51.

24. J. Conrad, *Nostromo*, 48.

25. J. Conrad, *Nostromo*, 328.

26. Said, *Culture and Imperialism*, xviii, xix, 24–30, 146, 165–66.

27. GoGwilt, *The Invention of the West*.

28. Mignolo, *The Darker Side*, xiii–xiv.

29. Wolin, "'Modernity,'" 748.

30. Said, *Culture and Imperialism*, 108; see also 98.

31. Stendhal, *The Red and the Black*, 292.

32. Manuel de Silva to Benito Juárez, Sevilla, 12 July 1867, in *Diario Oficial del Gobierno Supremo de la República*, 24 August 1867.

33. Félix Pyat, "Salutación de los Obreros Republicanos Franceses, al Presidente Benito Juárez," *La República* (Chihuahua), 11 October 1867.

34. Cluseret, *Mexico*, 90.

35. Cluseret, *Mexico*, 94.

36. Cluseret, *Mexico*, 109.

37. Association of Genoese Workers, "Felicitaciones á México," *La República* (Chihuahua), 25 October 1867.

38. Asociación de la Democracia Militante to Ciudadano Juárez, Brussels, 25 September 1867, in *La República* (Chihuahua), 20 December 1867.

39. Emilio Castelar, "Política de Napoleón en America," *La Bandera Nacional*, 14 May 1864.

40. Emilio Castelar, "Política de Napoleón en America," *La Bandera Nacional*, 14 May 1864. See also Hale, "Emilio Castelar and Mexico."

41. Victor Hugo to Benito Juárez, Hauteville-House, 20 June 1867, in *El Boyacense*, 7 September 1867. Hugo's letter was also published in *El Globo*, 8 August 1867.

42. J. Garibaldi, "Un saludo á México," *La República* (Chihuahua), 9 August 1867.

43. Zephaniah Kingsley to George H. Evans, Puerto de Plata, Haiti, 13 September 1835, first printed in *Working Man's Advocate* (Rahway, NJ), 17 October 1835, reprinted in Kingsley, *Balancing Evils Judiciously*, 90.

44. Zephaniah Kingsley to George H. Evans, Puerto de Plata, Haiti, 13 September 1835, first printed in *Working Man's Advocate* (Rahway, NJ), 17 October 1835, reprinted in Kingsley, *Balancing Evils Judiciously*, 90.

45. Stowell, introduction.

46. Zephaniah Kingsley to George H. Evans, Cape Haïtien, Haiti, 29 September

1835, first printed in *Working Man's Advocate* (Rahway, NJ), 31 October 1835, reprinted in Kingsley, *Balancing Evils Judiciously*, 93.

47. Zephaniah Kingsley to George H. Evans, Port-au-Prince, Haiti, 12 October 1835, first printed in *Working Man's Advocate* (Rahway, NJ), 21 November 1835, reprinted in Kingsley, *Balancing Evils Judiciously*, 95.

48. Will of Zephaniah Kingsley, Jacksonville, FL, 20 July 1843, Duval, File 1203.

49. On Haiti as barbarous, see Hunt, *Haiti's Influence on Antebellum America*; Fischer, *Modernity Disavowed*.

50. On the Haitian Revolution's influencing of others, see Geggus, *The Impact*; Nesbitt, *Universal Emancipation*.

51. Delany, *The Condition*, 182. See also Levine, *Martin Delany*.

52. Delany, *The Condition*, 181.

53. Delany, *The Condition*, 183.

54. Delany, *The Condition*, 187; see also 185–87.

55. Delany, *The Condition*, 189.

56. Guillermo Caution to the Congress of Nueva Granada, Chagres, 24 February 1849, AGNC-SR-FC, legajo 18, 724. Caution described himself as a manumitted slave from the United States.

57. Dorsch and over two hundred others, *Manifestación*, broadside in AHMRG-FII, #630.

58. A different Spanish translation of this letter appears in "Voto de gracias de los Alemanes Radicales de los Estados Unidos al Presidente Juárez," *La República* (Chihuahua), 20 September 1867.

59. "Speech of Gerrit Smith on the Nebraska Bill," Washington D.C., 6 April 1854, in *Frederick Douglass' Paper*, 12 May 1854.

60. McDougall, *French Interference in Mexico*, 22.

61. On the United States and Europe, see Doyle, *Aristocracy and Its Enemies*.

62. On the United States, see Bradburn, *The Citizenship Revolution*.

63. This literature has grown too vast for each item in it to be cited. For a bibliography, see Sanders, "Popular Movements."

64. Said, *Culture and Imperialism*, 217.

65. McNeill, *The Rise of the West*, 731.

66. Headley, *The Europeanization of the World*, 4–5. See also Fernández-Armesto, *The Americas*, 133–34. On an undemocratic Latin America, see Vargas Llosa, *Liberty for Latin America*, 28–33; Schneider, *Comparative Latin American Politics*, 16–21; Harrison, *The Pan-American Dream*; Wiarda, *The Soul of Latin America*, 7; Duncan, *Latin American Politics*, 17–18; Dealy, "Prolegomena."

67. See Cañizares-Esguerra, *Puritan Conquistadors*, 227; Annino, "El paradigma y la disputa," 1:130. On ignoring Latin America, see Besse, "Placing Latin America."

68. "AHR Roundtable." See also Kalyvas and Katznelson, *Liberal Beginnings*; Viroli,

Republicanism; Appleby, *Liberalism and Republicanism*; Headley, *The Europeanization of the World*.

69. Chakrabarty, "The Muddle of Modernity," 673.

70. Said, *Culture and Imperialism*, 199.

71. Mignolo, *The Darker Side*, 2–3, 14, 259; Mignolo, *Local Histories/Global Designs*, 296–97, 317–18; Chakrabarty, *Provincializing Europe*, 4. For a critique of such postcolonial assumptions, see S. Conrad, "Enlightenment in Global History," 1005–6.

72. Chakrabarty, *Provincializing Europe*, 4. For critiques of Europeans' assumed influence, see Cooper, *Colonialism in Question*, 121–22, 140; Coronil, *The Magical State*, 13–14.

73. Cooper, *Colonialism in Question*, 148.

74. Mignolo, *Local Histories/Global Designs*, 296–97.

75. Thomson, "Mid-Nineteenth-Century Modernities," 85.

76. F. Bilbao, "El evangelio americano," 2:383.

77. F. Bilbao, "El evangelio americano," 2:384. See also Forment, *Democracy in Latin America*, 239–84, 440–42. For a critique of obsessions with the origins of the Enlightenment and modernity, instead of practices, see S. Conrad, "Enlightenment in Global History."

Bibliography

ARCHIVAL SOURCES AND ABBREVIATIONS
ACC—Archivo Central del Cauca (Centro de Investigaciones Históricas "José María Arboleda Llorente"), Popayán, Colombia
ACSR—Archivo de "El Carnero," Sala República
AM—Archivo Muerto
FA—Fondo Arboleda
SM—Sala Mosquera

ACON—Archivo del Congreso, Bogota, Colombia (Since I used this archive, it has been moved into the Archivo General de la Nación, Sección Archivo Histórico Legislativo.)
C—Cámara
S—Senado

AGNC —Archivo General de la Nación, Bogota, Colombia
FC—Fondo Congreso
FEOR—Fondo Enrique Ortega Ricaurte
FJHL—Fondo José Hilario López
FLM—Fondo Libros Manuscritos y Leyes Originales
FMAN—Fondo Manumisión
FSCR—Fondo Salvador Camacho Roldán

SACH—Sección Academia Colombiana de Historia
SC—Sección Colecciones
SR—Sección República

AGNM—Archivo General de la Nación, Mexico City
FG—Fondo Gobernación Siglo XIX, Gobernación
FJJ —Fondo Justicia, Justicia
FJS—Fondo Justicia, Secretaría de Justicia
IG—Instituciones Gubernamentales: Epoca Moderna y Contemporánea, Administración Pública Federal Siglo XIX

AGNU, Archivo General de la Nación, Montevideo, Uruguay
AGA—Archivo General Administrativo, Fondo Ministerio de Gobierno
EAM—Ex Archivo y Museo Histórico Nacional

AHMC—Archivo Histórico Municipal de Cali, Cali, Colombia
ACM—Archivo del Concejo Municipal

AHMRG—Archivo Histórico del Museo Regional de Guanajuato-Alhóndiga de Granaditos, Guanajuato, México
FBPCM—Fondo Bandos, Proclamas, Circulares, Manifiestos, y Similares
FEM—Fondo Ejército, Maniobras Militares, Guerra
FII—Fondo Imprenta e Impresos

BLAA—Biblioteca Luis Angel Arango, Bogota, Colombia
M—Sala de Manuscritos, Manuscritos

BN—Biblioteca Nacional, Bogota, Colombia
FM—Fondo Manuscritos
R—Reparación

Duval—Duval County Courthouse, Jacksonville, FL, Probate Records

INCORA—Archivo del Instituto Colombiano de la Reforma Agraria, Bogota, Colombia
B—Bienes Nacionales

LC—Library of Congress, Washington
JSP—Manuscript Division, John M. Schofield Papers
RB—Rare Books, Broadside Collection

MHN—Museo Histórico Nacional, Montevideo, Uruguay, Archivo y Biblioteca Pablo Blanco Acevedo
CMHN—Colección Museo Histórico Nacional

UI—Universidad Iberoamericana, Acervos Históricos, Mexico City
CPD—Colección Porfirio Díaz

NEWSPAPERS CITED

Ariete (Cali, Colombia)

Boletín Republicano (Mexico City)

Brooklyn Daily Eagle (Brooklyn, NY)

Colombia Ilustrada (Bogota)

Comercio del Plata (Montevideo)

Correio Mercantil (Rio de Janeiro)

Diario de Cundinamarca (Bogota)

Diario de la Marina (Havana)

Diario Oficial del Gobierno Supremo de la República (Mexico City)

El 21 de Abril (Popayán, Colombia)

El Aguijón (Guanajuato, Mexico)

El Americano (Paris)

El Amigo del Pueblo (Guanajuato, Mexico)

El Amigo del Pueblo (Mexico City)

El Atratense (Quibdó, Colombia)

El Boyacense (Tunja, Colombia)

El Calavera (Guanajuato, Mexico)

El Campeón de la Fe (Guanajuato, Mexico)

El Cauca (Popayán, Colombia)

El Caucano (Cali, Colombia)

El Cernícalo (Popayán, Colombia)

El Ciudadano (Popayán, Colombia)

El Clamor Nacional (Popayán, Colombia)

El Comercio (Lima)

El Compás (Montevideo)

El Condor de Bolivia (Chuquisaca, Bolivia)

El Conservador (Bogota)

El Conservador (Montevideo)

El Constitucional (Montevideo)

El Correo Nacional (Bogota)

El Corresponsal del Ejército (Mexico City)

El Cosmopolita (Mexico City)

El Cronista de México (Mexico City)

El Cruzado (Mexico City)

El Defensor de la Independencia Americana (Miguelete, Uruguay)

El Demócrata (Palmira, Colombia)

El Escolar (Guanajuato, Mexico)

El Espectador (Pasto, Colombia)

El Estado de Guerra (Bogota)

El Estado de Guanajuato (Guanajuato, Mexico)

El Estandarte Liberal (Cali, Colombia)

El *Estandarte Nacional* (Mexico City)

El *Farol* (Puebla, Mexico)

El *Ferrocarril* (Cali, Colombia)

El *Ferrocarril* (Guanajuato, Mexico)

El *Garibaldi* (San Luis Potosí, Mexico)

El *Genio de la Libertad* (Veracruz, Mexico)

El *Globo* (Mexico City)

El *Grito de Guerra* (Guanajuato, Mexico)

El *Guaitara* (Pasto, Colombia)

El *Heraldo* (Bogota)

El *Hijo de la Revolución* (Montevideo)

El *Hombre* (Cali, Colombia)

El *Imparcial* (Guanajuato, Mexico)

El *Imperio* (Guanajuato, Mexico)

El *Indicador* (Veracruz, Mexico)

El *Juicio Público* (Guanajuato, Mexico)

El *Lampacense* (Lampazos de Naranjo, Mexico)

El *Monitor Republicano* (Mexico City)

El *Montañes* (Barbacoas, Colombia)

El *Montevideano* (Montevideo)

El *Nacional* (Montevideo)

El *Noticioso Diligente* (Guanajuato, Mexico)

El *Núcleo* (Bogota)

El *Obrero del Porvenir* (Guanajuato, Mexico)

El *Observador de la República Mexicana* (Mexico City)

El *Pabellón Nacional* (Mexico City)

El *Patriota* (Popayán, Colombia)

El *Pensamiento Popular* (Cali, Colombia)

El *Pensamiento Público* (Guanajuato, Mexico)

El *Porvenir* (Bogota)

El *Porvenir de México* (Mexico City)

El *Porvenir Nacional* (Mexico City)

El *Progreso* (Mexico City)

El *Quincenal* (Guanajuato, Mexico)

El *Republicano* (Mexico City)

El *Sentimiento Democrático* (Cali, Colombia)

El *Siglo* (Montevideo)

El *Siglo Diez y Nueve* (Mexico City)

El *Socialista* (Mexico City)

El *Sol* (Mexico City)

El *Taller* (Bogota)

El *Tambor de la Linea* (La Linea, Uruguay)

El *Telégrafo* (Durango)
El *Transcendental* (Mineral de Pozos, Mexico)
El *Ultimo Mohicano* (Guanajuato, Mexico)
Frederick Douglass' Paper (Rochester, NY)
Gaceta del Cauca (Popayán, Colombia)
Gaceta Oficial (Popayán, Colombia)
Gaceta Oficial del Cauca (Popayán, Colombia)
La *Alianza de la Frontera* (Chihuahua, Mexico)
La *Aurora* (Guanajuato, Mexico)
La *Bandera Nacional* (Matamoros, Mexico)
La *Chinaca* (Mexico City)
La *Cruz* (Mexico City)
La *Cuestión Social* (Mexico City)
La *Democracia* (Montevideo)
La *Fraternidad* (León, Mexico)
La *Frontera* (Manizales, Colombia)
La *Gaceta Comercial* (Mexico City)
La *Guerra* (Morelia, Mexico)
La *Hesperia* (Mexico City)
La *Libertad* (Mexico City)
La *Minerva Guanajuatense* (Guanajuato, Mexico)
La *Nación* (Montevideo)
La *Opinión Nacional* (Mexico City)
La *Palanca* (Mexico City)
La *Patria* (Morelia, Mexico)
La *República* (Chihuahua, Mexico)
La *República* (Mexico City)
La *Salud del Pueblo* (Mexico City)
La *Sociedad* (Mexico City)
La *Sombra* (Mexico City)
La *Unión* (Popayán, Colombia)
La *Voz del Comercio* (Guanajuato, Mexico)
La *Voz del Pueblo* (Cali, Colombia)
La *Voz del Pueblo* (San Cristóbal, Mexico)
La *Voz Nacional* (Guanajuato, Mexico)
Las *Máscaras* (Pasto, Colombia)
Los *Amigos del Pueblo* (Mexico City)
Los *Principios* (Cali, Colombia)
New Hampshire Sentinel (Keene, NH)
New York Times (New York)
Registro Oficial (Popayán, Colombia)
Revista Telegráfica de México (Mexico City)

Spirit of the Times (New York)
The Two Republics (Mexico City)

PUBLISHED PRIMARY SOURCES

Alamán, Lucas. Historia de Méjico, desde los primeros movimientos que prepararon su independencia en el año de 1808 hasta la época presente. 5 vols. 1849–1852. Mexico City: Fondo de Cultura Económica, 1985.

Alberdi, Juan Bautista. Cartas inéditas á Juan María Gutiérrez y á Feliz Frías. Edited by Jorge M. Mayer and Ernesto A. Martínez. Buenos Aires: Editorial Luz del Día, 1953.

Alberdi, Juan Bautista. El imperio del Brasil ante la democracia de América. Paris: Imprenta A. E. Rochette, 1869.

Alberdi, Juan Bautista. La barbarie histórica de Sarmiento. Buenos Aires: Ediciones Pampa y Cielo, 1964.

Alberdi, Juan Bautista. La monarquía como mejor forma del gobierno en Sud América, estudio preliminar y notas de Juan Pablo Oliver. Buenos Aires: A. Pena Lillo, 1970.

Alcaraz, Ramón. The Other Side: Or Notes for the History of the War between Mexico and the United States. Translated with notes by Albert C. Ramsey. New York: Burt Franklin, 1850.

Almonte, Juan N., and José Mariano de Salas. Mexicanos. Mexico City, 1864.

Altamira, Rafael. España y el programa americanista. Madrid: Editorial América, 1917.

Arango, Napoleon. The Cuban Revolution, Its History, Government, Resources, Object, Hopes and Prospects. No place or press, 1870.

Arboleda, Sergio. El clero puede salvarnos i nadie puede salvarnos sino el clero. Popayán, Colombia: Imprenta del Colejio Mayor, 1858.

Arboleda, Sergio. Rudimentos de geografía, cronología e historia. Bogota: Imprenta de El Tradicionalista, 1872.

Arias, Juan de Dios. Reseña histórica de la formación y operaciones del cuerpo de Ejército del Norte durante la intervención francesa. Mexico City: Imprenta de Nabor Chávez, 1867.

Bilbao, Francisco. "Ecce homo." In Las obras completas de Francisco Bilbao, edited by Manuel Bilbao, 2:492–94. Buenos Aires: Imprenta de Buenos Aires, 1865.

Bilbao, Francisco. "El evangelio americano." In Las obras completas de Francisco Bilbao, edited by Manuel Bilbao, 2:311–444. Buenos Aires: Imprenta de Buenos Aires, 1865.

Bilbao, Francisco. "El Presidente Obando: Su traición y su enjuiciamiento." In Las obras completas de Francisco Bilbao, edited by Manuel Bilbao, 1:181–94. Buenos Aires: Imprenta de Buenos Aires, 1865.

Bilbao, Francisco. "Emancipación del espíritu en América." In Las obras completas de Francisco Bilbao, edited by Manuel Bilbao, 2:545–51. Buenos Aires: Imprenta de Buenos Aires, 1865.

Bilbao, Francisco. "Iniciativa de la América: Idea de un Congreso Federal de las Repúblicas." In *Las Obras Completas de Francisco Bilbao*, edited by Manuel Bilbao, 1:285–304. Buenos Aires: Imprenta de Buenos Aires, 1865.

Bilbao, Francisco. "La América en peligro." In *Las obras completas de Francisco Bilbao*, edited by Manuel Bilbao, 2:171–278. Buenos Aires: Imprenta de Buenos Aires, 1865.

Bilbao, Francisco. *La Revista del Nuevo Mundo*. Buenos Aires: Imprenta J. A. Berheim, 1857.

Bilbao, Francisco. *Las obras completas de Francisco Bilbao*, 2 vols, edited by Manuel Bilbao. Buenos Aires: Imprenta de Buenos Aires, 1865.

Bilbao, Francisco. "Movimiento social de los pueblos de la América Meridional." In *Las obras completas de Francisco Bilbao*, edited by Manuel Bilbao, 1:169–79. Buenos Aires: Imprenta de Buenos Aires, 1865.

Bilbao, Francisco. "Sobre la revelación del porvenir." In *Las obras completas de Francisco Bilbao*, edited by Manuel Bilbao, 2:524–31. Buenos Aires: Imprenta de Buenos Aires, 1865.

Bilbao, Francisco. "Sociabilidad chilena." In *Las obras completas de Francisco Bilbao*, edited by Manuel Bilbao, 1:3–41. Buenos Aires: Imprenta de Buenos Aires, 1865.

Bilbao, Manuel. "Vida de Francisco Bilbao." In *Las Obras completas de Francisco Bilbao*, edited by Manuel Bilbao, 1:ix–clxxxv. Buenos Aires: Imprenta de Buenos Aires, 1866.

Bolívar, Simón. "A Glance at Spanish America (1829)." In *El Libertador: Writings of Simón Bolívar*, edited by David Bushnell, translated by Frederick H. Fornoff, 95–102. Oxford: Oxford University Press, 2003.

Bolívar, Simón. "Letter to Colonel Patrick Campbell, British Chargé d'Affaires: 'Plague America with Miseries.'" In *El Libertador: Writings of Simón Bolívar*, edited by David Bushnell, translated by Frederick H. Fornoff, 172–76. Oxford: Oxford University Press, 2003.

Bolívar, Simón. "Letter to General Juan José Flores: 'Ploughing the Sea.'" In *El Libertador: Writings of Simón Bolívar*, edited by David Bushnell, translated by Frederick H. Fornoff, 145–49. Oxford: Oxford University Press, 2003.

Brooks, N. C. *A Complete History of the Mexican War*. 1849. Chicago: Rio Grande, 1965.

Cervantes, P. P. *Observaciones a los "Apuntamientos para la historia de la Guerra de 1876 a 1877" escritos por el señor Constancio Franco V*. Bogota, 1877.

Chamberlain, Samuel E. *My Confession*. New York: Harper and Brothers, 1956.

Cluseret, G. *Mexico, and the Solidarity of Nations*. New York: Blackwell, 1866.

Comonfort, Ignacio. *El ciudadano Ignacio Comonfort, General en Gefe de la división del Ejército Restaurador*. Guanajuato: Albino Chagoyán, 1855.

Conrad, Joseph. *Nostromo: A Tale of the Seaboard*. 1904. New York: Penguin, 1983.

Constitución Federal de los Estados-Unidos Mexicanos, sancionada y jurada por el Congreso General Constituyente. Mexico City: Imprenta de Ignacio Cumplido, 1857.

de Castillo y Lanzas, Joaquín M. *Arenga cívica que en memoria del glorioso grito de Dolores pronunció en la plaza de Veracruz en 16 de setiembre de 1839*. Veracruz, Mexico: Imprenta Liberal, 1839.

de la Luz Rosas, José. *La Junta Patriótica Central de Guanajuato, á los habitantes del Estado*. Guanajuato, Mexico: Tip. de la Reforma, 1862.

de Villar y Bocanegra, José. *El prefecto político del Departamento del Valle de México, á sus habitantes*. Mexico City, 1864.

Delany, Martin Robison. *The Condition, Elevation, Emigration and Destiny of the Colored People of the United States*. 1852. New York: Arno, 1969.

Documentos relativos á la misión política encomendada á la Asamblea General de Notables, que dio por resultado la adopción del sistema monárquico en México. Mexico City: Imprenta Literaria, 1864.

Dorsch, Edward, et al. *Manifestación al Presidente Benito Juárez hechas por los alemanes radicales de los E. Unidos*. 1867. Guanajuato, Mexico: El Barretero, 1906.

Douglass, Frederick. *Lecture on Haiti*. Chicago: Violet Agents Supply, 1893.

Echeverría, Estevan. *Cartas a D. Pedro de Angelis, Editor del Archivo Americano por el autor del Dogma Socialista, y de la ojeada sobre el movimiento intelectual en el Plata desde el año 37*. Montevideo: Imprenta del 18 de Julio, 1847.

Estrada, José Manuel. *El catolicismo y la democracia: Refutación á La América en Peligro del Señor Francisco Bilbao*. Buenos Aires: Imprenta de Bernheim y Boneo, 1862.

Garibaldi, Giuseppe. *Autobiography of Giuseppe Garibaldi*. Vol. 1. 1850, 1872, 1876. Translated by A. Werner. New York: Howard Fertig, 1971.

Gibson, William Marion. *The Constitutions of Colombia*. Durham, NC: Duke University Press, 1948.

González Montes, P. *Prefecto Municipal de Guanajuato á todos sus habitantes*. Guanajuato, Mexico, 1865.

Grant, U. S. *Personal Memoirs of U. S. Grant*. 1885. Cleveland, OH: World, 1952.

Gutiérrez Estrada, José María. *Carta dirigida al excelentísimo Señor Presidente de la República, sobre la necesidad de buscar en una convención el posible remedio de los males que aquejan á la República*. Mexico City: Ignacio Cumplido, 1840.

Hernández, José María P. *El C. José M. P. Hernández*. Ciudad Guerrero, Mexico: Imprenta del Gobierno, 1857.

Herrera Olarte, José. *La administración Trujillo: Juicio histórico*. Bogota: Imprenta de Gaitán, 1880.

Honores fúnebres celebrados por el Ser. Gr. Or. y Sup. Cons. de la República O. del Uruguay al pod. É Il. H. José Garibaldi, 26 de Julio de 1882. Montevideo: Imprenta de El Ferro-Carril, 1882.

Hostos, Eugenio M. *A Carlos Holguín, autor del proyecto de Alianza Colombiana*. New York, 1870.

Ignotus [Enrique Cortés]. *La lección del pasado: Ensayo sobre la verdadera misión del Partido Liberal*. Bogota: Imprenta de Medardo Rivas, 1877.

Kendall, George Wilkins. *Dispatches from the Mexican War*. Edited by Lawrence Delbert Cress. Norman: University of Oklahoma Press, 1999.

Kingsley, Zephaniah. *Balancing Evils Judiciously: The Proslavery Writings of Zephaniah Kingsley*. Edited by Daniel W. Stowell. Gainesville: University Press of Florida, 2000.

Leoni, Francisco Colombo. *Gumersindo Saraiva: Comandante de la Legión Garibaldina*. Montevideo: Imprenta de El Siglo, 1894.

Lerdo de Tejada, Miguel. *Cuadro sinóptico de la República Mexicana en 1856*. Mexico City: Imprenta de Ignacio Cumplido, 1856.

López, José Hilario. *Mensaje del Poder Ejecutivo á las Cámaras Lejislativas*. Bogota: Imprenta del Neo-Granadino, 1852.

López, José Hilario. *Mensaje del Presidente de la Nueva Granada al Congreso Constitucional de 1852*. Bogota: Imprenta del Neo-Granadino, 1852.

Los criminales, al presidio. [Cali, Colombia]: Imprenta de Nicolás Pontón i Compañía, [1862].

Los Miembros de la Sociedad Republicana de Artesanos. *Una representación*. Cali, Colombia: Imprenta de Hurtado, 1868.

Los Verdaderos Constitucionalistas. *A los liberales de la provincia*. Popayán, Colombia: Imprenta Democrática, 1853.

Macedo, Miguel S. "Parte octava: El municipio, los establecimientos penales, la asistencia pública." In Miguel S. Macedo, *México: Su evolución social*, 2:665–725. Mexico City: J. Ballescá y Compañía, 1902.

Manini Ríos, Pedro. *Garibaldi*. Montevideo: Imprenta de Dornaleche y Reyes, 1900.

Mantilla, Foción. *Informe del Secretario de Hacienda a la Legislatura del Estado Soberano del Cauca en sus sesiones ordinarias de 1883*. Popayán, Colombia: Imprenta del Estado, 1883.

Martí, José. "My Race." 1893. In José Martí, *Selected Writings*, edited and translated by Esther Allen, 318–21. New York: Penguin, 2002.

Martí, José. "Our America." 1891. In José Martí, *Selected Writings*, edited and translated by Esther Allen, 288–96. New York: Penguin, 2002.

Martí, José, and Máximo Gómez. "The Montecristo Manifesto." 1895. In José Martí, *Selected Writings*, edited and translated by Esther Allen, 337–45. New York: Penguin, 2002.

McDougall, J. A. *French Interference in Mexico: Speech of Hon. J. A. McDougall, of California, in the Senate of the United States, on Tuesday, February 3d, 1863*. Baltimore, MD: John Murphy, 1863.

Mensaje del Poder Ejecutivo a las Cámaras sobre la desnacionalización y desarme de la Lejión de Voluntarios. Montevideo: Imprenta del Nacional, 1844.

Mercado, Ramón. *Memorias sobre los acontecimientos del Sur, especialmente en la Provincia de Buenaventura, durante la administración del 7 de marzo de 1849*. 1853. Cali, Colombia: Centro de Estudios Históricos y Sociales "Santiago de Cali," 1996.

Mexico Illustrated at Stoppani Hall. New York: George F. Nesbitt, 1848.

Muñiz, Manuel. *Protesta*. N.p.: Imprenta Z. Andrade, 1862.

Observaciones para servir á la historia de la administración del 7 de Marzo, i especialmente en lo que concierne á la polémica promovida por el Arzobispo de Bogotá con relación á algunas disposiciones lejislativas recientemente puestas en ejecución. Bogota: Imprenta del Neo-Granadino, 1851.

Oribe, Manuel. *Circular de D. Manuel Oribe á los Cónsules extrangeros, y observaciones sobre ella*. Montevideo: Imprenta del Nacional, 1843.

Peña, Belisario. *Oda al triunfo obtenido por el ejército del Sumo Pontífice Pío ix sobre Garibaldi*. Quito: Los Huérfanos de V. Valencia, 1867.

Peskin, Allan, ed. *Volunteers: The Mexican War Journals of Private Richard Coulter and Sergeant Thomas Barclay, Company E, Second Pennsylvania Infantry*. Kent, OH: Kent State University Press, 1991.

Pesqueira, Ignacio. *Ignacio Pesqueira, Gobernador Constitucional del Estado de Sonora*. Ures: Imprenta de Gobierno, 1857.

Pinzón, Cerbeleón. *Catecismo republicano para instrucción popular*. Bogota: Imprenta de "El Mosaico," 1864.

Ramírez, José Fernando. *Mexico during the War with the United States*. Translated by Elliot B. Scherr. Columbia: University of Missouri Press, 1950.

Rasgo patriótico de la milicia nacional de Guanajuato. Guanajuato, Mexico: Imprenta del Supremo Gobierno, 1829.

Roa Bárcena, José María. *Recuerdos de la invasión norteamericana (1846–1848)*. Vol. 2. 1883. Mexico City: Editorial Porrua, 1947.

Rodó, José Enrique. *Ariel*. Montevideo: Imprenta de Dornaleche y Reyes, 1900.

Romero, M. *The Situation of Mexico*. New York: Wm. C. Bryant, 1864.

Samper, José María. *Ensayo aproximado sobre la jeografía i estadística de los ocho estados que compondrán el 15 de septiembre de 1857 la Federación Neo-Granadina*. Bogota: Imprenta de "El Neo-Granadino," 1857.

Samper, José María. *Ensayo sobre las revoluciones políticas y la condición social de las repúblicas colombianas (Hispano-Americanas); con un apéndice sobre la orografía y la población de la Confederación Granadina*. Paris: E. Thunot, 1861.

Sarmiento, Domingo F. *Facundo, o civilización i barbarie*. 3 vols. 1845. Montevideo: Tipografía Americana, 1888–89.

Sarmiento, Domingo F. *North and South America: A Discourse Delivered before the Rhode-Island Historical Society*. Providence, RI: Knowles, Anthony, 1866.

Scarpetta, M. *El grito de un republicano*. Cali, Colombia: Imprenta de Velasco, 1854.

Sierra, Justo. *Obras completas: Vol. 12, Evolución política del pueblo mexicano*. Edited by Edmundo O'Gorman. 1900–1902. Mexico City: Universidad Nacional Autónoma de México, 1977.

Sierra, Justo. *Obras completas: Vol. 17, Correspondencia con José Yves Limantour*. Edited by Alfonso de María y Campos. Mexico City: Universidad Nacional Autónoma de México, 1996.

Sociedad Democrática de Palmira. *Estatuto de la Sociedad Democrática de Palmira, aprobado definitivamente en la sesión del día 19 de mayo de 1868*. Bogota: Imprenta de Echeverría Hermanos, 1868.

Stendhal. *The Red and the Black*. 1830. Translated by Lloyd C. Parks. New York: Signet, 1970.

Vallenilla Lanz, Laureano. *Cesarismo democrático y otros textos*. Edited by Nikita Harwich Vallenilla. Caracas: Biblioteca Ayacucho, 1991.

Vergara y Vergara, José María. "La Política." In *Obras escogidas de Don José María Vergara y Vergara*, 2:91–101. Bogota: Editorial Minerva, 1931.

Webster, Noah. *Letters of Noah Webster*. Edited by Harry R. Warfel. New York: Library, 1953.

Wright, Francisco Agustín. *Montevideo: Apuntes historicos de la defensa de la República*. Montevideo: Imprenta del Nacional, 1845.

Zamorano, Belisario. *Bosquejo biográfico del Jeneral David Peña*. Cali, Colombia: Imprenta de Eustaquio Palacios, 1878.

SECONDARY SOURCES

Abel, Christopher, and Nissa Torrents, eds. *José Martí: Revolutionary Democrat*. Durham, NC: Duke University Press, 1986.

Acree, William G., Jr., and Juan Carlos González Espitia, eds. *Building Nineteenth-Century Latin America: Re-Rooted Cultures, Identities, and Nations*. Nashville, TN: Vanderbilt University Press, 2009.

Adams, Julia, Elisabeth S. Clemens, and Ann Shola Orloff, eds. *Remaking Modernity: Politics, History, and Sociology*. Durham, NC: Duke University Press, 2005.

Adelman, Jeremy. "Between Order and Liberty: Juan Bautista Alberdi and the Intellectual Origins of Argentine Constitutionalism." *Latin American Research Review* 42, no. 2 (2007): 86–110.

Adelman, Jeremy. *Sovereignty and Revolution in the Iberian Atlantic*. Princeton, NJ: Princeton University Press, 2006.

Aguilar Rivera, José Antonio. *En pos de la quimera: Reflexiones sobre el experimento constitucional atlántico*. Mexico City: Fondo de Cultura Económica, 2000.

Aguirre, Carlos. *Agentes de su propia libertad: Los esclavos de Lima y la desintegración de la esclavitud, 1821–1854*. Lima: Pontificia Universidad Católica del Perú, 1993.

"AHR Roundtable: Historians and the Question of 'Modernity.'" *American Historical Review* 116 (June 2011): 631–751.

Alda Mejías, Sonia. *La participación indígena en la construcción de la república de Guatemala, S. xix*. Madrid: Universidad Autónoma de Madrid, 2002.

Alonso, Carlos J. *The Burden of Modernity: The Rhetoric of Cultural Discourse in Spanish America*. Oxford: Oxford University Press, 1998.

Alonso, Paula. "Voting in Buenos Aires (Argentina) before 1912." In *Elections before Democracy: The History of Elections in Europe and Latin America*, edited by Eduardo Posada-Carbó, 181–99. London: Institute of Latin American Studies, 1996.

Aminzade, Ronald. *Ballots and Barricades: Class Formation and Republican Politics in France, 1830–1871*. Princeton, NJ: Princeton University Press, 1993.

Anderson, Benedict. *Imagined Communities: Reflections on the Origin and Spread of Nationalism*. London: Verso, 1991.

Andrews, George Reid. *Afro-Latin America, 1800–2000*. Oxford: Oxford University Press, 2004.

Andrews, George Reid. *Blackness in the White Nation: A History of Afro-Uruguay*. Chapel Hill: University of North Carolina Press, 2010.

Annino, Antonio. "The Ballot, Land and Sovereignty: Cádiz and the Origins of Mexican Local Government, 1812–1820." In *Elections before Democracy: The History of Elections in Europe and Latin America*, edited by Eduardo Posada-Carbó, 61–86. London: Institute of Latin American Studies, 1996.

Annino, Antonio. " El paradigma y la disputa: La cuestión liberal en México y en la América hispana." In *Relatos de nación: La construcción de las identidades nacionales en el mundo hispánico*, edited by Francisco Colom González, 1:103–30. Madrid: Iberoamericana, 2005.

Appelbaum, Nancy P. *Muddied Waters: Race, Region, and Local History in Colombia, 1846–1948*. Durham, NC: Duke University Press, 2003.

Appelbaum, Nancy P. "Reading the Past on the Mountainsides of Colombia: Mid-Nineteenth-Century Patriotic Geology, Archaeology, and Historiography." *Hispanic American Historical Review* 93 (August 2013): 347–76.

Appelbaum, Nancy P., Anne S. Macpherson, and Karin Alejandra Rosemblatt, eds. *Race and Nation in Modern Latin America*. Chapel Hill: University of North Carolina Press, 2003.

Appleby, Joyce. *Liberalism and Republicanism in the Historical Imagination*. Cambridge, MA: Harvard University Press, 1992.

Arboleda, Gustavo. *Diccionario biográfico y genealógico del antiguo Departamento del Cauca*. Bogota: Biblioteca Horizontes, 1962.

Arciniegas, Germán. *Latin America: A Cultural History*. Translated by Joan MacLean. New York: Knopf, 1967.

Arias Vanegas, Julio. *Nación y diferencia en el siglo xix colombiano: Orden nacional, racialismo y taxonomías poblacionales*. Bogota: Universidad de los Andes, 2005.

Armitage, David, and Sanjay Subrahmanyam, eds. *The Age of Revolutions in Global Context, c. 1760–1840*. New York: Palgrave, 2010.

Ávila, Alfredo. "Liberalismos decimonónicos: De la historia de las ideas a la historia cultural e intelectual." In *Ensayos sobre la nueva historia política de América Latina, siglo xix*, edited by Guillermo Palacios, 111–45. Mexico City: El Colegio de México, 2007.

Ávila Quijas, Aquiles Omar. "La transición de la Nueva España al México republicano desde el concepto representación, 1750–1850." *Historia Mexicana* 60 (January 2011): 1453–89.

Bailyn, Bernard. *Atlantic History: Concept and Contours.* Cambridge, MA: Harvard University Press, 2005.

Baker, Paula. "The Domestication of Politics: Women and American Political Society, 1780–1920." *American Historical Review* 89 (June 1984): 620–47.

Bayly, C. A. *The Birth of the Modern World, 1780–1914.* Oxford: Blackwell, 2004.

Beattie, Peter M. *The Tribute of Blood: Army, Honor, Race, and Nation in Brazil, 1864–1945.* Durham, NC: Duke University Press, 2001.

Becker, Marc. "In Search of Tinterillos." *Latin American Research Review* 47, no. 1 (2012): 95–114.

Beezley, William H. *Judas at the Jockey Club and Other Episodes of Porfirian Mexico.* Lincoln: University of Nebraska Press, 1987.

Beezley, William H. "Kaleidoscopic Views of Liberalism Triumphant, 1862–1895." In *The Divine Charter: Constitutionalism and Liberalism in Nineteenth-Century Mexico,* edited by Jaime E. Rodríguez O., 167–79. Lanham, MD: Rowman and Littlefield, 2005.

Beezley, William H. "The Porfirian Smart Set Anticipates Thorstein Veblen in Guadalajara." In *Rituals of Rule, Rituals of Resistance: Public Celebrations and Popular Culture in Mexico,* edited by William H. Beezley, Cheryl English Martin, and William E. French, 173–90. Wilmington, DE: Scholarly Resources, 1994.

Beezley, William H., Cheryl English Martin, and William E. French, eds. *Rituals of Rule, Rituals of Resistance: Public Celebrations and Popular Culture in Mexico.* Wilmington, DE: Scholarly Resources, 1994.

Belnap, Jeffrey, and Raúl Fernández, eds. *José Martí's "Our America": From National to Hemispheric Cultural Studies.* Durham, NC: Duke University Press, 1998.

Ben-Dor Benite, Zvi. "Modernity: The Sphinx and the Historian." *American Historical Review* 116 (June 2011): 638–52.

Bentley, Michael. *Politics without Democracy, 1815–1914.* Oxford: Blackwell, 1996.

Bergquist, Charles. *Coffee and Conflict in Colombia, 1886–1910.* Durham, NC: Duke University Press, 1986.

Berman, Marshall. *All That Is Solid Melts into Air: The Experience of Modernity.* New York: Penguin, 1982.

Besse, Susan K. "Placing Latin America in Modern World History Textbooks." *Hispanic American Historical Review* 84 (August 2004): 423–30.

Beverley, John. *Against Literature.* Minneapolis: University of Minnesota Press, 1993.

Bhambra, Gurminder K. "Historical Sociology, Modernity, and Postcolonial Critique." *American Historical Review* 116 (June 2011): 653–62.

Blanchard, Peter. "The Language of Liberation: Slave Voices in the Wars of Independence." *Hispanic American Historical Review* 82 (August 2002): 499–523.

Bonnett, Alastair. *The Idea of the West: Culture, Politics and History.* Basingstoke, UK: Palgrave, 2004.

Borucki, Alex. "From Shipmates to Soldiers: Emerging Black Identities in Montevideo, 1770–1850." PhD diss., Emory University, 2011.

Borucki, Alex, Karla Chagas, and Natalia Stalla. *Esclavitud y trabajo: Un estudio sobre los afrodescendientes en la frontera uruguaya, 1835–1855*. Montevideo: Pulmón Ediciones, 2004.

Bradburn, Douglas. *The Citizenship Revolution: Politics and the Creation of the American Union, 1774–1804*. Charlottesville: University of Virginia Press, 2009.

Brading, D. A. *The First America: The Spanish Monarchy, Creole Patriots, and the Liberal State 1492–1867*. Cambridge: Cambridge University Press, 1991.

Brands, H. W. *American Colossus: The Triumph of Capitalism, 1865–1900*. New York: Doubleday, 2010.

Braudel, Fernand. *A History of Civilizations*. Translated by Richard Mayne. New York: Penguin, 1993.

Breña, Roberto. *El primer liberalismo español y los procesos de emancipación de América, 1808–1824: Una revisión historiográfica del liberalismo hispánico*. Mexico City: El Colegio de México, 2006.

Buck-Morss, Susan. *Hegel, Haiti, and Universal History*. Pittsburgh, PA: University of Pittsburgh Press, 2009.

Buenaventura, Manuel María. *Del Cali que se fue*. Cali, Colombia: Imprenta Departamental, 1957.

Burns, E. Bradford. *The Poverty of Progress: Latin America in the Nineteenth Century*. Berkeley: University of California Press, 1980.

Bushnell, David. Introduction. In *El Libertador: Writings of Simón Bolívar*, edited by David Bushnell, translated by Frederick H. Fornoff, xxvii–lii. Oxford: Oxford University Press, 2003.

Bushnell, David. *The Making of Modern Colombia: A Nation in Spite of Itself*. Berkeley: University of California Press, 1993.

Bushnell, David, and Neill Macaulay. *The Emergence of Latin America in the Nineteenth-Century*. Oxford: Oxford University Press, 1988.

Cancino, Hugo, ed. *Los intelectuales latinoamericanos entre la modernidad y la tradición, siglos xix y xx*. Madrid: Iberoamericana, 2004.

Cañizares-Esguerra, Jorge. *How to Write the History of the New World: Historiographies, Epistemologies, and Identities in the Eighteenth-Century Atlantic World*. Stanford, CA: Stanford University Press, 2001.

Cañizares-Esguerra, Jorge. *Puritan Conquistadors: Iberianizing the Atlantic, 1550–1700*. Stanford, CA: Stanford University Press, 2006.

Caplan, Karen D. *Indigenous Citizens: Local Liberalism in Early National Oaxaca and Yucatán*. Stanford, CA: Stanford University Press, 2010.

Carmagnani, Marcello. *The Other West: Latin America from Invasion to Globalization*. Translated by Rosanna M. Giammanco Frongia. Berkeley: University of California Press, 2011.

Casaús Arzú, Marta Elena, ed. *El lenguaje de los ismos: Algunos conceptos de la moderni-dad en América Latina*. Guatemala City: F and G Editores, 2010.

Castilho, Celso T. "Abolitionism Matters: The Politics of Antislavery in Pernam-buco, Brazil, 1869–1888." PhD diss., University of California, Berkeley, 2008.

Castro Klarén, Sara, and John Charles Chasteen, eds. *Beyond Imagined Communities: Reading and Writing the Nation in Nineteenth-Century Latin America*. Baltimore, MD: Johns Hopkins University Press, 2003.

Chakrabarty, Dipesh. "The Muddle of Modernity." *American Historical Review* 116 (June 2011): 663–75.

Chakrabarty, Dipesh. "Postcoloniality and the Artifice of History: Who Speaks for 'Indian' Pasts?" *Representations* 37 (winter 1992): 1–26.

Chakrabarty, Dipesh. *Provincializing Europe: Postcolonial Thought and Historical Differ-ence*. Princeton, NJ: Princeton University Press, 2007.

Chambers, Sarah C. *From Subjects to Citizens: Honor, Gender, and Politics in Arequipa, Peru, 1780–1854*. University Park: Penn State University Press, 1999.

Chassen-López, Francie R. *From Liberal to Revolutionary Oaxaca: The View from the South, Mexico, 1867–1911*. University Park: Penn State University Press, 2004.

Chasteen, John Charles. *Heroes on Horseback: The Life and Times of the Last Gaucho Caudillos*. Albuquerque: University of New Mexico Press, 1995.

Chatterjee, Partha. *The Nation and Its Fragments: Colonial and Postcolonial Histories*. Princeton, NJ: Princeton University Press, 1993.

Chiaramonte, José Carlos. "The 'Ancient Constitution' after Independence (1808–1852)." *Hispanic American Historical Review* 90 (August 2010): 455–88.

Ching, Erik, Christina Buckley, and Angélica Lozano-Alonso. *Reframing Latin America: A Cultural Theory Reading of the Nineteenth and Twentieth Centuries*. Austin: University of Texas Press, 2007.

Clark, Meri L. "The Good and the Useful Together: Colombian Positivism in a Century of Conflict." In *Latin American Positivism: New Historical and Philosophic Essays*, edited by Gregory D. Gilson and Irving W. Levinson, 27–48. Lanham, MD: Lexington, 2013.

Cohen, Jean L., and Andrew Arato. *Civil Society and Political Theory*. Cambridge, MA: MIT Press, 1992.

Colom González, Francisco, ed. *Relatos de nación: La construcción de las identidades nacionales en el mundo hispánico*. 2 vols. Madrid: Iberoamericana, 2005.

Connaughton, Brian, Carlos Illades, and Sonia Pérez Toledo, eds. *Construcción de la legitimidad política en México en el siglo xix*. Zamora, Mexico: El Colegio de Michoacán, 1999.

Connor, Walker. "When Is a Nation?" *Ethnic and Racial Studies* 13, no. 1 (1990): 92–103.

Conrad, Sebastian. "Enlightenment in Global History: A Historiographical Cri-tique." *American Historical Review* 117 (October 2012): 998–1027.

Cooper, Frederick. *Colonialism in Question: Theory, Knowledge, History*. Berkeley: University of California Press, 2005.

Coronil, Fernando. *The Magical State: Nature, Money, and Modernity in Venezuela*. Chicago: University of Chicago Press, 1997.

Cosío Villegas, Daniel. *Historia moderna de México*. Vol. 1, *La república restaurada, la vida política*. Mexico City: Editorial Hermes, 1959.

Dallmayr, Fred R. *G. W. F. Hegel: Modernity and Politics*. Lanham, MD: Rowman and Littlefield, 2002.

Davis, David Brion. *Inhuman Bondage: The Rise and Fall of Slavery in the New World*. Oxford: Oxford University Press, 2006.

de la Fuente, Alejandro. *A Nation for All: Race, Inequality, and Politics in Twentieth-Century Cuba*. Chapel Hill: University of North Carolina Press, 2001.

Dealy, Glen. "Prolegomena on the Spanish American Political Tradition." In *Politics and Social Change in Latin America: The Distinct Tradition*, edited by Howard J. Wiarda, 163–83. 2nd ed. Amherst: University of Massachusetts Press, 1982.

Di Tella, Torcuato S. *National Popular Politics in Early Independent Mexico, 1820–1847*. Albuquerque: University of New Mexico Press, 1996.

Domingues, José Maurício. *Latin America and Contemporary Modernity*. New York: Routledge, 2008.

Donoso, Armando. *El pensamiento vivo de Francisco Bilbao*. 1911. Santiago: Editorial Nascimento, 1940.

Dore, Elizabeth. "One Step Forward, Two Steps Back: Gender and the State in the Long Nineteenth Century." In *Hidden Histories of Gender and the State in Latin America*, edited by Elizabeth Dore and Maxine Molyneux, 3–32. Durham, NC: Duke University Press, 2000.

Doyle, William. *Aristocracy and Its Enemies in the Age of Revolution*. Oxford: Oxford University Press, 2009.

Drake, Paul W. *Between Tyranny and Anarchy: A History of Democracy in Latin America, 1800–2006*. Stanford, CA: Stanford University Press, 2009.

Dubois, Laurent. *A Colony of Citizens: Revolution and Slave Emancipation in the French Caribbean, 1787–1804*. Chapel Hill: University of North Carolina Press, 2004.

Ducey, Michael T. *A Nation of Villages: Riot and Rebellion in the Mexican Huasteca, 1750–1850*. Tucson: University of Arizona Press, 2004.

Duncan, W. Raymond. *Latin American Politics: A Developmental Approach*. New York: Praeger, 1976.

Dunkerley, James. *Americana: The Americas in the World, around 1850*. London: Verso, 2000.

Dunkerley, James, ed. *Studies in the Formation of the Nation State in Latin America*. London: Institute of Latin American Studies, 2002.

Dussel, Enrique. "Eurocentrism and Modernity (Introduction to the Frankfurt Lectures)." *boundary* 2 20 (fall 1993): 65–76.

Dym, Jordana. *From Sovereign Villages to National States: City, State, and Federation* in *Central America, 1759–1839.* Albuquerque: University of New Mexico Press, 2006.

Eakin, Marshall C. *The History of Latin America: Collision of Cultures.* New York: Palgrave, 2007.

Earle, Rebecca. "Rape and the Anxious Republic: Revolutionary Colombia, 1810–1830." In *Hidden Histories of Gender and the State in Latin America,* edited by Elizabeth Dore and Maxine Molyneux, 127–46. Durham, NC: Duke University Press, 2000.

Earle, Rebecca. *The Return of the Native: Indians and Myth-Making in Spanish America, 1810–1930.* Durham, NC: Duke University Press, 2007.

Eisenstadt, S. N. "Multiple Modernities." *Daedalus* 129 (winter 2000): 1–29.

Elderfield, John. *Manet and the Execution of Maximilian.* New York: Museum of Modern Art, 2006.

Escorcia, José. *Sociedad y economía en el Valle del Cauca. Vol. 3: Desarrollo político, social y económico, 1800–1854.* Bogota: Biblioteca Banco Popular, 1983.

Faber, Sebastiaan. "'La hora ha llegado': Hispanism, Pan-Americanism, and the Hope of Spanish/American Glory (1938–1948)." In *Ideologies of Hispanism,* edited by Mabel Moraña, 62–104. Nashville, TN: Vanderbilt University Press, 2005.

Fabián Mestas, Graciela. "Historia y educación en la construcción de la nación Mexicana. Segunda mitad del siglo XIX." In *La modernización en México: Siglos xviii, xix y xx,* edited by Hilda Iparraguirre and María Isabel Campos Goenaga, 123–40. Mexico City: INAH, 2007.

Falcón, Romana, ed. *Culturas de pobreza y resistencia: Estudios de marginados, proscritos y descontentos, México, 1804–1910.* Mexico City: El Colegio de México, 2005.

Falcón, Romana. "El arte de la petición: Rituales de obediencia y negociación, México, segunda mitad del siglo XIX." *Hispanic American Historical Review* 86 (August 2006): 467–500.

Falcón, Romana. "Rituals, Rules and the Attempt to Dominate Porfirian Mexico." *Journal of Iberian and Latin American Studies* 6 (December 2000): 27–43.

Fanon, Frantz. *The Wretched of the Earth.* Translated by Constance Farrington. New York: Grove, 1963.

Fernández-Armesto, Felipe. *The Americas: A Hemispheric History.* New York: Modern Library, 2003.

Ferrer, Ada. "Haiti, Free Soil, and Antislavery in the Revolutionary Atlantic." *American Historical Review* 117 (February 2012): 40–66.

Ferrer, Ada. *Insurgent Cuba: Race, Nation, and Revolution, 1868–1898.* Chapel Hill: University of North Carolina Press, 1999.

Figueroa, Pedro Pablo. *Historia de Francisco Bilbao: Su vida i sus obras.* Santiago: Imprenta de "El Correo," 1898.

Fischer, Sibylle. *Modernity Disavowed: Haiti and the Cultures of Slavery in the Age of Revolution.* Durham, NC: Duke University Press, 2004.

Florescano, Enrique. *Historia de las historias de la nación mexicana*. Mexico City: Taurus, 2002.

Flores-Quiroga, Aldo. "Legitimacy, Sequencing, and Credibility: Challenges of Mexico's Liberal Reforms in the Nineteenth Century." In *The Divine Charter: Constitutionalism and Liberalism in Nineteenth-Century Mexico*, edited by Jaime E. Rodríguez O., 339–49. Lanham, MD: Rowman and Littlefield, 2005.

Foner, Eric. *Reconstruction: America's Unfinished Revolution, 1863–1877*. New York: Harper and Row, 1988.

Forment, Carlos A. *Democracy in Latin America, 1760–1900: Vol. 1*. Chicago: University of Chicago Press, 2003.

Formisano, Ronald P. "Deferential-Participant Politics: The Early Republic's Political Culture." *American Political Science Review* 68 (June 1974): 473–87.

Foucault, Michel. *Discipline and Punish: The Birth of the Prison*. Translated by Alan Sheridan. New York: Vintage, 1977.

Franco, Jean. *The Modern Culture of Latin America: Society and the Artist*. New York: Praeger, 1967.

French, William E. "*Progreso Forzado*: Workers and the Inculcation of the Capitalist Work Ethic in the Parral Mining District." In *Rituals of Rule, Rituals of Resistance: Public Celebrations and Popular Culture in Mexico*, edited by William H. Beezley, Cheryl English Martin, and William E. French, 191–212. Wilmington, DE: Scholarly Resources, 1994.

Galeana, Patricia. "Encuentros y desencuentros de una historia compartida." In *Latinoamérica en la conciencia europea: Europa en la conciencia latinoamericana*, edited by Patricia Galeana, 92–104. Mexico City: Archivo General de la Nación, 1999.

Garrido, Margarita. *Reclamos y representaciones: Variaciones sobre la política en le Nuevo Reino de Granada, 1770–1815*. Bogota: Banco de la República, 1993.

Geggus, David P., ed. *The Impact of the Haitian Revolution in the Atlantic World*. Columbia: University of South Carolina Press, 2001.

Gellner, Ernest. *Nations and Nationalism*. Ithaca, NY: Cornell University Press, 1983.

Giddens, Anthony. *The Consequences of Modernity*. Stanford, CA: Stanford University Press, 1990.

Gluck, Carol. "The End of Elsewhere: Writing Modernity Now." *American Historical Review* 116 (June 2011): 676–87.

Gobat, Michel. "The Invention of Latin America: A Transnational History of Anti-Imperialism, Democracy, and Race." *American Historical Review* 118 (December 2013): 1345–75.

GoGwilt, Christopher. *The Invention of the West: Joseph Conrad and the Double Mapping of Europe and Empire*. Stanford, CA: Stanford University Press, 1995.

Goldberg, David Theo. *Racist Culture: Philosophy and the Politics of Meaning*. Oxford: Blackwell, 1993.

Gómez Pérez, Jorge Ramón. "Ceremonias cívicas en el ámbito ferrocarrilero mexicano del siglo XIX." In *La modernización en México: Siglos xviii, xix y xx*, edited by Hilda Iparraguirre and María Isabel Campos Goenaga, 239–55. Mexico City: INAH, 2007.

González Bernaldo, Pilar. "Los clubes electorales durante la secesión del Estado de Buenos Aires (1852–1861)." In *Ciudadanía política y formación de las naciones: Perspectivas históricas de América Latina*, edited by Hilda Sabato, 142–61. Mexico City: Fondo de Cultura Económica, 1999.

González Echevarría, Roberto. *The Voice of the Masters: Writing and Authority in Modern Latin American Literature*. Austin: University of Texas Press, 1985.

González Undurraga, Carolina. "De la casta a la raza: El concepto de raza: Un singular colectivo de la modernidad. México, 1750–1850." *Historia Mexicana* 60 (January 2011): 1491–525.

Goodrich, Diana Sorensen. *"Facundo" and the Construction of Argentine Culture*. Austin: University of Texas Press, 1996.

Gootenberg, Paul. "Order[s] and Progress in Developmental Discourse: The Case of Nineteenth-Century Peru." In *In Search of a New Order: Essays on the Politics and Society of Nineteenth-Century Latin America*, edited by Eduardo Posada-Carbó, 61–83. London: Institute of Latin American Studies, 1998.

Gotkowitz, Laura. *A Revolution for Our Rights: Indigenous Struggles for Land and Justice in Bolivia, 1880–1952*. Durham, NC: Duke University Press, 2008.

Graham, Richard, ed. *The Idea of Race in Latin America, 1870–1940*. Austin: University of Texas Press, 1990.

Grandin, Greg. *The Blood of Guatemala: A History of Race and Nation*. Durham, NC: Duke University Press, 2000.

Grandin, Greg. "The Liberal Traditions in the Americas: Rights, Sovereignty, and the Origins of Liberal Multilateralism." *American Historical Review* 117 (February 2012): 68–91.

Guardino, Peter. *Peasants, Politics, and the Formation of Mexico's National State: Guerrero, 1800–1857*. Stanford, CA: Stanford University Press, 1996.

Guardino, Peter. *The Time of Liberty: Popular Political Culture in Oaxaca, 1750–1850*. Durham, NC: Duke University Press, 2005.

Guerra, François-Xavier, ed. *Las revoluciones hispánicas: Independencias americanas y liberalismo español*. Madrid: Editorial Complutense, 1995.

Guerra, François-Xavier. "Mexico from Independence to Revolution: The Mutations of Liberalism." In *Cycles of Conflict, Centuries of Change: Crisis, Reform, and Revolution in Mexico*, edited by Elisa Servín, Leticia Reina and John Tutino, 129–52. Durham, NC: Duke University Press, 2007.

Guerra, François-Xavier. *Modernidad e independencias: Ensayos sobre las revoluciones hispánicas*. Madrid: Editorial Mapfre, 1992.

Guerra, François-Xavier, and Annick Lempérière, eds. *Los espacios públicos en Iberoamérica: Ambigüedades y problemas, siglos xviii–xix*. Mexico City: Fondo de Cultura Económica, 1998.

Guerra, Lilian. *The Myth of José Martí: Conflicting Nationalisms in Early Twentieth-Century Cuba*. Chapel Hill: University of North Carolina Press, 2005.

Guerrero Mendoza, Francisco Javier. *La impasibilidad cuestionada de Juárez: Su papel axial en la Reforma y la intervención francesa*. Mexico City: Instituto Nacional de Antropología e Historia, 2009.

Guha, Ranajit. "On Some Aspects of the Historiography of Colonial India." In *Selected Subaltern Studies*, edited by Ranajit Guha and Gayatri Chakravorty Spivak, 37–44. New York: Oxford University Press, 1988.

Guha, Ranajit. Preface. In *Selected Subaltern Studies*, edited by Ranajit Guha and Gayatri Chakravorty Spivak, 35–36. New York: Oxford University Press, 1988.

Guillén, Mauro F. "Modernism without Modernity: The Rise of Modernist Architecture in Mexico, Brazil, and Argentina, 1890–1940." *Latin American Research Review* 39, no. 2 (2004): 6–34.

Guzmán, Tracy Devine. "Our Indians in Our America: Anti-Imperialist Imperialism and the Construction of Brazilian Modernity." *Latin American Research Review* 45, no. 3 (2010): 35–62.

Habermas, Jürgen. "Modernity versus Postmodernity." Translated by Seyla Ben-Habib. *New German Critique* 22 (winter 1981): 3–14.

Habermas, Jürgen. *The Structural Transformation of the Public Sphere: An Inquiry into a Category of Bourgeois Society*. Translated by Thomas Burger. Cambridge, MA: MIT Press, 1989.

Hale, Charles A. "Emilio Castelar and Mexico." In *The Political Power of the Word: Press and Oratory in Nineteenth-Century Latin America*, edited by Iván Jaksic, 128–41. London: Institute of Latin American Studies, 2002.

Hale, Charles A. *Emilio Rabasa and the Survival of Porfirian Liberalism: The Man, His Career, and His Ideas, 1856–1930*. Stanford, CA: Stanford University Press, 2008.

Hale, Charles A. *Mexican Liberalism in the Age of Mora, 1821–1853*. New Haven, CT: Yale University Press, 1968.

Hale, Charles A. *The Transformation of Liberalism in Late Nineteenth-Century Mexico*. Princeton, NJ: Princeton University Press, 1989.

Hall, Stuart. "The West and the Rest: Discourse and Power." In *Modernity: An Introduction to Modern Societies*, edited by Stuart Hall, David Held, Don Hubert, and Kenneth Thompson, 184–227. Cambridge: Polity, 1995.

Halperín Donghi, Tulio. *The Aftermath of Revolution in Latin America*. New York: Harper and Row, 1973.

Halperín Donghi, Tulio. *The Contemporary History of Latin America*. Durham, NC: Duke University Press, 1993.

Halperín Donghi, Tulio. "Sarmiento's Place in Postrevolutionary Argentina." In *Sarmiento: Author of a Nation*, edited by Tulio Halperín Donghi, Iván Jaksic, Gwen Kirkpatrick, and Francine Masiello, 19–30. Berkeley: University of California Press, 1994.

Halperín Donghi, Tulio, Iván Jaksic, Gwen Kirkpatrick, and Francine Masiello, eds. *Sarmiento: Author of a Nation*. Berkeley: University of California Press, 1994.

Harrison, Lawrence E. *The Pan-American Dream: Do Latin America's Cultural Values Discourage True Partnership with the United States and Canada?* Boulder, CO: Westview, 1997.

Headley, John M. *The Europeanization of the World: On the Origins of Human Rights and Democracy*. Princeton, NJ: Princeton University Press, 2008.

Hebrard, Véronique. "Ciudadanía y participación política en Venezuela, 1810–1830." In *Independence and Revolution in Spanish America: Perspectives and Problems*, edited by Anthony McFarlane and Eduardo Posada-Carbó, 122–53. London: Institute of Latin American Studies, 1999.

Henderson, Peter V. N. *Gabriel García Moreno and Conservative State Formation in the Andes*. Austin: University of Texas Press, 2008.

Hernández Chávez, Alicia. "Monarquía-República-Nación-Pueblo." In *Ensayos sobre la nueva historia política de América Latina, siglo xix*, edited by Guillermo Palacios, 147–70. Mexico City: El Colegio de México, 2007.

Hibbert, Christopher. *Garibaldi: Hero of Italian Unification*. New York: Palgrave Macmillan, 2008.

Hobsbawm, Eric J. *The Age of Capital: 1848–1875*. New York: Vintage, 1996.

Hobsbawm, Eric J. *The Age of Revolution, 1789–1848*. Cleveland, OH: World, 1962.

Hobsbawm, Eric J. *Nations and Nationalism since 1780: Programme, Myth, Reality*. Cambridge: Cambridge University Press, 1990.

Hogan, Michael. *The Irish Soldiers of Mexico*. Guadalajara, Mexico: Fondo Editorial Universitario, 1997.

Holden, Robert H. "Priorities of the State in the Survey of the Public Land in Mexico, 1876–1911." *Hispanic American Historical Review* 70 (November 1990): 579–608.

Holt, Thomas C. "Marking: Race, Race-Making, and the Writing of History." *American Historical Review* 100 (February 1995): 1–20.

Horsman, Reginald. *Race and Manifest Destiny: The Origins of American Racial Anglo-Saxonism*. Cambridge, MA: Harvard University Press, 1981.

Hunt, Alfred N. *Haiti's Influence on Antebellum America: Slumbering Volcano in the Caribbean*. Baton Rouge: Louisiana State University Press, 1988.

Huntington, Samuel P. "Political Modernization: America vs. Europe." In *Modernity: Critical Concepts*. Edited by Malcolm Waters, 3:279–311. London: Routledge, 1999.

Huntington, Samuel P. *Who Are We? The Challenges to America's National Identity*. New York: Simon and Schuster, 2005.

Hylton, Forrest. "Reverberations of Insurgency: Indian Communities, the Federal War of 1889, and the Regeneration of Bolivia." PhD diss., New York University, 2010.

Ignatiev, Noel. *How the Irish Became White*. New York: Routledge, 2008.

Iparraguirre, Hilda. "Modernidad y religiosidad en la organización de la fuerza de trabajo en México: Segunda mitad del siglo xix y principios del xx." In *La modernización en México: Siglos xviii, xix y xx*, edited by Hilda Iparraguirre and María Isabel Campos Goenaga, 141–61. Mexico City: INAH, 2007.

Iparraguirre, Hilda, and María Isabel Campos Goenaga. "Presentación." In *La modernización en México: Siglos xviii, xix y xx*, edited by Hilda Iparraguirre and María Isabel Campos Goenaga, 5–26. Mexico City: INAH, 2007.

Jacobsen, Nils. *Mirages of Transition: The Peruvian Altiplano, 1780–1930*. Berkeley: University of California Press, 1993.

Jaksic, Iván, ed. *The Political Power of the Word: Press and Oratory in Nineteenth-Century Latin America*. London: Institute of Latin American Studies, 2002.

Jalif de Bertranou, Clara Alicia. *Francisco Bilbao y la experiencia libertaria de América: La propuesta de una filosofía Americana*. Mendoza, Argentina: EDIUNC, 2003.

Jaramillo Uribe, Jaime. *El pensamiento colombiano en el siglo xix*. Bogota: Editorial Temis, 1964.

Johannsen, Robert W. *To the Halls of the Montezumas: The Mexican War in the American Imagination*. New York: Oxford University Press, 1985.

Johnson, Lyman L. *Workshop of Revolution: Plebeian Buenos Aires and the Atlantic World, 1776–1810*. Durham, NC: Duke University Press, 2011.

Johnson, Paul. *The Birth of the Modern: World Society 1815–1830*. New York: Harper Collins, 1991.

Kalyvas, Andreas, and Ira Katznelson. *Liberal Beginnings: Making a Republic for the Moderns*. Cambridge: Cambridge University Press, 2008.

Katra, William H. *The Argentine Generation of 1837: Echeverría, Alberdi, Sarmiento, Mitre*. Madison, NJ: Fairleigh Dickinson University Press, 1996.

Kerber, Linda. "'I Have Don . . . much to Carrey on the Warr': Women and the Shaping of Republican Ideology after the American Revolution." In *Women and Politics in the Age of Democratic Revolution*, edited by Harriet B. Applewhite and Darline G. Levy, 227–57. Ann Arbor: University of Michigan Press, 1990.

Keyssar, Alexander. *The Right to Vote: The Contested History of Democracy in the United States*. New York: Basic, 2000.

Klor de Alva, J. Jorge. "The Postcolonization of the (Latin) American Experience: A Reconsideration of 'Colonialism,' 'Postcolonialism,' and 'Mestizaje.'" In *After Colonialism: Imperial Histories and Postcolonial Displacements*, edited by Gyan Prakash, 241–78. Princeton, NJ: Princeton University Press, 1994.

Knight, Alan. *The Mexican Revolution. Vol. 1, Porfirians, Liberals and Peasants*. Lincoln: University of Nebraska Press, 1986.

Knight, Alan. "The Peculiarities of Mexican History: Mexico Compared to Latin America, 1821–1992." *Journal of Latin American Studies* 24 (Quincentenary Supplement 1992): 99–144.

Knight, Alan. "When Was Latin America Modern? A Historian's Response." In

When Was Latin America Modern?, edited by Nicola Miller and Stephen Hart, 91–117. New York: Palgrave, 2007.

König, Hans-Joachim. *En el camino hacia la nación: Nacionalismo en el proceso de formación del Estado y de la Nación de la Nueva Granada, 1750–1856*. Bogota: Banco de la República, 1994.

Kraay, Hendrik. *Race, State, and Armed Forces in Independence-Era Brazil: Bahia, 1790s–1840s*. Stanford, CA: Stanford University Press, 2001.

Landers, Jane G. *Atlantic Creoles in the Age of Revolutions*. Cambridge, MA: Harvard University Press, 2010.

Landes, David S. *The Wealth and Poverty of Nations: Why Some Are So Rich and Some So Poor*. New York: W. W. Norton, 1999.

Landes, Joan B. *Women and the Public Sphere in the Age of the French Revolution*. Ithaca, NY: Cornell University Press, 1988.

Larrain, Jorge. *Identity and Modernity in Latin America*. Cambridge: Polity, 2000.

Larson, Brooke. *Trials of Nation Making: Liberalism, Race, and Ethnicity in the Andes, 1810–1910*. Cambridge: Cambridge University Press, 2004.

Lasso, Marixa. *Myths of Harmony: Race and Republicanism during the Age of Revolution, Colombia, 1795–1831*. Pittsburgh, PA: University of Pittsburgh Press, 2007.

Latin American Subaltern Studies Group. "Founding Statement." *boundary 2* 20 (fall 1993): 110–21.

Leal, Claudia. "Recordando a Saturio: Memorias del racismo en el Chocó (Colombia)." *Revista de Estudios Sociales* 27 (August 2007): 76–93.

LeGrand, Catherine. *Frontier Expansion and Peasant Protest in Colombia, 1830–1936*. Albuquerque: University of New Mexico Press, 1986.

Lempérière, Annick. "De la república corporativa a la nación moderna: México (1821–1860)." In *Inventando la nación: Iberoamérica siglo xix*, edited by Antonio Annino and François-Xavier Guerra, 316–46. Mexico City: Fondo de Cultura Económica, 2003.

Lepore, Jill. *The Story of America: Essays on Origins*. Princeton, NJ: Princeton University Press, 2012.

Levine, Robert S. *Martin Delany, Frederick Douglass, and the Politics of Representative Identity*. Chapel Hill: University of North Carolina Press, 1997.

Linebaugh, Peter, and Marcus Rediker. *The Many-Headed Hydra: Sailors, Slaves, Commoners, and the Hidden History of the Revolutionary Atlantic*. Boston: Beacon, 2000.

López-Alves, Fernando. "Modernization Theory Revisited: Latin America, Europe, and the U.S. in the Nineteenth and Early Twentieth Century." *Anuario Colombiano de Historia Social y de la Cultura* 38, no. 1 (2011): 243–79.

López-Alves, Fernando. *State Formation and Democracy in Latin America, 1810–1900*. Durham, NC: Duke University Press, 2000.

Lynch, John. *Argentine Caudillo: Juan Manuel de Rosas*. Wilmington, DE: Scholarly Resources, 2001.

Lynch, John. *The Spanish American Revolutions, 1808–1826.* New York: W. W. Norton, 1986.

Machado, Carlos. *Historia de los Orientales. Vol. 2, De la Guerra Grande a Saravia.* Montevideo: Ediciones de la Banda Oriental, 1997.

Maiguashca, Juan. "The Electoral Reforms of 1861 in Ecuador and the Rise of a New Political Order." In *Elections before Democracy: The History of Elections in Europe and Latin America,* edited by Eduardo Posada-Carbó, 87–115. London: Institute of Latin American Studies, 1996.

Maiztegui Casas, Lincoln R. *Orientales: Una historia política del Uruguay. Vol. 1, De los orígenes a 1865.* Montevideo: Planeta, 2004.

Mallon, Florencia E. *Peasant and Nation: The Making of Post-Colonial Mexico and Peru.* Berkeley: University of California Press, 1995.

Mallon, Florencia E. "Subalterns and the Nation." *Dispositio/n* 25, no. 52 (2005): 159–78.

Martínez, Frédéric. *El nacionalismo cosmopolita: La referencia europea en la construcción nacional en Colombia, 1845–1900.* Bogota: Banco de la República, 2001.

May, Robert E. *Slavery, Race, and Conquest in the Tropics: Lincoln, Douglas, and the Future of Latin America.* Cambridge: Cambridge University Press, 2013.

McCornack, Richard Blaine. "The San Patricio Deserters in the Mexican War." *Americas* 8 (October 1951): 131–42.

McEvoy, Carmen. "La experiencia republicana: Política peruana, 1871–1878." In *Ciudadanía política y formación de las naciones: Perspectivas históricas de América Latina,* edited by Hilda Sabato, 253–69. Mexico City: Fondo de Cultura Económica, 1999.

McGuinness, Aims. *Path of Empire: Panama and the California Gold Rush.* Ithaca, NY: Cornell University Press, 2008.

McGuinness, Aims. "Searching for 'Latin America': Race and Sovereignty in the Americas in the 1850s." In *Race and Nation in Modern Latin America,* edited by Nancy Appelbaum, Anne S. Macpherson, and Karin Alejandra Rosemblatt, 87–107. Chapel Hill: University of North Carolina Press, 2003.

McLean, David. "Garibaldi in Uruguay: A Reputation Reconsidered." *English Historical Review* 113 (April 1998): 351–66.

McNamara, Patrick J. *Sons of the Sierra: Juárez, Díaz, and the People of Ixtlán, Oaxaxa, 1855–1920.* Chapel Hill: University of North Carolina Press, 2007.

McNeill, William H. *The Rise of the West: A History of Human Community.* Chicago: University of Chicago Press, 1991.

Mehta, Uday Singh. *Liberalism and Empire: A Study in Nineteenth-Century British Liberal Thought.* Chicago: University of Chicago Press, 1999.

Mejías-López, Alejandro. *The Inverted Conquest: The Myth of Modernity and the Transatlantic Onset of Modernism.* Nashville, TN: Vanderbilt University Press, 2009.

Melgarejo Acosta, María del Pilar. *El lenguaje político de la regeneración en Colombia y México.* Bogota: Editorial Pontificia Universidad Javeriana, 2010.

Méndez, Cecilia. *The Plebeian Republic: The Huanta Rebellion and the Making of the Peruvian State, 1820–1850*. Durham, NC: Duke University Press, 2005.

Merino, Mauricio. "La formación del estado nacional mexicano: Pasado colonial, ideas liberales y gobiernos locales." In *Relatos de nación: La construcción de las identidades nacionales en el mundo hispánico*, edited by Francisco Colom González, 1:333–50. Madrid: Iberoamericana, 2005.

Merry, Robert W. *A Country of Vast Designs: James K. Polk, the Mexican War, and the Conquest of the American Continent*. New York: Simon and Schuster, 2009.

Mignolo, Walter D. *The Darker Side of Western Modernity: Global Futures, Decolonial Options*. Durham, NC: Duke University Press, 2011.

Mignolo, Walter D. *The Idea of Latin America*. Malden, MA: Blackwell, 2005.

Mignolo, Walter D. *Local Histories/Global Designs: Coloniality, Subaltern Knowledges, and Border Thinking*. Princeton, NJ: Princeton University Press, 2000.

Miller, Nicola. *In the Shadow of the State: Intellectuals and the Quest for National Identity in Twentieth-Century Spanish America*. London: Verso, 1999.

Miller, Robert Ryal. *Shamrock and Sword: The Saint Patrick's Battalion in the U.S.-Mexican War*. Norman: University of Oklahoma Press, 1989.

Montero García, Luis Alberto. "La modernización tecnológica de la industria azucarera en el Papaloapan veracruzano durante el siglo XIX." In *La modernización en México: Siglos xviii, xix y xx*, edited by Hilda Iparraguirre and María Isabel Campos Goenaga, 189–213. Mexico City: INAH, 2007.

Moore, Rachel A. *Forty Miles from the Sea: Xalapa, the Public Sphere, and the Atlantic World in Nineteenth-Century Mexico*. Tucson: University of Arizona Press, 2011.

Moraña, Mabel, ed. *Ideologies of Hispanism*. Nashville, TN: Vanderbilt University Press, 2005.

Morse, Richard M. "Claims of Political Tradition." In *Politics and Social Change in Latin America: Still a Distinct Tradition?*, edited by Howard J. Wiarda, 70–107. Boulder, CO: Westview, 1992.

Muller, Dalia Antonia. "Latin America and the Question of Cuban Independence." *Americas* 68 (October 2011): 209–39.

Múnera, Alfonso. *El fracaso de la nación: Región, clase y raza en el Caribe colombiano (1717–1810)*. Bogota: Banco de la República, 1998.

Múnera, Alfonso. *Fronteras imaginadas: La construcción de las razas y de la geografía en el siglo xix colombiano*. Bogota: Planeta, 2005.

Murray, Pamela. "Mujeres, género, y política en la joven república colombiana: Una Mirada desde la correspondencia personal del General Tomás Cipriano de Mosquera, 1859–1862." *Historia Crítica* 37 (January 2009): 54–71.

Nesbitt, Nick. *Universal Emancipation: The Haitian Revolution and the Radical Enlightenment*. Charlottesville: University of Virginia Press, 2008.

Novak, William J. "The Myth of the 'Weak' American State." *American Historical Review* 113 (June 2008): 752–72.

O'Brien, Thomas F. *Making the Americas: The United States and Latin America from* the *Age of Revolutions to the Era of Globalization*. Albuquerque: University of New Mexico Press, 2007.

O'Gorman, Edmundo. *The Invention of America*. Bloomington: Indiana University Press, 1961.

Ortega y Medina, Juan A. "Indigenismo e hispanismo en la conciencia historiográfica mexicana." In *Cultura e identidad nacional*, edited by Roberto Blancarte, 44–72. Mexico City: Fondo de Cultura Económica, 1994.

Ortiz, Renato. "From Incomplete Modernity to World Modernity." *Daedalus* 129 (winter 2000): 249–60.

Overmyer-Velázquez, Mark. *Visions of the Emerald City: Modernity, Tradition, and the Formation of Porfirian Oaxaca, Mexico*. Durham, NC: Duke University Press, 2006.

Palacios, Guillermo, ed. *Ensayos sobre la nueva historia política de América Latina, siglo xix*. Mexico City: El Colegio de México, 2007.

Palti, Elías José. *El momento romántico: Nación, historia y lenguajes políticos en la Argentina del siglo xix*. Buenos Aires: Eudeba, 2009.

Palti, Elías José. *La nación como problema: Los historiadores y la 'cuestión nacional.'* Buenos Aires: Fondo de Cultura Económica, 2003.

Palti, Elías José. *La política del disenso: La "polémica en torno al monarquismo" (México, 1848–1850) . . . y las aporías del liberalismo*. Mexico City: Fondo de Cultura Económica, 1998.

Pani, Erika. "Dreaming of a Mexican Empire: The Political Projects of the 'Imperialistas.'" *Hispanic American Historical Review* 82 (February 2002): 1–31.

Pani, Erika. *Para mexicanizar el Segundo Imperio: El imaginario político de los imperialistas*. Mexico City: El Colegio de México, 2001.

Pérez Martínez, Herón. "Hacia una tópica del discurso político mexicano del siglo xix." In *Construcción de la legitimidad política en México en el siglo xix*, edited by Brian Connaughton, Carlos Illades, and Sonia Pérez Toledo, 351–83. Zamora, Mexico: El Colegio de Michoacán, 1999.

Pérez-Rayón Elizundia, Nora. *México 1900: Percepciones y valores en la gran prensa capitalina*. Mexico City: Universidad Autónoma Metropolitana, 2001.

Piccato, Pablo. *The Tyranny of Opinion: Honor in the Construction of the Mexican Public Sphere*. Durham, NC: Duke University Press, 2010.

Pike, Frederick B. "Making the Hispanic World Safe from Democracy: Spanish Liberals and Hispanismo." *Review of Politics* 33 (July 1971): 307–22.

Poniatowska, Elena. *Tinisima*. Translated by Katherine Silver. New York: Farrar, Straus and Giroux, 1996.

Posada-Carbó, Eduardo. "Elections before Democracy: Some Considerations on Electoral History from a Comparative Approach." In *Elections before Democracy: The History of Elections in Europe and Latin America*, edited by Eduardo Posada-Carbó, 1–15. London: Institute of Latin American Studies, 1996.

Posada-Carbó, Eduardo, ed. *In Search of a New Order: Essays on the Politics and Society of Nineteenth-Century Latin America*. London: Institute of Latin American Studies, 1998.

Posada-Carbó, Eduardo. Preface. In *In Search of a New Order: Essays on the Politics and Society of Nineteenth-Century Latin America*, edited by Eduardo Posada-Carbó, 1–7. London: Institute of Latin American Studies, 1998.

Pratt, Mary Louise. "Modernity and Periphery: Toward a Global and Relational Analysis." In *Beyond Dichotomies: Histories, Identities, Cultures, and the Challenge of Globalization*, edited by Elisabeth Mudimbe-Boyi, 21–47. Albany: State University of New York Press, 2002.

Quijada Mauriño, Mónica. "From Spain to New Spain: Revisiting the *Potestas Populi* in Hispanic Political Thought." *Mexican Studies/Estudios Mexicanos* 24 (summer 2008): 185–219.

Quijada Mauriño, Mónica. "Los confines del *pueblo soberano*: Territorio y diversidad en la Argentina del siglo XIX." In *Relatos de nación: La construcción de las identidades nacionales en el mundo hispánico*, edited by Francisco Colom González, 1:821–48. Madrid: Iberoamericana, 2005.

Quijano, Aníbal. "Coloniality and Modernity/Rationality." *Cultural Studies* 21 (March–May 2007): 168–78.

Quijano, Aníbal. "Coloniality of Power, Eurocentrism, and Social Classification." In *Coloniality at Large: Latin America and the Postcolonial Debate*, edited by Mabel Moraña, Enrique Dussel, and Carlos A. Jáuregui, 181–224. Durham, NC: Duke University Press, 2008.

Quijano, Aníbal, and Immanuel Wallerstein. "Americanity as a Concept, or the Americas in the Modern World-System." *International Social Science Journal* 44, no. 134 (1992): 549–57.

Quirarte, Martín. *Historiografía sobre el imperio de Maximiliano*. Mexico City: Universidad Nacional Autónoma de México, 1993.

Racine, Karen. "'This England and This Now': British Cultural and Intellectual Influence in the Spanish American Independence Era." *Hispanic American Historical Review* 90 (August 2010): 423–54.

Rama, Angel. *La ciudad letrada*. Hanover, NH: Ediciones del Norte, 1984.

Rama, Carlos M. *Garibaldi y el Uruguay*. Montevideo: Nuestro Tiempo, 1968.

Rama, Carlos M., ed. *Utopismo socialista (1830–1893)*. Caracas: Biblioteca Ayacucho, 1977.

Ramírez, Francisco Eladio, *General David Peña*. Bogota: Imprenta Nacional, 1938.

Ramos, Julio. *Divergent Modernities: Culture and Politics in Nineteenth-Century Latin America*. Translated by John D. Blanco. Durham, NC: Duke University Press, 2001.

Reeves, René. *Ladinos with Ladinos, Indians with Indians: Land, Labor, and Regional Ethnic Conflict in the Making of Guatemala*. Stanford, CA: Stanford University Press, 2006.

Reina, Leticia, ed. *La reindianización de América, siglo xix*. Mexico City: Siglo Veintiuno, 1997.

Riall, Lucy. *Garibaldi: Invention of a Hero*. New Haven, CT: Yale University Press, 2007.

Rodgers, Daniel T. *Atlantic Crossings: Social Politics in a Progressive Age*. Cambridge, MA: Belknap Press of Harvard University Press, 2000.

Rodríguez Morales, Leopoldo. "La modernidad y el campo del constructor en el siglo xix: Ciudad de México." In *La modernización en México: Siglos xviii, xix y xx*, edited by Hilda Iparraguirre and María Isabel Campos Goenaga, 163–88. Mexico City: INAH, 2007.

Rodríguez O., Jaime E. "The Emancipation of America." *American Historical Review* 105 (February 2000): 131–52.

Rodríguez O., Jaime E. "Introduction: The Origins of Constitutionalism and Liberalism in Mexico." In *The Divine Charter: Constitutionalism and Liberalism in Nineteenth-Century Mexico*, edited by Jaime E. Rodríguez O., 1–32. Lanham, MD: Rowman and Littlefield, 2005.

Rodríguez O., Jaime E., ed. *Mexico in the Age of Democratic Revolutions, 1750–1850*. Boulder, CO: Lynne Rienner, 1994.

Roig, Arturo Andrés. "El positivismo en Hispanoamérica y el problema de la construcción nacional: Consideraciones histórico-críticas y proyecto identitario." In *Relatos de nación: La construcción de las identidades nacionales en el mundo hispánico*, edited by Francisco Colom González, 2:663–77. Madrid: Iberoamericana, 2005.

Rojas, Cristina. *Civilization and Violence: Regimes of Representation in Nineteenth-Century Colombia*. Minneapolis: University of Minnesota Press, 2002.

Rojas, Rafael. *Las repúblicas de aire: Utopía y desencanto en la revolución de Hispanoamérica*. Mexico City: Taurus, 2009.

Roldán Vera, Eugenia, and Marcelo Caruso. "Introduction: Avoiding the National, Assessing the Modern." In *Imported Modernity in Post-Colonial State Formation: The Appropriation of Political, Educational, and Cultural Models in Nineteenth-Century Latin America*, edited by Eugenia Roldán Vera and Marcelo Caruso, 7–28. Frankfurt: Peter Lang, 2007.

Ross, Paul. "Mexico's Superior Health Council and the American Public Health Association: The Transnational Archive of Porfirian Public Health." *Hispanic American Historical Review* 89 (November 2009): 573–602.

Sabato, Hilda, ed. *Ciudadanía política y formación de las naciones: Perspectivas históricas de América Latina*. Mexico City: Fondo de Cultura Económica, 1999.

Sabato, Hilda. "La reacción de América: La construcción de las repúblicas en el siglo xix." In *Europa, América y el mundo: Tiempos históricos*, edited by Roger Chartier and Antonio Feros, 263–79. Madrid: Fundación Rafael del Pino, 2006.

Sabato, Hilda. *The Many and the Few: Political Participation in Republican Buenos Aires*. Stanford, CA: Stanford University Press, 2001.

Safford, Frank. "The Problem of Political Order in Early Republican Spanish America." *Journal of Latin American Studies* 24 (quincentenary supplement 1992): 83–97.

Said, Edward W. *Culture and Imperialism*. New York: Knopf, 1993.

Salvatore, Ricardo D., and Carlos Aguirre, eds. *The Birth of the Penitentiary in Latin America: Essays on Criminology, Prison Reform, and Social Control, 1830–1940*. Austin: University of Texas Press, 1996.

Sanders, James E. "'Belonging to the Great Granadan Family': Partisan Struggle and the Construction of Indigenous Identity and Politics in Southwestern Colombia, 1849–1890." In *Race and Nation in Modern Latin America*, edited by Nancy Appelbaum, Anne S. Macpherson, and Karin Alejandra Rosemblatt, 56–86. Chapel Hill: University of North Carolina Press, 2003.

Sanders, James E. "'Citizens of a Free People': Popular Liberalism and Race in Nineteenth-Century Southwestern Colombia." *Hispanic American Historical Review* 84 (May 2004): 277–313.

Sanders, James E. *Contentious Republicans: Popular Politics, Race, and Class in Nineteenth-Century Colombia*. Durham, NC: Duke University Press, 2004.

Sanders, James E. "Popular Movements in Nineteenth-Century Latin America." In *Oxford Bibliographies: Latin American Studies*, edited by Ben Vinson. Oxford: Oxford University Press, 2014.

Sartorius, David. *Ever Faithful: Race and Loyalty in Nineteenth-Century Cuba*. Durham, NC: Duke University Press, 2014.

Schmidt-Nowara, Christopher. *The Conquest of History: Spanish Colonialism and National Histories in the Nineteenth Century*. Pittsburgh, PA: University of Pittsburgh Press, 2006.

Schmidt-Nowara, Christopher. *Slavery, Freedom, and Abolition in Latin America and the Atlantic World*. Albuquerque: University of New Mexico Press, 2011.

Schneider, Ronald M. *Comparative Latin American Politics*. Boulder, CO: Westview, 2010.

Scirocco, Alfonso. *Garibaldi: Citizen of the World*. Translated by Allan Cameron. Princeton, NJ: Princeton University Press, 2007.

Scott, Rebecca J. *Degrees of Freedom: Louisiana and Cuba after Slavery*. Cambridge, MA: Belknap Press of Harvard University Press, 2005.

Scott, Rebecca J., and Jean M. Hébrard. *Freedom Papers: An Atlantic Odyssey in the Age of Emancipation*. Cambridge, MA: Harvard University Press, 2012.

Sepúlveda Muñoz, Isidro. *Comunidad cultural e hispano-americanismo, 1885–1936*. Madrid: Universidad Nacional de Educación a Distancia, 1994.

Sewell, William H., Jr. "The French Revolution and the Emergence of the Nation Form." In *Revolutionary Currents: Nation Building in the Transatlantic World*, edited by Michael A. Morrison and Melinda Zook, 91–125. Lanham, MD: Rowman and Littlefield, 2004.

Shumway, Nicolas. "Hispanism Is an Imperfect Past and an Uncertain Present."

In *Ideologies of Hispanism*, edited by Mabel Moraña, 284–99. Nashville, TN: Vanderbilt University Press, 2005.

Shumway, Nicolas. *The Invention of Argentina*. Berkeley: University of California Press, 1991.

Sinisterra, Manuel. *El 24 de diciembre de 1876 en Cali: Narración de algunos de los principios acontecimientos ocurridos en esa fecha memorable*. Cali, Colombia: Impresa de Manuel Sinisterra, 1919.

Sinkin, Richard N. *The Mexican Reform, 1855–1876: A Study in Liberal Nation-Building*. Austin: University of Texas Press, 1979.

Skidmore, Thomas E., and Peter H. Smith. *Modern Latin America*. 6th ed. New York: Oxford University Press, 2005.

Staples, Anne. "La modernidad decimonónica." In *Constelaciones de modernidad*, edited by Pilar Gonzalbo Aizpuru, 17–28. Mexico City: Universidad Autónoma Metropolitana, 1990.

Stevens, Donald F. "Lo revelado y lo oscurecido: La política popular desde los archivos parroquiales." In *Construcción de la legitimidad política en México en el siglo xix*, edited by Brian Connaughton, Carlos Illades, and Sonia Pérez Toledo, 207–26. Zamora, Mexico: El Colegio de Michoacán, 1999.

Stevens, Donald F. *Origins of Instability in Early Republican Mexico*. Durham, NC: Duke University Press, 1991.

Stowell, Daniel W. Introduction. In Zephaniah Kingsley, *Balancing Evils Judiciously: The Proslavery Writings of Zephaniah Kingsley*, edited by Daniel W. Stowell, 1–22. Gainesville: University Press of Florida, 2000.

Suárez Argüello, Ana Rosa. "Una punzante visión de los Estados Unidos (la prensa Mexicana después del 47)." In *Cultura e identidad nacional*, edited by Roberto Blancarte, 73–106. Mexico City: Fondo de Cultura Económica, 1994.

Symes, Carol. "When We Talk about Modernity." *American Historical Review* 116 (June 2011): 715–26.

Taylor, Charles. *Modern Social Imaginaries*. Durham, NC: Duke University Press, 2004.

Tenenbaum, Barbara A. "Streetwise History: The Paseo de la Reforma and the Porfirian State, 1876–1910." In *Rituals of Rule, Rituals of Resistance: Public Celebrations and Popular Culture in Mexico*, edited by William H. Beezley, Cheryl English Martin, and William E. French, 127–50. Wilmington, DE: Scholarly Resources, 1994.

Tenorio-Trillo, Mauricio. *Mexico at the World's Fairs: Crafting a Modern Nation*. Berkeley: University of California Press, 1996.

Thibaud, Clément. "Entre les cités et l'État. Caudillos et pronunciamientos en Grande-Colombie." *Genèses* 62 (March 2006): 5–26.

Thibaud, Clément. *Repúblicas en armas: Los ejércitos bolivarianos en la guerra de independencia en Colombia y Venezuela*. Bogota: Planeta, 2003.

Thomas, Lynn M. "Modernity's Failings, Political Claims, and Intermediate Concepts." *American Historical Review* 116 (June 2011): 727–40.

Thompson, E. P. *Customs in Common.* New York: New Press, 1991.

Thomson, Guy. "Mid-Nineteenth-Century Modernities in the Hispanic World." In *When Was Latin America Modern?*, edited by Nicola Miller and Stephen Hart, 69–90. New York: Palgrave, 2007.

Thomson, Guy P. C., with David G. LaFrance. *Patriotism, Politics, and Popular Liberalism in Nineteenth-Century Mexico: Juan Francisco Lucas and the Puebla Sierra.* Wilmington, DE: Scholarly Resources, 1999.

Thurner, Mark. "After Spanish Rule: Writing Another After." In *After Spanish Rule: Post-Colonial Predicaments of the Americas*, edited by Mark Thurner and Andrés Guerrero, 12–57. Durham, NC: Duke University Press, 2003.

Thurner, Mark. *From Two Republics to One Divided: Contradictions of Post-Colonial Nationmaking in Andean Peru.* Durham, NC: Duke University Press, 1997.

Tilly, Charles. "Contentious Repertoires in Great Britain, 1758–1834." *Social Science History* 17 (summer 1993): 253–80.

Trevelan, G. M. *Garibaldi.* London: Longmans, Green, 1933.

Ugarte Figueroa, Elías. *Francisco Bilbao, agitador y blasfemo.* Santiago: Editorial Universitaria, 1965.

Urías Horcasitas, Beatriz. "Ideas de modernidad en la historia de México: Democracia e igualdad." *Revista Mexicana de Sociología* 53 (October 1991): 45–55.

Uribe-Uran, Victor M. "The Birth of the Public Sphere in Latin America during the Age of Revolution." *Comparative Studies in Society and History* 42 (April 2000): 425–57.

Valencia Llano, Alonso. *Estado Soberano del Cauca: Federalismo y regeneración.* Bogota: Banco de la República, 1988.

Valenzuela, J. Samuel. "Building Aspects of Democracy before Democracy: Electoral Practices in Nineteenth Century Chile." In *Elections before Democracy: The History of Elections in Europe and Latin America*, edited by Eduardo Posada-Carbó, 223–57. London: Institute of Latin American Studies, 1996.

Valero, Anthony. *Anita Garibaldi: A Biography.* Westport, CT: Praeger, 2001.

Van Der Veer, Peter. "The Global History of 'Modernity.'" *Journal of the Economic and Social History of the Orient* 41, no. 3 (1998): 285–94.

Van Young, Eric. *The Other Rebellion: Popular Violence, Ideology, and the Struggle for Independence, 1810–1821.* Stanford, CA: Stanford University Press, 2001.

Van Young, Eric. *Writing Mexican History.* Stanford, CA: Stanford University Press, 2012.

Vargas Llosa, Alvaro. *Liberty for Latin America: How to Undo Five Hundred Years of State Oppression.* New York: Farrar, Straus and Giroux, 2005.

Varona, Alberto J. *Francisco Bilbao: Revolucionario de América.* Buenos Aires: Ediciones Excelsior, 1973.

Vaughan, Mary Kay, and Stephen E. Lewis. Introduction. In *The Eagle and the Virgin: Nation and Cultural Revolution in Mexico, 1920–1940*, edited by Mary Kay Vaughan and Stephen E. Lewis, 1–20. Durham, NC: Duke University Press, 2006.

Vázquez, Josefina Zoraida. "Europa desde América." In *Latinoamérica en la conciencia europea: Europa en la conciencia latinoamericana*, edited by Patricia Galeana, 105–11. Mexico City: Archivo General de la Nación, 1999.

Véliz, Claudio. *The Centralist Tradition of Latin America*. Princeton, NJ: Princeton University Press, 1980.

Villavicencio, Susana. "Republicanismo y americanismo: Domingo Faustino Sarmiento y la emergencia de la nación cívica." In *Relatos de nación: La construcción de las identidades nacionales en el mundo hispánico*, edited by Francisco Colom González, 1:179–99. Madrid: Iberoamericana, 2005.

Viroli, Maurizio. *Republicanism*. Translated by Antony Shugaar. New York: Hill and Wang, 2002.

Wade, Peter. *Race and Ethnicity in Latin America*. London: Pluto, 1997.

Walker, Charles F. *Smoldering Ashes: Cuzco and the Creation of Republican Peru, 1780–1840*. Durham, NC: Duke University Press, 1999.

Warren, Richard A. *Vagrants and Citizens: Politics and the Masses in Mexico City from Colony to Republic*. Wilmington, DE: Scholarly Resources, 2001.

Wasserman, Mark. *Everyday Life and Politics in Nineteenth Century Mexico: Men, Women, and War*. Albuquerque: University of New Mexico Press, 2000.

Waters, Malcom. "General Commentary: The Meaning of Modernity." In *Modernity: Critical Concepts*, edited by Malcolm Waters, 1:xi–xxiii. London: Routledge, 1999.

Weber, Eugen. *Peasants into Frenchmen: The Modernization of Rural France, 1870–1914*. Stanford, CA: Stanford University Press, 1976.

Wiarda, Howard J. *The Soul of Latin America: The Cultural and Political Tradition*. New Haven, CT: Yale University Press, 2001.

Wiarda, Howard J., with Esther M. Skelley. *Dilemmas of Democracy in Latin America: Crises and Opportunity*. Lanham, MD: Rowman and Littlefield, 2005.

Winichakul, Thongchai. "The Quest for 'Siwilai': A Geographical Discourse of Civilizational Thinking in the Late Nineteenth and Early Twentieth-Century Siam." *Journal of Asian Studies* 59 (August 2000): 528–49.

Wolfe, Justin. *The Everyday Nation-State: Community and Ethnicity in Nineteenth-Century Nicaragua*. Lincoln: University of Nebraska Press, 2007.

Wolin, Richard. "'Modernity': The Peregrinations of a Contested Historiographical Concept." *American Historical Review* 116 (June 2011): 741–51.

Wood, Gordon. *The Radicalism of the American Revolution*. New York: Vintage, 1991.

Wood, James A. "The Republic Regenerated: French and Chilean Revolutions in the Imagination of Francisco Bilbao, 1842–1851." *Atlantic Studies* 3 (April 2006): 7–23.

Wood, James A. *The Society of Equality: Popular Republicanism and Democracy in Santiago de Chile, 1818–1851.* Albuquerque: University of New Mexico Press, 2011.

Worcester, Donald E. "The Spanish-American Past—Enemy of Change." In *Politics and Social Change in Latin America: Still a Distinct Tradition?,* edited by Howard J. Wiarda, 31–39. Boulder, CO: Westview, 1992.

Zahler, Reuben. *Ambitious Rebels: Remaking Honor, Law, and Liberalism in Venezuela, 1780–1850.* Tucson, AZ: The University of Arizona Press, 2013.

Zinn, Howard. *A People's History of the United States.* New York: New Press, 1997.

Index

Arias, Juan de Dios, 2, 4
aristocracy, 5, 44, 52, 71, 90–91, 93, 96,
  99–100, 105–6, 114, 117, 121, 142, 185,
  233–34. See also monarchy
army. See state, the
Arosemena, Justo, 79
Artigas, José Gervasio, 25
artisans, 14, 84, 97, 101, 105, 111, 117–18,
  120, 132, 139, 203, 221
Asia: conceptions of, 60, 84, 91, 98, 153,
  155, 181, 183
Atlantic history, 4–7, 9, 13, 16, 19, 22–23,
  38, 89, 144, 175, 223, 235
Atlantic world, 53–54, 56, 75, 83–85,
  100, 103–104, 136–46, 151–60,
  162, 185, 199, 206, 210–11, 214–15,
  223–24; international struggle in,
  34, 36–38, 78, 86–89, 95, 136, 138,
  140–51, 155–57, 226, 233
Austria (Austro-Hungarian Empire), 37,
  153, 156–57

Bailyn, Bernard, 9, 11
bargaining, 31–33, 58–59, 66, 108,
  113–27, 164–71, 175, 212–22. See also
  popular politics
Bayly, C.A., 9, 15
Baz, Juan José, 125
Bentham, Jeremy, 207
Berman, Marshall, 9, 15
Bilbao, Francisco, 3–4, 7, 20, 22, 77, 86,
  89–91, 93, 98, 113, 136–46, 152–57,
  172, 194, 205, 207, 233, 237
Bilbao, Manuel, 140–41
Bilbao, Rafael, 137, 139–40
Black Liberalism, 161–75, 229
Bolívar, Simón, 39–41, 49–50, 63, 156
Bolivia, 47, 51
Bossero, Luis, 93
Brands, H.W., 215
Braudel, Fernand, 11
Brazil, 21, 25–26, 31–32, 36, 74, 140,
  147, 152, 156, 160
Brooks, N.C., 65, 68
Bulnes, Manuel, 139, 156
Burbano, Miguel, 114

Burns, E. Bradford, 11
Bushnell, David, 10

Camarena, José María, 96–97
Campo, Ignacio del, 149
Cañizares-Esguerra, Jorge, 186
capitalism, 7, 9, 11, 13, 22, 41, 45, 74,
  88, 90, 93, 120, 125, 132–35, 148–50,
  166–69, 176–77, 180–82, 190–97,
  201, 203–5, 209–11, 213–16, 222–24,
  236–37, 243n53; foreign capital, 149,
  178, 181–83, 196–98, 210–11, 218,
  223–24
Caro, Miguel Antonio, 185
Carvajal de Peña, Dolores, 167
Castelar, Emilio, 6, 157, 194, 231–32
Caste War of the Yucatan, 49–50
Castilla, Ramón, 140
Castillo y Lanzas, Joaquín M. de, 45–46
Catholic Church. See Vatican, the
caudillos, 10, 34, 41, 44–46, 49, 51–52,
  60, 139, 154, 164, 198
Chakrabarty, Dipesh, 86, 235–36
Chaves, Antonio José, 150
Chile, 53, 81, 89, 135–40, 152, 215–16
Churubusco, battle of, 65, 67
científicos, 103, 197, 205, 218
citizenship, 5–6, 19, 28–33, 59–60, 94,
  101–4, 134, 172; popular conceptions
  of, 18, 29–30, 33, 38, 55–60, 107,
  117–27, 134, 168, 172–74, 202–3,
  217–18, 221–22, 226, 234–35; restrictions on, 53–55, 127–34, 148, 179,
  203–5, 208–16, 222–23; universalism
  and, 100–4, 172–74. See also gender:
  citizenship and; rights
civilization, 6, 16, 42, 49, 67–68, 72, 81,
  90, 92–95, 97–99, 106–7, 119–20,
  125–26, 129–30, 142, 146–51, 181–83,
  186, 191–92, 206, 211, 232, 234; barbarism and, 9, 11, 34, 41–43, 54, 68, 70,
  93, 99, 103, 106, 113, 125–26, 128–30,
  147–48, 151, 173, 189, 199–200, 210,
  214, 231–32; clash of different visions,
  22, 230–35. See also modernity
civil wars. See war

modernity: absence in Latin America, 1–3, 9–13, 29–46, 60–63, 179–97, 206, 211–12, 223–24; American origin of, 2–7, 18, 35–38, 81–89, 96, 154, 226–27, 230–37; concept of, 12, 15–17, 42, 84; European origin of, 1, 9–12, 34–35, 40–45, 146–47; meanings of, 3–6, 34–39, 42–45, 67–68, 71–72, 74, 77, 80, 89–98, 102, 115, 134–35, 147–51, 171–72, 175–77, 179, 184, 190–201, 205–6, 215–16, 222–24, 228, 231–33, 236–37; nations and, 100–101; popular conceptions of, 38, 55–56, 125–27, 166, 168–69, 219; power of, 15–19, 126–27, 135, 222, 225, 233–34, 236–37; Western origin of, 179–90, 193–96, 223–24, 228–30. See also American republican modernity; civilization; Europhile cultural modernity; Western industrial modernity

Modotti, Tina, 160

monarchy, 2, 34–37, 40, 46–50, 60–61, 63, 74–79, 81–90, 94, 100, 102, 106, 116–17, 131, 142, 144–47, 154, 156, 185, 204–5, 208, 231, 233–34

monopolies, 121, 165, 218

Monroe Doctrine, 77–79, 144

Morelos, José María, 172

Morse, Richard, 10

Mosquera, Manuel María, 167, 199

Mosquera, Tomás, 73, 83, 91, 157, 162–63, 166, 170, 191

Muñiz, Manuel, 116–17

Muñoz, Higinio, 101, 173

Murillo, Mariano, 101

Napoleon III, 6, 87–88, 98, 140, 145–47, 154, 156, 233

nation, 9, 17–19, 24–25, 28–29, 33, 38, 55–60, 69–70, 100–101, 105, 116–17, 121–22, 124, 126–27, 129–32, 173–75; patriotic nationalism and, 70–71, 79–80, 101, 185–90, 227–28, 230, 236; weakness in Latin America, 10–11, 39–40, 43, 45–46, 50–51,

60–63, 126–27, 151, 189–90, 206–7; youth and, 84. See also citizenship

national guards, 28–33, 123–124, 171, 207, 212–14, 220. See also war

nation and state formation, 17–18, 122, 124, 126–27, 135, 174–75, 197, 205–8, 214. See also nation; state, the

Nesbitt, Nick, 8

newspapers: advertisements in, 193–94; as distinct discourse, 13–15; reading of, 14–15, 51, 112; restrictions on, 204, 207; as sources, 242n45

New World, 20, 80; versus Old World, 6–7, 25, 35, 77–80, 83–90, 101, 117, 144–46, 153–57, 230–35. See also America(s)

Nicaragua, 191, 233

nineteenth century: symbolism of, 30, 42, 84, 94, 142, 202

Núñez, Rafael, 177, 189, 199–200

Obando, José María, 93

Obregón, Adolfo M. de, 207

Ocampo, Melchor, 14–15, 142, 155, 212, 220

Ojinaga, Manuel, 95

Old World. See New World

oratory, 13–15

order, 96, 133–34, 149–50, 196–208, 212–16, 221. See also anarchy

Oribe, Manuel, 26, 29, 31, 34

Ortiz, Gabino, 84, 95, 100–101

Ospina, Mariano, 110, 150

Ottoman Empire, 155

Pacheco y Obes, Melchor, 27

Padilla, José, 172

Palacios, Eustaquio, 200

Panama, 77, 132–33, 163

Pani, Erika, 147, 184–85

Payán, Eliseo, 200–203

Peña, David, 22, 111, 119, 161–70, 175, 229

Peru, 46, 78, 84–85, 87, 111, 137, 139–40, 144, 187, 200

petitions, 55–60, 111, 113, 116–27, 166, 209–10, 216–22